# CRITICAL CHALLENGES FOR HEALTH CARE REFORM IN EUROPE

D0165524

# STATE OF HEALTH SERIES

Edited by Chris Ham, Director of Health Services Management Centre, University of Birmingham

# CRITICAL CHALLENGES FOR HEALTH CARE REFORM IN EUROPE

EDITED BY
**Richard B. Saltman,
Josep Figueras and
Constantino Sakellarides**

OPEN UNIVERSITY PRESS
Maidenhead · Philadelphia

Open University Press
McGraw-Hill Education
McGraw-Hill House
Shoppenhangers Road
Maidenhead
Berkshire
England
SL6 2QL

and

325 Chestnut Street
Philadelphia, PA 19106, USA

First Published 1998
Reprinted 1999

*Library of Congress Cataloging-in-Publication Data*
Critical challenges for health care reform/edited by Richard B. Saltman,
    Josep Figueras, and Constantino Sakellarides.
        p.    cm. — (State of health)
    Includes bibliographical references and index.
        ISBN 0–335–19971–2. — ISBN 0–335–19970–4 (pbk.)
        1. Health care reform — Europe. 2. Medical care — Europe —
    Finance. 3. Medical policy — Europe. 4. Medical economics —
    Europe. I. Saltman, Richard B. 1947–    II. Figueras, Josep, 1959–
    III. Sakellarides, Constantino, 1941–    .  IV. Series: State of
    health series.    V. World Health Organization — WHO—Europe.
    RA395.E85C75    1998
    362.1'094 – dc21                                                    97–51880
                                                                                    CIP

Typeset by Type Study, Scarborough

Printed and bound in Great Britain by
Marston Lindsay Ross International Ltd,
Oxfordshire

# CONTENTS

# SERIES EDITOR'S INTRODUCTION

Health services in many developed countries have come under critical scrutiny in recent years. In part this is because of increasing expenditure, much of it funded from public sources, and the pressure this has put on governments seeking to control public spending. Also important has been the perception that resources allocated to health services are not always deployed in an optimal fashion. Thus at a time when the scope for increasing expenditure is extremely limited, there is a need to search for ways of using existing budgets more efficiently. A further concern has been the desire to ensure access to health care of various groups on an equitable basis. In some countries this has been linked to a wish to enhance patient choice and to make service providers more responsive to patients as 'consumers'.

Underlying these specific concerns are a number of more fundamental developments which have a significant bearing on the performance of health services. Three are worth highlighting. First, there are demographic changes, including the ageing population and the decline in the proportion of the population of working age. These changes will both increase the demand for health care and at the same time limit the ability of health services to respond to this demand.

Second, advances in medical science will also give rise to new demands within the health services. These advances cover a range of possibilities, including innovations in surgery, drug therapy, screening and diagnosis. The pace of innovation is likely to quicken as the end of the century approaches, with significant implications for the funding and provision of services.

Third, public expectations of health services are rising as those who use services demand higher standards of care. In part, this is stimulated by developments within the health service, including the availability of new technology. More fundamentally, it stems from the emergence of a more educated and informed population, in which people are accustomed to being treated as consumers rather than patients.

Against this background, policy makers in a number of countries are reviewing the future of health services. Those countries which have traditionally relied on a market in health care are making greater use of regulation and planning. Equally, those countries which have traditionally relied on regulation and planning are moving towards a more competitive approach. In no country is there complete satisfaction with existing methods of financing and delivery, and everywhere there is a search for new policy instruments.

The aim of this series is to contribute to debate about the future of health services through an analysis of major issues in health policy. These issues have been chosen because they are both of current interest and of enduring importance. The series is intended to be accessible to students and informed lay readers as well as to specialists working in this field. The aim is to go beyond a textbook approach to health policy analysis and to encourage authors to move debate about their issue forward. In this sense, each book presents a summary of current research and thinking, and an exploration of future policy directions.

Professor Chris Ham
Director of Health Services Management Centre,
University of Birmingham

# FOREWORD

The process of reforming health systems necessarily has a long learning cycle. It typically requires several years from the implementation of a particular initiative before it is possible to discern its impact – if indeed that impact can be separated from other changes taking place simultaneously in the same environment.

This long lead time often leaves policy makers in an uncomfortable position. They find themselves under considerable pressure to adopt reforms recently implemented elsewhere, reforms that may involve both politically and financially expensive changes, yet for the likely efficacy of which there is as yet little hard evidence. Similarly, academics and interested citizens find themselves with insufficient basepoints by which to assess current policy.

This volume is intended to help resolve these dilemmas by contributing to the development of evidence-based health policy making. Just as evidence-based medicine can make a major contribution to our understanding of what works well in a clinical setting, evidence-based health policy seeks to develop suitable conceptual basepoints with which to guide socially responsible as well as effective decision making. While evidence-based policy making is at an early stage in its development, the chapters in this volume demonstrate that it is already possible to make certain judgements about a number of policy options available to health sector decision makers.

The papers presented here can help set the stage for more effective health policy making. They draw on the conceptual skills of senior academics as well as the hands-on knowledge of real-world decision makers. This combination of expertise can forge a stronger link between the resources invested and the health outcomes achieved. In so doing, these papers help define the broader policy context within which WHO programmes seek to increase health gain across the entire WHO European Region.

J.E. Asvall
WHO Regional Director for Europe

# ACKNOWLEDGEMENTS

This volume presents a sub-set of revised background papers commissioned by the World Health Organization Regional Office for Europe for a study on recent experience in health care reform. The study was structured as an analysis of the critical challenges confronting national health policy decision makers in the second half of the 1990s. Its findings laid the foundation for the policy recommendations made at the WHO Conference on European Health Care Reforms held in Ljubljana in 1996, encompassed in the Ljubljana Charter[1] approved by the Member States.

We are very grateful to our authors who responded so effectively to our request to 'put on your multidisciplinary hats, cross national boundaries, be rigorous and tell us what you have learnt'. Our thanks also go to Professor Chris Ham, who helped develop the idea for this book and who later provided valuable advice on several chapters. We would like also to give our special thanks to Phyllis Dahl, who assisted editors and authors with professionalism and a sense of humour, and to Janice Edwards who has helped to prepare the final manuscript.

Finally, this book is dedicated to the late Professor Ferenc Bojan, who participated in the WHO study and allowed us to benefit from his great knowledge and understanding of public health.

## NOTE

1  WHO (1996) *European Health Care Reforms: The Ljubljana Charter on Reforming Health Care*. Copenhagen: WHO Regional Office for Europe.

# LIST OF CONTRIBUTORS

*Anders Anell* is Director of the Swedish Institute for Health Economics in Lund.

*Howard Barnum* is a Senior Economist in Population and Human Resources at the World Bank.

*Ferenc Bojan* was Professor of Social Medicine at the Medical University of Debrecen, Hungary, and Director of the Hungarian School of Public Health.

*Michael Calnan* is Director of the Centre for Health Services Studies and Professor in Sociology of Health Studies at the University of Kent at Canterbury.

*David Chinitz* is a Lecturer in Health Policy and Management at the Hebrew University–Hadassah School of Public Health.

*André-Pierre Contandriopoulos* is Professor and Director of the Department of Health Administration in the Faculty of Medicine at the University of Montreal.

*Nigel Edwards* is Policy Director of the National Health Service Confederation, London.

*Josep Figueras* is Regional Adviser for Health Care Systems at World Health Organization Regional Office for Europe and is Head of the Secretariat of the European Observatory on Health Care Systems.

*Janoz Halik* is Deputy Director at the National Centre for Health System Management, Warsaw.

*Chris Ham* is Professor of Health Policy and Management and Director of the Health Services Management Centre at the University of Birmingham.

*Petr Hava* is a Sociologist at Charles University, Prague.

*Martin Hensher* is a European Union Consultant in Health Economics for the Health Financing and Economics Directorate, Department of Health, Pretoria, South Africa.

*Frank Honigsbaum* is a Visiting Senior Research Fellow, Health Services Management Centre, University of Birmingham, United Kingdom and Vice-Chair, Westway Primary Care Group, one of the new administrative bodies created under the National Health Service.

*David J. Hunter* is Professor of Health Policy and Management and former Director of the Nuffield Institute for Health, University of Leeds.

*Panos Kanavos* is a Lecturer in Health Policy, Department of Social Policy and Administration and LSE Health at the London School of Economics and Political Science.

*Simo Kokko* is Head of Research and Development in Primary Care in STAKES, the National Research and Development Centre for Welfare and Health, Helsinki.

*Joseph Kutzin* is a Health Economist for Organizing Health Systems (OHS), Global Program on Evidence for Health Policy (GPE) at the World Health Organization, Geneva.

*Marju Lauristin* is Professor of Sociology at Tartu University.

*Ellen Leibovich* is a Research Associate in the Department of Health Administration in the Faculty of Medicine at the University of Montreal.

*Kimmo Leppo* is Director-General of the Department of Social and Health Services in the Ministry of Social Affairs and Health, Finland.

*Hans Maarse* is Professor of Health Care Administration at the University of Limburg.

*Martin McKee* is Professor of European Public Health at the London School of Hygiene and Tropical Medicine and co-director of the School's European Centre on Health of Societies in Transition.

*Elias Mossialos* is a Senior Lecturer in European Health Policy, Department of Social Policy and Administration and Director of LSE Health at the London School of Economics and Political Science.

*Vicente Ortun* is Professor of Economics at the University Pompeu Fabra, Barcelona.

*Alex Preker* is Principal Economist in the Health, Nutrition and Population Group of the Human Development Network at the World Bank.

*Tom Rathwell* is Director and Associate Professor at the School of Health Services Administration, Faculty of Health Professions, at Dalhousie University, Halifax, Nova Scotia.

*Lise Rochaix* is Professor in the Department of Economics at the University of West-Brittany and Associate Researcher in Health Economics at the University of Paris-Dauphine (LEGOS).

*Jolanta Sabbat* is Director of Health Care Policy at Merck, Sharp & Dohme, Warsaw.

*Constantino Sakellarides* is Director-General for Health of Portugal.

*Richard B. Saltman* is Professor in the Department of Health Policy and Management at Emory University School of Public Health in Atlanta, Georgia and a Research Director of the European Observatory on Health Care Systems.

*Serdar Savas* is Director of Programme Management at the World Health Organization Regional Office for Europe.

*Igor Sheiman* is Director for the Legal and Regulatory Reform Project for the Trustees of Boston University based in Moscow.

*Ellie Tragakes* is a Consultant in the Department of Health Policy and Services at the World Health Organization Regional Office for Europe.

*Mikko Vienonen* is the Special Representative of the Director-General of the World Health Organization to the Russian Federation.

*Gill Walt* is a Reader in Health Policy, Department of Public Health and Policy at the London School of Hygiene and Tropical Medicine.

*Jürgen Wasem* is Chair for Healthcare Management at the University of Greifswald, Germany.

*Ursula Werneke* is a former research fellow at the London Health Economics Consortium at the London School of Hygiene and Tropical Medicine.

*Miriam M. Wiley* is Head of the Health Policy Research Centre and Senior Research Officer at the Economic and Social Research Institute, Dublin.

*W. Cezary Wlodarczyk* is Professor and Director of the School of Public Health at Jagiellonian University, Cracow.

# INTRODUCTION

## Josep Figueras,
## Richard B. Saltman and
## Constantino Sakellarides

Many countries in Europe are under considerable pressure to review and restructure their health care systems. While the mix of pressures varies among countries, the interest in reform has spread to encompass nearly every dimension of present-day arrangements.

A central paradox of this expanding reform process has been the uncertainty of the reform principles upon which it should be based. This uncertainty can be attributed to a variety of technical causes, including the difficulty in separating specific health system influences, the complexity of intra-system relationships and the imprecision that accompanies some social science research methodologies (Figueras *et al.* forthcoming). A further factor, reflecting in part these technical dilemmas, has been the relatively small number of sophisticated cross-national analyses on specific health system issues (McKee and Figueras 1997).

This uncertainty over principles has contributed to a perception among national policy makers that it is decidedly more difficult to engage in health sector reform than to undertake change in nearly any other area of public policy. While this perception may also reflect the inherent character of health systems and the role they occupy within a democratic society, there remains a need for better policy tools if current pressures are to result in financially sustainable, socially equitable and, ultimately, politically successful health care reform.

This volume presents a set of commissioned papers which review the available evidence about past or expected outcomes from a wide range of health policy interventions. It seeks to dispel some of the uncertainty about what works, what doesn't work, how and why in the field of health care reform, and thereby to contribute to the development of what can properly be termed evidence-based health policy.

## THE PRESSURES FOR REFORM

The widespread nature of health care reform suggests that it is being generated by broad secular trends that cross national boundaries. Two types of factors have fed these trends. First, a number of pressures from outside the health sector affect the basic framework within which health-related policies are formulated. Reforms are influenced by a range of political, ideological, social, historical, cultural and economic factors, all of which need to be taken into consideration in understanding the context for reform. A second set of pressures relates to existing health and health sector problems. These include specific challenges to the health of the population along with increasing constraints on health spending as well as a number of organizational and structural challenges.

Health systems are strongly influenced by the underlying norms and values of the broader society within which they function. Health care services, like other human service systems, closely mirror the deeply rooted social and cultural expectations of the citizenry as a whole. A key indicator of a society's normative values is the very nature of health care itself. In some societies it is viewed as a predominantly social or collective good, in which all citizens benefit when an individual receives needed curative as well as preventive care. In other societies, influenced by the radical market-oriented thinking prominent during the 1980s, health care is increasingly perceived as a commodity to be bought and sold on the open market. This latter position emphasizes the technical and dynamic efficiency that market incentives can instil into the provision of health services, and the contributions these incentives are believed to make towards restraining future growth in health care expenditure. However, the concept of health services as a market commodity, while having been discussed in some policy-making circles, has not been adopted in any European country.

The condition of the overall national economy is a similarly important factor for the character of health reform. In western Europe, macroeconomic policy increasingly reflects intense concern about national competitiveness in a period of regionalization and globalization of industrial production and trade. For the Member States of the European Union, the Maastricht criteria for admission to the forthcoming European Monetary Union are also having a powerful effect on macroeconomic policy (Chapter 1). Both concerns have led economic policy makers to call for sharp reductions in public sector spending, particularly for human services such as health care.

In central and eastern European (CEE) countries, although several years of negative economic growth have now been replaced by improvements in overall gross domestic product (GDP), as of 1996 only Poland has reached levels of production that exceed their 1989 levels. In Commonwealth of Independent States (CIS) countries, economic productivity in 1996 is estimated to be barely more than half what it was in 1989 (EBRD 1996). These reduced levels of GDP reflect the painful economic restructuring that is underway, and help explain the sharp fall in state revenue available for the health sector.

A number of demographic and social pressures have played a significant role in triggering the current wave of reform. One important development throughout the region is the further ageing of the population. The percentage of people over 65 years of age, especially the very old, will continue to rise. Although the use of health services by the elderly varies by country and cohort, governments are concerned that higher numbers of elderly citizens will need a greater volume of health care services and that overall spending rates will increase. Another key factor is the increase in both invasive and non-invasive clinical innovations over the past decade. For reasons of safety, efficiency, quality of care and prestige, as well as of patient satisfaction, health care providers find themselves under pressure to adopt the latest available medical techniques.

Finally, a key contextual pressure for reform is the increased expectations of citizens and patients. Citizens in all parts of Europe are demanding a more patient-oriented approach to the delivery of health care services. In western Europe, patients' rights movements are growing and providers are expected to provide high-quality services, in line with international standards. In CEE and CIS countries, patients have strong views on the need for choice and quality in health services, often backing up these demands with out-of-pocket payments to providers.

In addition to these political, economic and social factors, national health policy makers are also confronted with a variety of specifically health and health sector dilemmas. The European region faces continuing and, in some areas, growing health challenges such as the increasing disparity in life expectancy and mortality between countries in the eastern and western parts of the region (WHO 1994). The shifting pattern of disease in Europe is another significant factor driving change in the configuration of health services both at micro and macro level. The latter is typified by concerns about the long-term financing of health services in the light of ageing populations and the rising levels of chronic disease (Chapter 1). Indeed, these factors, together with the pace of technology development and increased population expectations, have combined to exert persistent upward pressure on health expenditure.

Beyond health concerns and increasing costs, there are also structural and organizational challenges in how European countries finance and deliver health services. First, there are growing inequalities in health services – in terms of access to and quality of care – even in countries where health sector arrangements provide universal access to services. Second, a growing body of research evidence has raised questions about the appropriateness and/or cost-effectiveness of various clinical procedures, suggesting that up to 30 per cent of all delivered clinical services may be ineffective. Third, there are concerns about inefficient performance at the micro-institutional level. Finally, the growing focus on micro-level institutional activities has generated increased concern about the quality of services delivered.

## REFORM PATTERNS

In response to these contextual, health and health sector challenges, countries have developed a wide variety of strategies for policy intervention at different levels of the health system. Underlying these strategies and mechanisms, however, one can discern a similar pattern of policy interaction within most countries across the region. These interactions revolve around efforts to establish a viable balance between various market-oriented mechanisms in allocating resources and managing institutions, on the one hand, and a complicated mix of public sector decentralization, sharpened state vigilance, and greater citizen empowerment, on the other.

In the last decade many governments have re-examined the structure of governance and the place of market mechanisms within their health systems. While the pressure for change has been felt unevenly across the different parts of Europe, there appears to be a set of parallel trends regarding governance. Some state functions have been decentralized within the public sector to regional and/or municipal authorities. In certain cases, functions have been given over to private ownership. Conversely, in some countries where the state plays a less central role, there has been an increase in regulatory intervention in certain subsectors of the health care system.

The greatest pressure for change has been the increased role of the private sector in the provision and, in some countries, the funding of health care. A number of market-style mechanisms have been introduced within different sectors of the health system: in health care funding, or in one or more sub-sets of the production of health services (e.g. hospitals, primary health care, and/or in the allocation mechanisms that distribute finance to service providers) (Saltman 1994). Market incentives have been applied to both health personnel, in the form of performance-related payment, and to consumers through mechanisms such as cost sharing or increased patient choice.

Many European countries with publicly operated provider systems such as Finland, Sweden or the UK have begun to apply certain market-style incentives to these providers. This type of publicly planned market, which has been termed an internal market (Enthoven 1985), public competition (Saltman and von Otter 1987), provider market or quasi-market (Le Grand and Bartlett 1993), involves various forms of competition among public and/or private providers which may include the separation of purchaser from provider through the use of negotiated contracts (Chapter 6).

An accompanying trend reflecting the changing role of the state has been decentralization of responsibility to lower levels within the public sector. Disappointment with large, centralized and bureaucratic institutions is widespread throughout Europe. In nearly every country the same drawbacks of centralized systems have been identified: poor efficiency, slow pace of change and innovation and a lack of responsiveness to shifts in the external environment. Decentralized institutions can address some of these problems, yet experience in CEE/CIS countries demonstrates that successful decentralization requires a number of preconditions including sufficient local administrative and managerial capacity as well as financial decentralization (Chapter 13).

A second accompanying trend is an increasing role for the citizen and patient in various reform strategies. Patient empowerment has several dimensions. One concern is patient rights with regard to health care services. Patient choice is a second dimension. In some countries this has meant choice of physician and treatment facility, for primary or hospital care (Saltman and von Otter 1992). In a few western European countries, but in an increasing number of CEE and CIS countries, choice has been extended to the selection of a private insurance carrier. A third increasing trend in health systems involves patients' participation in clinical decision making (Chapter 14).

## POLICY CHALLENGES

The above reform trends have translated into a range of specific policy strategies at various levels of the health system. The analytic logic adopted in this chapter organizes these policies into four groups, each reflecting a key policy challenge encountered by decision makers as they seek to reform their health care systems.

### Dealing with scarcity

As the resources available for paying for health care have become more constrained and the pressures on health expenditure have increased, national decision makers have had to develop strategies to deal with resource scarcity. There are two basic and often complementary options. Countries may increase the amount of resources for health care either by shifting funds from other areas of public sector expenditure, or by increasing taxation or social insurance contributions. The issue of the 'right' level of funding is widely discussed in the current reform debate. Several formulaic approaches have been suggested, including incremental funding adjusted by additional needs due to demographic, technology and policy changes; funding according to 'affordability' by linking health expenditure to GDP growth; or using international comparisons to look at the level of resources that other economically similar countries commit to health care (Appleby 1992). None of these approaches seem to be completely satisfactory, since the 'right' level of funding inevitably depends on a series of organizational and political decisions.

Countries can control health care expenditure by pursuing a range of strategies that influence either the demand for, or the supply of, health care services. Cost-containment strategies that act on demand include cost-sharing arrangements, priority setting to ration access to services, incentives for private spending such as income tax concessions for those who use private services and the right to opt out of the collectively funded system (Abel-Smith *et al.* 1995). In general, these measures seek to reduce demand by shifting a portion of health care costs on to the individual, although this strategy necessarily generates substantial equity problems. Among the most controversial demand-shifting strategies are cost sharing and priority setting, which are addressed in Chapters 3 and 4.

Costs can also be contained by influencing the supply of health services. A wide range of reform strategies can be included in this category. These include: introducing competition among public providers; setting global expenditure ceilings or global budgets for providers; reducing the production of doctors and the number of hospital beds; controlling the cost of the human resources (e.g. salaries) or supplies (e.g. pharmaceuticals) used to provide care; introducing more effective delivery patterns, such as substituting outpatient and primary care for more expensive in-patient services; regulating the use of technologies; influencing the use of resources authorized by physicians; and changing the methods of remunerating professionals (Abel-Smith *et al.* 1995). Key supply-oriented strategies based on a more efficient allocation of resources are addressed in Chapters 6 to 10. The control of pharmaceutical expenditure is addressed in Chapter 11.

Cost-containment strategies have met with varying degrees of success in containing costs. Overall, experience to date indicates that setting budgets for the health system or for each main subsector, based on targets and on limiting workforce members, appears to be the most effective means of containing costs (Abel-Smith and Mossialos 1994).

### Funding systems equitably and sustainably

The effort to balance equitable and sustainable funding of health services with scarce resources is a major challenge to policy makers. Countries have adopted a variety of health care funding strategies to deal with this challenge. Countries in western Europe based on a Beveridge model have taken a number of paths to a predominantly tax-funded health system. These include Ireland, the Scandinavian countries and the UK as well as southern European countries (Greece, Italy, Portugal and Spain). A key element of this approach is universal or near-universal access to health care. Despite the tone of recent political debates, none of these countries has expressed an intention to shift away from taxation as the main source of funding for health care. The role of the public sector as the main provider of funds, ensuring universal access to health care and equitable geographical distribution of resources, is widely accepted by their populations.

Countries in western Europe based on a Bismarck model (Austria, Belgium, France, Germany, Luxembourg, the Netherlands and Switzerland) have long-established statutory insurance-based systems. Though inspired by similar principles, these social insurance systems differ significantly in their specific characteristics. In nearly all cases, however, they are subject to close regulation by government. Indeed, there has been a noticeable increase recently in the level of government control and regulation, on grounds either of cost containment (for instance, by putting a ceiling on premiums) or of equity and solidarity.

The need to maintain universal access and financial sustainability constitutes a particular challenge for CEE and CIS countries engaged in transforming their funding systems amidst formidable macroeconomic constraints. Most are moving towards health insurance funded largely through payroll taxation. The Socialist Federal Republics of Yugoslavia already had such a health insurance system, while Hungary and the Russian Federation (1991), the Czech Republic and Estonia (1992), Latvia and Slovakia (1993), Georgia (1995) and Kazakstan (1996) all adopted such systems during the 1990s (WHO 1996). Other countries such as Belarus, Bulgaria, Kyrgyzstan, Lithuania, Poland and Romania, which still rely principally on general revenue to finance health care, have national health insurance laws under consideration (WHO 1996). CEE/CIS countries shifting to insurance-based funding face a series of problems including substantial increases in expenditure together with structural deficits associated with insufficient transfer of funds and higher labour costs (Preker *et al.* 1995).

In recent years a small number of health insurance countries both in western and eastern Europe have sought to experiment with the application of market incentives to the funding of health care by introducing free choice of insurer together with competition among statutory insurers. It was believed that these measures would lead to more cost-effective purchasing practices and higher quality of services. Whether a society can base health care funding on competing insurers and, at the same time, maintain a high level of social solidarity is, however, not demonstrated (Chapter 2).

**Allocating resources effectively**

A number of countries in both the eastern and western parts of the region have begun to move from integrated models of provision to a separation of public or quasi-public third-party payers from health service providers. As direct managerial relationships between these actors weaken, third-party payers have to find ways to ensure that providers follow the objectives set for the health system. Hence, strategies aimed at the reform of resource allocation mechanisms have become increasingly central in enabling payers and policy makers to achieve objectives such as the macro-level control of expenditure and the improvement of micro-level institutional efficiency. Key strategies for allocating resources more effectively include contracting mechanisms, allocation of capital, payment systems for professionals and institutions and purchasing mechanisms for pharmaceuticals.

In an increasing number of countries in Europe, contracting is seen as a useful instrument to implement health policy objectives. It is a coordinating mechanism that offers an alternative to traditional command-and-control models of health care management. An essential element of contracting is that it facilitates a more market-oriented form of institutional resource allocation based on separating purchaser from provider. Contracting mechanisms bind third-party payers and providers to explicit commitments, and generate the economic motivation to fulfil these commitments (Chapter 6).

In some countries, the move to contracting is limited by insufficient information for an effective purchasing policy. The minimum information requirements for effective contracting cover patient flow data, cost and utilization information across specialties or diagnostic groups as well as demographic and risk groups. These information systems require large investments of funds and personnel, and the information must be disseminated appropriately if it is to facilitate a rational choice of providers. One potential consequence of contracting is rising transaction costs, including costs associated with the continuing interaction of purchasers and providers (needs assessment, performance analysis, negotiating, monitoring, etc.) (Robinson and Le Grand 1995; Ham 1996). The dilemma faced by countries considering the adoption of contracting is the extent to which this increase in information and transaction costs can be offset by expected increases in quality and efficiency.

A related group of allocation strategies addresses the payment of institutional providers and health personnel. In the development of payment systems, policy makers have to balance collective societal objectives against individual preferences of providers and users of services. An ideal payment system seeks to achieve microeconomic objectives of efficiency, quality and satisfaction while maintaining macroeconomic objectives of financial sustainability and cost containment. No single payment system for professionals – fee for service, salary or capitation – can meet all policy objectives. A major drawback of a retrospective open-ended (fee-for-service) system is supply-induced demand, which exerts significant upward pressure on costs. Although prospective payment systems (capitation and salary) have incentives to control expenditure and may lead to a better geographical distribution, these systems can also result in excessive referrals, over-prescribing, reduced access for sicker patients and – particularly with salaried practitioners – less responsiveness to patients. There is a visible tendency towards adopting mixed payment systems which appear to be more successful in combining macro- and micro-efficiency objectives. However, there is still substantial uncertainty about the impact of different combinations and some degree of trade-off will remain inevitable (Chapter 8).

Several key issues concerning payment of physicians also apply to payment of hospitals. Like physicians, hospitals can be paid retrospectively by fee-for-service, per diem fees or cases treated, or they can be paid prospectively via global budgets provided to the hospital for a given period of time. Traditionally, prospective budgets based on historically incremental norms have been typical of tax-based systems. However, during the 1980s and 1990s several insurance-based systems in western Europe adopted prospective global budget systems, incorporating some measures of hospital activity such as bed-days or cases (OECD 1993, 1994). In a growing number of countries, the prioritization of cost control is complemented by a concern for efficiency by applying some adjustment for activity/case mix within the budget framework. Similarly, countries with retrospective payment systems are addressing their cost-control problems by combining these open-ended arrangements with prospective pricing and with contracts that require hospitals to achieve specific cost control (Chapter 9).

### Delivering care efficiently

Policy makers also face major concerns about inefficient performance at the micro-institutional level. Problems include poor coordination among providers and across subsectors, lack of incentives for efficient service provision, lack of adequate information about the cost and quality of services, inadequate management of capital resources and insufficient or inappropriate management at the institutional level. Similarly there are increasing concerns about the quality of services delivered. Researchers have found wide variation in the utilization of particular procedures and in the outcomes achieved.

In recent years, health care reforms in Europe have paid increasing attention to these organizational problems. Changes have concentrated on improving managerial efficiency and health outcomes. The measures adopted have focused on developing quality of care programmes, restructuring the internal and external organization of hospitals, enhancing the capacities of primary health care and, where possible, substituting more appropriate for less appropriate forms of care. Related changes have also been introduced in the area of human resources.

There is increasing recognition across Europe that health reform should include efforts to improve both the process and the outcome of the care provided. Deference to medical judgement about how to deliver health care is giving way in the face of wide variations in how physicians actually provide care (McPherson *et al.* 1982; Wennberg 1987). This has led to three related sets of concerns. First, there are sizeable gaps in knowledge about which treatments result in improved health outcomes, with only an estimated 20 per cent of medical interventions having been evaluated in clinical trials. Second, many clinical interventions do not achieve the intended objectives, and sometimes result in poor health outcomes. Information is still fragmentary, but systematic reviews have demonstrated that commonly used interventions in a number of areas are either definitely or probably ineffective. Finally, there are still large gaps in understanding how to change professional behaviour so as to ensure that the most effective, efficient and humane treatments are provided. These concerns have given rise to a wide range of activities that have gone under terms such as health care technology assessment, evidence-based medicine, outcomes research, quality assurance and continuous quality development. Despite some differences in approach, all these activities have as a common aim the improvement of health outcomes.

A notable reform trend across the region is the decentralization of management functions to provider institutions, coupled with the development of more effective management within institutions through strengthening managerial expertise, introducing improved information systems and increasing financial autonomy. In several publicly operated health systems in western Europe, the traditional hierarchy between health authorities and hospital providers is being replaced by more decentralized management arrangements in the form of self-governing hospital trusts and public firms. While these strategies have achieved a certain degree of success, self-governing schemes are still at an early stage of development in both the western and eastern parts of Europe. Key issues include public accountability, the representativeness of management boards, and legal liability.

Patterns of health care organization and delivery across care settings (hospital, primary, community and home care) have been changing to reflect new circumstances, both on the demand- and supply-sides of services. The adaptation of health systems has occurred through a process of *substitution*, by which there has been a continual regrouping of staff, skills, equipment and information across care settings to achieve better results (Warner 1996). Some western European countries such as the Netherlands and the UK have had considerable experience with various substitution schemes. The potential advantages of substitution policies include increased patient satisfaction, improved clinical outcomes, greater efficiency and more appropriate management of certain diseases. However, there are substantial differences between the various substitution schemes, and in many cases there is little evidence as to their impact on health service objectives.

One related area that has been under close scrutiny is the appropriate role for hospitals. In nearly all western European countries, the total number of hospital beds fell significantly between 1980 and 1993, resulting from a combination of cost-containment policies, changes in technologies or treatment and an increased reliance on primary and social care. There is increasing awareness that there are more cost-effective alternatives to the care currently provided in hospitals and that consequently there is scope for a further reduction in hospital services. Policy makers thus face questions about the long-term role of the hospital, its future configuration and how changes in hospital systems can be implemented (Chapter 10).

One final aspect sometimes under-emphasized by policy makers is the development of human resources. The largest proportion of recurrent expenditure in health care systems is typically the cost of staff, making human resources a critical factor to be addressed in any reform of the delivery of health care. Successful health reform requires careful consideration of key human resource implications, such as planning of staffing levels and mix of skills, educational training and accreditation, incentive policies and industrial relations.

## Implementing change

Arguably, a major challenge faced by policy makers is the actual implementation of reform changes. Many reform efforts focus on the development of the content, neglecting the process of reform and the difficulties of implementing and managing change. Yet, a review of the evidence shows that reform failures often have little to do with the relative merits of the reform programme but rather reflect inadequate understanding of the process of reform implementation and of the management of change.

The implementation of reform in a specific country is influenced by a range of contextual factors including the macroeconomic situation, the socio-political environment and prevailing societal values – some of which were explored above under reform pressures. The process of implementation is directly affected by the system of government and the distribution of authority as well as the way in which the process itself is conducted (e.g. clarity of objectives, enabling legislation, allocation of managerial responsibility or financial incentives). One contentious issue has been the pace of implementation and the relative merits of 'big bang' versus 'incrementalist' implementation (Klein 1995). In addition, actors or stakeholders are often key determinants of policy change. Four groups have a major bearing on implementation: citizens, professionals, policy elites and interest groups (see Chapters 16 and 17).

## PLAN OF THE BOOK

The chapters that follow provide an evaluation of the central health reform challenges that confront policy makers across the European region. The selection of these issues has been based on three criteria: degree of uncertainty and controversy as to effects on health system performance; centrality and magnitude within a health system; and cross-national significance across reform programmes both in western and eastern Europe. On each of these issues, the authors have reviewed evidence from across the European region, focusing their analysis on those health systems with salient experiences. A common aim of these chapters has been to digest the available evidence into a carefully considered assessment of accomplishments to date as well as dilemmas yet to be addressed and/or resolved. Much emphasis is put on drawing lessons that can be applied in the development and management of health reforms in other countries.

The chapters are arranged on the basis of a conceptual framework with five parts: (1) the context of reforms; (2) demand-side strategies; (3) supply-side strategies; (4) the role of the state, citizen and society; and (5) implementation of reforms. A health system's present structure and capacity for future change reflect a variety of factors. In Part I, Kanavos and McKee explore two key contextual factors that influence health care reform in Europe: the macroeconomic environment and the changing health needs of the population. Chapter 1 discusses trends in health spending and resource allocation in western and eastern Europe and highlights the impact of macroeconomic pressures. It then reviews the main challenges to health status. The authors conclude with a detailed account of the likely impact of these two factors on the configuration of health services and the implications for health sector reform.

In response to contextual challenges, countries have adopted a series of policy strategies. These strategies can be structured via a conceptual shorthand that organizes them on two central parameters: policy interventions that are instituted on the demand- or on the supply-side of health care systems.

Part II, 'Demand-Side Strategies', focuses on the financial relationship between citizens and third-party funders, the latter providing health care coverage in exchange for a predictable financial contribution either in the form of taxation or insurance premium. In Chapter 2, Chinitz, Preker and Wasem assess alternative mechanisms for collecting financial contributions (i.e. funding the health system). They address a core concern of countries considering changes in their funding system: how to balance solidarity with increasing pressures to establish competition among insurers. In particular, the chapter explores issues which arise in seeking to maintain equity in terms of universal coverage and solidarity if competition is introduced among more than one financing agency. In addition to exploring the conceptual arguments, the authors provide a critical review of recent funding reforms in western and eastern European countries.

The next chapters deal with two main reform measures seeking to contain costs on the demand-side: introducing a financial barrier to access services (i.e. cost sharing), or by restricting third-party coverage by excluding services from the public package of care (i.e. rationing). Chapter 3 provides a comprehensive review of cost-sharing practices in the European region. Kutzin explores the conceptual issues underlying cost sharing and provides a detailed assessment of available evidence on the impact of cost sharing on utilization and health status.

Chapter 4 focuses on priority setting and rationing health services. Following an account of the rationale for priority setting and some of the main approaches employed, Ham and Honigsbaum focus their analysis on countries which have attempted to undertake priority setting in a more systematic way. Drawing on this analysis, the authors put forward a series of lessons including the merits and demerits of rationing by *exclusion vs. guidelines*, the use of techniques for priority setting, methodologies for public involvement and the issues involved in implementation, in particular the need to balance competing objectives.

The final chapter in this section moves the debate from individual patient-based to aggregate population-based demand. In Chapter 5, McKee and Bojan highlight the need to complement health care reform with effective public health strategies that can reduce total demand for health care services. While recognizing the importance of the broader public health function, the chapter focuses its analysis on public health services and considers the options for reform. It identifies five major public health functions: communicable disease control and environmental health; provision of services to specific groups; health promotion; commissioning and planning health services; and undertaking research. In each case, the authors trace the historical development, review developments across the region and suggest reform directions to be pursued.

Part III, 'Supply-Side Strategies', brings together strategies that encourage third-party purchasers to pursue more effective allocation of financial resources to service providers, and that encourage service providers to achieve more cost-effective and higher quality of care.

Chapters 6–9 explore allocation mechanisms central to the newly reformed health services environment. In Chapter 6, Savas, Sheiman, Maarse and Tragakes outline a rationale for contracting and suggest a typology to understand various types of contractual relationships. The authors then apply this typology in a comprehensive review of contracting patterns in the European region. These are grouped in four categories: Beveridge, Bismarck, southern European countries and CEE/CIS countries. The authors emphasize the issues involved in contracting in a competitive environment. This discussion is complemented by Chapter 7, which discusses the dynamic link between investments, capital and health service delivery. Anell and Barnum review patterns of capital investment in different parts of the region and highlight how health sector reform can contribute to optimal policies regarding appropriate use of existing capital and new investments.

The success of reforms concerning the production of services is contingent on appropriate management of human resources. Chapter 8 reviews a core element of these policies – the payment of professionals. Rochaix addresses the cornerstone of physician payment systems: how to combine macroeconomic objectives of cost containment while achieving efficiency, quality and patient satisfaction at the microeconomic level. After examining key characteristics of this segment of the labour market, the author provides a comprehensive review of empirical evidence on the impact of different payment systems and a critical evaluation of current payment arrangements. Rochaix concludes that a mixed payment mechanism tied to performance would be likely to lead to the most favourable outcomes.

Acute hospitals constitute the largest single component of health expenditure. Chapters 9 and 10 review the challenges and available strategies for reforming the provision of acute services. Wiley reviews the financing of acute hospital services, and explores the range of applications for prospective budgeting and service-based financing. The chapter provides a broad perspective on the relative advantages and disadvantages of the various approaches. In the next chapter, Edwards, Hensher and Werneke explore the future of hospital systems in Europe and examine the range of policy instruments available to bring about change. These are grouped according to their intended aim: to increase provider efficiency; to improve appropriateness of hospital admission, use and discharge; and to change the configuration of hospital services. The authors demonstrate that if policy makers are to succeed in changing the hospital system, they will require a mix of planned and market mechanisms operating both on the demand- and supply-side of the system.

This section concludes with a comprehensive analysis of the provision of pharmaceuticals (Chapter 11). Using the latest available data on consumption and expenditure in European Union countries, Mossialos evaluates the impact of a wide range of measures addressed at regulating expenditure and improving the cost-effectiveness of pharmaceutical provision. The author puts forward a framework of policy options both on the demand- and supply-side which affect the user, the providers and the industry, demonstrating that a drug policy needs to combine several different strategies to be effective.

Following this review of strategies, Part IV looks at the role of the state, the citizen and broad societal values in determining the shape of the reforms. In the first chapter of this section, Kokko, Hava, Ortun and Leppo explore the central role played by the state in generating effective and sustainable health sector reform. They review the appropriate functions for ministries of health and the changing expectations placed on ministries in the current, more market-oriented policy environment. The authors conclude that the irreducible minimum of necessary state responsibility is, in fact, quite substantial.

Chapters 13 and 14 explore two changes associated with the new role of the state: the decentralization of health services management to lower levels within the public sector and the increased role for the citizen. After exploring the theoretical basis for decentralization, Chapter 13 draws from European experience to evaluate several different approaches to decentralization. Hunter, Vienonen and Wlodarczyk also lay out a comprehensive list of questions that policy makers should consider before embarking on a decentralization process.

In Chapter 14, Calnan, Halik and Sabbat explore the demands of citizens and patients for a greater say in health services. The authors review salient European experience on three major types of policies aimed at citizen empowerment: first, mechanisms to protect patients' rights and quality of care; second, the extent of patient choice; and, finally, strategies to increase participation and representation in health policy formulation. The chapter examines the potential impact of these policy changes, drawing on evidence from a number of recent UK studies.

In the last chapter of Part IV, Contandriopoulos, Lauristin and Leibovich examine the social underpinnings of health sector reform. Drawing upon philosophical and sociological analyses, Chapter 15 presents a framework for the social construction of reality, and for the values that subsequently develop within that framework. The chapter also applies this logic to the case of

CEE/CIS countries, demonstrating some of the dilemmas which current efforts to reconstruct these health care systems confront.

Finally, Part V looks at the actual implementation of change. Chapters 16 and 17 utilize analytical tools drawn from political science to examine why some reforms are introduced successfully, while others, however well designed, never materialize. Walt uses a policy analysis framework to explore the influence of contextual factors, processes and actors on the implementation of reforms. The author demonstrates how the framework can be used to plan strategically so that policies may be more effectively executed. Subsequently, Rathwell uses this policy framework to examine the experience to date with implementation of health system reform. From this review, the author identifies a number of attributes that have made some governments more successful than others in implementing reform.

All 17 chapters in this volume seek to incorporate both theory and evidence in the pursuit of a wiser, more flexible and more equitable health reform process. It is our hope as editors that, together, they make a useful contribution toward this end.

## REFERENCES

Abel-Smith, B. and Mossialos, E. (1994). Cost containment and health care reform: A study of the European Union. *Health Policy*, 28, 89–132.

Abel-Smith, B., Figueras, J., Holland, W., McKee, M. and Mossialos, E. (1995). *Choices in Health Policy: An Agenda for the European Union.* Luxembourg and Aldershot: Office for Official Publications of the European Communities and Dartmouth Publishing Company.

Appleby, J. (1992). *Financing Health Care in the 1990s.* Buckingham: Open University Press.

EBRD (European Bank for Reconstruction and Development) (1996). *Transition Report: Infrastructures and Savings.* London: European Bank for Reconstruction and Development.

Enthoven, A. (1985). *Reflections on the Management of the NHS.* London: Nuffield Provincial Hospitals Trust.

Figueras, J., Saltman, R. and Mossialos, E. (forthcoming). Challenges in evaluating health sector reform: An overview. In M. McKee (ed.), *Public Health in Europe – Learning from the Experience of Others.* London: Avebury.

Ham, C. (1996). Contestability: A middle path for health care. *British Medical Journal*, 312, 70–1.

Klein, R. (1995). Big bang health care reform – does it work? The case of Britain's 1991 National Health Service reforms. *Milbank Quarterly*, 73, 299–337.

Le Grand, J. and Bartlett, W. (1993). *Quasi-markets and Social Policy.* London: Macmillan.

McKee, M. and Figueras, J. (1997). Comparing health care systems: How do we know if we can learn from others? *Journal of Health Services Research and Policy,* 2, 122–5.

McPherson, K., Wennberg, J. E., Hovind, D. B. and Clifford, P. (1982). Small area variations in the use of common surgical procedures: An international comparison of New England, England, and Norway. *New England Journal of Medicine,* 307, 1310–14.

OECD (Organisation for Economic Co-operation and Development) (1993). *The Reform of Health Care: A Comparative Analysis of Seven OECD Countries.* Paris: Organisation for Economic Co-operation and Development.

OECD (1994). *The Reform of Health Care Systems: A Review of Seventeen OECD Countries.* Paris: Organisation for Economic Co-operation and Development.

Preker, A. S., Goldstein, E., Chellaraj, G. and Adeyi, O. (1995). *Health Status, Health Services and Health Expenditure: Trends During the Transition in CEE.* Washington, DC: World Bank.

Robinson, R. and Le Grand, J. (1995). Contracting and the purchaser–provider split. In R. Saltman and C. von Otter (eds), *Implementing Planned Markets in Health Care: Balancing Social and Economic Responsibility.* Buckingham: Open University Press.

Saltman, R. B. (1994). A conceptual overview of recent health care reforms. *European Journal of Public Health,* 4, 287–93.

Saltman, R. B. and von Otter, C. (1987). Revitalizing public health care systems. A proposal for public competition in Sweden. *Health Policy,* 7, 21–40.

Saltman, R. B. and von Otter, C. (1992). *Planned Markets and Public Competition: Strategic Reform in Northern European Health Systems.* Buckingham: Open University Press.

Warner, M. (1996). *Implementing Health Care Reforms through Substitution.* Cardiff: Welsh Institute for Health and Social Care.

Wennberg, J. E. (1987). Population illness rates do not explain population hospitalisation rates: A comment on Mark Blumberg's thesis that morbidity adjusters are needed to interpret small area variations. *Medical Care,* 25, 354–9.

WHO (World Health Organization) (1994). *Health in Europe: The 1993/94 Health For All Monitoring Report.* Copenhagen: WHO Regional Office for Europe.

WHO (1996). *Health Care Systems in Transition (Country Profiles).* Copenhagen: WHO Regional Office for Europe.

# PART I

## THE CONTEXT FOR HEALTH REFORM

# 1

# MACROECONOMIC CONSTRAINTS AND HEALTH CHALLENGES FACING EUROPEAN HEALTH SYSTEMS

Panos Kanavos and
Martin McKee

## INTRODUCTION

This chapter explores two of the major pressures for health care reform in Europe, the macroeconomic environment and the changing health needs of populations. Inevitably, the nature and consequences of these factors vary widely between countries. For the purposes of the present chapter the countries of the European region have been brought together into three groups: European Union (EU) countries, the central and eastern European (CEE) countries and the Commonwealth of Independent States (CIS) – within which the countries face broadly similar challenges. It is important, however, to recognize that, while the use of these standard groupings illustrates distinct trends in macroeconomic policy directions and patterns of disease, there are also important national and regional variations (Chenet *et al.* 1996a).

The chapter first discusses trends in health spending in Europe. It continues by identifying the nature and extent of the macroeconomic pressures in the countries of the region. It then reviews the health challenges and concludes by drawing together the main implications for health policy and for the reform of health services.

## HEALTH SPENDING AND RESOURCE ALLOCATION

### European Union

Within the EU, spending on health care has been absorbing a rising share of GDP since the post-war era from an average of 3.6 per cent in 1960 to 7.8 per cent in 1995. In the advent of the first and second oil shocks in the early and late 1970s respectively, most western European countries started to seek policies that would contain ever rising (public) expenditure on health (Abel-Smith *et al.* 1995; OECD 1995). The principal factors underlying the expansion of health care spending are common to most countries in western Europe and include ageing populations with the growth of chronic diseases and increasing need for care, but increasingly recognized as even more important are the technological developments in health care, many of which are cost-increasing (Abel-Smith 1996).

There are major differences in expenditures on health care among the countries in the EU. The highest spending countries, France and Germany, each spend up to four times more per capita than the lowest (Greece, Ireland, Portugal and Spain). Even when the expenditure is expressed as a percentage of GDP, large disparities remain. France spent 9.9 per cent of GDP on health care in 1995, followed by Belgium, Finland, Germany, Italy and the Netherlands with health spending above the EU average of 7.8 per cent. At the other end Greece spends 5.7 per cent of GDP. Despite the well-known association between national income and health care expenditure (total and as a percentage of GDP), this pattern does not wholly reflect the wealth of individual countries. Wealthier countries such as Denmark and the UK have spent less as a proportion of GDP than 'poorer' countries such as Ireland and Portugal. However, despite the wide use of comparative statistics on GDP and health spending, caution must be exercised when comparing countries with others due to problems in the methodology of collecting data in different countries, the reliability of the data themselves and the existence of underground (health) economies in different countries, the extent of which is not known (Kanavos and Mossialos 1997).

All health systems in the EU continue to be publicly funded, with public financing exceeding 75 per cent of total health spending. Austria, Germany, Italy, the Netherlands and Portugal have considerable private health insurance markets, which in the latter two cases is compulsory for higher income earners. Over time, however, there is a trend for private health markets to increase their share of health expenditure (Figure 1.1). At the same time, several EU Member States including Belgium, Finland, France and the UK have experienced an increase of the share of health expenditure in total public spending.

Considerable variations exist between countries in the EU in the allocation of resources. Ambulatory care absorbs almost half of total health spending in Luxembourg, over 30 per cent in Belgium and Portugal, while in Ireland, Spain and the UK its share is less

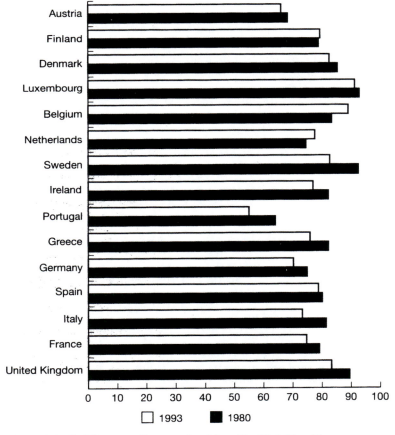

**Figure 1.1** Public expenditure on health as % of total health expenditure in EU countries, 1980–93

*Source*: OECD Health Data (1996)

than 15 per cent of the total. Pharmaceutical expenditure averages 16 per cent of total health spending in the EU, but ranges from 10 per cent in Austria to over 25 per cent in Portugal. Indicators of the physical volume of inputs also show a striking diversity. The ratio of doctors per 1000 population varies from 4.1 in Spain, followed by Greece and Italy, to 1.4 in the UK. The ratio of qualified nurses per 1000 population is highest in Finland (11.2) and Sweden (9.9), which have over three times the ratio of nurses than in Greece (3.5). The southern European Member States have the lowest doctor/nurse ratios with about one nurse per doctor compared with Ireland and the UK which have more than three nurses per doctor. While ratios of doctor employment in Greece, Italy and Spain are the highest among the EU, ratios of nurses are among the lowest. All countries are reducing in-patient bed rates, and reductions have been observed in acute hospital beds. Despite the fact that in-patient admissions as a percentage of the population have increased in most countries over the last 25 years, most countries in the EU have experienced a considerable decline in the average length of stay.

### Central and eastern Europe and the CIS

Most eastern European countries experienced an escalation in health spending, as a proportion of GDP, in the post-1989 era with the exception of Albania (Table 1.1). This was most obvious in the Czech Republic, where the total health expenditure as percentage of GDP rose from 4.6 per cent in 1987 to 7.8 per cent in 1994, while similar trends were observed in Hungary, Lithuania, Slovakia, Slovenia and less so in Bulgaria and Romania. In the CIS, health spending as a share of GDP is on average lower than the CEE average and ranges from 3 per cent in the Russian Federation to approximately 5.1 per cent in Uzbekistan in the early 1990s (World Bank 1993) although the figures must be treated with considerable caution because of poorly developed national statistical systems in some countries. In particular, there are major gaps in knowledge of the scale of private payments, subsidies by local enterprises and expenditure by other government departments.

Recorded spending in health care by most countries in the region remains low by OECD standards both in per capita terms and as a proportion of GDP (with the exception of Croatia, the Czech Republic and Slovenia). The reasons include the lower wages and incomes in the region, the (lower) prices of health supplies and/or

**Table 1.1** Health spending as % of GDP in EU, CEE and the CIS

| EU country | 1987 | 1995 | CEEC | 1987 | 1994 | CIS | 1994 | 1987 |
|---|---|---|---|---|---|---|---|---|
| Austria | 8.4 | 9.6 | Albania | 3.0 | 2.8 | Armenia | na | na |
| Belgium | 7.7 | 8 | Bulgaria | 3.3** | 4.0 | Azerbaijan | 3.8a | na |
| Denmark | 6.3 | 6.5 | Croatia | 8.4*** | 8.7 | Belarus | na | na |
| Finland | 7.5 | 8.2 | Czech Republic | 4.6 | 7.8 | Georgia | – | – |
| France | 8.5 | 9.9 | Estonia | 2.7*** | na | Kazakstan | 3.3a | – |
| Germany | 8.7 | 9.6 | Hungary | 4.7 | 6.9 | Kyrgyzstan | 4.4a | – |
| Greece | 4.3 | 5.2d | Latvia | 3.4a | 2.4b | Republic of Moldova | – | – |
| Ireland | 7.4 | 7.9d | Lithuania | 2.6 | 4.9 | Russian Federation | 3.0a | – |
| Italy | 7.4 | 7.7 | Poland | 4.0 | 4.9* | Tajikistan | – | – |
| Luxembourg | 6.4 | 5.8d | Romania | 2.1 | 3.7 | Turkmenistan | 0.8 | 3.2b |
| Netherlands | 8.1 | 8.8 | Slovakia | – | 7.0 | Ukraine | 7.7c | – |
| Portugal | 6.8 | 7.6d | Slovenia | – | 7.9 | Uzbekistan | 5.1c | – |
| Spain | 5.7 | 7.6 | The Former | 8.0a | 7.7 | | | |
| Sweden | 8.6 | 7.7 | Yugoslav Republic | | | | | |
| UK | 5.9 | 6.9 | of Macedonia | | | | | |

*Note:* *1993   **1988   ***1989   ****1989   a1990   b1991   c1992   d1994

*Sources:* OECD Health Data (1996); EBRD (1996); World Bank Reports

the lower amounts allocated to health care by national governments.

The main item of spending in most CEE countries and the CIS is salaries of health care professionals, often accounting for over 40 per cent of total health spending. The second largest element of the health budget is pharmaceuticals. CEE countries and the CIS countries are seeing their total expenditures allocated to drugs, medical supplies, technology and equipment rapidly rising. As an increasing proportion of these goods begins to reflect world prices, the share of total health spending allocated to them may rise disproportionately, as for instance in Hungary in 1994 where the proportion spent on drugs rose from 18 per cent to 30 per cent of total health spending. In addition to the foreign exchange burden, if the level of services is to remain constant, the share of health spending in GDP will have to increase and substantial domestic growth will have to occur. The alternative scenario (and in many cases the most likely one) is that the real wage in health is decreasing and the fall of resources is accompanied by lower quality of services, supply shortages and postponed facility maintenance.

Most countries in this part of the region suffer from excess capacity in terms of hospital beds and physicians per capita. The numbers of doctors per 1000 population in Latvia, Lithuania and Ukraine, for instance, was higher than in any EU country (4.3, 4.3 and 4.5 respectively) in 1992; similar trends hold for hospital beds. As noted in Chapter 10, it would be essential to withdraw unnecessary hospital beds from service and rationalize hospital service delivery by retaining only programmes relevant to service area needs. At the same time, it would be essential to reduce the annual intake of medical students and rationalize the number of medical school facilities, while recognizing that the pattern of medical employment is quite different from western Europe with many doctors in area-based polyclinics having low skill levels and undertaking work done by other health care workers elsewhere.

## MACROECONOMIC PRESSURES

### European Union

The EU Member States experienced high growth rates in the 1960s and 1970s averaging 5.1 per cent per annum in the 1960s and 3.7 per cent in the 1970s. Following recessions in the early and late 1980s, the 1990s were characterized by moderate growth which did not match the performance of the 1960s and 1970s (see Figure 1.2).

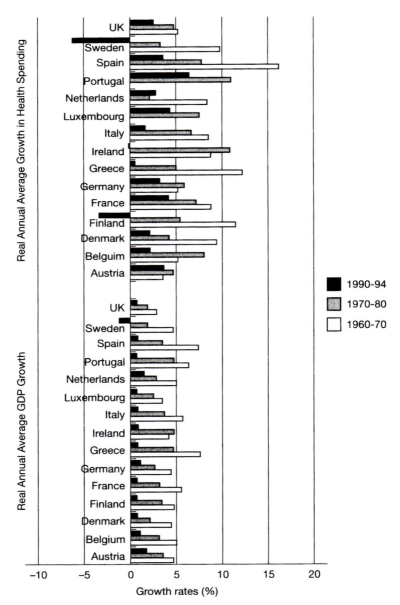

**Figure 1.2** Real annual average health expenditure growth (upper panel) and real annual GDP growth (lower panel) in EU countries, 1960–94

*Source*: OECD Health Data (1996)

Over time, therefore, growth rates have been declining, thereby exerting pressures on public expenditures and, in particular, in the allocation of resources to health, since health spending has tended to rise faster on average than national resources in most EU Member States (Figure 1.2).

Lower growth rates and economic policy choices aiming at keeping inflation under control are not, however, the only macroeconomic pressures on financing of health care in the EU. The debate about forming an economic and monetary union (EMU) is another. Although the 15 Member States could be divided into two categories according to their political stance on EMU, macroeconomic policy choices are similar regardless of the endorsement or not of the Maastricht Treaty and its requirements for such a union. Policy priorities include the control of inflation and the pursuit of macroeconomic stability, thereby implying drastic reduction of fiscal deficits and overall government debt levels. Concerns for both groups of countries have led economic policy makers to call for reductions and rationalizations in public sector spending, particularly for human services such as health care.

All EU Member States are currently implementing tight fiscal policies in order to control either their general government deficits or their overall debts or both, whilst at the same time trying to achieve or maintain price stability. It is generally accepted that most Member States are far from meeting the Maastricht requirements. The need to tighten fiscal policies further leads to the conclusion that governments are likely to introduce further cuts in expenditure in many areas of public finance which may include health care. Additionally, Member States need growth rates above the trend if long-term problems such as unemployment are to become less of a burden; otherwise the impact of tight fiscal policy on health care expenditure may be even more restrictive.

The implications therefore for health care financing are compelling. Health expenditure is part of the overall budget, which has been increasing in significance not only because health expenditures are rising faster than national resources, but also due to attempts by many countries to privatize other parts of the public sector in view of growing fiscal pressures, which has increased the relative importance of health within the state budget. Contractionary fiscal policies will mean that the health sector will be subjected to further pressures by national governments, which may imply the privatization of parts of the health economy, or the exercise of more explicit forms of rationing. The latter is actively on the agenda of many EU countries, together with the debate over appropriateness of care and the resulting development of clinical practice guidelines by professional bodies (Grol 1993; Thomas 1994; Le Fur and Sermet 1996).

Consequently, it is not surprising that health care reform in EU countries over the last 15 years has focused largely on cost containment (Abel-Smith and Mossialos 1994) and improving micro-efficiency. Evidence can be found from particular countries of the effectiveness of specific measures which were taken (Mossialos *et al.* 1997). Budget controls, targets and manpower limits can be quite effective. Budgets for hospitals have accelerated reductions in lengths of stay and budgets for doctors in Germany have reduced them. Increases in cost sharing can reduce demand except where there is substantial supplementary health insurance as in France. However, it is often difficult to distinguish the quantitative effect of particular measures because of other changes happening at the same time; for example, the introduction of a new technology or procedure may be cost-reducing in that it reduces the length of stay, but may also be cost-increasing in that it may require highly specialized staff, have high maintenance costs or transfer costs to the community.

### CEE and CIS countries

During the post-1989 era, most CEE/CIS countries in the region implemented macroeconomic reforms supplemented by institutional changes and enactment of new legislation aiming to complete the transformation at different paces. The willingness to implement reforms manifested itself in the adoption of 'big-bang' reforms in some countries, more gradually in others. The governments in most of the region have liberalized prices, external trade and currency arrangements, privatized small-scale economic units, introduced new tax systems and reformed their 'social safety net'. Most of the governments in eastern Europe began the implementation of stabilization policies (tight fiscal and monetary policies) between 1989 and 1992 (EBRD 1994). Most CIS countries followed similar policy patterns although they still find themselves at the early stages of market-oriented reform, either because of a different approach to reform or because of war or social unrest (e.g. in Armenia, Azerbaijan, Georgia).

In terms of macroeconomic performance, the countries in the region are diverging. An 'advanced' group consisting of the Baltic states, Croatia, the Czech Republic, Hungary, Poland, Slovakia and Slovenia are well into the recovery phase and have achieved substantial structural reform and macroeconomic stabilization. In an 'intermediate' group, major stabilization and reform efforts have been made but with mixed results; this is the case in Bulgaria, the Former Yugoslav Republic of Macedonia, the Republic of Moldova and Romania. Albania has recently experienced social unrest following a period of growth from 1993–6. The current environment in most of the above CEE countries can be characterized by relatively strong growth since 1992–3 (EBRD 1996), although short-term effects and external shocks (such as slow growth in the main export markets of western Europe) heavily affect the performance of these countries.

In the third group, comprising all other CIS countries, there has been little progress. Considerable changes still need to take place in order to change the command of this region's economies including privatization and restructuring of public finances and the legal framework. The common feature of CIS countries is zero or negative growth, although the prospects appear to be improving with a slowdown in 1995 and 1996 of output decline.

The trend of rising recorded health care spending in CEE countries in relation to GDP has to be balanced against the background of considerable decline in output and income during the 1989–94 period. The initial period of contraction was subsequently followed by relatively high growth rates for most of the countries in this group. During the same period, total health expenditures did not increase in real terms. It is therefore suggested that the increase in the share of health expenditure in eastern Europe was the result of a dramatic contraction in local GDP rather than a conscious rise in health sector investment (Kanavos 1997). For this purpose, the comparison between the rate of real GDP growth and the rate of growth of real health expenditures is quite striking. Table 1.2 shows that despite the severe contraction (or moderate expansion in the best of cases) in real GDP growth over the 1987–94 period, real health expenditures either grew faster or contracted slower than GDP only with the exception of Albania and the Former Yugoslav Republic of Macedonia, where health expenditures declined faster than GDP. The fact that health spending increased faster than GDP in the ensuing growth period (1994–6) in several countries including the Czech Republic, Croatia and Hungary reflects the health policy choices made during the previous years which led to an explosion of health care costs.

**Table 1.2** Growth rates of GDP and health expenditures in eastern European countries, 1987–94

| | 1987–90 | | 1991–4 | |
|---|---|---|---|---|
| | *GDP growth* | *Health expenditure growth* | *GDP growth* | *Health expenditure growth* |
| Albania | –7.9 | 4.5 | –34.4 | –57.7 |
| Bulgaria | –9.2[a] | 8.5[a] | –3.1 | 1.5 |
| Croatia | – | – | –23.6 | –8.8 |
| Czech Republic | – | – | –55 | 14.1 |
| Hungary | 4.6 | 26.8 | 2.3[c] | 4.9[c] |
| Lithuania | 0.3 | 7.5 | –48.9 | –33.3 |
| Poland | –2.0 | 17.8[b] | 5.6[c] | –4.8[c] |
| Romania | –12.7 | 18.7 | –5.5 | 3.5 |
| Slovakia | 0.5[a] | 6.8 | –21.2 | 31.8 |
| Slovenia | – | – | 0.0 | 51.8 |
| The Former Yugoslav Republic of Macedonia | – | – | –24.6[c] | –49.0[c] |

*Notes:* [a]1990/89
[b]Only capital health expenditures are available
[c]1993/91

*Source:* Chellaraj *et al.* (1996)

The immediate economic pressures that the CEE/CIS countries are facing are multiple and include among others the continuous pursuit of stabilization policies in order to control inflation (particularly in CIS), intensifying the efforts for structural reform and creation of viable employment opportunities for the region's populations, and addressing the tremendous infrastructure needs (particularly CIS) in order to make the economies of the region more competitive in the medium-to-long term (EBRD 1994). Many CEE countries aim to integrate themselves into the EU (Czech Republic, Estonia, Hungary, Poland and Slovenia in the 'first' wave), and this, apart from its resource implications for administration and legislation, may further suggest that macroeconomic performance indicators will be closely monitored and continually evaluated. This also implies that health care is one of the areas requiring attention by national governments. The resource issue becomes critical in this respect as all countries in the region become more price sensitive particularly to those parts of the health sector that cannot be produced locally (technology, supplies, medicines).

The continuing recession in some parts of eastern Europe (mainly Albania, Bulgaria and Romania) and many parts of the CIS (particularly the Russian Federation, Ukraine and most central Asian republics), has resulted in a severe undercapitalization of health insurance funds, due to the shrinking tax base, arrears and avoidance of contributions.

## HEALTH CHALLENGES

The configuration of health services in Europe, at both the micro and macro levels, is also being driven by the changing pattern of disease. The expansion of services for sexually transmitted diseases in the wake of the rise in HIV infection and AIDS is an example of changes at the micro level (Wellings 1994), whereas concerns about the long-term financing of health services in the light of ageing populations and the rising level of chronic disease are influencing organization at the macro level. The following section provides an overview of some of the major trends in health in Europe.

### Health trends in Europe[1]

In terms of overall trends in mortality, the most striking finding is the divergence in life expectancy between these three parts of the region (Figures 1.3 and 1.4). Between 1980 and 1995, male life expectancy at birth in the EU increased by 3.3 years from 70.7 to 74; for females, it increased by 3.2 years from 77.5 to 80.7. In contrast, in CEE countries, the figure for males increased by only 0.5 of a year, from an already low value of 66.8 to 67.3 years; the increase for females was 2 years, from 73.6 to 75.6 years. The situation in the NIS is the most disturbing, with life expectancy at birth actually falling: for men by 1.1 year from 62.2 to 61.1 years, and for women by 0.4 of a year from 72.5 to 72.1 years. There has since been a slight recovery.

These aggregate figures conceal considerable national and regional diversity. In general, life expectancy is greater in countries in the south of each of the regions, such as Greece, Italy and Spain in western Europe, Albania in the CEE countries, and the republics of the Caucasus in the NIS. In western Europe, Denmark experienced very little increase in life expectancy over the period (Chenet *et al.* 1996b), while the previously rapid improvement in Spain slowed down after 1981, due to increasing numbers of deaths in young people from accidents and HIV/AIDS (Chenet *et al.* 1997).

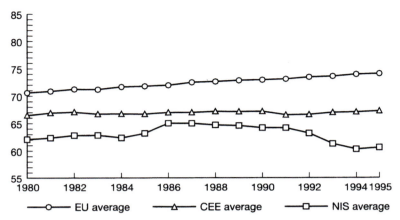

**Figure 1.3**  Life expectancy at birth in the WHO European region, males, 1980–95

*Source*: WHO (1996b)

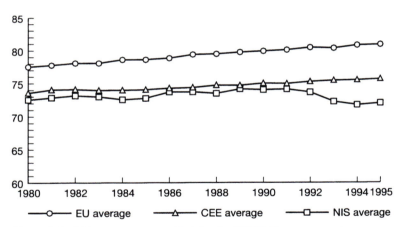

**Figure 1.4**  Life expectancy at birth in the WHO European region, females, 1980–95

*Source*: WHO (1996b)

The previous advantageous position of Greece is also being lost, largely due to the rise of smoking-related diseases. In CEE countries, the Czech Republic and Poland have experienced recent reversals of long-term downward trends in life expectancy while Hungary has not. Accidents and violence, as well as liver cirrhosis

– all strongly related to alcohol consumption – play an important role in Hungary but somewhat less so in Poland, where a popular campaign against alcohol consumption in the early 1980s halted a previously increasing trend in alcohol-related diseases (Varasovszky *et al.* 1997). In the NIS, the Russian Federation has experienced a particularly serious deterioration in male life expectancy at birth, losing seven years between 1986 and 1994, although this has ranged from a loss of 12 to 49 years, in some regions such as Tuva and Sakhalin, to a slight improvement in others, such as Dagestan. There have also been differences in trends over time, with a dramatic improvement in life expectancy in the NIS after 1985 that has subsequently been reversed (Figures 1.3 and 1.4). There is now compelling evidence that these fluctuations in mortality are not an artefact and are due, in very large parts, to changes in alcohol consumption. Deaths from accidents, violence and cardiac disease have been especially affected, with many of the cardiac deaths apparently due to acute toxic effects of alcohol superimposed on alcoholic cardiomyopathy rather than, as was previously thought, atheromatous coronary disease (Figure 1.5).

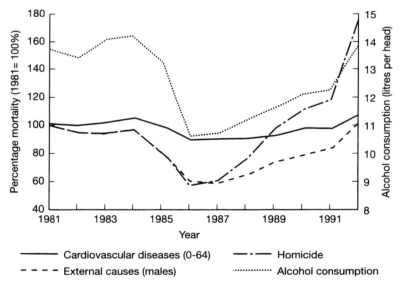

**Figure 1.5**    Alcohol consumption and mortality in the Russian Federation, 1981–92

*Source*: WHO (1996b)

Elsewhere in the NIS, in the central Asian republics, there are also major threats to the health of women, with a high prevalence of nutritional anaemia due largely to the consequences of differential distribution of food within families, with many women surviving predominantly on a diet of tea and bread.

Turning to specific causes of death, in any ranking of leading challenges to health in Europe, cardiovascular diseases feature strongly. They cause half of all deaths and a third of all permanent disability in the region, and are therefore responsible for a substantial proportion of total health care costs. Death rates vary widely within the region and, as with life expectancy, the trends are diverging (Figures 1.6 and 1.7). There are also large differences between the rates in males and females, partly due to the protective effect of female hormones which delay the onset of disease until after menopause, but also due to lower rates of smoking among women in many countries.

In the EU countries between 1981 and 1995, the age-standardized death rate from ischaemic heart disease among men aged 0–64 years decreased from 77.2 to 47.0 per 100,000 population. In females, there was also a decrease from 16.8 to 10.8. In the CEE countries, however, the figure for males increased from 86.2 in 1981 to 99.8 in 1995, with a smaller increase for women from 22.2 to 26.3 per 100,000. As with life expectancy, the situation in the NIS is

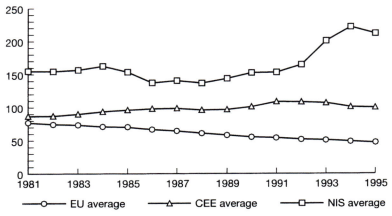

**Figure 1.6** Age-standardized death rates (SDR) from ischaemic heart disease in the WHO European region, males, 0–64 years, 1981–95

*Source*: WHO (1996b)

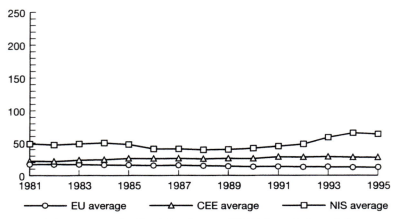

**Figure 1.7** Age-standardized death rates (SDR) from ischaemic heart disease in the WHO European region, females, 0–64 years, 1981–95
*Source*: WHO (1996b)

significantly worse, with an increase among men from 153.9 per 100,000 in 1981 to 203.0 in 1995; the corresponding figures for women are 47.1 and 58.2. Thus, in this age group, the death rates from heart disease among NIS citizens are now between four and five times those in the EU. Cardiovascular diseases account for approximately half of the difference in life expectancy between eastern and western Europe, although the risk factors for deaths from cardiac disease differ in the two halves of Europe.

Cancer is the second largest cause of death in the region, accounting for 20 per cent of all deaths. The overall trends conceal differences in cancers at different sites. Many cancers are related to aspects of lifestyle and thus preventable to varying degrees, although certain genetic susceptibilities render some individuals at greater risk than others. The role of lifestyle is most clearly demonstrated by tobacco consumption, which is an important cause of a wide range of cancers, and is the leading avoidable cause of cancer in Europe (Figure 1.8). Lung cancer rates offer a marker for the consequences of juvenile smoking, and in the NIS/CEE countries the aggressive marketing by tobacco companies will have major health consequences in the future. In each part of the region, death rates are much lower in women than in men, reflecting their somewhat later adoption of smoking on a large scale. There are inevitably large national variations partly reflecting cultural

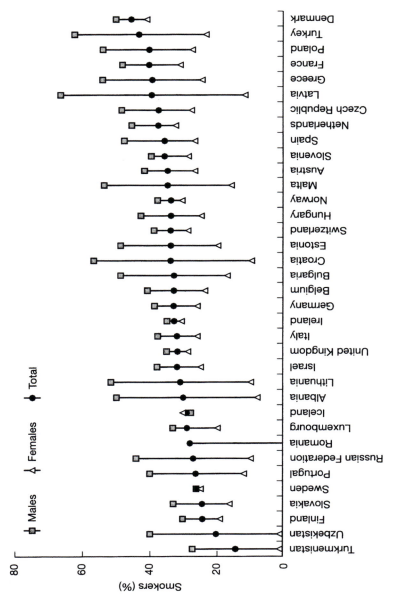

**Figure 1.8** Estimates of smoking prevalence in the WHO European region, early 1990s

*Source:* WHO (1996b)

**Table 1.3** Factors contributing to the gap in life expectancy between the CEE countries and NIS and western European countries

| Cause of death | Additional life expectancy in western Europe by age group (years) | | | | |
|---|---|---|---|---|---|
| | <1 year | 1–34 years | 35–64 years | >65 years | All ages |
| Infectious and parasitic diseases | 0.3 | 0.1 | 0.08 | -0.01 | 0.47 |
| Cancer | 0 | 0.05 | 0.25 | -0.35 | -0.05 |
| Cardiovascular diseases | 0 | 0.07 | 1.36 | 1.85 | 3.28 |
| Respiratory diseases | 0.68 | 0.2 | 0.15 | -0.5 | 0.97 |
| Digestive diseases | 0.02 | 0.03 | 0.08 | -0.04 | 0.09 |
| External causes | 0.04 | 0.64 | 0.71 | 0.03 | 1.41 |
| Undefined conditions | -0.1 | 0.01 | 0.04 | 0.18 | 0.12 |
| Other diseases | 0 | 0 | -0.02 | -0.2 | -0.22 |
| All causes | 0.93 | 1.09 | 2.63 | 1.4 | 6.06 |

*Source:* WHO (1996b)

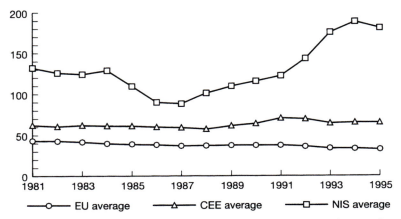

**Figure 1.9** Age-standardized death rates (SDR) from external causes in the WHO European region, 0–64 years, 1981–95

*Source*: WHO (1996b)

differences, and the gap between the sexes is rapidly closing in some countries such as Denmark. Furthermore, smoking may act synergistically with other causes of cancer such as exposure to asbestos and, in the case of cervical cancer, human papillomavirus.

Other aspects of lifestyle are also important. Diet contributes to cancer of the gastrointestinal tract and breast, and sexual activity, through viral infection, contributes to cancer of the cervix.

External causes of death, such as accidents, homicide and suicide are the third greatest cause of death in the region, and they are the second largest contributor to the gap in life expectancy at birth between eastern and western Europe (Table 1.3). They particularly affect adults in their thirties and forties, and thus have a disproportionate impact on families and on industrial productivity. They have risen dramatically in the NIS, largely due to increased consumption of alcohol. They have fallen in the EU and risen only slightly in the CEE countries. These trends are shown in Figure 1.9.

## IMPLICATIONS FOR HEALTH SERVICE REFORM

### Ageing populations

The changing demography of the European population is producing a substantial challenge to health services. The need for health care accelerates once people are over 75, although some evidence suggests that consumption of resources is related to the period before death at whatever age this occurs, suggesting that the consequences of ageing populations may be less than some have suggested. This argument is as yet unresolved but it is clear that the percentage of the population that is elderly is increasing in all parts of Europe, although increases will be especially great in southern and western Europe. This has implications both for total need for health care and for the pattern of diseases contributing to it.

The anticipated increased need for health care has important resource consequences. In many countries, this is compounded by falling birth rates, so that the number of working people able to contribute to health care funds will decrease just as need is increas- ing, and when other demands for social welfare, such as pensions, are also increasing. The scale of this problem will vary. Some coun- tries, such as the UK, will be affected relatively mildly, but others, like France, Germany and Italy, will face substantial challenges (Chand and Jaeger 1996). The dramatic decline in birth rates in many NIS/CEE countries is also likely to prove a major problem, since a smaller economically active population will be available to support growing numbers of elderly people.

**Macroeconomic constraints**

The macroeconomic environment provides the starting point for most sectoral analyses including the health sector. In health care, a resource intensive service, macroeconomic pressures may manifest themselves in a variety of ways ranging from the relaxation of health and safety rules to the deterioration in the quantity and qual- ity of services provided and the deterioration of health status.

Within the EU, it is clear that with a few exceptions such as Ireland and the Netherlands, fast economic growth is an experience of the past and most EU economies are characterized by slow growth rates combined with high unemployment; this creates the pressing need to keep public expenditure under control constantly, particularly those parts which have had the tendency to rise faster than GDP, including health spending. In addition, all Member States (with the exception of Luxembourg) are some distance from meeting the tough conver- gence criteria (budgetary, debt, inflation and interest rate) put for- ward for the EMU. This unavoidably implies contractionary fiscal policies not only in the run-up to monetary union but also during its implementation phase afterwards in order to keep within the prede- termined performance ranges. The reduction of current levels of deficit and debt requires further restrictive budgetary policies, which may result in attempts to reduce the size of public sectors further.

The macroeconomic environment in Europe has a number of implications for the financing and provision of health care. Despite the high levels of health expenditure in the EU, measured both in absolute terms and as a share of GDP, there are concerns about the quality of care and patient satisfaction (Mossialos 1997). The need for cost containment and greater micro-efficiency in different parts of the health sector are high on the agenda of policy makers throughout the EU (OECD 1994). Similar is the pressure to set priorities for services that can be reimbursed. The issue of health technology, its utilization and contribution to rising health care costs, poses additional pressures on health budgets and, increasingly, calls for an evaluation of its role (Davis 1974). Finally, if fiscal pressures intensify several countries may seek short-term savings by privatizing certain parts of the health service, or further excluding populations from publicly provided services.

The nature of the macroeconomic problem is substantially different in CEE/CIS countries than in the EU. The element in common across the board in CEE/CIS countries was the deep recession in all countries, following the demise of the socialist system of governance. This recession manifested itself with various degrees of intensity and was made evident through negative growth rates, high inflation or hyperinflation, high unemployment and limited employment opportunities. The tasks ahead for the majority of these countries are to reverse the negative output and high inflation trends and pursue actively a transformation of their economies, while at the same time maintaining fiscal and monetary stability.

The implications for health services of the macroeconomic environment in CEE/CIS countries are quite considerable. Most CEE countries experienced an increase in the costs of health care after 1989; however, the share of GDP spent on health tends to be higher in CEE countries than in developing countries at similar income levels (Goldstein *et al.* 1996). Yet the evidence suggests that most systems in the region are underfunded, resulting in poor quality of care. As the WHO reports in its *Health Care Systems in Transition* profiles, the health sector in most countries in transition faces serious problems in connection with both hospital facilities and medical equipment (WHO 1996a). Hospitals are deemed to be too old and ill-equipped and capital expenditures are largely insufficient to support existing facilities or introduce new technology where it is needed. Such a move would require an expansion and diversification of capital resources. By contrast, these are becoming a lesser fraction of spending over time, thus postponing necessary investment.

The conflict between macroeconomic limits on public budgets and the demand for ever-increasing care has spread amongst CEE countries the 'third revolution of health care' (i.e. cost containment) to the same extent that it has done in the EU. In this light, a restructuring of expenditure might be a more appropriate strategy for the short term. This restructuring implies constraints imposed on specific types of expenditures (positive lists and/or budgets for drugs, capitation payments for first contact doctors, making excess capacity redundant).

The potential strategy to use market forces in the health sector has both positive and negative implications (Preker and Feachem 1994). The health budget crisis which occurred in Poland in 1992, in part due to a sudden increase in the price of pharmaceuticals, and the cost explosion in the Czech Republic in 1992–5 pose serious warnings about the extensive use of market forces. Efficiency gains through market forces require accompanying tough regulatory measures, some public production and targeted subsidies to control the associated abuses and deficiencies (Enthoven 1988).

The introduction of health insurance has been characterized by some as a way to solve many of the financial problems of the health system. However, a health insurance scheme does not create new money in the economy for health care but introduces a set of complex dynamics into the health system that can adversely affect service delivery. Premature introduction of health insurance can lead to financial problems, the competitiveness of the transition economies, distortions in priority for service delivery and distraction away from the need to deal with more fundamental problems in the health system. The Czech Republic, Hungary and Slovakia are experiencing serious difficulties because of the ill-timed introduction of health insurance.

In the CIS, the continuing recession calls for solutions in financing health systems and allocating funds; instead of allocating according to the number of beds and personnel, ministries should base decisions on the number of patients treated related to population served or alternatively allocate funds on a per capita basis and allow payment for services to stimulate competition among health institutions.

## Changing patterns of health

The present pattern of disease in Europe has major implications for the organization and delivery of health services. The enormous burden of chronic disease in the CIS and, to a slightly lesser extent, in CEE countries, places a huge load on curative health services. This load is likely to be unsustainable, as illustrated by the financial crises affecting many health care systems in the region. This can only be tackled through a major reorientation of the health services: three major implications are identified here.

First, although there is growing evidence that health services are making a greater contribution to declining mortality in western Europe than was thought in the 1970s (Bunker 1995), in CEE/CIS countries it is necessary to recognize that health services *per se* can have only a relatively limited impact on the major determinants of health. Health status is largely determined by the interaction of four linked factors: genetic susceptibility, behaviour and lifestyle, socio-economic status and environmental conditions (Lalonde 1974).

Concentrating on health services entails the risk that important underlying factors may be ignored such as social position and socio-economic status. There is now convincing evidence that societal factors are important (Evans *et al.* 1994). The British Whitehall Study, which followed up a cohort of civil servants, found that death rates were higher among officials in lower grades, and this was true at all levels of employment. Furthermore, these higher death rates could only partly be explained by known risk factors such as diet and tobacco consumption (Smith *et al.* 1990). Similarly, there is a growing body of evidence in western Europe that inequalities in wealth are important determinants of differences in mortality between countries (Wilkinson 1992) and within them (Ben-Shlomo *et al.* 1996; Kaplan *et al.* 1996). Unemployment and the insecurity that accompanies it are also important predictors of ill health. Despite the sparse research in CEE/CIS countries, there is evidence that those at the margins of society and in relative poverty in the CEE – divorced men, for example – have been most adversely affected (Hajdu *et al.* 1995) and that stress is playing a significant part in the high levels of mortality (Bosma 1994).

Second, reformed health systems must incorporate mechanisms for tackling the major threats to health. There is a need to reorientate health services towards health promotion and prevention of disease. In particular, the increase in tobacco consumption presents

an enormous challenge to governments. The interval between starting smoking and developing lung cancer means that the health services of the twenty-first century will face an enormous burden from
tobacco-related disease. Efforts will also have to be directed at diet,
which is likely to be an extremely important factor, with generally
low levels of nutrition in the CEE/CIS countries (EURONUT-
SENECA 1991). Here there is some cause for optimism, with
decreasing consumption of animal fats and increasing consumption
of fruit and vegetables in some countries (Poland) but not to the
same extent in others (Hungary). In sum, there is a need for strong
public health services with the ability to monitor trends in diseases
and to support the development of integrated programmes, involving both preventive and curative services, to deal with them.

Third, as patterns of disease change over time, health services
will need to respond to these changes rather than remain trapped in
structures designed for a time when disease patterns were quite
different. Health services have regularly responded to new challenges. For instance, the spread of HIV infection and AIDS has
stimulated the development of health promotion activities and services directed at sexually transmitted diseases. While the record of
responses to abrupt changes in patterns of disease has often been
good, results have been less satisfactory in the face of longer-term
trends.

Patterns of disease will continue to change. There will be further
growth in the number of people suffering from heart disease, cere-
brovascular disease, cancer, dementia and, especially among
women, fractures. It will no longer be sufficient for health services
to respond reactively to these conditions. As research develops on
the effectiveness of specialized programmes to tackle the major
causes of disease, health services will have to reconfigure themselves accordingly with, for example, regionalized cancer services,
dedicated multidisciplinary stroke units (Indredavik *et al.* 1991) and
integrated packages of care that involve orthopaedic surgery, geriatric medicine and rehabilitation for patients with fractured hips. A
further consequence of ageing is that an increasing number of
people will suffer from multiple disorders, thus requiring a wide
range of treatments with potential for adverse interactions. This
presents health services with new challenges and emphasizes the
need to move away from a model of care that is based on individual
physicians to one involving multidisciplinary teams.

Changes in diet and lifestyle also present serious challenges to
health services. For many years, longevity has been greater in the

countries of southern Europe than in other parts of the region, even within groups of countries that are otherwise broadly similar. This is largely believed to be due to differences in diet (de Lorgeril *et al.* 1994). Unfortunately, the situation is changing in those countries that have historically enjoyed this advantage. The spread of northern European diets to countries such as Spain, containing high levels of animal fat rather than fresh fruit and vegetables, is likely to lead to increasing levels of heart disease and to other diet-related diseases such as breast cancer. It may become necessary, for example, to reassess the need for screening programmes in southern European countries with previously low levels of breast cancer.

Rising tobacco consumption in some parts of Europe is another way in which lifestyle changes create greater demands for cancer services and, where the increase is taking place in parallel with a breakdown of traditional family structures, a need for palliative care services. The growth of smoking in countries that are also experiencing dietary change, such as Greece and Spain, will exacerbate the rise in cardiovascular diseases. Smoking has many other consequences, however, including insidious effects on lung function that render many people less fit for general anaesthetics and more prone to postoperative chest infections leading to longer stays in hospital and to higher costs.

The growth of new and re-emerging infections presents a further challenge. It is important to note that the implications of the emergence of HIV/AIDS have not been confined to services for sexually transmitted diseases, but have affected nearly all aspects of health care including approaches to hospital infection control and the screening of blood products. The growth of multi-resistant bacteria in hospitals is likely to have major consequences for the way in which hospital services are provided. In some countries, the lack of appropriate, enforced antibiotic policies is causing large increases in the rates of hospital-acquired infections and consequently adding to both length of stay and costs.

Increased incidence of infectious diseases, however, is not confined to patients already in hospital. The breakdown of previous public health measures in the NIS has contributed to the re-emergence of poliomyelitis, diphtheria, cholera and malaria, with important implications for public health and primary health care services. All of Europe is facing an increasing incidence of tuberculosis, a disease many thought had almost disappeared. The emergence of a variant resistant to most common drugs is especially worrying, necessitating new approaches such as the supervised administration of medication and the prescription of expensive second-line drugs.

The preceding paragraphs give some examples of the changes in disease patterns that European health services are confronting. These changes will affect the countries' abilities to sustain existing levels of provision, as well as the way in which services are provided, and carry considerable implications for health care reform. Traditional hospital care, with treatment regimes based on a narrow medical model and with a wide range of diseases treated in general wards, is no longer appropriate. New structures and packages of incentives should reflect the demands currently facing providers and not reinforce obsolete models of care. This, in turn, makes it essential that those involved in health sector reform should incorporate into their debates evidence about trends in disease patterns and their implications for health services using the approaches described above.

In sum, the changing patterns of disease have a wide set of implications for those involved in health system reform. It is clear that many of the diseases that will contribute most to the burden of ill health in the coming decades are caused by factors outside the formal health sector. If they are to be most effective, cost-containment strategies should address demand both in terms of the numbers of people seeking care and of the health system's ability to return them rapidly to the community – prevention, the strengthening of primary health care and the reorientation of hospital services. To do so, they must ensure that reformed health systems have a strong public health component that can analyse trends in disease, identify explanations and propose and monitor effective responses. This will require effective support and trained individuals with an understanding of epidemiology, of health care evaluation and of approaches to changing professional behaviour. Without intersectoral action that can address the major underlying causes of ill health, the growing burden of disease will compromise efforts to achieve other government objectives such as economic growth.

## CONCLUSION

Health systems in the European region are facing considerable macroeconomic constraints that may impact on the ability of publicly funded health systems to keep pace with rising health care costs in the near future. Demand for health services has been increasing consistently over the past two decades, faster than national income in real terms, whilst at the same time real GDP growth rates have fallen considerably in the 1980s and 1990s compared with the 1960s and 1970s, particularly in eastern Europe which experienced a painful path towards transition. The need to meet an ever-increasing demand for health services from a total pool of resources which does not grow at the same rate contributes to the national economies' budget deficits and overall indebtedness.

A further source of macroeconomic pressure in the EU stems from the determination by most Member States to participate in Economic and Monetary Union. As most of them are still far from meeting the above criteria, policy responses put emphasis on fiscal policy not only in the run-up to Monetary Union, but also over the long term. Eastern Europe, by contrast, has only just begun to register positive growth rates, having had to undergo severe recession and structural reform. The latter is expected to continue in the foreseeable future, imposing pressures on national resources including total spending on health. As health systems in the EU are publicly financed, rising health costs and low growth rates impose additional pressures on national budgets, the deficits of which need to be curbed and kept consistently low. It is not surprising, therefore, that cost containment has gained priority in health policy decision making.

The European region also faces a number of evolving patterns in the causes of disease and death, which could impact on the ability of health services to deliver care in the near future. There are three such challenges. First, infectious diseases pose considerable threat to the extent that there are no effective treatments that cure the disease. Furthermore, many known conditions/infections exist that are resistant to many (or most of) known antibiotics, thereby increasing the cost of treatment and contributing to the need for additional drug testing, and for more prolonged hospital stays, as well as the use of non-antibiotic management, such as isolation techniques. Second, conditions such as diabetes and conditions of the central nervous system are gaining in importance. These conditions are to a certain extent associated with age, or psycho-social factors, and contribute considerably to the cost of treating patients as European populations age gradually and available treatments are more palliative than curative. Third, diseases related to diet, habits and lifestyles impose a further economic burden which is not strictly related to the health sector *per se*, but brings further spillover effects to the family and the social system.

The resource constraint, the health challenges and the ageing populations limit the flexibility of national governments in the entire European region to varying degrees. Difficult choices will have to be made regarding the funding of health services and the allocation of scarce resources to ever-increasing demand.

## NOTE

1 The epidemiological data given in this section are taken from the WHO Regional Office for Europe's Health for All database, in which statistics on the CIS countries and the Baltic states are combined to give a single figure for the newly independent states (NIS) of the former USSR (WHO 1996b).

## REFERENCES

Abel-Smith, B. (1996). Escalation of health care costs: How did we get there? In OECD Health Policy Studies No. 8 (*Health Care Reform: The Will to Change*). Paris: OECD.

Abel-Smith, B. and Mossialos, E. (1994). Cost containment and health care reform: A study of the European Union. *Health Policy*, 28, 89–132.

Abel-Smith, B., Figueras, J., Holland, W., McKee, M. and Mossialos, E. (1995). *Choices in Health Policy: An Agenda for the European Union*. Luxembourg and Aldershot: Office for Official Publications of the European Communities and Dartmouth Publishing Company.

Ben-Shlomo, Y., White, I. R. and Marmot, M. (1996). Does the variation in the socioeconomic characteristics of an area affect mortality? *British Medical Journal*, 312, 1013–14.

Bosma, J. H. A. (1994). *A Cross Cultural Comparison of the Role of Some Psychosocial Factors in the Etiology of Coronary Artery Disease. Follow up to the Kaunas Rotterdam Intervention Study (KRIS)*. Maastricht: Maastricht University Press.

Bunker, J. P. (1995). Medicine matters after all. *Journal of the Royal College of Physicians, London*, 29, 105–12.

Chand, S. K. and Jaeger, A. (1996). *Ageing Populations and Public Pension Schemes*. IMF Occasional Paper No. 147. Washington, DC: International Monetary Fund.

Chellaraj, G., Adeyi, O., Preker, A. S. and Goldstein, E. (1996). *Trends in Health Status, Health Services, and Health Finance: The Transition in Central and Eastern Europe*. World Bank Technical Paper. Washington, DC: World Bank.

Chenet, L., McKee, M., Fulop, N., Bòjan, F., Brand, H., Hort, A. and Kalbarcyzk, P. (1996a). Changing life expectancy in central Europe: Is there a single reason? *Journal of Public Health Medicine*, 18, 329–36.

Chenet, L., Osler, M., McKee, M. and Krasnik, A. (1996b). Changing life expectancy in the 1980s: Why was Denmark different? *Journal of Epidemiology and Community Health*, 50, 404–7.

Chenet, L., McKee, M., Otero, A. and Ausin, I. (1997). What happened to life expectancy in Spain in the 1980s? *Journal of Epidemiology and Community Health*, 51, 510–14.

Davis, K. (1974). The role of technology demand and labour markets in the determination of hospital costs. In M. Perlman (ed.), *The Economics of Health and Medical Care*. New York: John Wiley and Sons.

de Lorgeril, M., Renaud, S., Mamelle, N., Salen, P., Martin, J.-L., Monjaud, L. *et al.* (eds) (1994). Mediterranean alpha-linoleic acid-rich diet in secondary prevention of coronary heart disease. *Lancet*, 343, 1454–9.

EBRD (1994). *Transition Report*. London: European Bank for Reconstruction and Development.

EBRD (1996). *Transition Report: Infrastructures and Savings*. London: European Bank for Reconstruction and Development.

Enthoven, A. C. (1988). *Theory and Practice of Managed Competition in Health Care Finance*. Amsterdam: North Holland.

EURONUT-SENECA (1991). Nutrition and the elderly in Europe. *European Journal of Clinical Nutrition*, 45, 326–45.

Evans, R. G., Barer, M. L. and Marmor, T. R. (1994). *Why Are Some People Healthy and Others Not?* Berlin: de Gruyter.

Goldstein, E., Preker, A. S., Adeyi, O. and Chellaraj, G. (1996). *Trends in Health Status, Services and Finance: The Transition in Central and Eastern Europe*. Washington, DC: World Bank.

Grol, R. (1993). Development of guidelines for general practice care. *British Journal of General Practice*, 43, 146–51.

Hajdu, P., McKee, M. and Bojan, F. (1995). Changes in premature mortality differentials by marital status in Hungary and in England and Wales. *European Journal of Public Health*, 5, 259–64.

Indredavik, B., Bakke, F., Solberg, R., Rokseth, R., Haaheim, L. L. and Holme, I. (1991). Benefit of a stroke unit: A randomized controlled trial. *Stroke*, 22, 1026–31.

Kanavos, P. (1997). Health expenditures in eastern European economies in transition: Friend or foe? In R. Saltman and J. Figueras (eds), *European Health Care Reform: Analysis of Current Strategies*. Copenhagen: WHO Regional Office for Europe.

Kanavos, P. and Mossialos, E. (1997). *The Methodology of International Comparisons of Health Care Expenditures: Any Lessons for Health Policy?* Discussion Paper No. 3. London: LSE Health, University of London.

Kaplan, G. A., Pamuk, E. R., Lynch, J. W., Cohen, R. D. and Barbour, J. L. (1996). Inequality in income and mortality in the United States. Analysis of mortality and potential pathways. *British Medical Journal*, 312, 999–1003.

Lalonde, M. (1974). *A New Perspective on the Health of Canadians: A Working Document*. Ottawa: Canada Information.

Le Fur, P. and Sermet, C. (1996). *Medical References: The Impact on Pharmaceutical Prescriptions*. Paris: CREDES-CES.

Mossialos, E. (1997). Citizens' views on health care systems in the 15 Member States of the European Union, guest editorial. *Health Economics*, 6, 109–16.

Mossialos, E., Kanavos, P. and Abel-Smith, B. (1997). Will managed care work in Europe? *Pharmacoeconomics*, 11, 297–305.

OECD (1994). *The Reform of Health Care Systems: A Review of Seventeen OECD Countries*. Paris: Organisation for Economic Co-operation and Development.

OECD (1995). *New Directions in Health Care Policy*. Paris: Organisation for Economic Co-operation and Development.

OECD (1996). *Health Data 1996*. Paris: Organisation for Economic Co-operation and Development.

Preker, A. S. and Feachem, R. G. A. (1994). *Health and Health Care*. New York: World Bank.

Smith, D. G., Shipley, M. J. and Rose, G. (1990). The magnitude and causes of socio-economic differentials in mortality: Further evidence from the Whitehall Study. *Journal of Epidemiology and Community Health*, 44, 265–70.

Thomas, S. (1994). Standard setting in the Netherlands: Impact of the human factor on guideline development. *British Journal of General Practice*, 44, 242–3.

Varasovszky, Z., Bain, C. and McKee, M. (1997). Alcohol related mortality in Poland and Hungary: Differences and similarities. *Journal of Epidemiology and Community Health*, 51, 167–71.

Wellings, K. (1994). Assessing AIDS/HIV prevention. What do we know in Europe? General population. *Sozial- und Präventivmedizin*, 39, 14–46.

WHO (1996a). *Health Care Systems in Transition (Country Profiles)*. Copenhagen: WHO Regional Office for Europe.

WHO (1996b). *Health for All Database*. Copenhagen: WHO Regional Office for Europe.

Wilkinson, R. G. (1992). Income distribution and life expectancy. *British Medical Journal*, 304, 165–8.

World Bank (1993). *Ukraine: The Social Sector During Transition*. Washington, DC: World Bank.

# PART II

## DEMAND-SIDE STRATEGIES

# 2

# BALANCING COMPETITION AND SOLIDARITY IN HEALTH CARE FINANCING

David Chinitz, Alex Preker and Jürgen Wasem

## INTRODUCTION

A market typically consists of a straightforward transfer of goods or services from a supplier to a purchaser and of direct payments from purchaser to supplier. In most developed countries, this kind of arrangement plays only a minor role in the health sector. Rather, the health sector consists of a 'triangular' arrangement which includes patients, providers of care and payers (e.g. governments and public or private insurance agencies). Thus an effective health policy needs to deal with three different dimensions of health care financing: taxes or contributions (which citizens pay to purchasers of care), payment to providers by the funders of care, and out-of-pocket payments (which patients pay directly to providers).

Changes involving one or more of these three dimensions in health care financing have been at the centre of the health care reform debate in many European countries. Competition among providers and the methods used by governments and insurers to pay for health services has dominated much of the recent discussion about efficiency and effectiveness in health care systems. Less has been written about changes in the source of financing (how money is raised from patients, taxpayers or insurance members) or about the appropriate role for competition among financing agencies. Yet several recent proposals for health care reform in Europe have focused on this last dimension of health care financing (e.g.

Belgium, Germany, the Netherlands, Switzerland) which also have significant implications for both equity and efficiency in service delivery.

This chapter explores the issues which arise in seeking to maintain equity in terms of universal coverage (referred to in Europe as *solidarity*) when competition is introduced among more than one financing agency. The next section provides an overview of the origins of the concepts of solidarity and competition. Several examples of recent reforms in the source of health care financing in eastern Europe, western Europe and Israel are then briefly reviewed, followed by a summary of key observations and conclusions.

## SOLIDARITY AND COMPETITION IN HEALTH CARE FINANCING

### Concepts of solidarity and competition in health care

The concept of 'solidarity' has a variety of origins, ranging from socialist theory, conservative notions about social order and neo-liberal concepts about the social contract (Ashford 1986). This concept played an important role in nineteenth-century 'pre-welfare state' health care arrangements in Australia, Canada, the Friendly Societies in England and New Zealand, and in the company-based sickness funds in continental Europe. Solidarity subsequently became one of the central pillars of the emerging welfare states in twentieth-century Europe and elsewhere in the developed world.

The term 'solidarity' was originally used to describe some sort of collective arrangement. During the past 50 years, when most member states of the Organisation for Economic Co-operation and Development (OECD) (with the notable exception of the US) introduced universal coverage in health care financing, the term solidarity came to convey some vague notion about the welfare state. The nearly synonymous use of the term solidarity to mean universal risk pooling, in which health care costs are not financed individually, but rather *ex ante* through some sort of collective pooling of resources that protects the individual against the financial risks of illness (de Roo 1995), is very common across Europe.

Health insurance schemes that are characterized by the concept of solidarity do not adjust contribution rates for an individual's *ex ante* health status. Instead, the schemes are redistributive in the sense that contributions are adjusted according to income levels (ability to pay), although there is often a ceiling on such contributions. On the delivery side, such schemes typically provide benefits according to professional judgements about need rather than consumer notions about demand (Culyer 1993). In this article, health financing systems which provide redistribution between age groups, between income classes, between single individuals and families, and between good and bad health risks are considered to achieve solidarity. Health financing arrangements such as unregulated private health care markets, which use *ex ante* risk ratings and have little or no redistributive function, are considered as not achieving solidarity even if they provide protection to the individual through risk pooling.

There are four ways in which competition can occur in a health care system:

- competition among health care providers in relation to patients;
- competition among health care providers in relation to paying or purchasing agencies;
- competition among producers of health sector goods and services in relation to the producers of goods and services in other sectors which individuals may choose to buy;
- competition among funding agencies for tax or contributions made by individuals or employers.

The central question is: 'Can competition be introduced among two or more health care funding agencies without significantly compromising equity (solidarity) in sharing the financial burden of illness across population groups?' A related question is: 'Does such competition among health care financing agencies convey any benefits in terms of improving efficiency, effectiveness, quality or choice in health care delivery systems?'

### Methods of financing health care

The extent to which competition can be introduced into health care financing without significantly compromising equity has been the subject of recent debate. A brief review of the four main mechanisms for mobilizing financial resources for the health sector – general taxation, social insurance premiums, private risk-adjusted premiums and out-of-pocket payments – can provide some perspective on this question.

*Funding through general revenues*

General revenues are used to fund health care systems in a number of eastern and western European countries, as well as in Australia, Canada and New Zealand. In these countries, paying for health care is an integral part of the national (or regional) government's tax structure. The share of revenues devoted to health care is determined through the regular budgeting process with each health ministry or department lobbying the government for a share of total available resources.

Equity in funding health care through such a system is directly related to the progressivity of a country's tax system. The degree of progressivity of the tax system is in turn directly related to the mix of taxes used and the degree of tax compliance by the population. Wagstaff demonstrated that general revenues are usually the most equitable way to finance health care, although there are rare instances when a social insurance scheme may be more progressive than the tax structure (Wagstaff *et al.* 1992). For instance, in several former Soviet republics, tax collection mechanisms have collapsed and general revenues have dropped to less than 10 per cent of GDP. In such cases, general revenues may be more regressive than other sources of health care financing, since, in effect, the allocated sum is insufficient to provide an adequate level of health care service.

In Europe as well as the OECD generally, there are few examples of countries which rely heavily on general revenues as the main sources of health care funding that also utilize competition in the financing of health care, Australia being a notable exception.[1,2] One dimension of such systems that can have important implications for solidarity is the level of private health care insurance which operates alongside the publicly funded system. Where such a parallel system exists, there is, in effect, 'competition' between the two systems (de Roo 1995). Understanding the positive and negative elements of such competition is essential for policy makers involved in regulating both these systems.

*Funding through social insurance*

Social insurance is used as the main source of funding for health care in many continental European countries (Austria, Belgium, Croatia, Czech Republic, Germany, Hungary, the Netherlands and Slovenia) as well as in combination with general revenues in others (Canada, France, etc.). It is often referred to as the Bismarckian system, after Chancellor Otto Von Bismarck who introduced such a system in Germany in 1883. Funding health care through social insurance typically involves: (1) mandating payroll taxes or contributions on employers and employees' wages; (2) contributions from independent workers; and (3) transfers from other payroll tax-based programmes such as pension plans, unemployment schemes, etc. Sometimes a specific share of a general social insurance payroll tax is allocated to health. In other cases, earmarked premiums are used specifically to finance health care.

The process for negotiating the budget for a national health insurance scheme is much more complex than the competition which takes place among various government ministries in the case of general revenue-financed systems. The stakeholders in social insurance-based systems include: employers, trade unions, the medical profession, governments and the citizens. Several European countries, such as France, Germany and the Netherlands, use 'corporatist' mechanisms to set the contribution levels and resolve disputes. Although it is rare to have a consensus, payroll-based systems usually reflect social choices in health care financing to the extent that social insurance-based systems are transparent, require public accountability and depend on public consultations.

Wagstaff *et al.* (1992) found that social insurance-based systems for financing health care, with rare exceptions, are usually less progressive than general revenue-based systems. This is due to the fact that contribution rates are often a flat percentage of salaries or income, and that there is usually a ceiling on the income used to calculate premiums. As a result, those who earn above the ceiling pay an increasingly lower proportion of their total income. Equity is also affected by rules governing who is included in, who is excluded from, and who may opt out of the programme. If those with high incomes are not included in – or may opt out of – the system, it becomes even more regressive.

Often there is only one national health insurance agency, in which case there is no real competition. The same is true if there are several agencies, but people are assigned to a specific payer and are not allowed to switch or do not have any incentives to switch. Competition can be introduced into such a system by giving members a choice and by providing some incentive for switching through differences either in the premium levels or the benefits offered. In both of these cases equity is affected if either income level or health status affects the choices that individuals can make. Proposals for competition among the different sickness funds in Germany and the Netherlands have attempted to avoid such equity implications through limitations in the scope of the competition.

### Funding through private insurance

Europeans are often surprised when they learn that almost two-thirds of health care financing in the United States is provided collectively, that is, not through out-of-pocket payment by individuals.[3] As noted by Evans (1991), private health insurance in the US is organized *collectively*, though not necessarily publicly. When such private health insurance is also subsidized through 'tax credits', then it not only provides some protection against risk, but it is also partly public. Thus, private health insurance, insofar that it provides risk pooling and is often subsidized, can also be considered as providing some degree of social protection – and therefore could contribute to overall solidarity.

Unfortunately, in many countries (including the US), private health insurance exhibits substantial market failure which serves to undermine both equity and efficiency (Musgrove 1996). A chief cause of failure in private insurance markets is termed 'adverse selection'. Individuals who view themselves as 'good risks' opt out of insurance schemes which charge premiums high enough to cover 'bad risks,' which in turn drives up the premium for the latter.

In order to mitigate the effects of adverse selection, private health insurance premiums are often risk-adjusted by taking into account the health status of the individual prior to joining the plan or even adjusting the premium after episodes of certain illnesses. Under such a system, the chronically ill (if they manage to join at all) will pay more than healthy members. This clearly erodes the risk pooling and social protection provided by this form of insurance.

In all private insurance markets, successful competition relies either on the ability to adjust premiums in line with the assumed risk (risk rating in the case of health insurance) or to select low-risk cases and limit exposure to claims (cream skimming in the case of health insurance when risk rating is not allowed). When risk adjustment is allowed, competition among insurance companies concentrates on the accurate assessment of such risks so that premiums can be adjusted accordingly.

To reduce the negative social consequences of adverse selection, the state may introduce regulations to limit the degree of risk adjustment which is allowed. For example, regulators may mandate so-called 'community rating' which prohibits health-related risk rating by requiring that all individuals be covered for the same premium. In this case, competition among insurance companies concentrates on identifying low-risk cases and preventing higher-risk cases from gaining entry. Insurance companies that are unable to identify good risks and offer lower premiums to them end up with a high percentage of bad risks and are eventually driven out of the market (Pauly 1974; Rothschild and Stiglitz 1976).

There are a number of methods used by private insurance companies to sort out good from bad risks. One is to base premiums on 'experience ratings'. This involves charging higher premiums to those who *ex post* turn out to be high users of services. Experience rating also can be implemented *ex ante* by charging higher premiums to individuals who fall into risky categories such as the elderly, people who report a bad medical record at the time of signing an insurance contract, or who belong to certain professions which have become markers for high-risk profiles (e.g. groups perceived to be at high risk for HIV/AIDS). Risk adjustment based on experience rating makes it difficult for high-risk cases to get adequate insurance in a private health insurance market, especially individuals who are not members of groups large enough to buy group insurance (Dowd and Feldman 1992).

The degree to which these failures of a purely competitive health insurance market eat away at social protection depends on how much and how well the market is regulated. Some countries have tried to implement enough regulation to reach at least a minimally acceptable level of protection, however these regulations often bring new problems.

### Out-of-pocket payments

In most OECD countries, direct out-of-pocket payments by patients at the point of service constitute a limited but significant portion of total health care financing. In the Wagstaff study cited earlier, out-of-pocket payments accounted for less than 20 per cent of national health expenditure in six out of ten OECD countries.

In most instances, out-of-pocket payments are the most regressive form of financing for health care, because such payments constitute a much greater share of income for the sick and poor than for those who are healthy and better off. Since there is no risk pooling, to all intents and purposes there is little or no collective protection provided through out-of-pocket payments.[4] If regulatory guidelines exempt lower-income groups from co-payments, some element of social protection may be maintained.

In the case of out-of-pocket payments, of course, there is a degree of competition among providers for direct fees. Insurers may also compete by offering different combinations of premiums, co-payments and deductibles, with some trade-off between the two. Higher co-pays and deductibles may be used as tools to attract healthier and/or wealthier clients who prefer to pay lower premiums and accept the risk of having to pay what are for them affordable out-of-pocket fees.

### *Implications of mixed systems*

Most countries use a blend of the above methods to fund their health systems. Almost all OECD countries have to some degree a private system (private health insurance and out-of-pocket payments) which exists in parallel to the public system (general revenues or social insurance-financed). Since the collapse of communism, most countries in eastern Europe now have at least some parallel private elements as well in the financing of their health care systems.

In separate parallel systems, when the services provided in the private sector are of a significantly higher quality and efficacy than those in the public sector, questions arise about equity. With many medical procedures being relatively expensive, however, it is rare that more than a few individuals can afford a totally private system. In most countries outside the US, the private subsystems are not comprehensive but cover a select range of services (primary care, laboratory services, ambulatory diagnostic and mid-range hospital services). Ultimately, many of those insured in the parallel private system need to return to the public system when they confront serious illnesses. If they are allowed to 'opt out' of contributions to the public system while they are healthy or have only minor illnesses, they undermine both the equity and the fiscal sustainability of the public system.

In a number of countries, both public and private sources of financing may be intermixed in the provision of health services for the same individual. In such systems several prickly issues arise. To what extent will those with private insurance or private personal resources be allowed to 'cut in line', be more comfortable or have a greater choice (Evans 1991)? To what degree will patients who have private insurance or those able to pay out-of-pocket end up being

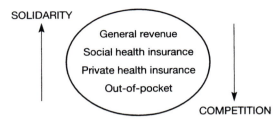

**Figure 2.1** Competition and solidarity

subsidized by public insurance and using public facilities (sometimes at the encouragement of providers seeking to supplement their income from private sources)?[5] In the latter case, the private sector is benefiting from the existence of the public sector without bearing any of the cost (Dowd *et al.* 1993).

At a theoretical and conceptual level, there is thus an inverse relationship between competition and equity in health care financing. Both the administrative feasibility and existence of competition increase as one moves on the spectrum from financing by general revenues at one end, through social and private insurance, and finally to direct out-of-pocket finance. Conversely, equity and solidarity erode (see Figure 2.1).

## EXAMPLES OF RECENT HEALTH FINANCING REFORMS

Having discussed the impact of various types of health care financing on competition and equity at the conceptual level, the next section reviews several recent financing reforms that have attempted to introduce competition into the financing of health care.

### Examples from western Europe and Israel

In western and northern Europe there has been significant debate during recent years about introducing various forms of competition into health care systems. This debate has been closely associated with a parallel debate about the future of the welfare state in Europe. Just as health care systems were an integral part of the creation of the welfare state, so the current pressure on the welfare state has called into question certain preconceived ideas about health care systems and in particular how health care is financed (OECD 1994). Several factors have contributed to this debate:

- The rising cost of health care and pressure on governments not to increase taxes or social insurance contributions.
- Ideological arguments that most of health care is a private rather than public good (Friedman and Friedman 1981).
- Insurance market failure and its implications, especially in relation to the cost-effective use of new technology (Weisbrod 1991).
- The shift in the age structure of most European countries with its associated increase in medical costs for chronic disease-related conditions.

In some countries, the scepticism about the welfare state has been combined with efforts to increase competition in the health care system (both on the service delivery side and in health care financing), while relying less on arguments about the special nature of health care as an economic good.

### Health insurance reform to promote equity in Israel

The Israeli health care system covered 96 per cent of the population through four private sickness funds, with one fund dominating the market. There was a limited right to choose between these funds. In recent years, competition increased among the funds with the largest fund losing market share to the smaller funds (Chinitz 1994).

Financing for the sickness funds and the health care system in 1992 came from several sources: earmarked employer-based health taxes and membership dues to the sickness funds (48 per cent), direct government funding (20 per cent) and private out-of-pocket payments (28 per cent) (Chernichovsky and Chintz 1995). Until 1990, the formula used to distribute employer health taxes among the sickness funds was predominantly based on the income of a fund's members. Subsequently, this was changed to reflect a weighting based on the age of members. The largest sickness fund, which was less restrictive in enrolling members, became saddled with the least wealthy and oldest population. Since this sickness fund insured the majority of the population, the government was often called upon to cover the fund's deficit, while the smaller funds often enjoyed a surplus despite spending more per capita than the main larger fund.

During the late 1980s and early 1990s, in order to reduce waiting times for elective surgeries, all four sickness funds introduced supplemental insurance to cover specific treatments for which there were queues. All the sickness funds sought to avoid raising premium rates for the relatively wealthy in order not to drive attractive members away. As a result, poorer sickness fund members were paying an ever higher percentage of their income to the funds, while the percentage borne by the wealthy was reduced.

Recent reforms in health financing in Israel have sought to rearrange these financial flows in order to promote more equity. Since 1995, employer and individual health taxes are paid into a central fund. These resources, combined with direct government contributions, are distributed on an age-adjusted capitation basis to the sickness funds. The largest fund now receives higher revenues, while the smaller funds receive lower. Moreover, funds are officially prohibited from being selective regarding enrolment. As a result of these changes, the overall financial position of the large fund has been improved, while the small funds must now cover all types of enrolees with lower revenues.

The National Health Insurance Law also allows the sickness funds to offer supplemental insurance to their members, under strict governmental regulation of both benefits and premiums. The supplemental insurance is permitted to cover only those services that are not included in the basic basket of services guaranteed to all citizens under the law. At the same time, however, commercial insurance companies can offer coverage of all services in exchange for premiums they set themselves (Chernichovsky and Chinitz 1995).

Although it is too early to evaluate the full impact of these changes, one outcome appears to have been a redistribution of the burden of health taxation. A recent survey revealed that only a small minority of those with the lowest incomes report that their health tax payments have increased, while most of the wealthy report an increase of their health tax payments (Berg *et al.* 1996a), indicating that the new law may be achieving one of its goals – increasing equity in the burden of health care financing.

There are also, however, several unresolved issues. Since all sources of income have been centralized and the payment rates determined by law, the amount available to the system is fixed. The government determines what the overall amount should be in order to cover the basic basket guaranteed by law. There is considerable controversy as to whether the guaranteed amount is sufficient in view of changes in health sector wage rates, the costs of new medical technologies and the ever-increasing demands resulting from socio-demographic changes such as an increase in the number of elderly requiring care.

In the supplemental insurance market, the funds can compete on price. As mentioned earlier, the National Health Insurance Law requires that supplemental insurance benefits be limited to items not included in the basic basket. Ambiguity regarding the distinction between supplemental and basic benefits raises difficult issues. The government is considering eliminating supplemental insurance entirely. Although purchase of private health insurance is limited, the small market is growing. The same is true of out-of-pocket payments which, as mentioned above, constitute 28 per cent of total health expenditures, having increased in proportion from 18 per cent in 1984 (Berg *et al.* 1996b).

To summarize, the recent changes in the Israeli system replaced multiple sources of finance, which led to a variety of inequities, with centralized financing of a basket of services guaranteed by law to all citizens. The new system is more progressive and, in addition, the government is required to fill in any gaps in funding which emerge. The new system allows little if any direct competition in the financing of the basic services, seeking instead to encourage competition among sickness funds over the quality of service. In reaction to the tight budgets of the mandatory schemes, additional sources of financing such as supplemental health insurance, private health insurance, and out-of-pocket payments have all increased in importance. The extent to which reliance on these sources will eat away at equity remains to be seen.

### Restructuring the sickness fund system in Germany

At the beginning of the 1990s, the public sickness fund system in Germany provided health care for about 90 per cent of the population, with the remainder (civil servants, the self-employed and high-income employees) being insured by private health insurance. At that time, there were about 1000 separate sickness funds, some regional, others occupational and the rest company-based. Whereas about 60 per cent of the insured (particularly white-collar workers) could choose their sickness fund, others were assigned to a particular fund by public regulation. Competition among the sickness funds was very limited.

The sickness funds were financed almost entirely by income-related social insurance premiums paid by the insured and their employers. These premiums were paid directly from the insured and their employers to each sickness fund, which in turn had to calculate its own contribution rate so that it had a balanced budget. The income-linked basis of premiums implied that sickness funds which attracted wealthier or healthier members could levy a lower contribution rate. The market share of regional funds decreased because they could not restrict membership to specific types of individuals and therefore had contribution rates that were higher than average.

In 1994, a risk-adjustment formulary was introduced which took into account the income, age and sex of the insured and whether they were recipients of invalidity pensions. Thus funds which had mainly young, wealthy and healthy members had to transfer part of their revenues to sickness funds which covered average to bad risks. This led to a considerable decrease in the contribution rates of some funds.

A second element of this same reform was to introduce greater freedom in choosing a sickness fund. Starting in 1996, more than 95 per cent of the insured are able to choose membership with one of the 15 largest sickness funds and are entitled to switch insurers on an annual basis. Furthermore, there is mandatory open enrolment now, so these sickness funds cannot deny access to applicants.

Although much of the academic debate among health economists during the 1980s in Germany focused on the introduction of free choice among sickness funds and risk-adjustment systems, inspired by American ideas of managed competition (Enthoven 1980), the major political reason for introducing these measures was not to stimulate competition but (as in Israel) a concern for equity (Wasem 1993). The introduction of a right to choose among sickness funds, however, also led to greater competition. The regional funds, in particular, feared that many of those who had previously been obliged to be insured by them would use their new right and switch to another insurer.

Despite these changes, actual competition among the funds remains limited. Today, all the sickness funds are calling for a deregulation in their relationship with health care providers in an effort to improve their chances to compete with each other. Some funds also want new provisions which would allow them to provide supplemental insurance.

## Maintaining solidarity in the Netherlands

Whereas changes in the sickness fund systems in Germany and Israel were driven primarily by problems of equity, reforms in the Netherlands explicitly targeted a market-oriented approach. In the original proposal of the 1987 Dekker Commission, the health insurance funds would play a central role as agents who competed for resources and contracts with health care providers in their bid to attract members (van de Ven 1987).

The Dutch sickness fund system had been based on a solidarity principle which promoted equity in access to health care (de Roo 1995). Had the recommendations of the Dekker report come into effect, they would have combined competition with a system seeking to preserve equity at the same time. The report recommended that legal rules which until then prevented competition should be eliminated. It also proposed an additional income-independent premium (a 'nominal premium') which could differ between the different sickness funds (this would have been separate from the common payroll tax rate and ceiling applied to all sickness fund members).

Whereas the income-dependent premium reflected concern for equity, the income-independent premium would reflect concern for competition and efficiency. The underlying principle was that sickness funds that behaved as 'prudent buyers' in the health care market would have a lower nominal premium than those which had more expensive contracts with providers.

The Dekker report recommended that equity concerns be strengthened by including everybody in a mandatory insurance programme for a basic package of services. Under this scheme, both the sickness funds and private insurers would be allowed to offer this basic package. Had this recommendation come into effect, it would have been quite different from the separation existing then between public and private health insurance schemes. In particular, under the system which existed at that time, all employees whose income exceeded a certain level were obliged to leave the public system and become insured in the private sector. The previous system thus required higher income groups not to contribute to the redistributive public system.

Although most of the Dekker reform recommendations have not been implemented, several have had a significant impact. Health insurers have started to compete against each other to a greater extent than before (even as mergers between sickness funds reduced the total number of competitors). The pooling of income-related premiums in a central equalization fund with a reallocation based on a risk-adjustment formulary has contributed to overall equity. Finally, since the sickness funds are at risk for only part of their health expenditures, inequity introduced through differences in the nominal premiums are minimal (van de Ven *et al.* 1994). The integration of those earning above the income ceiling into the overall system, however, has not been attempted, and the sickness funds do not compete as 'prudent buyers' (de Roo 1995).

## Examples from the CEE countries and the newly independent states (NIS) of the former USSR

*Historical context*

The former socialist CEE countries and the NIS can be divided into two groups. The first group comprises those countries which had virtually no system of risk pooling prior to the Bolshevik Revolution in 1917. These countries include Albania, Belarus, Georgia, the Republic of Moldova, the Russian Federation and most Asian Republics of NIS. In these countries, the organization and financing of health care had been *laissez-faire* at best. By 1935, the Russian constitution had called for a government-run national health service, financed through general revenues and staffed by doctors and other health care professionals who were employed as civil servants by the state. In the countries which belong to this group, none of the health care professionals and only very few individuals remember health care as it was prior to the socialist era.

The second group comprises those countries which had already introduced fairly elaborate systems of risk pooling prior to the socialist era, through splintered Bismarckian-styled or employment-based health insurance schemes. These countries include the Baltic states, Bulgaria, Czechoslovakia, Hungary, Poland, the Socialist Federal Republic of Yugoslavia, and to a lesser extent Romania and the Ukraine. In most of these countries, this 'social insurance system' of financing health care continued well into the 1960s and in some cases into the early 1970s before it was finally replaced by a general revenue-financing arrangement.

By the early 1970s, most of the NIS and CEE countries had switched to financing health care mainly through general revenues (the one exception being the Socialist Federal Republic of Yugoslavia, where many of the states continued to rely in part on payroll tax health care financing). One of the achievements of this era was universal risk pooling and entitlement of the entire regional population (over 350 million) to health services. This system of financing health care provided the broadest possible risk pooling for the population and a low-cost administrative system for the mobilization of financial resources for the health sector.

Although the communist system secured universal access to a comprehensive range of health services, the lack of appropriate incentives in the service delivery system eventually led to serious problems. In countries where health care professionals and patients still remembered the Bismarckian health insurance system, there was a wave of nostalgia which confused the problems in the health care delivery system under centralized planning with the system used for risk pooling and resource mobilization. Poor performance of the delivery system thus undermined equity in health care financing.

*Transition in health financing in the NIS and CEE countries*

The reforms initiated since the onset of the transition have aimed at redefining the role of the state, health care providers and individuals. The reforms have sought to break the monopoly which governments previously had over the ownership and financing of health services, make health care providers more accountable for the effective and efficient use of scarce resources and increase the responsibility of individuals for their own health and the financing of health care (Preker and Feachem 1995).

One main trend has been a shift away from financing health care through general tax revenues towards a significant reliance on national health insurance funded through payroll taxation (Preker *et al.* 1995). The Socialist Federal Republic of Yugoslavia had such a health insurance system before the transition, while the Czech Republic (1992), Estonia (1992), Hungary (1991), Kazakstan (1996), Kyrgyzstan (1992), Latvia (1993), the Russian Federation (1991) and Slovakia (1993) have all adopted such systems during the 1990s. Other countries such as Belarus, Bulgaria, Lithuania, Poland and Romania, which still rely on general revenues as the principal source of health care financing, have national health insurance laws under development or under consideration. Although most of the countries which have introduced national health insurance continue to rely on general budgetary revenues as well, the use of a narrower contribution base through payroll taxes has on the whole been a regressive shift in health care financing.

There have been discussions in some NIS and CEE countries about allowing part of the population to opt out of mandatory insurance. To date this has not yet occurred, avoiding the negative consequences for equity of 'de-insuring' part of the population or turning to private health insurance as the main source of health care financing. Many NIS and CEE countries have, however, seen a significant growth in private health care. Since services in the private sector are provided only for those who can afford it, ability to pay is playing an increasing role in the financing of health care. In most countries, however, the standard package offered through the public sector remains sufficiently comprehensive that the equity implications of the private sector remain a marginal issue.

In addition to the negative impact on equity of private services, the shift from general revenues to payroll taxes for financing health care in the NIS and CEE countries has been associated with three other adverse effects. First, although a full analysis has not been done, several of the new health insurance funds appear to have a significant structural deficit as part of their design. Second, the shift in the source of financing for health care from the state budget to payroll taxes has also significantly increased labour costs. This has major implications for international competitiveness and the informalization of the economy as both employers and employees seek ways to avoid the resulting heavy tax burden. Third, the financial resources for the health sector, in countries which use health insurance and co-payments, are now channelled in a complex way through several intermediate agencies, making application of expenditure controls difficult.

It is still too early to evaluate the full impact of these health financing reforms on equity, health gain, efficiency and quality of care. This is especially true because rising rates of unemployment, poverty and structural changes in the economy also have impacts on health and the health care system that are difficult to separate from the effects of changes in the source of financing. Thus far, none of the changes in health care financing in NIS and CEE countries have led to significant competition among financing sources.

### Regulating private health insurance markets in Europe

In most European countries, private health insurance plays a role only as supplemental insurance, since most of the population is included in the publicly mandated schemes. Although health economists sometimes argue that supplemental insurance 'is not a matter of social concern' (Pauly 1974: 14), regulation of private health insurance remains a clear area of public sector policy in both western and eastern Europe due to extensive market failure.[6]

In some European countries (Germany, Ireland, the Netherlands),[7] private health insurance is the only form of risk pooling available to part of the population. In these cases, governments have tried to introduce regulation which provides some *ex ante* social protection. For example, since 1986 in the Netherlands, all private insurers are required to provide open enrolment under a Standard Package Policy (SPP). An equalization system allows some transfer of resources among the private insurance funds to cover high-risk cases under the SPP (Okma 1995).

In Ireland, until recently there was a virtual monopoly on the supply-side in the private health insurance market. A new law introduced in 1994 requires mandatory open enrolment, a risk-adjusted capitation system and community ratings for all health insurers who might enter the market (Kennedy 1996).

Since 1995, people in Germany who are insured with private health insurance companies have also been obliged to subscribe to a universal insurance scheme for long-term care. Privately insured persons who are already old or in need of long-term care cannot be excluded from this programme on the basis of their pre-existing condition. To cover their costs, insurance companies use a system of inter-generational transfers from younger and healthier members. An equalization pool is used to spread the risk of this programme across the private insurance funds (Wasem 1995).

In these examples, the regulations needed to increase equity and risk pooling limit certain dimensions of competition. Although the impact of these measures on objectives like equity, efficiency, health gains and quality of care has not yet been adequately evaluated, the negative implications of an unregulated private health insurance market are well known.

The NIS and CEE countries have been slow to adopt these lessons. Hungary is currently the only country which has passed legislation for the creation of voluntary insurance (non-life, including health and pensions). Even in the case of Hungary, there is virtually no regulatory framework to control for market distortions in the private health insurance sector (cream skimming, adverse selection, moral hazard etc.).

## CONCLUSIONS

This paper has reviewed the relationship between competition and solidarity (equity) in health care financing. In the case studies, proposals for reform in health care financing have attempted to balance a concern for social protection with a desire for greater sustainability and efficiency in the mobilization and allocation of scarce health care resources. A tension clearly exists between efficiency, gained through market forces and competition, and equity. This is probably a healthy tension that policy makers must struggle to reconcile.

As noted earlier, competition among health care insurers (regardless of whether they are private or public) tends to erode equity in health care financing since health insurers seek to select good risks. A central theme of more recent health financing reforms has been to reduce the impact of this problem. One common proposal has been mandatory open enrolment. Another closely linked effort has been to introduce an equalization fund intended to counter the effects of risk selection. Although technical procedures differ among countries, the central idea is to try to eliminate individual health risks as much as possible from the competitive arena.

Since many of the health financing reforms involving competition are relatively new, and concrete data are not readily available, it is difficult to prove empirically if recent reforms have had their desired impact on health, equity, access, efficiency, quality of care and choice. The following are, however, some general observations.

- Existing risk-adjustment formulae are far from perfect (van de Ven *et al.* 1994). Differences in morbidity are in most cases only measured by age (as is presently the case in Israel) and in some cases sex, which are at best very crude indicators. Differences in nominal premium (Netherlands) or in contribution rate (Germany), as explained above, are often associated with uneven risk structures. This in itself erodes equity and violates the desired allocative signalling.
- Since different risk structures are not neutralized completely by the risk calculations and equalization payments system, health insurers still have strong incentives to cream skim. They do this by developing marketing strategies that attract good risks and that cannot be easily monitored by the regulatory system (de Roo 1995). For example, they may, by tailoring benefit packages and contracts with providers, make them particularly attractive

to certain groups that they prefer to insure. This is one reason that proponents of managed competition in the US call for a standardized benefits package.

• Competition among health insurers only makes sense if they are both freed from detailed hierarchical regulation on contracts with providers and exposed to a full range of risks. If health insurers are not exposed to a full range of both benefits and risks, including the benefit of being more competitive if they provide improved health gains or the risk of going broke, it is unlikely that market-based reforms introduced through competition will have their desired impact.

If policy makers were to take away a single lesson from this discussion on competition and solidarity in health care funding, it would be that the introduction of markets in health care financing is a risky game. The chances of creating serious problems when introducing markets in the source of financing for health care systems are high, while the potential benefits are not yet proven. It is possible that one of the critical success factors is universal coverage through a pre-existing public scheme. Countries that have not yet secured universal coverage, or whose universal coverage is fragile, would be well advised to look at other ways to improve their health care systems than to turn to competitive market forces as the source of their health care financing. Countries with universal schemes should proceed with caution, aware of the implications for solidarity of the introduction of competition in the finance of health care.

## NOTES

1 In pure general revenue-financed systems, of course, there is an active budgetary competition which goes on between the health sector and other sectors which rely equally on government revenues. Furthermore, internal markets can also exist among providers in such systems as has been seen in the UK and some Scandinavian countries (Saltman and von Otter 1995).

2 In Australia, the premium-based Medibank Private competes actively with the general revenues-based public Medicare programme. A further splintering and competition among the resulting public schemes is currently under consideration. Despite much political rhetoric, competition between Medibank Private and the public Medicare programme does not appear to have compromised equity in health care financing in Australia. Competition between the public and private

systems appears to have provided an impetus for the public system to cater more to patient satisfaction than would have been the case had there been no such competition. To date, the Australian experience has not led to a collapse in the public system and may, therefore, be viewed as an example that competition and equity in health care financing can coexist under special circumstances (the critical factor being universal coverage through a pre-existing public scheme). In other countries the coexistence of private health insurance in parallel to, and in competition with, public schemes has been fraught with more problems (see subsequent sections).

3 Risk pooling through private insurance is a form of collective protection even if it may be considered regressive and typically has many disclaimers which undermine the social protection provided by it.

4 This includes medical savings accounts which, by forcing individuals to save during the earlier and healthier part of their lives for expenses which will be incurred later when they are less productive and have greater medical needs, do offer some protection in terms of income smoothing, but without risk-sharing or income redistribution among groups of individuals.

5 For these reasons it is prohibited in Canada to sell private insurance for services that are included in the publicly financed basket (Evans 1993).

6 Within the EU, Member States may regulate supplemental insurance to a limited extent only.

7 In the Irish case, there is a controversy between the Irish government and the EU Commission on the question of whether the Irish private health insurance is a full alternative for provision of care within the NHS or whether it is just supplemental insurance.

# REFERENCES

Ashford, D. E. (1986). *The Emergence of the Welfare State*. New York: Oxford University Press.

Berg, A., Rosen, B., Gross, R. and Chinitz, D. (1996a). *Public Perception of the Health System following Implementation of the National Health Insurance Law: Selected Preliminary Findings from a Survey of the General Population (an Executive Summary of a Research Report)*. Jerusalem: Brookdale Institute.

Berg, A., Rosen, B. and Ofer, G. (1996b). *Changes in Household Expenditure on Health between 1986/87 and 1992/93*. Jerusalem: JDC/Brookdale Institute.

Chernichovsky, D. and Chinitz, D. (1995). The political economy of health system reform in Israel. *Health Economics*, 4, 127–41.

Chinitz, D. P. (1994). Reforming the Israeli health care market. *Social Science and Medicine*, 39, 1447–59.

Culyer, A. J. (1993). Health, health expenditures, and equity. In E. van Doorslaer, A. Wagstaff and F. Rutten (eds), *Equity in the Finance and Delivery of Health Care. An International Perspective*. Oxford: Oxford University Press.

de Roo, A. A. (1995). Contracting and solidarity: Market-oriented changes in Dutch health insurance schemes. In R. B. Saltman and C. von Otter (eds), *Implementing Planned Markets in Health Care*. Buckingham: Open University Press.

Dowd, B. and Feldman, R. (1992). Insurer competition and protection from risk redefinition in the individual and small group insurance market. *Inquiry*, 29, 148–57.

Dowd, B., Feldman, R., Christianson, J. and Shapiro, J. (1993). *Development of the Competitive Pricing Proposal for Medicare*, Final Report. Institute for Health Services Research, University of Minnesota.

Enthoven, A. C. (1980). *Health Plan. The Only Practical Solution to the Soaring Cost of Medical Care*. Reading, MA: Addison Wesley.

Evans, R. G. (1991). Life, death, money and power. In T. J. Litman and L. S. Robins (eds), *Health Policy and Politics*. Albany: Delmar.

Evans, R. G. (1993). Canada: The real issues. *Journal of Health Politics, Policy and Law*, 17, 739–63.

Friedman, M. and Friedman, R. (1981). *Free to Choose*. New York: Free Press.

Kennedy, A. (ed.) (1996). *Private Health Insurance in Ireland. The Advent of a Competitive Market and a Risk Equalisation Scheme*. Brussels: Alliance National des Mutualités Chrétiennes.

Musgrove, P. (1996). *Public and Private Roles in Health*. Washington, DC: World Bank.

OECD (1994). *The Reform of Health Care Systems: A Review of Seventeen OECD Countries*. Paris: Organisation for Economic Co-operation and Development.

Okma, K. G. H. (1995). *Regulating the Private Insurance Market in The Netherlands*. Rijswijk: Ministry of Health and Welfare, The Netherlands.

Pauly, M. V. (1974). Overinsurance and public provision of insurance: the role of moral hazard and adverse selection. *Quarterly Journal of Economics*, 88, 44–62.

Preker, A. S. and Feachem, R. G. A. (1995). *Market Mechanisms and the Health Sector in Central and Eastern Europe*. Technical Paper No. 293. Washington, DC: World Bank.

Preker, A. S., Goldstein, E., Chellaraj, G. and Adeyi, O. (1995). *Health Status, Health Services and Health Expenditure: Trends During the Transition in CEE*. Washington, DC: World Bank.

Rothschild, M. and Stiglitz, J. (1976). Equilibrium in competitive insurance markets: An essay on the economics of imperfect information. *Quarterly Journal of Economics*, 90, 629–49.

Saltman, R. and von Otter, C. (1995). *Implementing Planned Markets in Health Care: Balancing Social and Economic Responsibility*. Buckingham: Open University Press.

van de Ven, W. P. M. M. (1987). The key role of health insurance in a cost-effective health care system. Towards regulated competition in the Dutch medical market. *Health Policy*, 7, 253–71.

van de Ven, W. P. M. M., van Vliet, R. C. J. A., van Barnevald, E. M. and Lamers, L. L. (1994). Risk-adjusted capitation: Recent experiences in the Netherlands. *Health Affairs*, 13, 120–36.

Wagstaff, A., van Doorslaer, E., Calonge, S., Christiansen, T., Gerfin, M., Gottschalk, P., Janssen, R., Lachaud, C., Leu, R. E., Nolan, B. *et al.* (1992). Equity in the finance of health care: Some international comparisons. *Journal of Health Economics*, 11, 361–87.

Wasem, J. (1993). Der kassenartenübergreifende Risikostrukturausgleich – Chancen für eine neue Wettbewerbsordnung in der GKV. *Sozialer Fortschritt*, 42, 31–9.

Wasem, J. (1995). Gesetzliche Krankenversicherung und private Krankenversicherung – auf dem Weg zur Konvergenz? *Sozialer Fortschritt*, 44, 89–96.

Weisbrod, B. A. (1991). The health care quadrilemma. An essay on technological change, insurance, quality of care, and cost containment. *Journal of Economic Perspectives*, 29, 523–52.

# 3

# THE APPROPRIATE ROLE FOR PATIENT COST SHARING

## Joseph Kutzin

### INTRODUCTION

Cost sharing refers to any direct payment made by users of health services to the providers of those services. This paper describes the cost-sharing practices of countries in the European region and attempts to assess the consequences of these policies on the sectoral objectives of efficiency, equity, and health status. For this assessment, the major issues addressed include the impact of cost sharing on utilization levels and patterns, health expenditures and health status. The analysis draws on evidence from non-European (especially US) and European countries.

The relative importance that a country attaches to the various possible objectives of cost-sharing policies (i.e. cost containment, efficiency, or resource mobilization) depends on a number of factors. One of the most important of these is the overall macroeconomic context and, more specifically, the budgetary outlook for the national health service or social insurance scheme. Cost-sharing objectives are also likely to vary with the extent to which the population is covered with a reasonably well-functioning health service (again, either a public system or one financed through taxes or social insurance contributions), the extent and role of private insurance, and with the methods used to pay providers under these systems.

## CONCEPTUAL FRAMEWORK

### Definitions

Patient cost sharing refers to a group of specific policy tools that act on the demand-side of the market for health care services. Usually, these tools are applied in the context of (public or private) insurance or a national health system. The three main forms or mechanisms of patient cost sharing are the following (Rubin and Mendelson 1995):

- *deductible*: amount that must be paid out-of-pocket before benefits of the insurance programme become active;
- *co-payment*: flat amount that the beneficiary must pay for each service used;
- *co-insurance*: percentage of the total charges for a service that must be paid by the beneficiary.

Other policies are often associated with these forms of cost sharing and can also affect the level of out-of-pocket expenditures made by patients to providers. These include (adapted from Rubin and Mendelson 1995):

- *benefit maximum*: a defined limit on the amount that will be reimbursed by the insurer for a defined period, over and above which the patient is entirely liable for payment;
- *out-of-pocket maximum*: a defined limit on the total amount of out-of-pocket spending for which an insured person or household will be liable for a defined period, over and above which all expenses are paid by the insurer (Schoenman 1993);
- *extra billing*: charges by the provider that are higher than the maximum reimbursement levels set by insurers, leaving patients liable to pay the difference;
- *pharmaceutical reference pricing*: a price list established by the insurer for therapeutically comparable drugs that establishes a maximum reimbursement level per item prescribed, leaving patients financially responsible if more expensive items are chosen;
- *coverage exclusions*: services or methods of using services that are not covered in the benefit package of public or private insurance plans, leaving individuals liable for their full costs or the costs over and above what is covered.

These various cost-sharing options are potential policy tools. That is, they can constitute options for progressing toward the achievement of specific objectives. For many western European countries, the main objective of cost sharing is to reduce demand for services in order to contain costs. For many central and eastern European (CEE) countries and the Commonwealth of Independent States (CIS), the main objective is to raise additional revenues to help sustain their health services. Caution is warranted with regard to over-generalizing about the motivations of countries in either region, however. Some western European countries see resource mobilization as an objective of their cost sharing, and some CEE/CIS countries see these measures as tools for demand management.

## Cost sharing in theory

Economists are split as to whether cost sharing can be an effective tool for improving efficiency and containing costs. There is more general agreement, however, that unless accompanied by compensating measures for low-income persons, cost sharing will be inequitable in terms of both the finance and the receipt of care. In countries that do not have a functioning universal health care system, the rationale for cost sharing may be less one of demand management than of revenue raising to sustain and expand service provision. For some of these countries, this may also reflect a history of informal payments ('grey market') for services and supplies.

### Efficiency and cost containment: the great debate

The fundamental rationale for the use of cost sharing is as a tool to ration the demand for care in the presence of public or private insurance. As reflected in Figure 3.1, the socially optimal level of consumption would occur at point A, where the marginal cost (reflected in the supply curve) of producing services equals the marginal benefit (reflected in the demand curve) of consuming them. At this point, $Q_1$ of services are consumed at a price of $P_1$, which is equal to the marginal cost of supply at that quantity of output. With insurance, price is less than marginal cost, and so the level of consumption implied by this occurs at a point where the cost to society of producing the services is greater than the value of their consumption (Feldman and Dowd 1993).[1] If insurance fully protects consumers from the price of health services, the quantity of services demanded will be that which would exist at a zero price ($Q_2$ in the

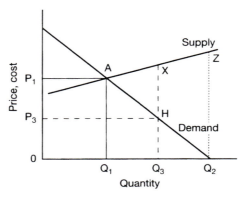

**Figure 3.1**   Welfare consequences of insurance and cost sharing in the neo-classical model

figure). At this point, marginal cost (corresponding to point Z on the supply curve) is far greater than marginal benefit (which is essentially zero). Standard neo-classical economic theory implies that this would result in a loss of welfare to society equal to the area contained in the triangle $AZQ_2$. This is why some economists postulate that the demand for care exceeds socially desirable levels when services are fully covered by insurance. Cost-sharing measures introduce prices back into the medical market ($P_3$ in the figure) in an attempt to limit the excessive demand[2] and consequent welfare loss believed to exist as a result of insurance.[3] With cost sharing at price $P_3$ in the figure, the quantity demanded is $Q_3$, and thus the welfare loss is reduced to the area of triangle AXH.

Some economists and others have questioned whether the above conclusion derived from neo-classical economic theory about the welfare loss from complete insurance coverage (and the implied welfare gain from cost sharing) is valid in practice. The theoretical rationale for cost sharing has been refined based on an analysis of 'health services' from the perspective of welfare economics. Health services are not monolithic; they are comprised of various goods and services with different economic characteristics. One dimension upon which health services vary as an 'economic good' is the extent to which the benefits of consumption are limited to the individual who receives a service (Akin *et al.* 1987; Preker and Feachem 1995). Some health services are purely *private* goods, in that the health benefits of consumption accrue solely to the individual receiving a service, and those who do not receive the service are *excluded* from the associated benefits. An example of this would be an aspirin purchased for treatment of a headache. For this type of good, welfare economics implies that marginal cost pricing (as in the standard neo-classical model described above) yields an optimal allocation of resources.

Alternatively, some health services are pure *public* goods, that is, the benefits of the service accrue to all the members of society. If the service is provided, no one can be excluded from the associated benefits. Examples of public goods would be some environmental health interventions, such as control of air and water pollution. Charging 'users' for these services is not feasible because non-payers would get the same benefits as those who pay, so there would be no incentive for any individual to pay.[4]

Finally, many health services can be characterized as mixed goods; the individual receives the benefits of consumption, but some others who are not directly involved in the transaction between provider and consumer benefit as well.[5] An example of a mixed good is treatment of a communicable disease, such as tuberculosis or syphilis. Such treatment not only protects the individual being treated but also those persons that he or she would have infected if no treatment was obtained. Social benefits exceed private benefits for these types of services, so marginal cost pricing will result in a lower level of consumption than is socially optimal. Therefore, a subsidy is desirable to raise private demand to the level that will equate social benefits with social costs and thus maximize welfare (Arrow 1963; Jimenez 1987), and the implications for cost-sharing policy are mixed. This subsidy may entail varying degrees of out-of-pocket payments by consumers ranging from zero to a substantial percentage of marginal cost.

The market for health care services is imperfect because the unregulated activities of producers and consumers do not result in a socially desirable quantity, mix, and distribution of services. As suggested by the above discussion, one reason for this is the diversity of specific services in terms of the capture of the benefits of consumption. There is an additional element of market failure that is particularly relevant for a discussion of the effects of cost sharing. This is 'information failure', which manifests itself in the health care market by the reliance/dependence of consumers on providers for information regarding the services they 'need'. This asymmetry in information may lead to 'supplier-induced demand', i.e. demand for services that would not have occurred if the consumer's agent, the provider, had not encouraged the consumer to demand the services (Mooney and Ryan 1993). The assumption of supplier-induced demand implies that it is provider preferences that determine at least some of the demand for health care services. The existence, precise definition, effects, and appropriate policy response to supplier-induced demand is a topic of considerable interest and debate among health economists (see Labelle *et al.* 1994; Pauly 1994 for a review and debate of the issues).

Although some economists remain unconvinced that there is sufficient empirical evidence to demonstrate conclusively that supplier-induced demand exists (Pauly 1994), most accept that providers do use their power to affect consumers' demand for care through their agency function (Fuchs 1986; Mooney 1994). If supplier-induced demand exists, the use of the standard supply–demand paradigm to measure welfare loss may be inappropriate, since one of the underlying assumptions of that model is that supply and demand are independently determined. Therefore, given the asymmetry of information between the provider and consumer and the agency role played by the provider, the debate among economists is whether the demand curve is really an appropriate tool for measuring consumer welfare. Some argue that the demand curve should not be used for measuring welfare because of these information problems (Evans 1984; Rice 1993; Mooney 1994). Others say that there will never be perfect information, and that an estimated demand curve always incorporates existing levels of information. Therefore, the demand curve can still be used to measure the welfare consequences of insurance and cost sharing because it reflects consumers' welfare-maximizing decisions based on the information they have at any point in time (Feldman and Dowd 1993; Pauly 1994; McClellan 1995).

Understanding this debate about supplier-induced demand is relevant to an assessment of the likely effects of cost sharing, which is a demand-side policy tool. Supplier-induced demand is not inherently 'bad'; indeed, providing the lay person with information about his or her medical needs is a very important function of physicians, and providing medical training to the entire population would not be an economically efficient use of resources, even if it were feasible. However, if the analysis indicating that cost sharing reduces society's welfare loss is based upon a flawed model, then the use of cost sharing for this purpose is called into question. Consequently, some believe that the scope for achieving efficiency gains from cost sharing are very limited due to the diversity of health services and the potential for supplier-induced demand (Evans *et al.* 1993a, 1993b; Mooney 1994).

The reason why many believe that supplier-induced demand compromises the usefulness of cost sharing is as follows. If cost sharing initially reduces consumer demand for care, provider incomes will be threatened (in health systems where some or all providers are paid according to the volume of services). To the extent that they can induce demand for additional services, providers could compensate for a reduction in consumer-driven demand in order to maintain their level of income (see Fahs 1992 for a description of this aspect of supplier-induced demand). This 'supply response' will negate the demand-dampening effects of patient charges, which will, therefore, along with other measures that act on the consumer side of the market, be an ineffective policy tool. Thus, some have argued (e.g. Evans *et al.* 1993a, 1993b) that in systems in which providers are reimbursed retrospectively, they will respond to any generalized reduction in consumer-driven demand by increasing the volume and/or intensity (number of items of service provided per contact with the health system) of services provided in order to maintain their income levels. Therefore, these authors maintain that incentives and/or regulations affecting the supply-side of the market are likely to be much more powerful tools for cost containment. Others believe that there is scope for an appropriate demand-side policy response to the potentially harmful effects of information asymmetry between providers and consumers. This is not to provide more complete insurance coverage (i.e. reduce cost sharing) but instead to arm consumers with more information (Feldman and Dowd 1993).

In trying to extend this theoretical analysis, it is important to remember that health care services are not homogeneous. As indicated above, they are comprised of a mix of goods and services with diverse market characteristics in terms of the capture of the benefits of consumption. There are large numbers of personal health services with characteristics of private or mixed goods for which, therefore, cost-sharing policies might be appropriate for purposes of demand management. Examples of these services include inpatient care, hospital-based outpatient care, ambulatory care in a non-hospital setting, physician services, pharmaceuticals etc. However, health care services are also heterogeneous in the extent to which information asymmetry, and thus supplier-induced demand, applies to each specific service. Because of this, the appropriateness of cost sharing as a demand-rationing tool is likely to vary across services.

For each specific service, the key issue to consider is the extent to which demand is driven by consumers or providers. Given the reliance of consumers upon their provider–agents for information that affects their demand for certain services, the theoretical basis for applying cost sharing as a demand-rationing tool to services that are largely provider-determined (such as referral services, for example) is weak (Mooney 1994), unless investments are made to increase consumer knowledge of the likely effects of alternative diagnostic and treatment options (Feldman and Dowd 1993). However, it seems unrealistic to believe that, given the specialized nature of medical knowledge, the information gap between providers and consumers can be narrowed appreciably. There is not, therefore, a strong theoretical rationale for applying cost sharing to a broad variety of services for the purpose of improving efficiency and welfare. These considerations suggest that a selective approach to cost sharing is more appropriate where the purpose is demand management and the objective is efficiency improvement. The selection of services for which cost sharing would be appropriate for this purpose should therefore depend on the extent to which the demand for each specific service is driven by consumers or providers.

### Efficiency in the pattern of service use

Aside from the debate over the potential welfare gains from cost sharing and the role of supplier-induced demand in limiting these gains, there is clearly scope for selective cost sharing to improve efficiency by using price signals to channel demand in desired directions. The mechanism of coverage exclusions is especially appropriate for this. Excluding cost-ineffective services or patterns of utilization from the benefit package will reduce government subsidies to services outside a defined basic benefit package and can encourage the use of appropriate referral channels.

### Raising revenues for health services

For countries where most providers are part of the public sector, an objective of cost-sharing policies may be to raise revenues in order to improve the quality and availability of the health services. This is most likely to be a policy objective in situations where government resources are inadequate to fund the network of service providers, leading to a greater reliance on direct charges to the users of services to meet operating costs. This is currently the case in most of the CEE/CIS countries where the macroeconomy has deteriorated in recent years. In this situation, cost sharing is operationalized as user fees that are not necessarily related to any public or private insurance scheme. This may also be viewed as a cost-containment objective, albeit one where the goal is to limit government rather than total expenditures (Schoenman 1993). Implicit in the use of patient charges to raise revenues is an assumption that, at the level of prices being charged to users, utilization will not fall to such an extent as to offset the revenues from higher prices. In other words, it is assumed that the demand for care is inelastic (the percentage decrease in utilization will be less than the percentage increase in price).

### Equity

Cost sharing raises obvious concerns about equity with regard to both the finance and the receipt of care. It can cause inequity in financing because of the potential for the burden of cost sharing to fall on households or individuals irrespective of their ability to pay. It can cause inequity in the consumption of health care services by reducing access by persons in lower socio-economic groups. The differential impact of patient charges on lower-income persons assumes that utilization by poorer people is more responsive to price changes than is that by higher-income persons (i.e. elasticity rises as income falls). This is an empirical question, but it is reasonable to expect that price would be more of a deterrent to use when it implies a greater percentage of a household's budget. Absolute reductions in utilization or delays in seeking treatment can lead to inequities in health status for lower-income individuals to the extent that use of health services would have had beneficial health effects.

## COST-SHARING POLICIES AND PRACTICES IN EUROPEAN COUNTRIES

The countries of the European region employ a variety of approaches to cost sharing; however, the context, the objectives of these policies, and the way cost sharing is implemented in practice tend to be different in the countries of western Europe as compared to the CEE/CIS countries.

A combination of conditions both within and external to the health sector determine the likely effects that cost-sharing policies will have. These conditions also affect strongly the main objectives that countries assign (implicitly or explicitly) to cost sharing as part of their national health policies and systems. An overriding contextual factor is the broad macroeconomic environment. This includes such features as the levels and rates of growth of per capita income, income inequality, formal sector employment, and inflation. Some of these economic characteristics relate closely to the budgetary situation of a national health service or national/social insurance institutions. They also directly affect a second key contextual factor: the extent to which the population is covered with a well-functioning health service. Where the health services are operating at low levels of quality or are inaccessible for a significant proportion of the population, the revenue-raising objective will tend to dominate other aims of cost sharing. These conditions have set the context for overall policies on health financing, including choices on funding sources, risk sharing, provider payment options, and methods to ensure access to care for the poorest members of society. These in turn have implications for the role and likely consequences of cost sharing. For example, in systems using retrospective reimbursement of providers, there is likely to be a greater reliance on cost sharing to achieve policy aims than in systems where doctors and hospitals are paid prospectively, since prospective systems (salaries, budgets, or capitation, for example) build in cost-containment objectives on the supply-side. Cost sharing is only one feature of broader health financing policies. To understand its role and effects, it is essential to understand the motivating forces driving these broader policies.

### Cost sharing in western European countries

Nearly all of the countries of western Europe provide universal coverage[6] for health care costs to their population through general tax-funded national health systems or compulsory social insurance programmes. This coverage has been achieved as a consequence of historical factors, including cultural values of social solidarity and universality, plus a long period of relatively stable macroeconomic growth. Stable macroeconomic performance has meant that for the most part, western European countries do not need to rely on out-of-pocket payments to raise revenues for the provision of health services. They also focus their cost-containment efforts on the

**Table 3.1** Patient cost sharing in western European health care systems

| Country | Type of provider | | |
|---------|-----------------|--|--|
| | *First contact* | *Referral* | *Pharmaceuticals* |
| Austria[a] | 80% of the population has no cost saving; the rest has co-insurance or is exempt due to low income | Mix of co-payment and co-insurance (with exemptions). Out-of-pocket liability limited to first 28 days in hospital | Co-payment for prescribed drugs. Non-prescription drugs are excluded |
| Belgium[b,c,d] | Narrow range of co-payments or co-insurance (less for low-income persons). Extra billing allowed | Variable co-payments according to fee schedule (lower co-payment for low income persons) | Co-payment or co-insurance with rates ranging, by type of drug, from 0% to 85%; drugs not on positive list are excluded from cover |
| Denmark[a] | None | None | Variable co-insurance rate (0–50%) applied to reference price. Drugs not on formulary excluded from cover |
| Finland[a] | Municipalities may choose none, annual prepayment or co-payment, or co-payment with out-of-pocket maximum | Maximum payment levels per hospital day and per specialist visit | Co-insurance |
| France[c] | Co-insurance; extra billing allowed for defined categories of physicians | Co-insurance for per diem rate plus co-payment to cover meals. No out-of-pocket liability after 30 days | Most subject to co-insurance; no coverage for items not on national list of approved drugs |
| Germany[f,g] | None | Flat co-payment for up to 14 days per year; thereafter no out-of-pocket liability | Variable co-payment; reference pricing; no coverage for items on negative list |

| | | | |
|---|---|---|---|
| Greece[a] | None, although extra billing is common among private doctors | None for in-patient hospital care. Some funds have co-insurance for diagnostic services | Co-insurance |
| Iceland[a] | Co-payment, with higher rate for visits outside normal working hours. Higher co-payment for home visits. Out-of-pocket maximum | None for in-patient hospital care. Mix of co-payment and co-insurance for specialist and hospital outpatient care. Co-payment for diagnostic services. Out-of-pocket maximum | Mix of deductible per 'day' of prescription, plus co-insurance, up to a defined out-of-pocket maximum. Some items entirely free and others excluded from coverage |
| Ireland[b,d,h] | None for 'Category I' population (37% in 1987). Full charges for others, unless they buy insurance. Insured persons face an annual deductible, which also serves as an out-of-pocket maximum | None for 'Category I' population in public hospitals. For the rest, co-payment for first hospital outpatient visit per episode and co-payment per diem for the first 10 days of public hospital care per year. Insurance buys free care in public and private hospitals | None for 'Category I' population. Others face a monthly deductible, which also serves as an out-of-pocket maximum for the month. Items on the negative list of drugs are excluded from coverage |
| Italy[a,b] | None | None for in-patient care. Cost sharing was introduced in 1990 in public hospitals for diagnostic procedures, specialist visits and spa treatment | Deductible only for essential drugs. Most other drugs have a deductible plus co-insurance. Some drugs excluded from coverage |
| Luxembourg[b] | Co-insurance | Per diem co-payment indexed to inflation | Co-insurance for outpatient drugs, except for 'special diseases'. In-patient drugs are free |

**Table 3.1** continued

| Country | Type of provider | | Pharmaceuticals |
|---|---|---|---|
| | First contact | Referral | |
| Netherlands[f] | None for publicly insured; varies for privately insured | None for publicly insured; varies for privately insured | Reference price system; no coverage for excluded items |
| Norway[a] | Cost sharing, with annual out-of-pocket maximum for all services | None for in-patient care. Cost sharing for diagnostic services | Reference price system for essential drugs |
| Portugal[a,b] | Cost sharing | Cost sharing | Two co-insurance rates according to type of drug. Also, some items are free, but others are excluded from coverage |
| Spain[b] | None | None | Co-insurance. Items not on approved list are excluded from coverage |
| Sweden[f,i] | Co-payment, with annual out-of-pocket maximum for all services except in-patient | Co-payment per diem for in-patient care. Co-payments for therapeutic referrals | Co-payment for first item prescribed; greatly reduced co-payment for additional items. Reference pricing for items with generic equivalents |
| Switzerland[a] | Annual deductible plus co-insurance | Co-payment per diem for hospital care | Cost sharing varies among insurers. Items on negative list are excluded from coverage |
| Turkey[a] | Mostly private providers who charge on a fee-for-service basis | Social insurance schemes cover all charges; uninsured face user fees | All social insurance schemes have co-insurance for outpatient drugs |
| United Kingdom[f] | None | None, except for amenity hospital beds | Co-payments, but 83% of prescriptions are exempt. Items on negative list are excluded from NHS coverage |

*Sources:* [a]OECD (1994); [b]Abel-Smith and Mossialos (1994); [c]Abel-Smith (1992); [d]OECD (1992); [e]Rodwin and Sandier (1993); [f]Rubin and Mendelson (1995); [g]United States General Accounting Office (1994); [h]Nolan (1993); [i]Jönsson and Gerdtham (1995)

supply-side of the market, usually through budgetary controls (especially for hospital care) and by requiring primary care physicians to act as gatekeepers[7] to referral-level care. Thus, with the exception of France and Portugal (Abel-Smith *et al.* 1995), western European countries rely very little on cost sharing as a tool for either raising revenues or containing costs for physician and hospital services. On the other hand, cost sharing for pharmaceuticals is widespread, and though the objectives of such policies are rarely stated explicitly, their main purpose seems to be to shift some or much of the cost of drugs to users. Indeed, an analysis of cost sharing for prescription drugs in the British National Health Service states that the main purpose of such charges 'is to raise additional revenue to supplement the NHS budget' (Hughes and McGuire 1995).

The cost-sharing policies of western European countries are summarized in Table 3.1. The organization of the table is driven by the prior discussion of the theoretical basis for cost sharing.

About half of these countries use some form of cost sharing for first contact care, and about half also apply cost sharing to inpatient and specialty outpatient care. The most common forms of direct cost sharing are co-payments and co-insurance; only in Switzerland is use made of deductibles. Irrespective of the extent to which cost sharing is used, virtually all of the countries of western Europe use some form of out-of-pocket maximum to limit the liability of individuals or households for medical care costs, and none employ benefit maximums. Hence, income protection is a strong feature of these systems.

Extra billing by physicians is not legal in the health systems of most western European countries. Exceptions to this are Belgium, France, and the 'Group 2' programme of Denmark.[8] More common is the use of coverage exclusions to limit the financial obligations of the insurance programme and encourage appropriate channels of service use. This is a feature of many countries' pharmaceutical benefit programmes where purchases of items on a 'negative list' (e.g. Germany, Ireland) or not on a 'positive list' (e.g. Belgium, Spain) are not reimbursed. In countries such as Finland and the UK that use general practitioners or primary care centres as gatekeepers to referral services, use of other providers for first contact care is excluded from the benefit package. Citizens are entitled to go out of their defined referral channels but must finance such services privately. Similar in concept are the practices of a number of county councils in Sweden. They have imposed higher charges for specialists than for GPs with the intention of discouraging patients from self-referring directly to specialists (Ham and Brommels 1994).

Pharmaceutical reference pricing has been implemented in Denmark, Germany, the Netherlands, Norway and Sweden. In Germany, the Health Care Reform Act of 1989 established a maximum reimbursement level (the reference price) for each drug, with consumers liable for the difference between the retail price and the reference price (United States General Accounting Office 1994). In a way, then, reference pricing is a special case of a coverage exclusion. Under this system, the health system's (or insurer's) expenditure per item is explicitly limited, but consumers are free to choose among the available products on the market.

A policy with implications for the effects of cost sharing is the role allowed for voluntary (not-for-profit or for-profit) health insurance. In most countries of western Europe, such insurance is either not allowed (e.g. Belgium, Norway, Sweden) or it can only be used to purchase private services not included in the standard benefit package of the national health service or social insurance system (e.g. Austria, Italy, UK). In Denmark and France, however, individuals are allowed to purchase insurance that covers the cost sharing obligations of the national insurance systems. In Denmark, about 26 per cent of the population uses private insurance to cover cost sharing for pharmaceuticals and dental services (OECD 1994). In France such coverage is widespread: 84 per cent of the population has complementary private coverage provided by commercial carriers or *mutuelles*. Thus, even though France makes extensive use of cost sharing (*ticket moderateur*) in its national health insurance system, only a small percentage of the population is affected by these charges. Indeed, voluntary insurance in France not only covers the cost-sharing requirements of national insurance, but most insurers also cover any extra billing charged by providers (Rodwin and Sandier 1993).[9] This feature of the French health system eliminates any potential demand-reducing effects of cost sharing, except for that part of the population that is unable to obtain private insurance coverage.

Virtually all western European countries reduce or eliminate cost-sharing obligations for persons identified as belonging to a disadvantaged group. Exemption from charges is commonly made on the grounds of individual or household income and age.

In most countries, policies are determined centrally by the national health service or on behalf of the social insurance schemes. In countries with multiple compulsory social insurance institutions, cost-sharing obligations may vary across schemes, as in Austria (OECD 1994). In Finland (OECD 1994) and Sweden (Rubin and Mendelson 1995) political systems are highly decentralized, and decisions on cost sharing are made by local (municipal or county) governments.

Greece and Turkey are exceptions to the general picture of countries providing universal coverage for access to well-functioning health systems. In Greece, coverage with social insurance is universal, but great geographic disparities in the distribution of providers means that many citizens do not have ready access to services. Moreover, the practice of illegal extra billing ('envelope payments') by staff in hospitals and elsewhere is common, reflecting low pay levels for health professionals (Abel-Smith *et al.* 1994). In Turkey, only 60–65 per cent of the population is covered by a social insurance scheme. All persons are entitled to use government health facilities, but user charges apply to a wide range of services (Project General Coordination Unit 1995). In both of these countries, therefore, official and unofficial charges are widespread and exist mainly for the purpose of raising additional revenues to fund health service provision.

### Cost sharing in the CEE/CIS countries

In the current period of economic transition, revenue raising has been the principal concern of most of the CEE/CIS countries. Although insurance or general taxation are better methods for raising resources than are direct charges to patients, falling levels of employment have reduced the scope for mandatory contributions to social insurance, since these are usually financed by the contributions of employers and employees. Similarly, there are limits to the amount of revenues that could be generated through general taxes. Thus, many (though not all) of the CEE/CIS countries are using direct charges to patients primarily as a means to provide additional resources to sustain the health services. At the same time, the available evidence suggests that providers are increasing their reliance on informal 'side payments' from patients.[10] Table 3.2 describes the cost-sharing policies of those countries for which information could be obtained. This table is organized in a similar fashion to Table 3.1, but it has an additional column that identifies the presence (and if possible, the extent) of informal payments.[11]

It is apparent from the table that informal payment for services is common in the CEE/CIS countries. These payments are related to

**Table 3.2** Patient cost sharing in selected CEE/CIS countries

| Country | Type of provider | | | Side payments |
|---|---|---|---|---|
| | First contact | Referral | Pharmaceuticals | |
| Bulgaria[a] | None in public sector; full payment in private sector (no insurance coverage) | None, but private donations are common | Patients often pay for drugs that are officially free | Widely used |
| Croatia[b,c] | Low levels of co-insurance, but likely to increase | Low levels of co-insurance, but likely to increase | Low levels of co-insurance, but likely to increase | |
| Czech Republic[d] | Modest cost sharing for specific PHC services, with out-of-pocket maximum. Private doctors can charge extra | Plan to introduce cost sharing with out-of-pocket maximum | Cost sharing; positive list of reimburseable drugs | Yes |
| Estonia[ ] | Modest cost sharing | None for in-patient care; modest levels for specialist outpatient care | High co-insurance with exemptions and reductions for specific groups | Yes |
| Hungary[e] | No formal charges | Modest cost sharing for in-patient care | Cost sharing with exemptions | Widely used |
| Kyrgyzstan[f] | 25% pay official charges; the rest are exempt or not charged | 25% pay official admission charges; the rest are exempt or not charged. Families often provide food | Most patients pay for drugs; prices vary widely | Yes, and growing |
| Latvia | Modest cost sharing | Modest cost sharing for in-patient and outpatient care, with exemptions for specific groups | Cost sharing | Yes |

the low levels of remuneration of providers in these countries which exist as a consequence of historical factors and also because of the recent economic decline. They also reflect a willingness (by those who are able) to pay something for health care. In Bulgaria, systematic underfunding of public sector services has led to widespread reliance on illegal payments and 'voluntary donations'. Payments are often made by patients for drugs and medical supplies, food, clinical tests, and other services that are ostensibly free (Balabanova 1995). In Hungary, the payment of 'gratitude money' to health service providers has become widespread as their salary levels have dropped in real terms (Kincses 1995). The low level of salaries for medical personnel in Poland contributes to the continuation of informal payments (Marek 1995). Household survey data from Kazakstan reveal that patients often have to supply goods and services in-kind during their hospital stays that are supposed to be provided by the government health system. Fifty-seven per cent of these patients also had to purchase or bring the medicines required during their hospitalization (Novak 1996).

The CEE/CIS countries do not have a uniform context and experience, however. In the Czech Republic, for example, macroeconomic performance has improved more rapidly than in many neighbouring countries. A universal compulsory insurance programme was introduced at the beginning of 1992 but was soon followed by a cost explosion, largely because of the incentives of a fee-for-service reimbursement system. A package of supply-side and demand-side reforms has been introduced (or is planned) in an attempt to contain costs. This policy package includes low levels of cost sharing (limited by an out-of-pocket maximum), ostensibly as a complement to other cost control policies (von Bredow 1995). Thus, the main purpose of cost-sharing policy in the Czech Republic appears to be cost containment rather than resource mobilization.

The rapid introduction of market mechanisms in the health systems of the CEE/CIS countries raises concern about the ability of poorer citizens to meet the formal and informal charges required to access health services. Moreover, the economic decline associated with the transitional period has led to a growth in the percentage of the population that is poor. In Hungary during the 1990s for example, economic growth has declined, there has been a rapid increase in unemployment, and demographic changes have occurred leading to an increase in the number of pensioners. One consequence of these changes has been the economic polarization of the population. Higher-income persons are more able to pay, more likely to be insured, and less likely to be deterred from using health services than are lower-income persons. To provide some protection for disadvantaged persons, certain drug items are exempt from official charges. These include drugs for specified chronic conditions and specified communicable diseases, plus prescribed drugs for the 'socially needy', whose status has been verified and who consequently hold a public health provision identity card (Kincses 1995).

## EVIDENCE ON THE EFFECTS OF COST-SHARING POLICIES

The most detailed assessment of the effects of cost sharing on utilization, costs and health status comes from a US study that used a truly experimental design. It is generally referred to as the Rand Health Insurance Experiment (HIE), and it was implemented during the 1970s and early 1980s in six sites (Newhouse 1974; Manning *et al.* 1987).[12] While this is probably the most widely cited study that has ever been done on the effects of cost sharing, several authors have noted that the effects of cost sharing observed in the HIE cannot be directly translated into the expected outcomes of national reforms involving cost sharing. The main reason for this is that, in each experimental site, the number of patients of any individual practitioner who were involved in the experiment was too small to have had a noticeable impact on provider behaviour. Thus, the experiment was not able to incorporate possible supplier response to any changes in demand induced by changes in cost-sharing requirements. If national reforms involving cost sharing led to a reduction in consumer-led demand, however, this might directly threaten physician incomes (depending, of course, on how physicians are paid), leading them to induce increases in either the volume or intensity of services provided (Evans *et al.* 1993a; Rice and Morrison 1994).

### Efficiency and cost containment

*Effect of cost sharing on utilization*

Several studies have examined the effects of cost sharing on levels and patterns of health service use. To summarize the effects of cost sharing on efficiency, three aspects of these utilization effects are described here: (1) effect on total utilization levels; (2) effect on necessary (appropriate) vs. unnecessary (inappropriate) service use; and (3) effect on the use of first contact vs. referral services.

*Total utilization*
Based on their extensive review of the (mostly US) literature on the effects of cost sharing, Rice and Morrison found that 'The literature is unanimous in its conclusion that cost sharing results in decreased utilisation' (Rice and Morrison 1994: 263). Studies from other countries show similar results. An analysis of the impact of the use of co-payments for physicians' services from 1968 to 1971 in the Canadian province of Saskatchewan showed that this caused a slight reduction in utilization (Beck and Horne 1980). Similarly, data from Japan show that the co-payment in their national health insurance system had a small negative effect on total service utilization (Kupor *et al.* 1995).

Household survey data from Ireland in 1987, a period when GPs were reimbursed on a fee-for-service basis, facilitated a comparison of utilization behaviour across persons facing different cost-sharing requirements. The part of the population entitled to free care had 6.8 visits per capita, whereas the other groups had only 2.8. Although the free care group had a higher proportion of older persons, utilization rates within age groups remained large (for example, 5.9 vs. 2.7 visits for ages 35–44, 9.4 vs. 4.0 visits for ages 55–64). A multivariate analysis that controlled for variations in both demographic and health status indicated that being in the category of persons facing no cost-sharing obligations (predominantly but not exclusively poor persons) was significantly and positively related to a higher probability of having had a GP visit during the year. Voluntary insurance coverage (which reimbursed expenditures above a defined out-of-pocket maximum) was also positively and significantly related to this probability but to a lesser extent than fully free care (Nolan 1993).

*'Necessary' vs. 'unnecessary' utilization*
Part of the rationale for the use of cost sharing as a demand management tool is that it will not merely reduce the overall level of utilization, but will reduce the use of services that are not medically necessary to a greater extent than more 'appropriate' services. If this were true, cost sharing could help to contain costs without harmful health effects. Unfortunately, those studies that

have attempted to examine this issue have found that cost sharing is a blunt rather than a fine policy tool. Analyses of the HIE, for example, showed that a reduction in contacts occurred for both appropriate and inappropriate care, measured as services considered to be 'highly effective' or 'rarely effective' (Lohr *et al.* 1986; Siu *et al.* 1986). Thus, 'Cost-sharing did not seem to have a selective effect in prompting people to forego care only or mainly in circumstances when such care probably would be of relatively little value' (Lohr *et al.* 1986).

In Iceland, where physicians are paid on a full salary basis and thus have no financial incentives to increase the number of patient visits, new, higher cost sharing for GP and specialist services introduced in 1993 led to a reduction in the number of specialty visits of approximately 10 per cent. There is no clear evidence as to whether this decline was for 'unnecessary' services, but there was a 17 per cent decline in the number of women receiving screening for cervical cancer. This raises some concerns about the possible impact of increased cost sharing on the use of necessary preventive care (OECD 1994).

*First contact vs. referral services*
Analyses of the utilization effects of cost sharing disaggregated in this manner are essential for examining the issue of supplier-induced demand and, by extension, the scope and limitations of cost sharing as a tool for enhancing health system efficiency. In their analysis of the HIE, Manning *et al.* found that while cost sharing reduced the number of both outpatient and in-patient contacts, there was no difference in the intensity of care (i.e. the number and type of services per contact) used by persons with different cost-sharing requirements after the initial decision to seek care was made (Manning *et al.* 1987). In other words, once a person was in the care of a physician, cost sharing had no effect on utilization patterns for the rest of that episode of illness.

Studies from outside the US also suggest that, as might be expected, the utilization rate of consumer-initiated services (i.e. primary care) is more sensitive to cost sharing than is that of provider-initiated (i.e. referral) services. For example, Kupor *et al.* (1995) conclude that in-patient utilization in Japan was much less sensitive to cost sharing than outpatient medical and outpatient dental care. From their analysis of the data on the effects of co-payments in Saskatchewan, Beck and Horne found that the in-patient co-payment levied between 1968 and 1971 had no effect on either the number of hospital admissions or the length of hospital stays (Beck and Horne 1980).

Two other US studies highlight the importance of distinguishing between first contact and referral services. Furthermore, they illustrate the possibility that, faced with a reduction in consumer-initiated utilization (and income) resulting from cost sharing, providers can and will induce increases in the intensity of referral care. Analysis of utilization before and after the introduction, in 1967, of a 25 per cent co-insurance requirement (where none had existed previously) for all services covered by the Group Health Plan of Stanford University (California) showed that per capita physician visits and costs declined by about 24 per cent, whereas outpatient ancillary service visits declined by only 11 per cent and costs by 11.5 per cent. The number and costs of surgical hospitalizations decreased by 5 and 8 per cent respectively, while those of medical hospitalizations declined by 3 and 15 per cent respectively (Scitovsky and Snyder 1972). Thus, the decline in the per capita volume and cost of services that require referral by a physician fell by less than the decline in physician visits. This suggests that cost sharing has a much greater effect on consumer-initiated services than on referral services, or that physicians attempted to offset the reduction in visits by increasing the intensity of referral services prescribed per visit.[13]

An analysis of utilization and costs at one physician group practice in the US, the income of which depended upon the total volume of services provided to users,[14] suggests that if utilization falls as a consequence of the introduction of cost sharing to one group of patients, physicians can induce greater utilization by persons to whom cost sharing does not apply. In mid-1977, miners and their families covered by the United Mine Workers' (UMW) Health and Retirement Fund became subject to a co-payment for each physician visit, after having had no cost-sharing obligations for the previous 25 years. An analysis was made of utilization and costs at one medical group practice for the year prior and two years after the introduction of cost sharing for UMW members and their families. The clients of the group practice were comprised largely (more than 80 per cent) of mine workers, steelworkers, and their families. Unlike the UMW members, the health insurance benefits of steelworkers remained constant over the study period. The study found that while utilization by UMW members and their dependents decreased, utilization, price and costs of the rest of the practice's clients increased. In particular, for non-UMW patients, hospital length of stay and cost per case increased, the recommended interval between ambulatory visits decreased, and reimbursement rates for ambulatory care increased. Thus, physicians changed their practice patterns in an attempt to maintain their incomes in response to a fall in demand by a large segment of their client population due to cost sharing. This implies that the utilization and cost reductions implied by cost-sharing policies (as in the HIE analyses) may be less at an overall system level than would be the case if physicians did not respond (Fahs 1992).

*Effect of cost sharing on total health expenditures*

Evidence suggests that cost sharing does reduce utilization but does not contain costs. Overall costs are not contained because cost sharing is a set of demand-side policies, and costs are primarily driven by supply-side factors. Cross-country comparisons indicate that the US has a lower rate of physician contacts and per capita bed-days than many other countries, such as Canada, France, Germany, Japan and the UK, but costs in the US are much higher relative to GDP than in these other countries (see Table 3.3). This strongly suggests that it is the intensity of care provided per contact in the US that is responsible for this apparent paradox (Rasell 1995). The US has the highest level of out-of-pocket expenses, much of which is to meet cost-sharing obligations, and also has the highest overall costs. Other countries have lower cost sharing and higher utilization rates, but lower costs. This does not mean that cost sharing

**Table 3.3**   Health care utilization and expenditures, ca. 1990

| Country | Physician contacts (per capita) Number | Use of acute in-patient care (per capita) Number of bed-days | Health care expenditures % of GDP |
|---|---|---|---|
| Canada | 6.9 | 1.5 | 9.5 |
| France | 7.2 | 1.5 | 8.8 |
| Germany | 11.5 | 2.3 | 8.3 |
| Japan | 12.9 | – | 6.7 |
| UK | 5.7 | 0.9 | 6.2 |
| US | 5.5 | 0.9 | 12.2 |

*Source:* Rassell (1995)

causes higher costs; it means that measures other than cost sharing (supply-side measures such as budgetary controls) are much more effective cost-containment mechanisms.

The HIE suggests that cost sharing is associated with a decrease in total health expenditures, but the design of the experiment does not really enable strong conclusions to be drawn as to the consequences for total expenditures of broad national implementation of cost sharing within a retrospective reimbursement system. The reason is that providers can compensate for a reduction in consumer-initiated demand by inducing increases in service volume or intensity, as shown by the analyses of the Stanford (Scitovsky and Snyder 1972) and UMW (Fahs 1992) experiences described above. Cross-country data (Rasell 1995) suggests that consumer-initiated demand is not the major factor driving health care costs. Instead, it appears to be the intensity of services provided. Since intensity is largely provider-initiated, there is little scope for cost sharing to have much of an impact on the overall level of expenditures.

Limited evidence on the effects of pharmaceutical cost sharing from European countries also suggests that this is a weak tool for overall cost containment. In Sweden, the introduction of the reference price system led to a rapid decline in pharmaceutical prices. Generic market share for items covered by the reference price system increased from 35 to 49 per cent during the first six months of 1993. The estimated annual savings to government resulting from this change was about 5 per cent of its total pharmaceutical costs. However, total drug expenditures continued their previous rate of annual increase as additional costs were shifted to patients (Jönsson and Gerdtham 1995). Similarly in the Czech Republic, pharmaceutical costs were completely covered until 1992, when cost sharing was introduced. This had very little effect on overall drug expenditures, however, which still account for about 30 per cent of total health spending (von Bredow 1995).

## EQUITY

### Equity in finance

Has cost sharing led to a relatively greater burden of health care financing falling on lower income households? Based on data from the 1980s, Switzerland and the US were found to have the most regressive health financing system of ten OECD countries studied (van Doorslaer and Wagstaff 1993). This finding was attributed to their heavy reliance on both private health insurance and private out-of-pocket payments. The latter were found to be very regressive in these two countries because, in most instances, cost-sharing obligations apply irrespective of patient income.

The equity consequences in France are unclear because there is not a straightforward direct relation between income and complementary insurance coverage. Employees in small firms and young people, as well as the unemployed, tend to be less likely to have complementary insurance. This suggests that voluntary complementary insurance that covers the cost-sharing obligations of a national insurance system can lead to a disproportionate financing burden (and probably inequitable access as well) for those unable to purchase voluntary coverage.

Evidence from Kyrgyzstan suggests that the mix of formal and informal charges to users of health services worsened inequities in financing. The out-of-pocket requirements of an episode of illness could pose a substantial burden for many households. In 20 per cent of cases, the total costs of an illness episode for an individual exceeded the monthly income of his or her entire household. Almost 50 per cent of in-patients reported severe difficulties in finding the money to pay for their stay, and one-third of in-patients borrowed to pay for their hospital charges. Capital items were often sold (farm animals in rural areas, consumer durables in urban areas) to come up with the necessary funds. Overall, there is evidence that the incidence of out-of-pocket payments for health is inequitable (i.e. it is creating more of a burden for poorer households and individuals) (Abel-Smith and Falkingham 1995).

### Equity in access and health status

In Ireland, the absence of cost sharing for GP services for the persons in the group entitled to free care played an important role in their having higher consultation rates than the rest of the population (Nolan 1993). Thus, the Irish system explicitly promoted greater financial access for persons from lower-income groups, and this appears to have been effective at raising utilization.

The survey data from Kyrgyzstan suggests that user charges are reducing access for the poorest groups and thus worsening equity in the receipt of services. The survey data indicate (like all surveys to date) that persons from poorer households are less likely to seek care when sick than those from richer households. Sixty-three per cent of ill persons in the richest income quintile sought care outside the home, compared with 41 per cent of ill persons in the poorest quintile. In addition, 5 per cent of persons who required in-patient care said that they were not able to go to the hospital. Most of these people said that they could not afford it, and all of them were in the bottom half of the income distribution (Abel-Smith and Falkingham 1995).

Has cost sharing led to reduced access and worse outcomes due to delay or non-use for persons from lower socio-economic groups? Evidence from the HIE study suggests that cost sharing has harmful effects on health status for poor people who are at high risk for ill health. Conversely, free care can provide health benefits for this same population. For the least healthy 25 per cent of people participating in the study,[15] those not subject to cost sharing had a mortality risk that was 10 per cent less than those who did face out-of-pocket obligations, primarily as a result of better control of high blood pressure among those in the free care group. For other health status measures, however, there were no significant differences between cost sharing and free care plans among persons of average income (Brook *et al.* 1983).

The study also indicated that cost sharing had negative health consequences for persons who were in the lowest 40 per cent with respect to income and the lowest 40 per cent with respect to initial health status. Prevalence of specific tracer conditions and symptoms (e.g. chest pain when exercising, bleeding not caused by accidents, and shortness of breath during light exercise or work) was 21 per cent higher for persons in this group who were subject to cost sharing than for those who had access to free care. Moreover, the study showed that free care (absence of cost sharing) can improve health status for the poor. For the relatively low-income and unhealthy group mentioned above, persons without cost-sharing obligations had similar levels of serious symptoms to those of less healthy persons in higher-income groups (Shapiro *et al.* 1986).

Thus, even within its selected sample that excluded the elderly population, the Rand study found that cost sharing reduced access to necessary care, especially for relatively poor people. For the poorest one-third of the population, adults facing cost-sharing obligations were 59 per cent as likely to seek 'highly effective care for acute conditions' as were those entitled to free care. This difference was 71 per cent for middle-income and upper-income groups. The utilization differences of cost sharing on children of different income groups were more dramatic: appropriate utilization with cost sharing was 56 per cent of free care levels for the poorest one-third, whereas the impact of cost sharing on appropriate use by children in other income groups was not significant (Lohr *et al.* 1986).

The study also found that cost sharing reduced access to personal preventive care. Low-income adults who faced cost-sharing obligations had only 54 per cent as many general medical examinations as persons in the same income group who had free access, whereas this figure was 71 per cent for non-poor adults. For children, the comparable figures were 68 per cent and 79 per cent respectively (Lohr *et al.* 1986). Similarly, the introduction of 25 per cent co-insurance in the Stanford University Group Health Plan caused a much greater reduction in the per capita number of annual physical examinations by adult men and children in the lowest socio-economic category than in the other two categories (Scitovsky and Snyder 1972).

One conclusion that can be drawn from the HIE is that cost sharing had harmful health effects for the poor when these measures deterred or delayed access to physician care for conditions that are amenable to direct diagnosis or treatment by physicians. The HIE design caused income effects to be understated because the out-of-pocket maximum was defined as a percentage of family income. Consequently, poor households were more protected than rich ones from high absolute levels of health expenditures (Schoenman 1993). The HIE suggests that no cost sharing (i.e. free care) for the sick poor can improve health equity. However, there may be ways of doing this through a targeted subsidy or other special programme that might be less administratively costly than through the cost-sharing system.

## CONCLUSIONS

The appropriateness and likely effects of cost sharing depend on the services to which it is applied and the extent of effective coverage of the population by a well-functioning national health or insurance system. The evidence suggests that in countries with universal or near-universal coverage, as in most countries of western Europe, cost sharing is a weak instrument for promoting efficiency and cost containment and has detrimental effects on equity in the finance and use of health services. Cost sharing is likely to have similar weaknesses in countries without near-universal effective insurance or health system coverage, as in most CEE/CIS countries. In these countries, however, formal or informal cost sharing is a coping strategy used to supplement the incomes of underpaid (or irregularly paid) health workers and/or to ensure that needed inputs are available for effective treatment. In this context, cost sharing has the potential to improve the quality and availability of services, but with stark adverse effects on equity in the finance and receipt of care, and probably on health status as well.

The evidence presented in this paper indicates that, by itself, cost sharing does not provide a very powerful policy tool for improving efficiency or containing health sector costs. Because of the importance of providers in influencing the demand for many services, especially those that are the main drivers of health sector costs, policies that address the supply-side of the market are much more powerful than those that work solely on the demand-side. Cost sharing will reduce consumer-initiated utilization, but such reductions will not be effective for cost containment. This is because the main driver of health care costs is service intensity, which is a provider-driven characteristic. In systems in which providers are reimbursed retrospectively, reductions in consumer-initiated utilization caused by cost sharing will lead providers to increase the volume of services per patient contact (i.e. service intensity) in order to maintain their incomes. In this context, therefore, cost sharing does little to restrain cost growth because providers can respond to a drop in consumer-initiated utilization by inducing an increase in the use of diagnostic and therapeutic services. In systems where providers are prepaid, there are no obvious incentives for this supplier response, but the effects of cost sharing are still likely to be marginal because supply-side incentives are sufficient to restrain expenditure growth.

Without specific measures to exempt low-income groups from out-of-pocket charges, cost sharing causes inequity in the finance and receipt of health services. Evidence from countries around the world shows consistently that service use by poorer people is deterred to a greater extent by direct charges than is that by richer people. These limitations on access may result in adverse health effects for poorer and sicker segments of the population. The challenges of implementing compensatory measures to protect access (and incomes) of poorer members of society should not be underestimated. Experience from developing countries, where measures to exempt low-income persons from user fees have proven largely ineffective, suggests that there are considerable administrative, informational, economic and political constraints to overcome (Gilson *et al.* 1995).

## ACKNOWLEDGEMENTS

I am grateful to Dr Gyula Kincses for his work in collecting and summarizing cost-sharing practices in a number of CEE/CIS countries as part of the preparation of this paper. I also thank the many participants of the Workshop on European Health Care Reforms held at the WHO Regional Office for Europe in December 1995 for their comments on an earlier draft of this paper. Written and oral comments received from Richard Saltman and Alex Preker were particularly helpful.

## NOTES

1 'Moral hazard' is the term used to describe the cause of the additional use of health care arising from insurance coverage.
2 Technically, 'excessive demand' does not refer to demand for services that are medically unnecessary or potentially harmful. Indeed, the additional services consumed may yield positive health benefits. But, in economic terms, utilization is considered to be excessive if the marginal social cost of providing this additional service is greater than the marginal social benefit arising from the consumption of the service. In other words, the resources used to provide the additional unit of service (e.g. a physician visit) could have yielded a greater benefit to society if they were used for some other purpose. Despite this, many researchers (including several economists) have tried to operationalize a definition of excessive demand by testing whether the utilization deterred by cost sharing was for 'necessary' services or had harmful health effects. Although this definition of excess demand differs from that used in economics, it has intuitive appeal. The implications of this approach are that if cost-sharing mechanisms are successful at reducing demand with no effect on health status, one can conclude that economic efficiency has been improved. The policy will have led some costs to be shifted to users, but overall costs would be reduced while benefits remain unchanged.
3 Of course, insurance also produces a social welfare gain by protecting people from the risk of financial loss due to high health expenditures (Hammer and Berman 1995), so it leads to both a welfare gain from risk reduction and a welfare loss from excess consumption of health care services. The theoretical case for cost sharing is that it can reduce the latter without affecting the former.
4 This is called the 'free-rider' problem.
5 These benefits that accrue to non-market participants are called 'externalities'.

6  In several countries, coverage is not quite universal. However, more than 99 per cent of the population is covered in virtually all countries of western Europe.

7  Notable exceptions to this are Belgium, France and Germany.

8  In this programme, patients have complete free choice of providers, but doctors are free to charge rates above the defined reimbursement levels. Less than 4 per cent of the population opted for this programme in 1991 (OECD 1994).

9  This is more broadly true with respect to physician services. Many *mutuelles* do not cover fully the in-patient per diem (Sandier 1996).

10  These informal payments are called by a variety of names, including 'black money', 'under-the-table payments', 'gratitude money', etc.

11  A questionnaire was mailed to knowledgeable persons in the CEE/CIS countries in an attempt to obtain consistent information on both formal and informal cost-sharing practices. Unless otherwise indicated in Table 3.2, responses to this questionnaire are the source of the information. I am grateful to Dr Gyula Kincses for collecting and summarizing this information.

12  For the HIE study, about 5800 persons (excluding those who chose not to participate before the experiment began and who may have had higher health risks) were assigned randomly to one of several fee-for-service insurance plans with different cost-sharing levels (plus one HMO group) for a three to five-year period. Persons over 62 years of age were excluded from the sample, as was the richest 3 per cent of the population. The different experimental groups varied by level of co-insurance rate (0 per cent, 25, 50 and 95 per cent) and out-of-pocket maximum (which were set at either 5, 10 or 15 per cent of annual family income, but never to exceed $1000) for plans that had some cost sharing. There was also one plan that had a $150 annual deductible per person for outpatient services but no in-patient cost sharing. The list of services covered was the same for each of the plans.

13  This conclusion is strengthened by the fact that the insurance scheme being studied only reimbursed services provided by one integrated medical clinic, and this clinic provided physician visits in and out of the hospital, laboratory and radiology services, echo cardiogram and electro encephalograph services, and physiotherapy. Thus, the increased number of referrals for ancillary services (even though these were also subject to a 25 per cent co-insurance rate) meant greater income for the medical clinic as a whole.

14  The group practice employed its full-time physicians on a salaried basis. However, the group received fee-for-service reimbursements from third-party payers. The doctors received no outside income, so the ability of the group to pay their salaries depended on the total revenues that were paid to the practice. Thus, there was a collective incentive to increase service provision.

15 This definition was based on an assessment of four categories of health status measures: self-reported general health, self-reported health habits, physiologic health, and mortality risk factors (Brook *et al.* 1983).

## REFERENCES

Abel-Smith, B. (1992). *Cost Containment and New Priorities in Health Care: A Study of the European Community.* Aldershot: Avebury Ashgate.

Abel-Smith, B. and Falkingham, J. (1995). *Financing Health Services in Kyrgyzstan: The Extent of Private Payments.* London: London School of Economics.

Abel-Smith, B. and Mossialos, E. (1994). Cost containment and health care reform: A study of the European Union. *Health Policy*, 28, 89–132.

Abel-Smith, B., Calltorp, J., Dixon, M., Dunning, A., Evans, R., Holland, W. *et al.* (1994). *Report on the Greek Health Services.* Athens: Ministry of Health and Social Welfare of Greece: Pharmétrica SA.

Abel-Smith, B., Figueras, J., Holland, W., McKee, M. and Mossialos, E. (1995). *Choices in Health Policy: An Agenda for the European Union.* Luxembourg and Aldershot: Office for Official Publications of the European Communities and Dartmouth Publishing Company.

Akin, J., Birdsall, N., de Ferranti, D. *et al.* (1987). *Financing Health Services in Developing Countries: An Agenda for Reform.* World Bank Policy Study. Washington, DC: World Bank.

Arrow, K. (1963). Uncertainty and the welfare economics of medical care. *American Economic Review*, 53, 941–73.

Balabanova, D. (1995). Health care reforms in Bulgaria: Current problems and options for development. *Eurohealth*, 1, 25–8.

Beck, R. G. and Horne, J. M. (1980). Utilization of publicly insured health services in Saskatchewan before, during and after copayment. *Medical Care*, 18, 787–806.

Brook, H., Ware, J. E., Rogers, W. H. *et al.* (1983). Does free care improve adults' health? *New England Journal of Medicine*, 309, 1426–34.

Evans, R. G. (1984). *Strained Mercy: The Economics of Canadian Health Care.* Toronto: Butterworths.

Evans, R. G., Barer, M. L. and Stoddart, G. L. (1993a). *User Charges, Snares and Delusions: Another Look at the Literature.* Toronto: Ontario Premier's Council on Health, Well-being and Social Justice.

Evans, R. G., Barer, M. L. and Stoddart, G. L. (1993b). *User Fees for Health Care: Why a Bad Idea Keeps Coming Back.* Working Paper No. 26. Toronto: Canadian Institute for Advanced Research Program in Population Health.

Fahs, M. C. (1992). Physician response to the United Mine Workers' cost-sharing program: The other side of the coin. *Health Services Research*, 27, 25–45.

Feldman, R. and Dowd, B. (1993). What does the demand curve for medical care measure? *Journal of Health Economics*, 12, 193–200.

Fuchs, V. R. (1986). Physician-induced demand: A parable. *Journal of Health Economics*, 5, 367.

Gilson, L., Russell, S. and Buse, K. (1995). The political economy of user fees with targeting: Developing equitable health financing policy. *Journal of International Development*, 7, 369–401.

Ham, C. and Brommels, M. (1994). Health care reform in the Netherlands, Sweden, and the United Kingdom. *Health Affairs*, 13, 105–19.

Hammer, J. S. and Berman, P. A. (1995). Ends and means in public health policy in developing countries. In P. A. Berman (ed.), *Health Sector Reform in Developing Countries: Making Health Development Sustainable*. Boston: Harvard University Press.

Hughes, D. and McGuire, A. (1995). Patient charges and the utilisation of NHS prescription medicines: Some estimates using a cointegration procedure. *Health Economics*, 4, 213–20.

Jimenez, E. (1987). *Pricing Policy in the Social Sectors: Cost Recovery for Education and Health in Developing Countries*. Baltimore, MD: Johns Hopkins University Press.

Jönsson, B. and Gerdtham, U. G. (1995). Cost sharing for pharmaceuticals: The Swedish reimbursement system. In N. Mattison (ed.), *Sharing the Costs of Health: A Multicountry Perspective*. Basle: Pharmaceutical Partners for Better Health Care.

Kincses, G. (1995). *The Role of Co-payment. The Possibilities and Barriers of Adaptation in Central–Eastern Europe*. Budapest: Ministry of Welfare, National Information Center for Health Care.

Kupor, S. A., Liu, Y., Lee, J. and Yoshikawa, A. (1995). The effect of copayments and income on the utilization of medical care by subscribers to Japan's national health insurance system. *International Journal of Health Services*, 25, 295–312.

Labelle, R., Stoddart, G. and Rice, T. (1994). A re-examination of the meaning and importance of supplier-induced demand. *Journal of Health Economics*, 13, 347–68.

Lohr, K. N., Brook, R. H., Kamberg, C. J. *et al.* (1986). Use of medical care in the Rand Health Insurance Experiment: Diagnosis- and service-specific analyses in a randomized controlled trial. *Medical Care*, 24, Supplement 1–87.

McClellan, M. (1995). The uncertain demand for medical care: A comment on Emmett Keeler. *Journal of Health Economics*, 14, 239–42.

Manning, W. G., Newhouse, J. P., Duan, N., Keeler, E. B., Leibowitz, A. and Marquis, M. S. (1987). Health insurance and the demand for medical care: Evidence from a randomized experiment. *American Economic Review*, 77, 251–77.

Marek, M. J. (1995). Remuneration in ambulatory health care. Paper presented at the Workshop on European Health Care Reforms, 7–9 December. Copenhagen: WHO Regional Office for Europe.

Mooney, G. (1994). *Key Issues in Health Economics*. Hemel Hempstead: Harvester Wheatsheaf.
Mooney, G. and Ryan, M. (1993). Agency in health care: Getting beyond first principles. *Journal of Health Economics*, 12, 125–35.
Newhouse, J. P. (1974). A design for a health insurance experiment. *Inquiry*, 11, 5–27.
Nolan, B. (1993). Economic incentives, health status and health services utilisation. *Journal of Health Economics*, 12, 151–69.
Novak, J. (1996). *South Kazakstan Oblast Health Demand Survey Results*. ZdravReform Program Special Report No. CAR/KAZ-5. Bethesda, MA: Abt Associates, Inc.
OECD (1992). *The Reform of Health Care: A Comparative Analysis of Seven OECD Countries*. Health Policy Studies, No. 2. Paris: Organisation for Economic Co-operation and Development.
OECD (1994). *The Reform of Health Care Systems: A Review of Seventeen OECD Countries*. Paris: Organisation for Economic Co-operation and Development.
Pauly, M. V. (1994). Editorial. A re-examination of the meaning and importance of supplier-induced demand. *Journal of Health Economics*, 13, 369–72.
Preker, A. S. and Feachem, R. G. A. (1995). *Searching for the Silver Bullet: Market Mechanisms and the Health Sector in Central and Eastern Europe*. Washington, DC: World Bank.
Preker, A. S. and Herbert, W. B. (1995). Healing the wounds. In L. Paine (ed.), *New World Health*. London: Sterling Publications.
Project General Coordination Unit (1995). *Health Care Reform in Turkey*. Ankara: Ministry of Health of Turkey.
Rasell, M. E. (1995). Cost sharing in health insurance – a reexamination. *New England Journal of Medicine*, 332, 1164–8.
Rice, T. (1993). Demand curves, economists, and desert islands: A response to Feldman and Dowd. *Journal of Health Economics*, 12, 201–4.
Rice, T. and Morrison, K. R. (1994). Patient cost sharing for medical services: A review of the literature and implications for health care reform. *Medical Care Review*, 51, 235–87.
Rodwin, V. G. and Sandier, S. (1993). Health care under French national health insurance. *Health Affairs*, 12, 111–31.
Rubin, R. J. and Mendelson, D. N. (1995). A framework for cost-sharing policy analysis. In N. Mattison (ed.), *Sharing the Costs of Health: A Multicountry Perspective*. Basle: Pharmaceutical Partners for Better Health Care.
Sandier, S. (1996). Personal communication.
Schoenman, J. A. (1993). Use of patient cost sharing as a means of controlling health care costs. Paper presented at Project HOPE/Western Consortium Conference on Health Reforms in Central Europe: National Strategies for Cost Containment, Prague, 15 May.

Scitovsky, A. A. and Snyder, N. M. (1972). Effect of coinsurance on use of physician services. *Social Security Bulletin*, 35, 3–19.

Shapiro, M. F., Ware, M. F. and Sherbourne, C. D. (1986). Effects of cost sharing on seeking care for serious and minor symptoms. *Annals of Internal Medicine*, 104, 246–51.

Siu, A. L., Sonnenberg, F. A., Manning, W. G. *et al.* (1986). Inappropriate use of hospitals in a randomized trial of health insurance plans. *New England Journal of Medicine*, 315, 1259–66.

Stobbelaar, F. (1995). Ensuring value for money from pharmaceuticals. Draft paper presented at the Workshop on European Health Care Reforms, 7–9 December. Copenhagen: WHO Regional Office for Europe.

United States General Accounting Office (1994). *German Health Reforms: Changes Result in Lower Health Costs in 1993*. Report GAO/HEHS-95-27. Washington, DC: Committee on Governmental Affairs, US Senate.

van Doorslaer, E. and Wagstaff, A. (1993). Equity in the finance of health care: Methods and findings. In E. van Doorslaer and A. Wagstaff (eds), *Equity in the Finance and Delivery of Health Care: An International Perspective*. Oxford: Oxford University Press.

von Bredow, L. (1995). The reform of health care in the Czech Republic. *Eurohealth*, 1, 22–5.

# 4

# PRIORITY SETTING AND RATIONING HEALTH SERVICES

## Chris Ham and Frank Honigsbaum

### INTRODUCTION[1]

The need to make choices on the allocation of resources between competing demands exists in all health care systems. Decisions on resource allocation reflect the relative priority attached to different services. As the resources available for paying for health care have become more constrained, particularly following the oil crisis of the 1970s, there has been increasing interest in priority setting or rationing.[2] In recent years this has been illustrated by the initiative taken by governments in a number of countries such as the Netherlands, New Zealand, Norway, Sweden and the UK to examine priority setting on a more systematic basis.

Policies pursued in relation to rationing are only one strand in the movement to reform health care systems. A range of other strategies have been pursued including the establishment of planned and internal markets, changes to payment systems and budgetary incentives and policies to strengthen the management of health services (Ham *et al.* 1990; OECD 1992; Saltman and von Otter 1992; OECD 1994; Ham 1997a). In this context of widespread reform, the significance of the rationing debate is that it is beginning to open up fundamental questions about the future scope of publicly funded health service provision. At a time when the future of welfare services as a whole is coming under close scrutiny, the ability of governments to continue to support universal and comprehensive health services is once more the subject of debate. Not least, it is suggested by some analysts that there should be a move away from government to individual responsibility and a retreat from the post-war expansion of state-financed health systems. This view, however, remains strongly contested and the necessity of rationing health services by excluding services from public funding is by no means universally accepted.

Against this background, this chapter explores in more detail the issues involved in priority setting and rationing health services. The core of the paper is a review of experience in those European countries which have attempted to approach priority setting in a systematic way. The paper seeks to summarize developments in these countries and to distil the lessons which emerge. This leads to recommendations for a research agenda and for the way forward. To begin with, however, the chapter briefly reviews the reasons why priority setting is on the agenda and some of the main approaches to priority setting.

## WHY RATIONING IS INEVITABLE

In recent years there has been a surge of interest in priority setting with a large body of work which reviews the theoretical and empirical issues involved in it. However, analysis of this issue can be traced back over many years (Fuchs 1974; Cooper 1975). Current debates stem most directly from the mid-1970s when the afore-mentioned oil crisis led to a reappraisal of health services financing and the introduction of policies to curb the high levels of expenditure growth. The dilemmas facing policy makers were highlighted in an analysis by Maxwell which reviewed international trends in health and health services (Maxwell 1974). Maxwell's analysis has been echoed in subsequent reports to the extent that the existence of 'infinite demand and finite resources' has become part of the conventional wisdom among health policy analysts (Thwaites 1987). The need to make choices in health care has presented particular challenges to politicians, managers and clinicians who have had to reconcile available funding with the needs and demands of patients and citizens.

Rationing has taken a number of forms in the past. A common approach in many countries has been to create waiting lists for non-urgent treatment. Attempts have also been made to limit demand through cost-sharing arrangements (see Chapter 3). Other approaches have included shifting costs away from the health service budget to other parts of the public sector or to individuals and their families, as well as containing expenditures in areas such as pharmaceuticals (see Chapter 11).

As the demands on the health sector grow, decisions on priorities have posed an even greater challenge. Three factors have contributed to this challenge:

- *Demographic changes*, particularly the ageing population. The growth in the proportion of the population aged 65 and over in many developed countries adds to the pressures on limited health service budgets.
- *Developments in medical technology*. This is illustrated by the introduction of new forms of diagnosis and treatment which enable additional services to be provided.
- *Rising public expectations*. Fuelled in part by awareness of developments in medical technology and in part by demands for greater choice and increased service responsiveness, these have led to pressure for additional resources to be allocated to health care.

Yet before accepting as a given the inevitability of rationing, it is important to acknowledge the existence of alternative positions in the literature. First, there is the argument that rationing would not be necessary if additional funding were available. Funding restrictions might be removed by a change of public expenditure priorities or by increases in taxation or social insurance. Either way it is argued that the effect would be to channel more resources into health care and to obviate the need to set priorities.

Second, there is the argument that rationing could be avoided if resources were used more efficiently. This position draws on evidence of variations in clinical practice (Ham 1988) and on the awareness that there are large gaps in knowledge of which treatments are most effective. This evidence suggests that there is scope to redeploy resources to more cost-effective interventions. Thus, a greater investment in health technology assessment and quality assurance activities such as clinical guidelines would result in more appropriate use of existing health care resources.

Both of these arguments are important, yet neither is entirely convincing. Additional expenditure on health services would certainly ease the process of priority setting but even countries which spend a relatively high proportion of national income on health services have to make choices at the margin and there is no reason to believe that these can be avoided (Maxwell 1995). Equally, while the opportunities to use resources more efficiently should not be ignored, there is no health care system in the world which has succeeded in squeezing out all sources of inefficiency. Also the scope for redeploying resources through evidence-based medicine remains uncertain.

## APPROACHES TO PRIORITY SETTING

The literature on priority setting draws on a wide range of disciplines. Apart from economics, the most significant contributions have come from political science, philosophy and epidemiology.

In the case of *epidemiology* two themes are important. First, by analysing patterns of mortality and morbidity, epidemiology helps to inform decision making by identifying the main causes of death and disability and the burden of disease this represents. One way of doing this is through the use of disability-adjusted life years (World Bank 1993). Second, epidemiology also contributes to the analysis of the effectiveness of clinical procedures. The results of evaluative studies carried out by epidemiologists in this way help to inform decision making by providing information on those interventions which are most likely to bring benefits to patients.

The contribution of *economics* is in enabling comparisons to be made of the cost-effectiveness of different procedures. One well-publicized approach is to analyse the quality adjusted life years (QALYs) associated with carrying out particular interventions. Data from a range of studies can then be combined with information about the cost of these interventions to produce cost per QALY league tables. An example (Maynard 1991) is displayed in Table 4.1.

Another contribution of economics is in the application of programme budgeting and marginal analysis (Mooney *et al.* 1992). These are techniques which compare health service expenditure by programmes (for example, mental health) in order to illustrate the distribution of spending between different services. Marginal analysis seeks to show the effects of small changes in expenditure within programmes on the health of the population. In this way, economics provides a set of tools to aid decision making on priorities.

An approach which brings together the contributions of epidemiology and economics is disease mapping. This combines

**Table 4.1** Cost per QALY of some NHS interventions (£, August 1990 prices)

| Treatment | Cost per QALY (£) |
|---|---|
| Cholesterol testing and diet therapy (ages 40–69) | 220 |
| Neurosurgery for head injury | 240 |
| Advice to stop smoking from GP | 270 |
| Neurosurgery for subarachnoid haemorrhage | 490 |
| Antihypertensive treatment to prevent stroke (ages 45–64) | 940 |
| Pacemaker implantation | 1,100 |
| Valve replacement for aortic stenosis | 1,140 |
| Hip replacement | 1,180 |
| Cholesterol testing and treatment | 1,480 |
| Coronary artery bypass graft (left main vessel, severe angina) | 2,090 |
| Kidney transplant | 4,710 |
| Breast cancer screening | 5,780 |
| Heart transplant | 7,840 |
| Cholesterol testing and incremental treatment (ages 25–39) | 14,150 |
| Home haemodialysis | 17,260 |
| Coronary artery bypass graft (one vessel disease, moderate angina) | 18,830 |
| Continuous ambulatory peritoneal dialysis | 19,870 |
| Hospital haemodialysis | 21,970 |
| Erythropoietin treatment for anaemia (dialysis patients, assuming ten per cent reduction in mortality) | 54,380 |
| Neurosurgery for malignant intracranial tumours | 107,780 |
| Erythropoietin treatment for anaemia (dialysis patients, assuming no reduction in mortality) | 126,290 |

*Source*: Maynard (1991)

information on the number of patients suffering from particular diseases with evidence on service use and costs. When combined with data on cost-effectiveness, the resulting analyses illustrate both the need for health care in different areas and the opportunities available for achieving improvements in health within available resources (Raftery 1992).

*Political scientists* and policy analysts have often been critical of the work of epidemiologists and economists, arguing that priority setting cannot be reduced to a technical exercise as in essence it involves a debate about values. Political scientists therefore see techniques as only one element in the decision-making process and not necessarily the most important. Writers such as Klein emphasize the importance of the process by which decisions are made and the role of different groups in this process (Klein 1991). They also maintain that techniques can be misleading if the basis on which they are constructed is not understood. According to this school of thought the aim should be to muddle through elegantly (Hunter 1993) and to ensure that the debate about priorities is open and fair.

In highlighting the role of values in priority setting, political scientists enter the territory of *philosophers* whose contribution to the literature has grown in importance in recent years. Philosophers draw attention in particular to the moral basis of decision making and the ethical principles which underpin choices in health care. This includes different concepts of justice such as utilitarian and needs-based approaches. Like political scientists, philosophers are often critical of the work of economists, arguing that this work is based on questionable moral assumptions and fails to recognize that each person is as important as any other (Harris 1987).

A growing number of studies draw on empirical research to begin to conceptualize about approaches to priority setting. For instance, Rudolf Klein has argued that there are different levels of priority setting in health care (Klein 1993). At the macro or systems level there is the priority to be attached to health care in relation to other competing claims on resources. Next there are choices on the allocation of the budget for health care between different geographical areas and services. At a further level decisions have to be taken on the allocation of resources to particular forms of treatment within service areas (e.g. the priority to be given to heart transplants vs. open heart surgery). Then there are choices on how to prioritize access to treatment between patients if treatment cannot be administered immediately. Finally, priorities have to be set for individual patients, particularly in the case of innovative or expensive procedures when it may be necessary to decide whether a treatment should be provided at all and if so for how long.

Klein's categorization offers a useful framework for analysing priority-setting processes in health care. While decisions at the micro level are influenced by decisions at the macro level, discussion of priority setting often fails to distinguish between different levels and results in a lack of clarity about the nature of the choices being made and responsibility for those choices. The responsibility of politicians at the macro level is paralleled by the responsibility of clinicians at the micro level. In between, at the intermediate levels of priority setting, a range of political, clinical and managerial influences operate and vary between systems. The role and influence of these different actors is contingent on the balance that is struck between planning and competition as strategies for allocating resources. In planned systems the influence of politicians is particularly important both in determining priorities at the macro level and in shaping the way in which decisions are taken at lower levels. In contrast, in competitive systems patients and clinicians have a significant influence on decision making and the role of politicians is commensurately weaker.

## TRENDS AND DEVELOPMENTS

The manner in which decisions on priorities are made is not always easy to understand because of lack of transparency in the processes involved. The main and partial exception to this concerns those countries which have adopted a more systematic approach to priority setting at the macro level. In the Netherlands the government appointed a committee (the Dunning Committee) in 1990 to examine how to put limits on new medical technologies and how to deal with problems caused by scarcity of care, rationing of care and the necessity of selection of patients for care (Dunning 1992).

In its report the Dunning Committee acknowledged that it was possible to make more money available for health care but it concluded that this option was limited. A second possibility was to become more efficient and the committee attached high priority to this. A third option was to make explicit choices about care, for example by excluding certain treatments from funding. The committee reached the view that this was painful but necessary, if only to ensure basic health care for all.

In considering how choices should be made, the committee concluded that the best way forward would be to apply four tests to determine whether care should be included in the basic health care package. These tests, illustrated in Figure 4.1, included asking whether the care was necessary from the community's point of view, whether it was effective and efficient, and whether it could be left to personal responsibility. If services passed these tests then they would be included in the care package. If they did not they would be left to individuals to purchase from their own resources.

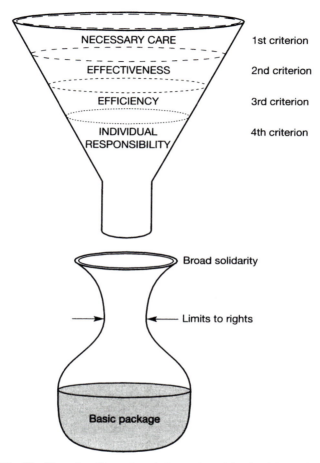

**Figure 4.1**   The Dunning Committee's four 'sieves' for health services

Using this framework, the Dunning Committee argued that dental care for adults, homeopathic medicines and *in vitro* fertilization could be left out of the care package. It also emphasized that the government should protect by law the quality of care for vulnerable groups such as the mentally and physically disabled. Beyond these proposals, the committee argued that priorities should be set by assessing the effectiveness of health care technologies and by devising explicit criteria for determining access to waiting lists and from waiting lists into hospital. It also called on the health care professions to take the lead in drawing up guidelines for the provision of services.

Most of these recommendations have been accepted by the Dutch government. Although the initial reaction to the report was cautious, action has been taken to improve arrangements for technology assessment and to research the nature of waiting lists. In parallel, the government has accepted that dental care for adults and homeopathic medicines should be excluded from coverage. An intensive debate is taking place about other services such as *in vitro* fertilization, physiotherapy and certain pharmaceuticals. Within the Netherlands, influencing doctors' decisions in order to promote more effective clinical practices is seen as the key to further progress (Mulder 1995).

Priority setting in Sweden has been strongly influenced by work originally undertaken in Norway. In both countries – as in the Netherlands – the desire to reduce waiting lists was one of the factors which led to action by policy makers. In its final report in 1994, the Parliamentary Priorities Commission (Swedish Parliamentary Priorities Commission 1995) concluded that priority setting should be based on a sound and explicit ethical platform. To this end, it proposed three principles as the starting point:

- *human dignity*: all human beings have equal dignity and the same rights, regardless of their personal characteristics and their functions in the community;
- *need and solidarity*: resources should be committed to those fields where needs are greatest and special attention should be paid to the needs of those groups unaware of their human dignity or who have less chance than others of making their voices heard or exercising their rights;
- *cost-efficiency*: when choosing between different options, one should aim for a reasonable relation between cost and effect. This principle should only be applied in comparisons of methods for treating the same disease.

These principles are listed in rank order and this means that in practice the cost-efficiency principle is given relatively low priority. As the commission emphasized, 'the cost-efficiency principle cannot justify refraining from or impairing the quality of care given to the dying, the severely and chronically ill, old persons, dementia patients, the mentally retarded, the severely handicapped or other persons for whom care would not "pay" '.

The commission also emphasized that certain criteria were not acceptable as a basis for prioritization. These included advanced age, self-inflicted injuries and social position. On this basis the commission outlined a number of priority categories, dividing these between those that should apply at the political/administrative level and those that should apply at the clinical level. Highest priority was attached to the treatment of life-threatening acute diseases and to the treatment of chronic disease and severe mental disorders, followed by prevention activities with a documented benefit. Lowest priority was given to mild disorders and illnesses where self-care was sufficient and to care for reasons other than disease or injury.

In the UK there has been no national initiative of the kind found in the Netherlands and Sweden. Nevertheless, there has been a great deal of interest and activity in relation to priority setting, particularly at a local level. This has grown out of the reforms introduced in the National Health Service in 1991 which had the effect of separating responsibility for purchasing and providing health care (Ham 1997b). As a result of this change, priority setting has become more explicit. Furthermore a number of well-publicized cases of patients being denied care or having to wait for treatment has brought to public attention what has long been known to clinicians and managers: rationing is a pervasive feature of the NHS.

Health authorities have been at the forefront of efforts to develop a more systematic approach to priority setting and a number of studies have reviewed their experience (Klein and Redmayne 1992; Ham *et al.* 1993; House of Commons Health Committee 1995). The findings of these studies indicate that there is considerable variation in the methods used. Increasingly health authorities are arriving at decisions after consulting key interests in their area including local people and general medical practitioners. They are also undertaking epidemiologically-based health needs assessments to aid decision making. In some cases this has resulted in decisions to exclude services from funding but more commonly health authorities have made incremental changes to their plans and have shifted priorities only at the margins.

A key objective has been to ensure that clinical decisions are informed by research findings (Department of Health 1995). In this respect health authorities have been asked to develop the use of guidelines and clinical protocols in their work with providers. There is a close similarity here with the recommendation of the Dunning Committee that priority should be given to the use of guidelines to ensure that care is provided appropriately. One other feature of the UK approach has been the introduction of clinical audit as a means of reviewing professional practices and promoting high standards. As with many of the other initiatives that have been taken, the focus of audit is the clinical or micro dimension of rationing.

Other systems outside Europe have also attempted to set priorities in a more systematic manner (Honigsbaum *et al.* 1995). Box 4.1 summarizes the experiences in the State of Oregon in the United States and in New Zealand.

---

**Box 4.1    Priority setting outside Europe**

In **Oregon** a State Health Commission was appointed in 1989 to make recommendations to the state legislature on how Medicaid coverage could be expanded and how priorities could be set within the Medicaid programme. The Commission tried out a number of methods for setting priorities, beginning with an approach based on economic evaluation. This produced such anomalous results that it was abandoned and the Commission resorted to a judgemental approach supported by a number of exercises in public consultation. The resulting list of almost 700 condition–treatment pairs was presented to the legislature and, after amendments were made to satisfy the federal government and to avoid infringing disability legislation, the Oregon plan was implemented in 1994. At the time of writing some 565 treatments are funded under the plan and population coverage has been extended in line with the expectations of the plan's architects. What has not yet happened is the extension of the Oregon list beyond the Medicaid programme to form the basis of health insurance throughout the state. A key element of the Oregon approach is the attempt to involve the public in priority setting through public hearings and community meetings. In practice concerns were expressed at the lack of representativeness of those attending the meetings and this is something that has been addressed in subsequent work (Oregon Health Services Commission 1991; Kitzhaber 1993).

In **New Zealand** the government appointed a Core Services Committee in 1992 to advise on the services that should be included within the publicly funded health system. The Committee decided that it would not be appropriate to draw up a list of services Oregon-style. Instead it argued that the services

---

currently provided were those that should be provided and it set in train a process for determining priorities within specific areas of provision. This was done through a range of methods including consensus conferences, reviews of published research and international evidence, expert practitioner evaluation of contemporary practice, closed workshops, contested public hearings, and public consultation. In most cases the aim is to draw up guidelines on the service concerned. These guidelines are then offered as advice to the Health Minister. The Committee's view was that whole categories of care should not be excluded because this might discriminate against those who could benefit from receiving such care. One of the purposes of the guidelines that have been prepared is to identify those most likely to benefit from receiving a service, thereby targeting resources where they can achieve the most health gain. By the middle of 1995 18 areas had been systematically reviewed. The next stage of the Committee's work will examine the question of priorities between services or treatment areas and will involve implementing priority criteria for waiting lists (National Advisory Committee on Care 1994).

## EMERGING LESSONS

Different countries have approached priority setting in different ways. Much of the work that has been done is at an early stage of development and its impact therefore remains uncertain. Nevertheless certain lessons have emerged and in this section these are brought together under five major headings: (1) rationing by exclusion vs. guidelines; (2) using techniques and debate; (3) involving the public; (4) balancing competing objectives; and (5) implementing decisions.

- *Rationing by exclusion vs. guidelines.* There is a key distinction to be made between rationing services by exclusion and rationing by guidelines (Ham 1995). Only Oregon has chosen to ration by exclusion, defining in detail the care package that should be funded. Moreover, this rationing process is limited to the Medicaid programme. In contrast, the New Zealand Core Services Committee has rejected exclusions and instead has put the emphasis on drawing up guidelines for specific services and for waiting lists. The Netherlands has sought to combine these two approaches by excluding some services from the care package while at the same time attaching priority to the development of guidelines by professional associations.

• *Using techniques and debate.* In all systems there is a concern to combine the use of techniques for determining priorities with public debate about the choices that should be made. While greater emphasis is given to technical approaches in some systems than others, everywhere there is recognition that priority setting cannot be reduced to a technical exercise. This applies particularly to the use of economic approaches, the role of which is widely acknowledged – but as only one contribution to the process of priority setting. Box 4.2, which is drawn from research into priority setting in the UK, illustrates the pressures which impinge on policy makers in that country and the need to balance a range of factors in the process of making choices. The figure shows in simplified form the forces which guide rationing decisions in planned health care systems and the need to reconcile different influences.

• *Involving the public.* Methodologies for involving the public in the process of priority setting are at various stages of development. A wide variety of approaches have been used (see Box 4.2) and there is little apparent agreement on those that are most effective. Much depends on the aim of involving the public and whether the purpose is to use the public's views to shape decision making or to

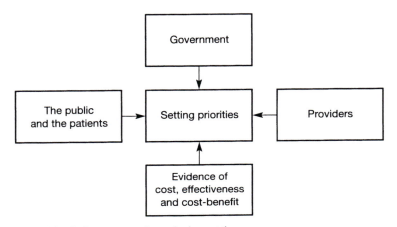

**Figure 4.2** Influences on the priority-setting process

*Source*: Heginbotham and Ham (1992), adapted from Cochrane *et al.* (1991)

inform the public about the need to make choices. Evidence from the UK suggests that a majority of the public are reluctant themselves to be involved in priority setting and would prefer decisions to be left to the medical profession (Heginbotham 1993).

Despite this, significant efforts have been made to engage the public in debate, both in the UK and elsewhere, and this seems likely to continue in the future. One of the reasons is the need to legitimize rationing decisions. Decisions on priorities are essentially value judgements and they will vary between individuals and groups. Legitimacy therefore rests on the process by which decisions are made. This process is more likely to be seen as legitimate if it is open and enables different interests to contribute to decision making.

As this happens and the need to ration scarce resources becomes more apparent, those who are seen to be responsible for decision making risk unpopularity. Experience suggests, however, that having brought decision making out into the open, it may be difficult to take it back behind closed doors. This is certainly the case in the Netherlands, where the debate engendered by the Dunning Committee has raised public awareness of and interest in rationing to the point of no return.

---

**Box 4.2   Public involvement in priority setting**

Public involvement in rationing has taken a number of forms. In **Oregon** the methods used included public hearings, community meetings and telephone surveys. An organization known as Oregon Health Decisions was commissioned to help with this work. One of the methods used was focus groups in which participants drawn from different sections of the community discussed some of the choices that had to be made. Oregon Health Decisions concluded that this was a particularly effective way of extracting information from the community about values. However, because of the small numbers involved, it was less effective as a method of engaging the community at large.

In the **United Kingdom** a variety of approaches have been tried at a local level (Ham *et al.* 1993). These include public meetings, postal questionnaire surveys, delphi techniques, consultation with the public and general practitioners in small

areas or localities, the use of consensus conferences, consultation with community health councils, market research, rapid
appraisal, and focus group discussions. As in Oregon, focus
groups have been found to be particularly effective (Barker
1995).

In the **Netherlands** an extensive period of public consultation was established following publication of the Dunning
Committee's report. About 60 organizations were involved in
discussions on choices in health care. This started in 1991 and
ended in 1995. An evaluation of the process concluded that
about one-third of the population was reached by the public
discussions. As a consequence, there were changes in public
opinion. For example, in 1990 55 per cent of the population
believed that all treatments must be possible, irrespective of
costs, whereas in 1994 this percentage fell to 44 per cent. Less
positively, the results of the exercise were not used by the
Dutch government within the decision-making process on
choices in health care.

In **Sweden** the work of the Parliamentary Priorities Commission was informed by a number of surveys of the public and
health care professionals. The survey of the public was carried
out by questionnaire in January 1994 and involved a random
sample of 1500 people. A 78 per cent response rate was
achieved. A majority of respondents felt that medical care
should be devoted mainly to people with the severest illnesses.
A majority of respondents also agreed with the Commission's
recommendation that terminal care should be given the same
high priority as emergency health care. Services which the
public felt might be restricted included cosmetic surgery,
harmless birthmarks, smoking cessation programmes and *in
vitro* fertilization. Overall the questionnaire survey strongly
endorsed the principles set out in the Commission's first report.

• *Balancing competing objectives.* Setting priorities involves
making trade-offs between objectives such as comprehensiveness, universality, equity, health gain and choice. As an example,
the Oregon plan was designed to bring in to the Medicaid scheme
groups in the population who were previously excluded. In this
case, comprehensiveness for the Medicaid population was sacrificed in the pursuit of extended population coverage.

Similar considerations apply in the Netherlands, albeit in a different policy context. As the Dunning Committee noted, choices in health care have to balance the aim of achieving basic care for all and the need to contain health care costs. In the case of the Netherlands, a degree of comprehensiveness has been sacrificed in the pursuit of cost containment. The same applies in the UK even though the debate has not been framed in this way. The effect of government policies to limit the growth of expenditure in the NHS has been to remove or limit the provision of certain low-priority services (for example, infertility treatment), thereby bringing into question the ability of the NHS to provide services 'from the cradle to the grave'.

The UK experience also illustrates the impact of priority-setting policies on equity. The absence of a national initiative in that country has meant that health authorities are responsible for determining priorities at a local level. Health authorities have approached this task in different ways and this has resulted in variations in the services that are purchased. In the absence of a national menu of NHS services, patients' access to particular services depends in part on where they live. Locating responsibility for priority setting at a local level has therefore undermined the pursuit of geographical equity, a goal that has always proved elusive.

In contrast, in both the Netherlands and Sweden, equity or solidarity is explicitly mentioned as one of the key principles which should guide priority setting. In both countries particular priority has been attached to care for vulnerable groups. In the Netherlands the Dunning Committee proposed that the position of these groups should be protected in law while in Sweden the Parliamentary Priorities Commission emphasized the need to ensure that cost-efficiency was not pursued at the expense of equity. Again, this illustrates the trade-offs inherent in priority setting. While the aim of achieving greater efficiency in the use of resources is widely acknowledged in different countries, it is one objective among many and has to be weighed against other considerations.

Health gain has been addressed in much of the work that has been undertaken through the emphasis given to health promotion and disease prevention. These activities are seen as a high priority in all systems. In Sweden, for instance, prevention is identified as the second priority out of five priority categories, and its importance has also been recognized in the UK in the national health strategy published in 1992. Health gain has also guided much of the work done at a local level in the UK as health authorities have developed priorities for their own populations (Ham *et al.* 1993).

In all systems the concern to maximize the health gain achieved within available resources has led to increasing attention being given to clinical practice patterns in order to eliminate ineffective procedures and to concentrate resources where they will achieve the most health benefit. This is one of the factors behind the use of guidelines and protocols. A key purpose of practice guidelines is to improve the quality of care by reducing inappropriate interventions and promoting cost-effective practices. Among the countries reviewed here, New Zealand has given most attention to the development of guidelines but little is known as yet of their impact on quality.

The emphasis given to health gain and equity may have the effect of constraining consumer choice. Much of the work that has been done focuses on priority setting from the population or community perspective. To the extent that priority setting seeks to achieve the greatest health benefit for the population, so individual preferences may be sacrificed for the greater good. Against this, the emphasis placed in Sweden on the principle of human dignity and the concern to increase choice as part of other health care reform policies appears to run counter to population-based rationing strategies which limit choice.

- *Implementing decisions.* Priority setting is inherently complex and is not amenable to a quick fix solution. As our discussion has shown, a strategic approach is needed which includes action on the different levels of rationing decisions that have been identified. Some of this action will be at the political level in terms of setting priorities for the system as a whole. Some will be at the clinical level in terms of ensuring that decisions on which patients to treat and in what order of priority are informed by research-based evidence. A continuing effort is required at all levels if decisions are to be soundly based and defensible. This is best illustrated by experience in the Netherlands where national debate on the care package is combined with an investment in technology assessment, the development of practice guidelines and the establishment of criteria to govern waiting lists.

Research indicates that there is often a gap between the conclusions reached by national committees and what happens in practice. This is not always the case, and the report of the

Dunning Committee in the Netherlands illustrates how the work of an expert committee can act as a force for debate and change. Nevertheless, it is important to recognize that establishing a national framework is only one step in the process. A way then has to be found of translating the framework into action and, most importantly, of influencing clinical decisions. In practice, as we have emphasized, it is not a question of seeking to change clinical decisions *or* developing a national framework but how the two can best go hand in hand. What is also important is the way in which the recommendations and principles set out in national reports are implemented, particularly when these principles are expressed in general terms and are open to competing interpretations.

## THE RESEARCH AGENDA

On the basis of these emerging lessons, what are the priorities for research and for future work in this field? To begin with, it would be valuable to examine the impact of priority-setting developments in a wider range of systems, such as those in central and eastern Europe whose experience has been studied to a much lesser extent.

A further priority is to continue to track developments in the systems reviewed in this chapter (e.g. the Netherlands, New Zealand or Sweden). These are at an early stage in their evolution and could develop in a number of directions. More work is needed to assess in particular the extent to which the recommendations of national committees are followed in practice.

It would also be valuable to take specific aspects of the priority-setting process and explore these in more detail in a comparative context. One example is the attempt to involve the public in debates on priorities. What different methods are used to engage the public and what has been their effect?

Another issue worth investigating is the availability of particular services in different systems. This was the subject of a widely cited review of health services in the UK and the US (Aaron and Schwarz 1984) and it would be of value to update this over a larger number of systems and for a range of services. Such a study might include examination of the impact of rationing on access to services like renal dialysis and heart surgery where it appears that there are wide differences in provision between systems.

This is linked to a further topic, namely the way in which

clinicians respond to resource constraints. This has been examined in a few studies, including an analysis of renal provision in the UK (Halper 1989). It would be valuable to extend this work to explore in greater detail the interaction between macro decisions on priority setting and clinical decisions at the micro level. The latter remain implicit in all systems and little is known about the criteria used by clinicians in making decisions.

## THE WAY FORWARD

This chapter began by arguing that the debate about priority setting is raising fundamental questions about the scope of publicly-funded health service provision. The evidence indicates that in no system has this yet led to the state retreating from a commitment to play a major part in funding and regulating health services. Rather the aim has been to increase the efficiency with which resources are used and to make changes to the services available in an incremental manner.

This analysis has shown that priority setting is more like a marathon than a sprint. A continuing effort is needed over a relatively long time before the results become apparent. In this process, there is a case to be made for policy makers learning from each other's experience. This will require an investment in networks and information exchange, building on what already exists. While there is some evidence that this is happening (EU Council and EU Ministers for Health 1991; Abel-Smith *et al.* 1995), more can and should be done. There is a role for WHO here both in conducting studies of priority setting and in organizing meetings of interested parties.

Ultimately, each country will need to find its own solution to the priority-setting dilemma, reflecting different starting points, levels of expenditure and expectations. What works in Oregon cannot easily be transplanted to Europe, and much the same applies within Europe. It is also the case that priority-setting issues have to be revisited on a regular basis since the dynamic nature of health care means that these issues can never be solved 'once and for all'. The processes that are established to support priority setting therefore need to be sufficiently well designed to stand the test of time.

Those elected into public office have to use their best judgements in determining priorities. Their decisions will be shaped by the availability of resources, an assessment of what is politically feasible, and of course by the values they bring to bear. The one clear message from international experience is that rationing health care cannot be divorced from values and to pretend otherwise is to ignore the evidence presented here and in other places. The key issue is whose values should prevail, and how should the debate on this question be conducted?

## NOTES

1   This paper draws on various sources including a review prepared for the World Health Organization on the research agenda in relation to priority setting (Ham 1996).
2   In the literature the terms *rationing* and *priority setting* tend to be used interchangeably and this convention has been followed in this chapter. Both terms are used to describe the process by which choices in health care are made, particularly in circumstances where the demand for health care exceeds the resources available.

## REFERENCES

Aaron, H. J. and Schwarz, W. B. (1984). *The Painful Prescription*. Washington: Brookings Institution.
Abel-Smith, B., Figueras, J., Holland, W., McKee, M. and Mossialos, E. (1995). *Choices in Health Policy: An Agenda for the European Union*. Luxembourg and Aldershot: Office for Official Publications of the European Communities and Dartmouth Publishing Company.
Barker, J. (1995). *Local NHS Health Care Purchasing and Prioritising from the Perspective of Bromley Residents – a Qualitative Study*. Bromley: Bromley Health Authority.
Cochrane, M., Ham, C. J., Heginbotham, C. and Smith, R. (1991). Rationing: At the cutting edge. *British Medical Journal*, 303, 1039–42.
Cooper, M. (1975). *Rationing Health Care*. London: Croom Helm.
Department of Health (1995). *Government Response to the First Report for the Health Committee Session 1994–95*. London: HMSO.
Dunning, A. (1992). *Choices in Health Care: A Report by the Government Committee on Choices in Health Care. Executive Summary*. Rijswijk: Ministry of Welfare, Health and Culture.
EU Council and EU Ministers for Health (1991). Resolution of meeting within the Council of 11 November 1991, concerning fundamental health policy choices. *Official Journal of the European Communities*, 304/5–6.
Fuchs, V. (1974). *Who Shall Live?* New York: Basic Books.

Halper, T. (1989). *The Misfortunes of Others*. Cambridge: Cambridge University Press.

Ham, C. J. (1988). *Healthcare Variations*. London: King's Fund Institute.

Ham, C. J. (1995). Health care rationing. *British Medical Journal*, 310, 1483–4.

Ham, C. J. (1996). Priority setting in health. In K. Janovsky (ed.), *Health Policy and Systems Development: An Agenda for Research*. Geneva: World Health Organization.

Ham, C. J. (ed.) (1997a). *Health Care Reform: Learning from International Experience*. Buckingham: Open University Press.

Ham, C. J. (1997b). *Management and Competition in the NHS*. Oxford: Radcliffe Medical Press.

Ham, C. J., Robinson, R. and Benzeval, M. (1990). *Health Check*. London: King's Fund Institute.

Ham, C. J., Honigsbaum, F. and Thomson, D. (1993). *Priority Setting for Health Gain*. London: Department of Health.

Harris, J. (1987). QALYfying the value of life. *Journal of Medical Ethics*, 13, 117–23.

Heginbotham, C. (1993). Health care priority setting: A survey of doctors, managers and the general public. In R. Smith (ed.), *Rationing in Action*. London: BMJ Publishing Group.

Heginbotham, C. and Ham, C. J. (1992). *Purchasing Dilemmas*. London: King's Fund Institute.

Honigsbaum, F., Calltorp, J., Ham, C. J. and Holmström, S. (1995). *Priority Setting Processes for Healthcare*. Oxford: Radcliffe Medical Press.

House of Commons Health Committee (1995). *Priority Setting in the NHS: Purchasing*. Report HC 134-1. London: HMSO.

Hunter, D. (1993). *Rationing Dilemmas in Health Care*. Birmingham: National Association of Health Authorities and Trusts.

Kitzhaber, J. A. (1993). Prioritising health services in an era of limits: The Oregon experience. *British Medical Journal*, 307, 373–7.

Klein, R. (1991). On the Oregon trail: Rationing health care. *British Medical Journal*, 302, 1–2.

Klein, R. (1993). Dimensions of rationing: Who should do what? *British Medical Journal*, 307, 309–11.

Klein, R. and Redmayne, S. (1992). *Patterns of Priorities*. Birmingham: National Association of Health Authorities and Trusts.

Maxwell, R. (1974). *Health Care: The Growing Dilemma*. New York: McKinsey.

Maxwell, R. (ed.) (1995). Rationing health care. *British Medical Bulletin*, 51, 4.

Maynard, A. (1991). Developing the health care market. *Economic Journal*, 101, 177–86.

Mooney, G., Gerard, K. and Donaldson, C. (1992). *Priority Setting in Purchasing*. Birmingham: National Association of Health Authorities and Trusts.

Mulder, J. (1995). Priority setting in health care: The Dutch experience. Unpublished paper, prepared for an international seminar at the Health Services Management Centre, University of Birmingham, 1 May.

National Advisory Committee on Care (1994). *Third Report: Core Services of 1995/96*. Wellington: Health and Disability Support Services.

OECD (1992). *The Reform of Health Care: A Comparative Analysis of Seven OECD Countries*. Health Policy Studies No. 2. Paris: Organisation for Economic Co-operation and Development.

OECD (1994). *The Reform of Health Care Systems: A Review of Seventeen OECD Countries*. Paris: Organisation for Economic Co-operation and Development.

Oregon Health Services Commission (1991). *Prioritisation of Health Services*. Portland: Oregon Health Services Commission.

Raftery, J. (1992). Disease Mapping, Comparative Analysis and Purchasing for Health Gain by Disease. Unpublished paper.

Saltman, R. B. and von Otter, C. (1992). *Planned Markets and Public Competition. Strategic Reform in Northern European Health Systems*. Buckingham: Open University Press.

Swedish Parliamentary Priorities Commission (1995). *Priorities in Health Care*. Stockholm: Ministry of Health and Social Affairs.

Thwaites, B. (1987). *The NHS: The End of the Rainbow?* Southampton: Southampton University.

World Bank (1993). *World Development Report 1993. Investing in Health*. New York: Oxford University Press.

# 5

# REFORMING PUBLIC
# HEALTH SERVICES

## Martin McKee and
## Ferenc Bojan

### INTRODUCTION

The perceived imbalance between demand for health services and
the ability to provide them poses a challenge to governments in all
countries. A recent report to the European Commission on the
health policy choices facing Member States identified a series of
possible strategies to meet this challenge (Abel-Smith *et al.* 1995)
and highlighted the need to complement health care reform with
strategies that reduce the demand for health services through effective public health action.

Although many countries have formally adopted policies on both
health care reform and the World Health Organization's health for
all (HFA) concept, the two are rarely coordinated. Dekker has
noted how health care reform has ignored health as a determinant
of demand (Dekker 1994). However many healthy public policies
have been shown to reduce the burden on health services. The
growing recognition of the complex interplay between social factors and the development of disease, its rate of progression, and the
patient's adherence and response to treatment (Evans *et al.* 1994),
as well as the blurring of the distinction between curative and preventive interventions, such as integrated breast cancer screening
programmes, make it necessary for health sector reform to encompass both curative and preventive interventions.

This chapter seeks to provide an overview of public health and its
potential relationship with health sector reform. It is focused on what
is usually termed the public health service. As this has no explicit

definition, for the present purposes an admittedly somewhat tauto-logical definition has been adopted. It is taken to mean those roles in which individuals with formal public health training are employed with the objective of improving the health of the population.

This is not to ignore the broader public health function which is the responsibility of many sectors, such as transport, housing and education. This function is not seen in the same way everywhere and few have given it formal recognition, such as the responsibility given to the Ministry of Health in Denmark to coordinate health promotion activities across government departments and the inter-ministerial committee on Health of the Nation in the UK (Robinson *et al.* 1996). In contrast, in countries such as the Netherlands, absence of effective inter-ministerial coordination has been seen as an obstacle to implementing healthy public policies (de Leeuw and Polman 1995).

This chapter will concentrate on the roles that public health professionals have adopted. In each case it will review how they developed into their present form and will suggest how they might be reformed in the future. They can be considered under five headings: (1) communicable disease control and environmental health; (2) provision of services to specific groups; (3) health promotion; (4) advising on commissioning and planning of health services; and (5) undertaking research (McCarthy and Rees 1992).

## COMMUNICABLE DISEASE CONTROL AND ENVIRONMENTAL HEALTH

Communicable disease control and environmental health are widely seen as the core roles of public health. The idea that the environment may play a part in the development of disease can be traced back at least as far as Hippocrates, who noted the association between certain diseases and, for example, diet, water and the weather. Communicable disease and environmental health often remain the focus of public health services. The emergence of new infections has re-emphasized the importance of this role. Indeed, HIV/AIDS has been seen by some as galvanizing societies in a way not seen since the black death. In some countries, such as France and Switzerland, it has been responsible for a substantial strengthening of the public health function at national level. But despite the long tradition of public health involvement, there are enormous differences in its detailed implementation.

Countries differ in whether responsibility is in local government (as in Germany and Scandinavia), in the health service (as in Italy and in the former socialist countries of central and eastern Europe), or split between the two (as in the UK, where public health medicine is part of the health service but environmental health is a local government responsibility). There is little evidence about which approach is best. What is more important is that there are very strong links with other agencies involved and between those who deliver services and those who develop policies.

There are also considerable differences in the methods used in surveillance and investigation of outbreaks and these differences are arguably rather more important than structural considerations. Many systems fall far short of best practice. Few countries have well-developed surveillance systems with rapid transmission of information from hospital laboratories (Desenclos *et al.* 1993). This is especially difficult where there are private microbiological laboratories but it can also be problematic where laboratories are in the same public system, as in the former socialist countries. How outbreaks are investigated also differs. In some countries outbreak investigation is based on microbiological testing. This will often fail to identify avoidable risk factors and is ineffective where organisms with special culture requirements are involved and epidemiological clues are needed to suggest their involvement. Many western European countries recognize that laboratory input is essential but place much more emphasis on a coordinated approach including case-control studies and developing policy to eliminate identified risk factors.

The approach to environmental health also differs. The optimal model has environmental control based on integrated exposure and health status monitoring, and implementation of appropriate policy responses encompassing economic, educational and regulatory approaches. No European country achieves this ideal but some, such as the Netherlands, have made much more progress than others.

**Potential reforms**

Communicable disease control is seen by many as somewhat peripheral to health care reform, but each impact on the other. Failure of communicable disease control may have considerable economic consequences, both in the direct cost of treating patients who acquire infections outside hospital, through longer stays of those acquiring nosocomial infections and through the consequences of measures to contain established outbreaks (Dixon 1987). There are also the indirect costs to society of outbreaks, such as those that have led to the closures of food factories, with consequences for national economic growth (Roberts and Sockett 1994).

But health sector reform can also affect communicable disease surveillance and control. Many countries, especially those with multiple providers, have been unable to develop integrated comprehensive surveillance systems, causing outbreaks to go unrecognized. Health sector reform that leads to fragmentation of laboratory networks, such as privatization, may compromise existing surveillance activities (O'Brien *et al.* 1993).

Some environmental health responses, such as central and eastern European San-Epid stations, have very limited impact. They should develop multi-disciplinary approaches, involving geography, economic and policy analysis, and mathematical modelling, and should move from the existing model of medical dominance.

The wide variation in the quality of communicable disease control and environmental health is a matter of great concern. The EU is supporting projects to develop agreed definitions to be used in surveillance and to develop rapid communication networks, partly because of the recognized threats from increasing mobility within Europe as well as the emergence of new diseases such as HIV/AIDS and Bovine Spongiform Encephalopathy. But many national governments also need to take action to ensure that effective systems are in place.

## PROVISION OF SERVICES TO SPECIAL GROUPS

The second area in which public health may be involved is the provision of services for specific groups, such as children (including school health), the elderly, those with learning impairments, and those with certain diseases such as tuberculosis. Traditionally this role arose from the inability to design financial incentives to persuade independent physicians to care for these groups. This should serve as a warning of the risks of market-based systems. As a consequence, the state took responsibility for them. In countries adopting social insurance systems this was perhaps unsurprising as many schemes were, initially, limited to those in employment, who were mostly men, so that the public health system was left to provide services for mothers and children. But even in those countries where government was responsible for all health services, such as the post-1948 UK or the Soviet Union, the systems remained separate.

Increasingly these services are being integrated with mainstream health services. This is, first, because of the recognition that separate vertical systems frequently duplicated existing services and provided a second-rate service (Heinz-Trossen 1991). Second, there is recognition of the benefits of integrated models of primary care. Consequently public health is withdrawing from this role. For example, in Germany since the early 1970s there has been a steady transfer of responsibility of services from public health to sickness funds (Rosewitz and Webber 1990). In the UK, child health surveillance and immunization have become the responsibility of general practitioners. High levels of immunization have been achieved by contractual payments to general practitioners based on certain targets, with monitoring by public health staff who provide advice and support if targets are not being met. A caveat is required. It is not sufficient simply to abolish the vertical systems that are still common in the NIS and CEE countries and assume that they will be taken over by the mainstream service. It is essential to remember that the reason these systems were established was because of the failure of the market to meet the needs of disadvantaged groups. Consequently such integration should be undertaken within a framework of explicit, measurable objectives, with those responsible for change given scope to use a wide range of mechanisms to bring it about, and with detailed monitoring of the consequences. There is concern in some countries, such as Switzerland, that this has been overlooked. Even in those countries that have made most progress, it is over-simplistic to think that this process has been completely successful.

**Potential reforms**

Where public health continues to manage health services in separate vertical programmes there is a strong case for integrating these activities with mainstream health services. This will be difficult in the absence of a highly developed primary care network but the role of the gatekeeping function by general practitioners, in cost containment, makes such a development a legitimate goal in its own right. Often it will be necessary to work within a contractual relationship between purchasers and providers, requiring a complex combination of incentives and regulation. Experience indicates the need for clearly identified objectives and effective monitoring and feedback systems. There may, however, be a case for some parallel services such as family planning aimed at teenagers and sexually transmitted diseases where prevailing cultural attitudes might inhibit people from seeking care from a family doctor.

As with communicable disease control, greater pluralism carries considerable risks. In countries with integrated services, introduction of competing providers may break down carefully cultivated relationships that cross what were simply administrative boundaries but which have become commercial ones. The solutions to this problem are complex but, as a first step, it should be recognized and monitored.

## HEALTH PROMOTION

The third area in which public health is commonly involved is health promotion. Accumulating information on the ability to prevent disease led to the growth of two parallel but often uncoordinated activities: health education, undertaken largely in public health departments, and preventive medicine, focused largely on secondary prevention such as screening for hypertension. These approaches were especially strong during the 1960s, when many new drugs were becoming available and there was optimism about the role of scientific medicine, typified by the concept of a 'clinical iceberg' (Last 1963), with only the tip showing itself to the medical profession.

Both approaches were based on a medical model of the determinants of health and disease, with little concession to how social factors determine behaviour and risk of disease. A seminal report in 1974 by the Canadian government, *A New Perspective on the Health of Canadians* (Lalonde 1974) introduced the health field concept, in which health is a product of lifestyles, the environment, human biology and health care. It provided a basis for the subsequent development of the WHO HFA programme. Here, public health enables individuals and communities to increase control over the determinants of health and thereby to improve it (WHO 1986).

At its centre is an intersectoral approach to health. It reasoned that, as many of the determinants of health were outside the scope of health services, those promoting the health of the public must work with agencies such as those responsible for transport and the environment. The gulf between preventive and curative services widened further. There was also growing realization that scientific medicine was failing to deliver what it promised. McKeown's revisionist study of the decline of infectious disease offered support for this view (McKeown 1976). Greater awareness of iatrogenesis and, in the field of mental health, the deleterious consequences of institutionalization, led to a backlash against health care providers, articulated most effectively by Illich (Illich 1976).

**Potential reforms**

Many countries have adopted a model of health promotion based on an intersectoral approach, drawing on a range of disciplines, including epidemiology, social policy, psychology, marketing, anthropology and economics. In a few, however, activities are based on the obsolete medical model consisting of poorly coordinated programmes of preventive medicine and health education. Those working in health promotion must bridge the gap between health services and other elements of society. They must assess the major health challenges facing their populations, on the basis of sound epidemiological evidence, develop prioritized programmes for action, and develop and implement policies that draw on all methods available to change knowledge, attitudes and practice. Such a strategy will present particular difficulties for countries of central and eastern Europe where many of these skills are weak and where the few with expertise in areas such as marketing and economics will be in great demand from the commercial sector who can offer salaries far in excess of those in the public sector.

## COMMISSIONING AND PLANNING HEALTH SERVICES

Having moved away from a direct managerial role in health services, now that they no longer provide health services, public health professionals are increasingly directing health services through planning or commissioning. This reflects the growing awareness of evidence of underuse of effective interventions and overuse of ineffective interventions, variations in outcomes and unequal access to care. The introduction of systems based on the concept of 'quasi-markets' (Le Grand and Bartlett 1993) or 'planned markets' (Saltman and von Otter 1992) has strengthened the need for these skills. Quasi-markets seek to use market-based incentives to achieve socially desirable goals but must act within a tightly regulated structure if they are to avoid the adverse consequences of market failure.

This role for public health is seen in an increasing number of countries. In Scandinavia, there is input from public health professionals at county and national level but it is perhaps most highly developed in the UK, where public health plays a central role in health care purchasing: assessing health needs of their populations, deciding priorities for meeting these needs, placing contracts to meet these needs and evaluating their performance, and otherwise promoting health. These roles have been somewhat slower to develop in some other countries. In France, the *Schéma Régionale d'Organisation Sanitaire* is coordinating regional priorities with plans of health care providers but this is difficult in a pluralist system (Bach 1994). In Germany, research institutes of sickness funds are developing this role but, to date, their focus has been more narrowly on control of pharmaceutical expenditure (Graf von der Schulenburg 1994). In many other countries this role has yet to develop but in some, such as Belgium, it has been advocated by health policy analysts to overcome identified problems of market failure (Nonneman and van Doorslaer 1994).

**Potential reforms**

All systems have someone acting as third-party purchasers, at least to prevent market failure. They must be able to act as an agent for the patient and identify the needs of their populations, determine how to meet these needs, identify ways to change behaviour by providers and evaluate outcomes. Specifically, they need skills to monitor and evaluate research, including the extent to which it can be applied to local circumstances. This is becoming even more pressing with the advent of expensive technologies and the rapidly increasing complexity of medical interventions such as those directed at the genetic and cellular mechanisms of many diseases. Evidence that research is often not acted on has highlighted the need for skills such as epidemiology, economics, sociology and policy analysis.

Unfortunately, the skills and knowledge required to manage health care markets are in very short supply in all countries. Even where there is the greatest experience of quasi-markets, public health professionals are still on a steep learning curve (McKee and Clarke 1995). As with health promotion, there are particularly great problems in central and eastern Europe where these skills are likely to be in great demand from the commercial sector. Integrated packages to train and retain staff are needed including competitive remuneration and well-defined career structures. Isolated training programmes are insufficient.

## PUBLIC HEALTH RESEARCH

The final public health role is to undertake research. Modern health services are driven by advances in biomedical research and public health research must keep pace. Inevitably, the direction of research will be influenced by how public health is seen in each country. In its broadest sense, it includes use of epidemiological methods to describe the health needs of a population, to identify hazards to health and social determinants of disease. It also involves supporting the development of policies to tackle these hazards and determinants, including evaluation of specific interventions. In practice, this research is undertaken in relatively few countries and even then is rarely part of a coordinated strategy.

The need for research is especially pressing as many health care reforms are driven by concerns about upward pressure on costs. For a long time it was argued that the policy that 'prevention is better than cure' could not be sustained on economic grounds (Russell 1986). More recent analyses have questioned this, suggesting, for example, that the low prevalence of chronic disease in Japan consequent on lifestyle factors may be a major factor in the low cost of the health system there and arguing that a model of a health care system that fails to include the demand for care is incomplete (Evans and Stoddart 1994). Unfortunately, economic evaluation of public health interventions is difficult. Interventions typically have a long time frame, with expenditure now leading to benefits far in the future. Decision makers often have much shorter time horizons (Rosen and McKee 1995). This short-termism is accentuated by discounting benefits in economic evaluations, despite the absence of an empirical basis for doing so (Krahn and Gafni 1993).

A further problem is the lack of good economic evaluations of preventive interventions. Available evidence is often of limited generalizability. But evidence does exist, such as studies of workplace health promotion in the US (Pelletier 1991), which have been shown to reduce health care costs. Finally, health systems have little incentive to spend money if savings accrue to individuals or to other sectors. There are also obstacles to developing health services research. Funding bodies are often dominated by basic medical scientists, with little regard for applied work and that involving a multi-disciplinary approach. Some countries have attempted to overcome this problem with new structures that prioritize objectives and have dedicated funding, as in the Netherlands and the UK (Peckham 1991).

**Potential reforms**

Dependence on responsive research funding is inefficient, leading to duplication of effort and waste. Countries should identify the major public health challenges facing their population and the gaps in research required to intervene in them. This research should address the health needs of populations, effectiveness of interventions and the best ways of bringing about change. They must also establish means by which public health advice can be brought to the attention of decision makers.

The opening of borders in Europe provides both challenges and opportunities for public health research (Normand and Vaughan 1993). Challenges include the need to address the health of migrants and, in the EU, the consequences of the single market. Opportunities include the scope for comparative epidemiological and policy research, drawing on diversity. Much research is underway, such as that supported by the EU BIOMED programme (Baert *et al.* 1995). But this is still largely responsive and there is scope for a strategic overview of the major research questions facing Europe. There is also a need to ensure that this research is available to decision makers at a regional and European level.

## WHY HAVE DIFFERENT COUNTRIES ADOPTED DIFFERENT MODELS?

This chapter has not sought to categorize national public health systems, partly because of the difficulty in developing an unambiguous definition about what should be included in each country and also because of the lack of published information. In general, however, public health is strongest in Ireland, the Netherlands, Scandinavia, Switzerland and the UK. In some others, such as Italy and Spain, there is considerable variation with a strong public health contribution in some regions. Although there are differences in structures and processes, all of these countries have modern communicable disease surveillance and control systems, well-developed health promotion programmes, and have developed mechanisms to get public health input into the organization of health services. Some other countries are undertaking initiatives to strengthen their public health function, either through major training programmes or restructuring of services. These include Denmark, France, Germany, Hungary and Poland. Others, such as Austria, Greece and Portugal have done much less, although, again, there are some places where services are well developed. In the countries of the former Soviet Union the San-Epid system remains with its focus on traditional hygiene, a narrow laboratory-based approach and a failure to tackle major challenges to health (Beller 1992; Bojan *et al.* 1994; Steensberg 1994). The combination of challenges from societal disruption and reduced funding has led to failure even in those areas where they previously enjoyed some success, such as communicable disease control, with outbreaks of diseases such as diphtheria. In central and eastern Europe the picture is more complicated. Hungary has undertaken an extensive restructuring of the previous San-Epid system to encompass health promotion and non-communicable disease epidemiology although the process of change has been difficult (Bojan *et al.* 1994). Romania has reintegrated components of the service. Other countries, such as Bulgaria, the Czech Republic and Slovakia, have effectively ignored this sector.

Detailed examination of reasons for these differences is beyond the scope of this chapter and would be hampered by the lack of comparative research. There are some factors which are specific to a country or region. These include the imposition of a soviet model on the countries of central and eastern Europe in the post-war period, the previously low status of public health in Germany arising from its role during the second world war (Light *et al.* 1986) and, in some parts of the former soviet bloc, official rejection of the possibility of social inequalities in a communist system (Csaszi 1990), although in practice this view was increasingly challenged in many countries, such as Hungary and Poland, during the 1980s.

Apart from these specific factors, a major factor is how the state is involved in overall health policy. All health services are decentralized to some extent but the nature of this decentralization varies (Mills *et al.* 1990). In some countries, such as the UK, health and health care policy are developed in one department of central government and are disseminated through a deconcentrated hierarchical system to district health authorities, who must develop strategic frameworks in the light of national policies and priorities and local information on patterns of disease and of service availability. Here, public health input is found at governmental level and with local health authorities. The situation is similar in Italy and Scandinavia, where responsibility for curative and preventive services are also brought together but at the level of regions (Italy) or counties and municipalities (Scandinavia). In these countries, the powers of central government are limited but, again, public health is represented at both levels.

The situation is more complex where curative services are funded from social insurance, with the financing and delivery of care largely delegated or privatized. There is often a strong independent medical profession which rejects the idea that its work should be directed by public health concerns. National and local governments have, however, intervened to either persuade or compel sickness funds to adopt public health-related policies, such as when the Belgian Federal Minister for Social Affairs negotiated changes in the reimbursement scheme with the *Institut National d'Assurances contre la Maladie et l'Invalidité*, a statutory body representing health care professionals and *mutualities*, to alter the balance of primary and secondary care. In these countries public health input to government is needed, whether national or local. Such an input generally exists but varies considerably. It is relatively strong in the Netherlands and in some German *Länder* but less so elsewhere. It is arguable, by analogy with countries with purchaser–provider splits within the context of taxation-based systems, that there is a case for a public health presence at the level of sickness funds.

In theory, it should be somewhat more difficult to implement public health policies in a delegated or privatized system. Consequently, many governments have simply reconciled themselves to developing vertical systems to achieve specific public health objectives. Certainly the tools available are more limited. It is, however, still possible to use financial incentives creatively to bring about change, as in the UK immunization programme.

### Does it matter?

As diversity reflects differences in the health care environment, it may not matter. The different approaches adopted might be equally effective. But that is not so even for communicable disease control, the most fundamental public health role, with major deficiencies in surveillance and outbreak investigation in some systems.

Furthermore, commentators are increasingly calling for public health input into decisions by third-party payers in health care systems. Many public health policies have been shown to reduce mortality (Tuomilehto *et al.* 1986). It is less easy to identify consequences of failure to develop public health functions because of the absence of comparative research. Indeed, there is a striking absence of even basic descriptive research on services in many European countries, with even less evaluation of interventions. Some idea of the effect of variation in the development of services may, however, be gleaned from the following examples.

Sudden infant death syndrome (SIDS) is one of the leading causes of infant deaths in industrialized countries. Traditionally, infants were placed to sleep on their backs but during the 1960s, physiological research suggested that there may be advantages, especially to premature babies, of sleeping in the prone position (Engelberts and de Jonge 1990). These studies had many weaknesses but, despite their limitations, prompted paediatricians in many countries to advocate placing all infants face down. This was associated with a progressive rise in the incidence of SIDS. In contrast, by the mid-1980s, studies from Australia (Cameron and Williams 1986; McGlashan 1986), Belgium (Kahn *et al.* 1984), Germany (Saternus 1985) and Hong Kong (Davies 1985) suggested that prone sleeping could actually increase the risk of SIDS, although these studies were criticized by many paediatricians. The available evidence was deemed sufficient to justify a change in policy in the Netherlands in 1987 (de Jonge *et al.* 1989) but received little official attention elsewhere until a series of large prospective case-control studies were published from Tasmania (Dwyer *et al.* 1991), New Zealand and the UK in 1991.

There is now very strong evidence that infants should be placed on their backs. Despite this, only some countries, such as Ireland, New Zealand, Scandinavia, UK and parts of Austria, Germany and Switzerland, have mounted campaigns to increase awareness while others, in southern, central and eastern Europe have done almost nothing. Where these campaigns have been evaluated they have been shown to have been associated with substantial falls in death rates (de Jonge *et al.* 1993; Mitchell *et al.* 1994; Irgens *et al.* 1995).

HIV/AIDS offers another opportunity to study the relationship between public health policies and outcome. A detailed study of national responses to HIV/AIDS (Wellings 1994) has shown how some countries were able to mount effective and sustained campaigns early, such as Norway and Switzerland, while others acted relatively late, such as Finland, France and Portugal. The differing speed of response was not related to the prevalence of infection but an important factor was the presence of a public health infrastructure on which to base interventions, as in the Netherlands and Norway (or, as in Belgium and France, the absence of one).

Many other areas offer some indication of different levels of success in developing health policies, such as the large variations in smoking rates and deaths from road traffic accidents. There is also evidence of the effect of change over time, such as the way in which UK public health professionals have been able to disinvest in health care interventions shown to be ineffective, such as much of child health surveillance (Hall 1989). They have also been able to use the contracting process to support effective interventions, such as increased use of thrombolysis in patients with myocardial infarctions.

These examples illustrate that some countries are more easily able than others to develop and implement healthy public policies. In the case of HIV/AIDS, those countries that introduced schemes earliest had a strong public health presence at the relevant decision-making tier. In addition, it appears to have been easier to implement a service in an integrated health service, as in Scandinavia or the UK. SIDS and HIV/AIDS also appear to illustrate the importance of a strong public health function, although in both, non-governmental organizations and clinicians have played an important role in some countries (McKee *et al.* 1996).

It would, of course, be naive to assume that policy making is always strictly rational and based on evidence (Walt 1994). Decision makers must take many factors into account. This chapter advocates greater integration of public health and health care reform. Those adhering to a libertarian philosophy would argue that the state should not have any role in promoting healthy public policies and individuals should be 'free to be foolish' (Leichter 1991). Others, such as the representatives of the tobacco industry (Baggott 1987) and the food industry (Ziglio 1986) may be less explicit but, through their influence with governments, can obstruct such policies. As noted above, however, these views can be rejected as a basis for government action as all European governments have signed up to the principles of HFA and a detailed comparison of health policy in Germany and the UK has shown that, paradoxically, health sector reforms based on the idea of promoting individualism may increase public health interventions (Freeman 1995), suggesting that such strategies may reflect public choice.

So if it is legitimate for governments to pursue healthy public policies, this chapter seeks only to argue that some appear to be able to act more rationally than others. These differences cannot be attributed solely to the presence of a particular model of health care financing. The Netherlands, with a system based on social insurance, and Scandinavia and the UK, with national health services, albeit with differences in the degree of decentralization, have all had success in implementing research-based evidence. They each have developed their own methods of ensuring access to high-quality and timely information and have secured the ability to analyse it and present it to decision makers in a way that is comprehensible and supports formulation of policy. Of course, even in these countries political factors intervene, such as the frequently noted absence of research to underpin the reforms of the British National Health Service.

## WHERE NOW FOR PUBLIC HEALTH?

The development of public health in Europe is extremely patchy. In places it is well developed with many trained professional staff able to assess need, advise on effectiveness of interventions, and evaluate their implementation. Elsewhere it is marginalized, limited to relatively ineffective surveillance of communicable disease and responsible for what are often second-class services for disadvantaged groups.

There is an urgent need to increase the availability of skills in those countries introducing market-based reforms. Otherwise providers may adopt entirely rational tactics of cream skimming and promoting supplier-induced demand, often for ineffective services (Roberts 1993). Only the most extreme libertarian believes that health care can be treated like any tradable good. Organizations responsible for paying for care, whether they be German sickness funds, Scandinavian counties or UK health authorities, will need individuals with skills to assess need, advise on priorities for competing claims for resources and evaluate value for money. Those responsible for defined populations must monitor access to care for emerging inequities. Public health professionals with these skills and the opportunities to use them can make a major contribution to health care reform.

This chapter presents a case for a new model of public health, encompassing an improved approach to communicable disease and environmental health, a withdrawal from the delivery of health services as they are integrated into mainstream services, an intersectoral and multi-disciplinary approach to health promotion and greater involvement in planning and commissioning health services. It leaves open the question about whether these roles should be integrated or distributed among different organizations. This will depend on the context. It is more important that there is a mechanism for coordination that works.

A caveat is necessary. There is often a tension between those advocating greater development of intersectoral activities and those involved in commissioning health services. The two can work together, as in the UK where contracting has been used to purchase health promotion services (Killoran 1992). In practice, however, the relationship has often been unsatisfactory. In some countries this has led to a lengthy debate about the nature of public health and, especially, whether it should treat health services solely like any other public function or whether it should be part of them, seeking to improve health through both influence on delivery of care and links with other organizations. For example, in the UK, public health practitioners tread a finely balanced path between their managerial role in implementing government policies and their advocacy role, in which they must speak for the public on public health issues (Whitty and Jones 1992). Admittedly, this problem has been compounded by the highly centralized nature of UK government (Jenkins 1995) and the high political profile of the National Health Service, but the underlying tensions are likely to apply elsewhere.

Reform of the public health function will only succeed if professional staff have appropriate skills. These encompass a range of disciplines including epidemiology, economics, demography, sociology and policy analysis. Only a few countries have well-developed training programmes although some, such as the Baltic States, Denmark, Germany (Kolip and Schott 1994), Hungary (McKee *et al.* 1993) and Romania have recently strengthened their capacity. In some cases these are supported by international bodies such as the World Bank or the EU TEMPUS programme. There are relatively few international collaborative training programmes, such as the European Training Consortium in Public Health (Colomer *et al.* 1995). The European Public Health Association, which brings together almost all of Europe's national public health associations, also plays a part.

Strengthened training requires a complementary strategy for

research, with priorities based on epidemiological knowledge and systematic reviews of existing evidence. At present, much biomedical research is reactive, duplicates work elsewhere, and is of little relevance to major public health issues. Such a programme should incorporate adequate support to develop research infrastructure and to support training.

European public health services face major challenges. A few are in a position to respond to them. For many others, there is still much to do. In the totality of health sector reform, it is important that public health services are not forgotten.

## ACKNOWLEDGEMENTS

This work is supported in part by the EU COPERNICUS Programme [Contract number CIPACT930247 (ERB 3510 PL 92 4074)]. We are grateful to Naomi Fulop and Renée Danziger for helpful comments.

## REFERENCES

Abel-Smith, B., Figueras, J., Holland, W., McKee, M. and Mossialos, E. (1995). *Choices in Health Policy: An Agenda for the European Union.* Luxembourg and Aldershot: Office for Official Publications of the European Communities and Dartmouth Publishing Company.

Bach, S. (1994). Managing a pluralist health system: The case of health care reform in France. *International Journal of Health Services*, 24, 593–606.

Baert, A.-E., Baig, S. S., Bardoux, C., Fracchia, G. N., Hallen, M., Le Dour, O. *et al.* (eds) (1995). *European Union Biomedical and Health Research.* Amsterdam: IOS Press.

Baggott, R. (1987). Government–industry relations in Britain: The regulation of the tobacco industry. *Policy and Politics*, 15, 137–46.

Beller, M. (1992). Epidemiology and public health in the Yogodnoye district. *Alaska Medicine*, 34, 21–7.

Bojan, F., McKee, M. and Ostbye, T. (1994). Status and priorities of public health in Hungary. *Zeitschrift für Gesundheitswissenschaften*, 1, 48–55.

Cameron, M. H. and Williams, A. L. (1986). Development and testing of scoring systems for predicting infants with high risk of sudden infant death syndrome in Melbourne. *Australian Paediatric Journal*, 22 (Supplement), 37–45.

Colomer, C., Lindstrom, B. and O'Dwyer, A. (1995). European training in public health. *European Journal of Public Health*, 5, 113–15.

Csaszi, L. (1990). Interpreting inequalities in the Hungarian health system. *Social Science and Medicine*, 31, 275–84.

Davies, D. P. (1985). Cot death in Hong Kong: A rare problem? *Lancet*, 2, 1346–9.

de Jonge, G. A., Engelberts, A. C., Koomen-Liefting, A. J. M. and Kostense, P. J. (1989). Cot death and prone sleeping position in the Netherlands. *British Medical Journal*, 298, 722.

de Jonge, G. A., Burgmeijer, R. J., Engelberts, A. C., Hoogenboezem, J., Kostense, P. J. and Sprij, A. J. (1993). Sleeping position for infants and cot deaths in the Netherlands 1985–91. *Archives of Diseases in Childhood*, 69, 660–3.

Dekker, E. (1994). Health care reforms and public health. *European Journal of Public Health*, 4, 281–6.

Desenclos, J.-C., Bijkerk, H. and Huisman, J. (1993). Variations in national infectious disease surveillance in Europe. *Lancet*, 341, 1003–6.

Dixon, R. E. (1987). Costs of nosocomial infections and benefits of infection control programs. In R. P. Wenzel (ed.), *Prevention and Control of Nosocomial Infections*. Baltimore: Williams and Williams.

Dwyer, T., Ponsonby, A.-L. B., Newman, N. M. and Gibbons, L. E. (1991). Prospective cohort study of prone sleeping position and sudden infant death syndrome. *Lancet*, 337, 1244–7.

Engelberts, A. C. and de Jonge, G. A. (1990). Choice of sleeping position for infants: Possible association with cot death. *Archive of Diseases in Childhood*, 65, 462–7.

Evans, R. G., Barer, M. L. and Marmor, T. R. (eds) (1994). *Why Are Some People Healthy and Others Not?* Berlin: de Gruyter.

Evans, R. G. and Stoddart, G. L. (1994). Producing health, consuming health care. In R.G. Evans *et al.* (eds), *Why Are Some People Healthy and Others Not?* Berlin: de Gruyter.

Freeman, R. (1995). Prevention and government: Health policy making in the United Kingdom and Germany. *Health Policy*, 20, 745–65.

Graf von der Schulenburg, J.-M. (1994). Forming and reforming the market for third-party purchasing of health care: A German perspective. *Social Science and Medicine*, 39, 1743–81.

Hall, D. M. B. (ed.) (1989). *Health for All Children: A Programme for Child Health Surveillance. The Report of a Joint Working Party on Child Health Surveillance*. Oxford: Oxford University Press.

Heinz-Trossen, A. (1991). *Zur Reglementierung der Prostiten – insbesondere zur Arbeit der Gesundheitsämter der Bundesrepublik Deutschland West*. Bonn: Öffentliches Gesundheitswesen.

Illich, I. (1976). *Limits to Medicine*. London: Marion Boyars.

Irgens, L. M., Markestad, T., Baste, V., Schreuder, P., Skjaerven, R. and Oyen, N. (1995). Sleeping position and sudden infant death syndrome in Norway 1967–91. *Archives of Diseases in Childhood*, 72, 478–82.

Jenkins, S. (1995). *Accountable to None: The Tory Nationalization of Britain*. London: Hamish Hamilton.

Kahn, A., Blum, D., Hennart, P. *et al.* (eds) (1984). A critical comparison of the history of sudden-death infants and infants hospitalised for near miss for SIDS. *European Journal of Paediatrics*, 143, 103–7.

Killoran, A. (1992). *Putting Health into Contracts: The Role of Purchasing Authorities in Commissioning Health Promotion and Disease Prevention Services*. London: Health Education Authority.

Kolip, P. and Schott, T. (1994). Gesundheitswissenschaften in Deutschland: Universitäre Ausbildungsangebote. *Zeitschrift für Gesundheitswissenschaften*, 2, 81–90.

Krahn, M. and Gafni, A. (1993). Discounting in the economic evaluation of health care interventions. *Medical Care*, 31, 403–18.

Lalonde, M. (1974). *A New Perspective on the Health of Canadians: A Working Document*. Ottawa: Canada Information.

Last, J. M. (1963). The iceberg: 'Completing the clinical picture' in general practice. *Lancet*, ii, 28–31.

Leeuw de, E. and Polman, L. (1995). Health policy making: The Dutch experience. *Social Science and Medicine*, 40, 331–8.

Le Grand, J. and Bartlett, W. (1993). *Quasi-markets and Social Policy*. London: Macmillan.

Leichter, H. M. (1991). *Free To Be Foolish*. Princeton: Princeton University Press.

Light, D. W., Liebfried, S. and Tennstedt, F. (1986). Social medicine vs professional dominance: The German experience. *American Journal of Public Health*, 76, 78–83.

McCarthy, M. and Rees, S. (1992). *Health Systems and Public Health Medicine in the European Community*. London: Royal College of Physicians.

McGlashan, N. D. (1986). Sleeping position and SIDS. *Lancet*, i, 106.

McKee, M. and Clarke, A. (1995). Guidelines, enthusiasms, uncertainty, and the limits to purchasing. *British Medical Journal*, 310, 101–4.

McKee, M., Bojan, F. and Normand, C. (1993). On behalf of the TEMPUS consortium for a new public health in Hungary. A new programme for public health training in Hungary. *European Journal of Public Health*, 3, 58–63.

McKee, M., Fulop, N., Bouvier, P., Hort, A., Brand, H., Rasmussen, F. *et al.* (eds) (1996). Preventing sudden infant deaths – the slow diffusion of an idea. *Health Policy*, 37, 117–35.

McKeown, T. (1979). *The Role of Medicine: Dream, Mirage or Nemesis?* Oxford: Blackwell.

Mills, A., Vaughan, J. P., Smith, D. L. and Tabibzadeh, I. (1990). *Health System Decentralization: Concepts, Issues and Country Experience*. Geneva: World Health Organization.

Mitchell, E. A., Brunt, J. M. and Everard, C. (1994). Reduction in mortality from sudden infant death syndrome in New Zealand: 1986–92. *Archives of Diseases in Childhood*, 70, 291–4.

Nonneman, W. and van Doorslaer, E. (1994). The role of the sickness funds in the Belgian health care market. *Social Science and Medicine*, 39, 1483–95.

Normand, C. E. M. and Vaughan, J. P. (eds) (1993). *Europe without Frontiers. The Implications for Health*. Chichester: Wiley.

O'Brien, J. M., O'Brien, S. J., Geddes, A. M., Heap, B. J. and Mayon-White, R. T. (1993). Tempting fate: Control of communicable disease in England. *British Medical Journal*, 306, 1461–4.

Peckham, M. (1991). Research and development for the national health service. *Lancet*, 338, 367–71.

Pelletier, K. (1991). A review and analysis of the health and cost-effectiveness outcome studies of comprehensive health promotion and disease prevention programmes. *American Journal of Health Promotion*, 5, 311–15.

Roberts, J. A. (1993). Managing markets. *Journal of Public Health Medicine*, 15, 305–10.

Roberts, J. A. and Sockett, P. N. (1994). The socio-economic impact of human *salmonella enteriditis* infection. *International Journal of Food Microbiology*, 21, 117–29.

Robinson, M., McKee, M. and Coyle, E. (1996). *Health of the Nation: Every Government Department's Business*. London: RSM Press.

Rosen, R. and McKee, M. (1995). Short termism in the NHS. *British Medical Journal*, 311, 703–4.

Rosewitz, B. and Webber, D. (1990). *Reformversuche und Reformblokaden im deutschen Gesundheitswesen*. Frankfurt-am-Main: Campus-Verlag.

Russell, L. B. (1986). *Is Prevention Better than Cure?* Washington, DC: Brookings Institution.

Saltman, R. B. and von Otter, C. (1992). *Planned Markets and Public Competition. Strategic Reform in Northern European Health Systems*. Buckingham: Open University Press.

Saternus, K.-S. (1985). *Plötzlicher Kindstod – eine Folge der Bauchlage?* Heidelberg: Kriminalstatistik Verlag.

Steensberg, J. (1994). Post-Soviet public health administration in Estonia. *World Health Forum*, 15, 335–8.

Tuomilehto, J., Geboers, J., Salonen, J. T., Nissinen, A., Kuulasmaa, K. and Pushka, P. (1986). Decline in cardiovascular mortality in North Karelia and other parts of Finland. *British Medical Journal*, 293, 1068–71.

Walt, G. (1994). How far does research influence policy? *European Journal of Public Health*, 4, 233–5.

Wellings, K. (1994). Assessing AIDS/HIV prevention. What do we know in Europe? General population. *Sozial- und Präventivmedizin*, 39, 14–46.

Whitty, P. and Jones, I. (1992). Public health heresy: A challenge to the purchasing orthodoxy. *British Medical Journal*, 304, 1039–41.

WHO (1986). Ottawa Charter for Health Promotion. *Health Promotion*, 1, 73–6.

Ziglio, E. (1986). 'Uncertainty' in health promotion. Nutrition policy in two countries. *Health Promotion International*, 1, 257–68.

# PART III

## SUPPLY-SIDE STRATEGIES

# 6

# CONTRACTING MODELS AND PROVIDER COMPETITION

Serdar Savas, Igor Sheiman,
Ellie Tragakes and
Hans Maarse

## INTRODUCTION

Health care reforms under way in many European countries incorporate contracting relationships between payers and providers of health care. The contracting model is increasingly considered to be a coordinating mechanism which offers a promising alternative to traditional forms of command-and-control coordination in health care management.

An essential element of the new approach is a move from hierarchical or highly integrated forms of service delivery and finance towards models based upon purchaser–provider separation. Contracting is seen as a tool to help achieve this separation. Through contracting mechanisms, third-party payers and providers are bound by explicit commitments and also acquire economic motivation to follow these commitments.

In many countries, contracting between third-party payers and suppliers of health services has long served as a common coordinating mechanism. In Germany and the Netherlands, for instance, complex institutional structures have been created in which representative organizations of health insurers and physicians negotiate contracts on payment schemes for physicians' services to patients. Recently, however, stronger emphasis is being placed on the role of contracting as a planning tool and also as a way to encourage provider competition.

## CONCEPTIONAL ISSUES IN CONTRACTING

### Why contracting?

There are at least five reasons for the move from integrated models to contractual relationships in health care systems.

- *Encourages decentralized management.* A study of contracting in the NHS in the UK points out that contracting has great potential to delegate more responsibility, giving providers and lower-level managers more decision-making authority (Harrison 1993). Two mechanisms used to decentralize management through contracting are clear specification of commitments by contracting parties in terms of services to be provided, and risk-sharing arrangements between purchasers and providers. These mechanisms make the providers' commitments actual rather than declarative. Providers are bound by contractual provisions in terms of the outcomes rather than inputs for performance. Commitments are linked to the financial resources available, which is particularly important for the CEE and CIS countries where the health sector has been greatly underfunded. Providers require some level of autonomy to decide (within effective rules and regulations) on the size, skill mix and pay of the staff, bed capacity, types of equipment purchased, and other work characteristics.

  The role of health authorities in this contracting model is limited to specification on the demand-side (e.g. population needs assessment, analyses of resources available) and negotiating them with potential providers. They are not formally obliged to contract with local providers, and can select providers based on performance.

  Contracts constitute an essential link between purchasers and providers through provisions on risk-sharing arrangements. The traditional responsibility of the third-party payer to cover unpredicted expenditures gives way to contractual sharing of risks between purchasers and providers. This transforms the latter into risk bearers, thereby encouraging them to look for ways to increase their own operating efficiency.

- *Exerts more control over the performance of providers.* At first sight, this intention appears to conflict with decentralization of management. However, the mechanisms of contracting can resolve this conflict by changing key relationships within integrated delivery systems. Clear-cut contractual provisions can overcome blurred responsibilities between the parties and give payers levers to steer the providers' behaviour.

Contracting should be based on monitoring and evaluation with special emphasis on performance indicators. For example, contracting in the NHS in England formalizes the process of monitoring and evaluation through specification of targets and performance indicators (Donaldson and Mooney 1991). This enables purchasers to substantiate claims for better performance by providers and also to settle disputes. A major limitation to implementation of this kind of control is the availability of data.

- *Improves planning of health care development.* In recent years, planning systems have encountered problems which have substantially reduced their ability to meet health care objectives (Saltman and von Otter 1992). The rationale for using contracting as a planning tool is that it provides a direct link between planning and resource allocation, as providers become economically motivated to follow the planning strategy embodied in contractual arrangements.

  Contracting can be regarded as an alternative way to do some things which traditionally have been accomplished by planning. The incorporation of contracting into planning can break deadlocks that planning can sometimes encounter. Plans can be more effectively translated into action: for example, purchasers engaging in health needs assessment can pay selected providers to deliver services which best meet the needs of resident populations. Another innovation of a contract-based model of planning is that it can rationalize the use of new facilities according to actual needs. Contracting can also encourage the development of information systems.

- *Improves management of care.* A major objective of contracting is to generate changes in the pattern of care provision, in particular to shift from in-patient to outpatient care, and also to adopt more cost-effective medical interventions. This strategy is of particular importance for the CEE/CIS countries. Decades of bureaucratic control over these health systems have caused substantial distortions of health care provision structure, unknown to western countries (for example, in-patient care expenditures in the Russian Federation amount to around 70 per cent of health expenditures against the OECD average of 44 per cent for hospitals and 55 per cent for hospitals plus long-term care). Contracting instruments are designed to increase allocative efficiency of health care provision by setting up a vertical network of hospital–physician groups and funding them on a capitation basis.

As purchasers, health authorities are free to represent the interests of the citizenry they serve, as they are no longer directly responsible for the provider side of health services delivery. Payers can therefore engage in assessment of health needs for their resident populations, and can establish priorities for allocating resources among alternative uses. The traditional epidemiological approach to setting priorities, based on a measure of the population's ill health, can be complemented by the incorporation of cost-effectiveness considerations. Purchasers can appraise options for delivery of required services, and engage in negotiations with providers in order to best secure delivery of these services. By representing the consumer of health services, purchasers can secure the most appropriate pattern and balance of curative, health promotion, and disease prevention services for their populations.

- *Encourages local choice over health care.* The move to contracting has placed emphasis on forms of collective choice exercised by the purchaser on behalf of the subscribers. Contracting also can encourage competition among purchasers. For example, insurance companies could offer health insurance policies with various options increasing the number of medical benefits for subscribers. This would make the role of contracting between health insurers and the public more prominent.

By separating the functions of purchasing from functions of provision of care, contracting can overcome the traditional dominance of providers over consumers and payers. Contracting can make purchasers the champions of the citizenry. Contracting also changes the balance of power between payers and providers. Administrative dominance gives way to discussion, negotiation, risk sharing and exchange of information on needs and on providers' performance.

## Contracting from a public health point of view

### Equity

Contracting offers opportunities for supporting equity through the assessment of needs, which can take explicit account of vulnerable and disadvantaged groups, as well as underserved communities. However, contracting has also raised concerns about dangers which can undermine equity. Services which are less profitable, as opposed to less efficient, may be underemphasized or phased out. Services for acute conditions with rapid throughput could increase in importance relative to services for the chronically ill. Providers could try to avoid disadvantaged communities if serving them might generate losses. Services in deprived areas could be of a lower quality in order to keep costs within budget, as disadvantaged groups may be more costly to treat than the average (Whitehead 1990).

Possible benefits from contracting stem from the role of purchasers as representatives of the interests of their populations, who will allocate resources in accordance with the needs of their citizenry. Assessments of needs can take into consideration the socio-economic distribution of poor health, of risk factors, and determinants of health. They can therefore identify inequalities in provision which can be ameliorated through appropriate service specification. In addition, the inclusion into contracts of quality specifications can be used to raise standards of care for underprivileged areas and communities.

### Community participation

Community participation in contracting can generate a democratization process in health services, increase the accountability of governments and the medical profession, and make health policy more relevant to the priorities of society. The process of contracting can be divided into three stages: the pre-contracting stage, the actual contract or written agreement stage, and the post-contracting stage. Community participation can take place in all three of these stages.

### Intersectorality

Intersectorality is rarely present in contracting as currently practised, since contracting today focuses mainly on curative care. Yet numerous aspects of curative care are linked with other activities such as education, labour affairs and social protection mechanisms. Contracting could therefore be used as a mechanism to introduce the different interfaces of these activities into health care. In addition, there are potentials for contracting to be implemented in areas other than health care, e.g. community and environmental

health services. In this context, contracting could be an implementation tool which can help transform intersectorality from an
abstract notion into a reality. Contracting clarifies and makes
explicit the duties, obligations and rights of concerned parties, thus
offering the potential to bring out clearly the responsibilities of the
different areas/sectors and their possible linkages.

## Two approaches to contracting

Two basic approaches to contracting are possible. First, contracting
can be seen as an instrument of health care planning and management in both competitive and non-competitive environments. This
approach implies that contracts can be an integral part of the planning process, irrespective of the role market mechanisms play in
resource allocation. In the second approach, contracting can be
seen as a tool of informed selection of providers. This type of contracting is implemented in competitive environments and designed
to encourage local choice through competitive tendering.

Contracting can offer certain advantages in health policy
implementation in the absence of any significant competitive pressures. Contracts can be incorporated into the planning and management process, provided that medical facilities are paid for the
precise mix of services specified in the contract. However, this type
of contracting can serve only as the first step in changing the performance incentives of providers. The second and major step is to
make contracting competitive. Competition can be seen as a means
of promoting productive efficiency by ensuring that inefficient
providers are not awarded contracts. By making contracting more
selective, its potential to affect quantity, quality and cost of care can
be increased.

The two approaches do not contradict each other. The requirements placed by purchasers in the course of competitive tendering
may include provisions designed to improve planning and management.

## Typology of contracting relationships

Contracts define relationships between many categories of participants in a health care system. The types of contracts vary widely. A
typology of contracting relationships could be based on the following criteria: (1) contracting parties; (2) legal status of contracts;
(3) the contents of contracting; and (4) comprehensiveness of

contracting (that is, the level and scope of contractual relationships, e.g. bilateral vs. multilateral relationships).

*Contracting parties*

In the Beveridge model, the demand-side is represented by government at all levels, as well as by health authorities. A recent innovation in the Russian Federation, Sweden and the UK is that primary care providers are acting as purchasers of care as well. On the supply-side are providers at all levels. The subject of a contract might be not only in-patient or outpatient care, but also public health, community care or programmes for specific diseases. In the Bismarck model, the scope of contracting by government is much narrower, as statutory insurers act as the purchasers of care. Contracting here is between these statutory insurers and employers or individual subscribers, and also between insurers and providers of care. This might be supplemented by contracts between insurers and the government for provision of subsidies, and also between insurers and central insurance agencies.

In the Bismarck model, purchaser–provider relationships may be regulated by collective rather than individual contracting, for example contracts between physician associations and insurers (or their associations). Sometimes collective contracting is also used in countries with a predominant model of individual contracting. In the US in recent years, a so-called 'umbrella contracting' has been used for loose associations of physicians. In this format, the physician authorizes a loose association of peers to negotiate physician services contracts with purchasers. This contract specifies the general rules of contracting and spares individual contractors from negotiating too many provisions (Kongstvedt 1993). In Russia, agreement between regional government, insurance funds and an association of health providers similarly may provide the basis for individual contracts.

*The legal status of contracts*

There is a distinction between 'hard' and 'soft' contracting. Under hard contracting, the contracting parties are relatively autonomous and press their interests actively. Under soft contracting, contracts have a lower degree of formality, and contracting parties have a closer identity of interests. The relationship between third-party payers and providers depends more strongly on cooperation, mutual support, trust, and continuity in relations, as opposed to competition and opportunism (Saltman and von Otter 1992). Soft contracts are less likely to be legally binding. For example, in the contractual relationships emerging following the reforms of the UK NHS, contracts are not legal documents, and the government did not intend that they should be legally enforceable. As such, they could also be described as 'service agreements' and 'understandings', and would not be defined as 'contracts' in the legal sense defined above. Contracting may therefore be more precisely specified as a process of negotiations between at least two parties consisting of third-party payer(s) and provider(s), and resulting in a mutual agreement involving specified rights and obligations. This agreement may or may not be legally binding, and it may be a hard or soft variant.

The role of purchasers in contracting differs depending on the legal status of providers. When contracting with independent or autonomous providers (e.g. hospital trusts), health authorities are acting as purchasers with all rights and responsibilities which apply to the relationships between entities, each of which is deliberately engaging in an exchange. When contracting with state-owned providers, health authorities are acting as 'commissioners', fulfilling their agreed duties as a representative of the government in relationships with providers. In the former case there is a purchaser–provider split, in the latter a commissioner–provider split. This is a functional rather than institutional separation of duties.

The distinction between purchasing and commissioning can be related to the distinction noted earlier between hard and soft contracts. Purchaser–provider relationships can be based on either hard or soft contracts. By contract, commissioner–provider relationships are more likely to be less formal, and to be based on trust, continuity, and cooperation, thus involving a soft variant of contracting.

### The content of contracts

Three types of contracts are normally used in a purchaser/commissioner–provider split:

- *Block contracts.* These can be likened to a budget for a defined service. The purchaser (or commissioner) agrees to pay a fee in exchange for access to a broadly defined range of services. This type of contract predominates because of deficiencies in information (such as on the cost-effectiveness of treatments, and treatment cost structures). In the simplest block contracts, there is no specification of the number of patients (volume) and cost per patient. Increasingly, however, indicative levels of service as well as more detailed specifications are being written into block contracts. These may include an agreed specification of the number of patients to be treated, or of the services or specialties to be offered by the provider. Block contracts may additionally concern the volume of services to be provided and also assessment/monitoring of quality.

• *Cost and volume contracts.* These represent a refinement of block contracts in that payment for specific services is more explicitly related to the services offered. For example, they may entail an agreement for the purchaser (or commissioner) to pay a specified amount for a specified number of persons to be treated by one specialty. In a further refinement, the payments may be differentiated in accordance with the service rendered (for example, high-cost, medium-cost and low-cost categories).

• *Cost per case contracts.* A single cost is set for each item of service. To date, limited use is made of this type of contract as it requires cost information at a level of detail that is not currently available. Cost information systems are in the process of being developed and are increasingly being used in connection with efforts toward more effective resource management.

### Comprehensiveness of contracting

This relates to the scope of relationships regulated by contracting. The usual case is that the purchaser contracts with the individual provider. Correspondingly the provisions of the contract specify the commitments of the individual provider irrespective of the commitments of other providers.

An alternative to this type of individual contract is a comprehensive contract between a purchaser and a group of providers integrated into a vertical closed panel (hospitals, polyclinics, freestanding physicians, diagnostic centres, day-care centres, etc.). The group is funded on a capitation basis for provision of a defined set of medical benefits. This integrated approach to contracting seeks closer interactions among providers to achieve more cost-effective strategies of health care provision. In the US, this strategy is termed managed care, which has been manifested in Health Maintenance Organization-type settings. The major ideas behind this concept also influenced the NHS reform in the UK and are under consideration in some CEE/CIS countries.

Comprehensive contracting implies two sets of contracts: (1) between final purchasers and the integrated group of providers; (2) between providers within the group. For example, in the experiment with HMOs under the Zdrav Reform Programme for the Russian Federation in Kemerovo Region 10, contracts are signed within the integrated system (primary care providers–specialists, polyclinics–pharmacies, etc.). All units of the integrated system are subject to risk and incentives arrangements that create a common interest in the most cost-effective strategies. The set of contractual provisions goes beyond volume, cost and quality characteristics, and includes risk arrangements, targets for decreasing hospital utilization, specialist and hospital admissions referral authorization, quality management mechanisms and requirements for collection of data on outcomes and patient satisfaction.

## THE IMPLEMENTATION OF CONTRACTING

### Present patterns

In Europe, the countries divide into four groups regarding funding: countries following the Beveridge model, countries following the Bismarck model, southern European countries with a mixed model, and the CEE/CIS countries. The rationale for forming a special group for these last countries is that their health systems are in a transitional stage that does not easily fit into traditional typologies.

### *Beveridge model[1]*

These health systems are predominantly tax-financed, and have predominantly publicly operated health services providing comprehensive services. Contracting has traditionally played no role in the relationship between third-party payers which are government units and providers which are for the most part public, as both financing and delivery have been subsumed within the same organizational structure.

Health care reforms introducing contracting in this group of countries attempt to break the 'command and control' elements of this model. Contracting entails the introduction of a split between third-party payers and providers. Three countries in this group have introduced one or another form of contracting: Finland, Sweden and the UK.

## The UK

The contracting parties include District Health Authorities (DHAs), which previously were involved with the financing and management of hospital and community services, and fundholding general practitioners, consisting of large group practices (originally with over 9000 patients) who have exercised the option to receive the funds available for hospitals. The two groups of payers contract with quasi-public, self-governing hospital trusts,[2] with public hospitals managed by the NHS, private hospitals, and community services.

According to the above classification of contracts, DHAs act as commissioners rather than purchasers. However, the intention of health reform planners in the UK has been that eventually all public hospitals heretofore managed by the NHS will become autonomous hospital trusts. GP fundholders, on the other hand, act in the capacity of purchasers only.

Block contracts were the predominant type of contract at the initial stage of the reform. The idea was to avoid dramatic changes in the mix of services and patient flows in the absence of reliable information. But even block contracts differ from previous budget-based arrangements. They place more specific requirements on provider performance, and they also provide for ceilings and floors for activity levels. Moreover, beyond specified ceilings, cost and volume limitations come into operation.

## Finland

Finance and provision of health care in Finland have been formally the responsibility of municipalities. As part of a 1993 reform which altered the system of state subsidies, municipalities have been given greater freedom to organize the provision of services and take on a more active role vis-à-vis providers, though they still maintain overall responsibility for provision of health (and social) services. As a result of this reform, hospital operating revenues are now linked to the volume and type of services requested by the municipalities.

Key objectives of these reforms include increasing municipal (local level) flexibility in service provision with a corresponding reduction in central government control, and go hand-in-hand with efforts to strengthen the position of municipalities vis-à-vis hospital providers. It is likely that these reforms will lead to a fully-fledged commissioner–provider split.

### Sweden

Since 1983, health policy has been the formal responsibility of county councils (regional level government bodies). As part of efforts to explore new ways of financing and organizing health care, a number of counties at the end of the 1980s introduced the separation of financing from provision between counties and hospitals. Other reform elements included: (1) increasing contracting relationships between local governments with private providers; (2) having primary care providers in some counties act as purchasers of in-patient care ('Dalamodel'); and (3) giving consumers new opportunities to choose outpatient care settings and maternity clinics (Saltman and von Otter 1992).

### The Bismarck Model[3]

Health care systems adhering to this model are predominantly financed by social insurance. Financing and delivery are institutionally separated, and contractual arrangements govern the relationships between social insurance organizations (the third-party payer) and providers. These systems are characterized by a relatively high degree of pluralism (Cichon and Normand 1994).

Within this environment, contracting typically involves negotiating and bargaining over prices, remuneration levels, quality, and the global budget. Associations of sickness funds (the purchasers) contract with physicians' organizations for ambulatory care. In the case of hospital care, while associations of sickness funds negotiate the terms of contracts with hospital associations, the actual contracts are concluded between individual sickness funds and individual hospitals.

Health care reform is quite limited in this group of countries which directly involve contracting, with the exception of the Netherlands and to a lesser extent Germany.

### The Netherlands

Reform proposals of 1988 (the Dekker reforms) sought to use contracting as a tool to increase the accountability of sickness funds (the purchasers) by shifting the balance of power between purchasers and providers in favour of the former. The requirement that the sickness funds conclude contracts with all interested providers was to be abolished, and sickness funds were to be allowed to contract selectively with providers. Such selective contracting would transform insurers from passive administrators/funders into more active purchasers/managers. While sickness funds have already been granted the freedom to contract selectively with physicians, this has yet to be implemented with respect to hospitals (van de Ven *et al.* 1994).

The proposed contracting scheme would change the pattern of relationships between sickness funds and the public. The former now attempt to expand their market share by offering minor additional medical benefits, such as the option of annual check-up, the option of cross-border care in order to limit waiting time, and extended medical services which go beyond the basic package. This is a new development, as until recently in the Netherlands (and in other Bismarck model countries) the contract has been determined nearly 100 per cent by government regulation. The freedom of choice of insurers for the public was not seen as important.

Another development is the increasing role for employer-based contracts. Employers negotiate contracts with health insurers for their employees. These contracts may also include health insurance and other health-related insurances (e.g. sick leave payment), and are sometimes referred to as all-care contracts. The latest development is that they may include other non-health components as well (e.g. life insurance, liability insurance, banking facilities).

*Germany*

An effort to increase insurers' discretionary power over providers was initiated following the 1989 Health Care Reform Act. Sickness funds were given the freedom to cancel contracts with more expensive hospitals, although the collective (as opposed to selective) nature of contracting remains. An additional relevant provision in the Act was that hospitals were obliged to publish price lists.

In the Bismarck group of countries generally, contracting between third-party payers and providers tends to focus on levels of remuneration of providers. In Germany, for example, remuneration of physicians in the ambulatory sector is in accordance with the points system. Contracts concluded at the national level between federal sickness fund associations and federal physicians' associations establish a fee schedule, which includes about 2500 items of service, and a relative points scale. These are infrequently revised. State-level sickness fund associations (the purchasers) negotiate and agree with state-level physicians' associations to pay a prospective lump sum which is distributed to physicians in accordance with the nationally negotiated fee schedule and the volume of services produced by each physician. Physicians are reimbursed on a fee-for-service basis using the fee schedule, the relative points value scale, and a monetary value per point. Since the total amount to be transferred to the physicians' association is fixed in the agreement, the fee per point is inversely proportional to the volume of services produced collectively by the physicians. Hospital remuneration is determined by contracting between hospital associations and sickness fund associations, and is based on an agreed average daily rate to be paid for each patient day. Volume, however, is controlled through prospective global budgeting.

Contracts in the hospital sector can additionally include agreements concerning the quality of services. However, the remuneration mechanisms discussed above do not allow purchasers to specify what services are to be provided (in both the hospital and ambulatory sectors), or limits on volume (in the ambulatory sector). In the ambulatory sector, the kinds of services provided are determined by the nationwide relative points value scale, while volume is determined by physicians jointly with patients, both of whom have incentives to maximize volume.

*Southern European countries*

Greece, Israel, Italy, Portugal, Spain and Turkey have mixed systems, combining elements of both the Bismarck and Beveridge models. The first four of these are in a process of transition from primarily insurance-based to primarily tax-based financing. In Spain, 1991 reform proposals included provisions for a purchaser–provider split which would have led to the development of contracting, but the recommendations were not accepted and no national action has since been taken on them. Turkey is in the process of extending insurance coverage to previously uncovered segments of the population. Recent health care reform proposals include arrangements for purchaser–provider contracting. The proposals provide that insurance premiums (which are to be subsidized by tax revenues), collected from four insurance funds (three existing funds plus a new one to be established for the purpose of extending coverage), are to be transferred to provincial health directorates. The third-party payers will therefore be the provincial health directorates, which will contract with selected hospital providers. The selected hospitals, for their part, are to be autonomously managed. These proposals have not yet been implemented.

## CEE/CIS countries

Health care systems in these countries have historically been based on a variant of the Beveridge model known as the Semasko model. A number of countries in this group are planning or have already begun implementing a partial changeover to a social insurance-based system inspired by the Bismarck model. A few are attempting to implement contracting between third-party payers and providers in the context of their newly established health insurance systems. Many of the issues surrounding the contractual arrangements between insurers and providers have yet to be worked out. Countries which are attempting to implement contracting through a purchaser–provider split include Bulgaria, the Czech Republic, Estonia, Hungary, Romania and the Russian Federation. Further analysis is based on the Russian experience. Most of its contractual developments apply to other CEE/CIS countries (Ensor 1993).

### Russian Federation

According to 1991 Health Insurance Legislation, mandatory health insurance (MHI) is introduced on a highly decentralized basis. Each of 88 regions builds up its own system of MHI. However, the major elements of the system are determined by the federal legislation country-wide. These are: (1) employers make income-related contributions to the Regional Fund of MHI for their employees; (2) local authorities make contributions to this Fund for the non-working population and also finance directly a number of health programmes and providers; (3) the Regional Fund allocates resources to competing insurers based on a weighted capitation formula; (4) insurers (in some regions the branches of the Fund) pay health providers (Sheiman 1994).

According to this pattern of financial flows, four areas of contractual relationships arise: (1) employers and insurers; (2) insurers and the MHI Regional Fund; (3) local government and insurer (or the Fund); and (4) insurers and health providers. In some regions, regional or local health authorities contract directly with medical providers. These contracts are relatively rare, however, because health authorities tend to allocate resources directly. Thus the major purchaser is the insurer or the branch of the Fund.

The types of contracts with providers are similar to those used in the UK. But the emphasis is on different versions of cost per case contracts for hospitals and capitation contracts for polyclinics. Quality control and consumer complaints settlement are also included in the contracts. Providers are committed to perform according to the approved clinical standards and are subject to monitoring by insurers. There are specific provisions on the financial sanctions for the violation of standards, and also on the procedure of quality control. The scope of decentralization of management for hospitals, according to the contract, is not less than for the British medical trusts.

In most of the regions, contracts provide for purchasers to be the major risk bearers. They are committed to pay for each case of in-patient care and in some regions for each service of some polyclinics (e.g. in Moscow). To make this possible, the contracts require each party to withhold reserves to pay for unpredicted expenditures. However there is evidence of growing interest in risk arrangements between insurers and providers. For example, in the Kemerovo region, polyclinics are close to becoming fundholders for all types of outpatient care and specified portions of in-patient care, and thereby share risks with the insurers as final purchasers.

The regional MHI scheme is regulated by the collective contract (agreement) between regional government, the Fund and medical associations. It specifies the general rules of funding and management of the MHI system, including the methods and rates of payment and the basic package of medical benefits. The major provisions of the collective agreement deal with the mechanisms of equalization of funding across insurers and, correspondingly, across subscribers. Thus the system is designed to introduce contractual relationships with providers while sticking to the principles of solidarity and equity.

## CONTRACTING IN A COMPETITIVE ENVIRONMENT

Contracting in many European countries is connected with the concept of market competition in health care – both on the purchasing and provision sides. Contracts are increasingly seen as a coordinating mechanism in a market, ordering competitive interactions.

The introduction of market principles in health care has been at the forefront. 'Market principles' do not refer to the extreme organizational structure of a highly competitive market,[4] but rather to the relatively new development in health care of a planned or internal market. This entails the intentional development of a market by the exercise of state power for the purpose of achieving state policy objectives through selective and limited use of market instruments. Such a market involves decentralization of the planning process, as well as 'the partial replacement of bureaucratic administrative mechanisms with market-derived incentives' (Saltman and von Otter 1992).

The UK was the first country in which contracting was introduced in the context of a competitive framework produced by a planned or internal market. Since then, many issues regarding the introduction of market forces and competition in the NHS have been debated (Maynard 1994). These have included the feasibility of provider competition in systems which have been based on the principles of command-and-control and the evidence of emerging competition.

### Institutional constraints to competition

There are many reasons to doubt whether the new competitive forces can be easily 'switched on' in health systems with deeply-rooted traditions of central planning. The CEE/CIS countries can serve as examples of the institutional constraints to competition. To a lesser degree, these constraints also apply to western European countries with integrated systems.

CEE/CIS countries health systems have established a hierarchy of providers on a geographical basis, with clear specification of the role of each type of medical facility. In the Russian Federation, for example, the hospital sector is regionalized and divided between general and specialized hospitals with relatively little overlapping of their roles (Rowland and Telyukov 1991). They differ in equipment, skills of personnel and the package of services. In rural areas, low quality of communication and transportation makes a substantial number of hospitals into local monopolies, with little potential of competition between them.

In addition, in countries with an emerging contracting model there are economic and regulatory barriers to the entry to the market of new providers: high start-up costs; regulation of the deployment of resources such as new bed capacity and purchasing major equipment; a lack of effective labour markets with inadequate staff resources and low rates of pay; and rigid regulation regarding payment rates to providers. There is also some fragmented evidence of economies of scale in specialized health care provision, which may make big specialized hospitals more cost-effective. Thus dismantling certain monopolies may be inappropriate.

## Evidence of emerging contracting in the Russian Federation

A transition to the health insurance model in the context of market reforms in the economy has brought the first elements of competition in different sectors of health care. The most radical changes have taken place in pharmacies, drugs and medical equipment industries. Lifting price controls, along with privatization and liberalization of foreign trade, has created a market for these goods and services with vigorous competition among producers and dealers.

In primary care, new legislation allows free choice of polyclinic and of physician within the polyclinic. In practice, in most regions, very little is done to ensure patient choice. Physicians in polyclinics have no strong incentives to increase the list of patients; rigid catchment areas still exist for each polyclinic and physician within the polyclinic; open enrolment procedures are not implemented; patients lack information to make rational choices; and there is no alternative to big state-owned polyclinics. Thus consumer choice and competition in primary care is so far only a declaration of intent. Fragmented experiments in a few regions with decentralization of management in polyclinics seem to be promising for encouraging competition, but their scope is negligible.

It is worth mentioning that, contrary to the British version, a fundholding scheme has been designed primarily to encourage polyclinics to take on the major burden of health care rather than to encourage competition among hospitals. In the specific case of Russia, this is also a way to strengthen primary care provision and to reduce excess beds and physicians. Experiments in a few regions have managed to achieve this goal. But lack of competition among primary care providers resulted in evidence of denial of appropriate referrals to hospital (Sheiman 1995). In the hospital sector, the purchasing policy has not been designed to encourage competition either. Contrary to the British reform, regulation in the Russian Federation does not give much scope for price competition. Hospitals are paid according to authorized rates.

A major constraint to competitive tendering is that insurers as purchasers of care are contracting with employers rather than individuals, therefore they do not compete for subscribers through traditional market mechanisms. The prevailing model is that insurers negotiate with the Fund in their catchment area, and base their purchasing decisions on the local health resources rather than patients' preferences. In addition, great underfunding does not leave much space for increasing the package of medical benefits beyond basic services. The only area of substantial competition is the private sector, where hospitals, polyclinics and also private health insurance companies compete for patients and subscribers.

In spite of the lack of competition, there are signs of revitalization of the Russian health sector in terms of increasing efficiency. The growing tendency is to apply performance-related methods of payment to hospitals. Currently, more than 60 per cent of hospitals are paid by insurers on cost per case method (regional versions of the DRG method). This has created strong incentives for increasing occupancy in hospitals and reducing average length of stay. Polyclinics are increasingly paid by capitation (25.3 per cent of polyclinics) and fee-for-service (33.6 per cent) (Sheiman *et al.* 1996). The impact of performance-related methods of payment on the allocative efficiency and the structure of health care is not clear. But the internal efficiency of both hospitals and polyclinics has been positively affected in that they are now interested in increasing their workloads. The shift from input to output-based indicators also has started the process of reducing unnecessary bed capacity, deployment of day-care centres and other alternatives to costly in-patient care.

Quality control has become tougher. For example, in Kemerovo Region around 8 per cent of in-patient cases are currently subject to quality control by insurers with penalties for poor quality (Kemerovo Medical School 1995). Insurers are increasingly acting as champions of patients' interests. They set up special units which are responsible for settlement of patients' claims.

This positive evidence can hardly be attributed to growing competition. Rather, this is the result of the move from input-based allocation of resources to contracting mechanisms based on performance-related methods of payment, new information requirements, decentralization of management and monitoring of performance.

The Russian case suggests that contracting can have positive results in both competitive and non-competitive environments. In the former case, the increase in efficiency and resource allocation has been achieved through competitive mechanisms; in the latter case, through the new instruments of planning, management and payment of providers. The pressure of the market is needed to realize the potential of contracting, but even in the absence of this pressure a great deal can be gained in terms of efficiency and quality. This can serve as a starting point for collecting the information needed for more selective and more competitive contracting. At further stages of reform implementation, it will be easier to ensure 'the exit' of unnecessary capacity and more cost-effective medical interventions.

In summary, the scope and range of competition differs across countries and across sectors of health systems within each country. There are more elements of competition in outpatient care than in the in-patient care sector. Hospitals are increasingly exposed to new forces, driven by health reforms. However, the responsiveness of hospitals to these forces does not now support strong generalization. The feasibility of competition and its impact on efficiency and quality of care are largely dependent on the design of reforms as well as on the economic and political context within which they are implemented.

## CONCLUSIONS

The growing interest in contracting can be attributed to disappointment with traditional command-and-control patterns of resource allocation. In response, contracting has been implemented in both competitive and non-competitive environments. In both cases, contracting can be regarded as a type of planning and management tool. Contracting thus represents a new and different way to do many of the things with which the management of health care has traditionally been preoccupied, and a way that can simultaneously redress certain difficulties of traditional planning methods, while achieving a number of public health objectives.

The actual implementation of the contractual process does not always match theoretical expectations. Contracting confronts many obstacles, of which the most important are the lack of information, difficulty in managing health purchasers and providers, high transaction costs and (in CEE/CIS countries) inadequacy of public funding.

## NOTES

1 The Beveridge group includes the following countries: Denmark, Finland, Iceland, Norway, Sweden and the UK.
2 One of the elements of the UK reforms has been the opportunity offered to NHS hospitals to become autonomous, self-governing trusts.
3 The Bismarck group includes the following countries: Austria, Belgium, France, Germany, Luxembourg, the Netherlands and Switzerland.
4 As has been extensively discussed in the literature (Saltman 1992), the perfectly competitive market model is neither attainable nor desirable for health care.

## REFERENCES

Abel-Smith, B. (1995). The reforms of the British National Health Service. *Eurohealth*, October, 4–5.
Cichon, C. and Normand, C. (1994). Between Beveridge and Bismarck: Options for health care financing in central and eastern Europe. *World Health Forum*, 15(4), 323–8.
Donaldson, C. and Mooney, G. (1991). Needs assessment, priority setting, and contracts for health care: An economic view. *British Medical Journal*, 303, 1529–30.
Ensor, T. (1993). Health system reform in former socialist countries of Europe. *International Journal of Health Planning and Management*, 8, 169–87.
Harrison, A. (1993). *From Hierarchy to Contract*. Newbury: Policy Journals.
Hsiao, W. Abnormal economics in the health sector. *Health Policy*, 32, 125–40.
Kemerovo Medical School (1995). Quality Assurance of Health Care (in Russian). Kemerovo, 40.
Kongstvedt, P. R. (1993). *The Managed Health Care Handbook*. Gaithersburg, MD: Aspen.
Le Grand, J. (1995). Markets and quasi-markets in health care. *Eurohealth*, October, 3.
Maynard, A. (1993). Competition in the UK NHS: Mission impossible? *Health Policy*, 23, 193–204.
Maynard, A. (1994). Can competition enhance efficiency in health care? Lessons from the reform of the UK National Health Service. *Social Science and Medicine*, 39, 1438–45.
Robinson, R. and Le Grand, J. (1995). Contracting and the purchaser–provider split. In R. B. Saltman and C. von Otter (eds), *Implementing Planned Markets in Health Care*. Buckingham: Open University Press.

Rowland, D. and Telyukov, A. V. (1991). Soviet health care from two perspectives. *Health Affairs*, 10, 71–86.

Saltman, R. B. and von Otter, C. (1992). *Planned Markets and Public Competition. Strategic Reform in Northern European Health Systems.* Buckingham: Open University Press.

Sheiman, I. (1994). Forming the system of health insurance in the Russian Federation. *Social Science and Medicine*, 10, 1425–32.

Sheiman, I. (1995). New methods of financing and managing health care in the Russian Federation. *Health Policy*, 32, 167–80.

Sheiman, I., Skerski, V. and Zefkovitch, R. (1996). Methods of payment for outpatient care. *The Journal of Health Administration Education*, 2, 182.

Smee, C. (1995). Self-governing trusts and GP fundholders. The British experience. In R. B. Saltman and C. von Otter (eds), *Implementing Planned Markets in Health Care.* Buckingham: Open University Press.

van de Ven, W. P. M. M., Schut, F. T. and Rutten, F. F. H. (1994). Forming and reforming the market for third-party purchasing of health care. *Social Science and Medicine*, 39, 1405–12.

Whitehead, M. (1990). *The Concepts and Principles of Equity and Health.* Copenhagen: WHO Regional Office for Europe.

# 7

# THE ALLOCATION OF CAPITAL AND HEALTH SECTOR REFORM

Anders Anell and
Howard Barnum

## INTRODUCTION

Rapid technological change and overall growth have characterized developments in the health sector over the past several decades in countries throughout Europe. Associated with this development is the accumulation of capital in hospitals, clinics and other facilities. The shape of today's health system, and the kind of services delivered, is both supported and constrained by the existing capital infrastructure. Similarly, today's investments will determine the structure of health service delivery in the future. With this in mind it becomes important to explore how health sector reform can contribute to optimal policies regarding proper use of existing capital and investments in new technologies.

Whether in the CEE/CIS countries, where the primary objective is to restructure the previous hierarchical system, or in western Europe, where key objectives focus on deregulation, cost containment and control of technology, health sector reforms have a common set of characteristics. In both cases reforms are concerned with achieving greater efficiency in the delivery of services while retaining or increasing equity. And in both cases an important part of the reform agenda also involves dissatisfaction with present allocation of capital and use of technology. A common goal is to develop and strengthen alternatives to hospital care (e.g. primary care and day-care centres), and to make better use of existing resources within the hospital sector. But there are also important differences between countries (e.g. when it comes to institutional characteristics, reform policies and more specific problems).

This chapter discusses the dynamic link between investments, capital and health service delivery, in relation to past patterns of investments and current health sector reforms in Europe. In addressing this link, the chapter limits itself to physical infrastructure and does not include human capital. In many aspects, human capital can be treated conceptually in the same way as physical capital, with training and skills as the key concepts instead of investment and capital. Some non-conceptual details differ, however, and human capital should be treated separately.

## CONCEPTUAL FRAMEWORK

Economists distinguish between capital, investment, and depreciation. Capital refers to the existing *stock* of productive assets. Investment, in contrast, is a *flow* and refers to additions to capital. Depreciation is also a flow, and refers to subtractions from capital as the value of productive assets decreases over time. The distinction between these concepts is important because it identifies investment as a critical dynamic activity adjusting the capital structure of the sector. This adjustment of capital stock usually occurs only slowly over time. Investment exceeding 5–10 per cent of the existing capital stock would be unusual. Thus, it has taken many years to form the present capital infrastructure of hospitals and other facilities in Europe.

The level of technology in health care can be defined on the basis of the ability to understand, influence and prevent diseases (Table 7.1). The framework proposed by Thomas provides a useful

**Table 7.1**    Level of technology/knowledge in health services

| Level | Knowledge | Examples of care |
|---|---|---|
| Non-technologies | Limited; no therapy to counteract or cure | Caring of patients with incurable diseases |
| Halfway technologies | Basic knowledge; ability to counteract unfavourable effects | Organ transplants and treatment of cancer and diabetes |
| High technologies | Full knowledge; ability to cure or prevent | Vaccines |

*Source*: Thomas (1975)

starting point for discussing past patterns of investment and present allocation of capital in the health sector. At the initial level, among the so-called *non-technologies*, health services are characterized by taking care of sick people and nursing them. Knowledge of the pathological process is usually slight. In any event there is not much one can do about the progress of the illness in question. Examples in this area would be caring for patients with incurable diseases (e.g. AIDS) but also minor diseases without effective medical treatment (e.g. common colds and coughs). The next level is that of *halfway technology*. It offers the possibility of at least counteracting the unfavourable effects of diseases or postponing deaths, but there is no complete cure. For that, the available knowledge of the disease mechanisms of illness is not sufficient. Here we find several examples of what are termed high-tech care in ordinary language (e.g. organ transplants and treatment of cancer or diabetes). At the final level, among the *high technologies*, a genuine understanding of the disease mechanism does exist. Therefore, it is possible to cure the illness in question completely, or prevent it. Vaccines for many epidemic and other diseases as well as antibiotics offer good examples.

The framework put forward by Thomas is limited to linkages between the knowledge of disease mechanisms and technologies, and excludes, for example, care of traumas. Further, the definition of 'technology' is rather narrow and specifically based on the understanding of diseases. From an economist's point of view, 'technology' should be defined more broadly and include techniques and methods as well as organizational and administrative arrangements. In spite of these limitations, the framework can be used as a starting point for discussing the dynamic linkages between technology, costs and capital in the health sector.

**A dynamic process**

At any given point in time, health services comprise a mix of different forms of technologies based on the current knowledge and understanding of diseases and traumas. Using the three levels proposed by Thomas, some services are based on non-technologies, others are halfway technologies, and yet other are based on high technologies. The mix of different forms of technologies also has important linkages to expenditures and allocation of capital in the sector. In medieval hospitals, work was almost entirely non-technological in character; sick people were taken in and, if lucky, given nursing care. From those early days, evolution has proceeded as new knowledge became available. In particular, there seems to have been a substantial shift since the Second World War. The modern hospital, thanks to the use of modern medicines and procedures, has been able to treat and cure more, sicker and older patients. As knowledge has been developed further, care has been transferred to outpatient departments or primary care facilities, or disease prevented.

One useful example is supplied by the treatment of patients with tuberculosis and epidemic diseases. In the early twentieth century, there were a large quantity of special hospitals throughout western Europe for the treatment of patients whose illnesses were hard to cure. When someone had an infectious disease or suffered from TB, there was not a great deal that anyone could do, except to provide good nursing and hope that the progress of the disease would be halted. Then came sulpha drugs in the 1930s, which were able to exert a partial influence on the way some infectious diseases developed. The real breakthrough came with penicillin and other antibiotics introduced in the 1940s. The level of technology altered sharply, and in parallel there was a marked change when it came to demands for the allocation of capital. Many infectious diseases now could be effectively treated in outpatient settings, and the demand for beds at special hospitals dropped.

In the example of infectious diseases and antibiotics, total health care expenditures decreased as long-term care at special hospitals could be transferred to cost-effective treatment with drugs in outpatient settings. In most cases, however, technological breakthroughs can be defined as developments from non-technologies to halfway technologies. Burton Weisbrod argued that it is plausible that the cost function associated with a disease, as knowledge grows from non- to halfway and high technology, in most cases is inverted-U shaped (Weisbrod 1991). This means that health care expenditures are highest for the halfway technologies. In addition, new technologies and methods which *per se* entail lower costs may result in a greater volume of services performed due to more widespread use of the technology, and thus an increase in total expenditure.

This framework suggests several important statements about the ideal relation between investments, health technologies, capital and health sector reforms. First, allocation of capital should be guided by the given level of technology and knowledge. When a technological breakthrough allows a certain disease to be treated more cost-effectively in outpatient settings, or prevented through the use of vaccines or other measures, the in-patient facilities where patients formerly were treated should be sealed down or closed, and investments should be made in outpatient settings or preventive measures. Second, investments made in the health sector should promote developments towards high technology. Costly but inefficient halfway technologies should be avoided. This will also send important signals to the medico-industrial complex on how they should allocate their budgets for research and developments. Third, reform policies should make certain that reinvestments in capital are carefully balanced with operating expenditures to make certain that an appropriate stock of capital is maintained over time. Lacking such a balance, two types of problems are likely to appear. If too many resources are invested into new capital stock, too little will be left for operating expenditures. In the worst scenario, there will be no money left to start up the new activity in question. On the other hand, if too little of available resources are invested, capital stock will deteriorate, with negative effects on the quality of services and quite possibly also operating expenditures.

## PAST INVESTMENTS IN HEALTH

Although the hospital industry comprises the preponderance of health sector capital, a great deal of health care is actually received outside hospitals in clinics, medical offices, schools, workplaces and homes. Figure 7.1 depicts a health system pyramid that emphasizes that tertiary hospitals are an end point in a referral system in which basic care is received at the community and home level. Hospitals, by providing the technical support for referral care, can enhance the effectiveness of services available at the lower step of the pyramid. Their overemphasis in the system and misapplication to specific disease problems, however, can unnecessarily increase health costs.

Large tertiary regional hospitals and teaching facilities are usually located in urban areas. These hospitals have specialized staff

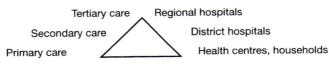

**Figure 7.1**   The health system pyramid – where services are provided

and advanced technical equipment, high staff-to-bed ratios and hundreds of beds. District hospitals are dispersed more widely and have fewer specialists which may be limited to internal medicine, paediatrics, obstetrics and general surgery. The district hospital, in concept, is the first referral from primary care providers. Community capital is much more modest in scale, consisting of outreach capacity, neighbourhood clinics, pharmacies and school or workplace health units. Different curative, preventive and public health functions may be performed at all levels of the system. Even though treatment is the main function of hospitals, a lot of treatment occurs in the household. Most public health activities are carried out in the community, but central specialized laboratories are an essential part of epidemiological surveillance, and educational services need national level organization and media programmes as well as specific community programmes.

The greater concentration of capital in the hospital industry is partly explained by more capital intensive production in comparison with primary care services. But in many countries, the past pattern of investments across the health sector concentrated on halfway technologies and tertiary facilities. Regional specialized hospitals, teaching facilities and new technology have absorbed major parts of available investment funds. By the late nineteenth century, the hospital had already become the symbol of modern medicine, and has since then attracted most investments in health. According to Victor Fuchs there has been a strong 'technological imperative' in the health sector, meaning that at least during the past several decades there has been a tendency to adopt new technologies just because they are new (Fuchs 1968). The quality of care during the same period has certainly improved, but at high costs.

In particular, significant investments, guided by technological progress, were made after the Second World War. The 1950s to 1960s saw the development of vaccines, anti-hypertensive drugs, blood-replacement substances, and analgesic, anaesthetic and antispasmodic drugs. The development of new drugs was also a prerequisite for the introduction of modern surgery and intensive care in the 1960s. At the same time, diagnostic services such as radiology made rapid progress. The 1970s to 1980s witnessed further improvements in all branches of hospital services. Even in countries where the increase in the level of technology has not been as rapid, building programmes have emphasized the accumulation of hospital beds at all levels, often without a clearly determined relation to improved health status.

It is difficult to quantify the extent of capital accumulation in health. Measures of the value of capital are not readily available across countries. Some information on physical measures of buildings, the number of beds and equipment of specific types, is available which can serve as a proxy for a direct measure of the value of capital. Another indicator of the allocation of capital comes by implication from the functional distribution of operating expenditures.

The physical measures and the distribution of operating expenditures give only an approximate indication of capital allocation that makes cross-country comparisons and generalizations difficult. Three critical reasons for this are differences in definitions and forms of care across countries, the difficulty in measuring quality and differences in the level of technology in use. For example, a common proxy for hospital capital is the number of beds, but in one country the number of beds may aggregate long-term and acute beds while in another the classifications are separate. A bed in a small, understaffed and under-equipped rural hospital is also not comparable to a bed in a large, well-equipped facility with skilled staff. Further, it would be hard to compare data directly as regards, for example, length of stay between central, eastern and western Europe, since the provision of health services in part is based on different levels of technology. These caveats notwithstanding, the existing literature contains ample qualitative observations that can temper and enhance the existing data and make useful generalizations possible. The pattern that emerges from this literature indicates both some similarities and some important differences between western Europe and the former socialist economies of central and eastern Europe.

## Central and eastern Europe

Prior to reform policies, the majority of health sector resources in central and eastern Europe were controlled by the ministries of health (MOH). Throughout the region, well over 90 per cent of hospitals and polyclinics were MOH facilities with the remainder controlled by enterprises and other ministries. Local control of either investment or operating expenditures was limited. Only a small number of hospitals, clinics and dental units were 'self accounting' or administered as cooperatives with autonomous management. Thus, the central government controlled the vast majority of medical institutions and managed the flow of inputs and the accumulation of real resources in the sector. The structure of the system was determined by service norms such as beds per thousand, medical doctors per thousand or number of hospitals and polyclinics. These norms also formed the basis on which performance was judged, and the basis for investment planning and budgeting. The result was, and remains, high hospital capacity in terms of number of beds and doctors.

## Hospitals

Throughout central and eastern Europe the number of beds grew rapidly through the 1980s. Since 1989 there have been slight reductions in the number of beds per capita as countries re-examine their previous policies. Still, the bed ratio remained in the vicinity of 100–130 per 10,000 population for most of the CIS countries in 1993. This is considerably higher than many western European countries. The number of physicians also grew throughout the same period (most of them allocated to the hospital sector) and remains high withy 48 per 10,000 population in Estonia, 33 in Kyrgyzstan and 45 in the Russian Federation (1993). In central Europe, beds and physicians per capita are lower than in the CIS. In Hungary there are 101 beds per 10,000 (in 1989), in Poland 57 and in Romania 89. Physician ratios are also lower in eastern Europe with 29 per 10,000 in Hungary, 21 in Poland and 18 in Romania (1989).

Some indication of inefficiency is given by the relatively high lengths of stay but only moderate occupancy rates. Occupancy rates average 60–85 per cent, with higher rates in central tertiary hospitals and district secondary hospitals and considerably lower rates in rural hospitals. In Estonia, the average length of stay in 1989 was 17.3 days, in Hungary 9.9 (1989), in Kyrgyzstan 15.6 (1994), Poland 12.6 (1989) and the Russian Federation 16.2 (1991). This is relatively long in comparison with practices in acute hospitals in western Europe. Further, there is a high rate of use of in-patient care. In the Russian Federation the 1989 average was 4.0 in-patient days per capita. This compares to 2.7 days for the median OECD country.

The long length of stay and high rate of use of in-patient care suggests that large gains in efficiency could be obtained by reducing length of stay and examining current guidelines for the use of in-patient services. It should however be noted that the level of technology in use is not directly comparable between central, eastern and western Europe. Thus, it is not possible to use data from hospitals in western Europe as 'benchmarks' for the whole European region. Statements of possible short-term gains in efficiency should in practice be made with great care. Investment in technology in central and eastern Europe has not followed the same pattern as in the western region. High-cost equipment, specialized surgical facilities and advanced pharmacology is not as widely available. This also means that the accumulation of technology has not been as critical a factor in driving health sector costs as it has been in western European countries. Access to the limited number of centres with high-cost new technology that do exist in central and eastern Europe is rationed either by connections or income.

Throughout the CIS there are many specialized hospitals that complement services of the acute hospitals. In Russia, there are over 1000 specialized hospitals, including 160 tuberculosis, 288 psychiatric, and 305 obstetric hospitals. In most OECD countries there has been a reduction in the use of specialized beds, for example for tuberculosis or mental health, over the last several decades. In parallel, the knowledge vested in different forms of specialized hospital has been integrated into the acute general hospital. The difference between the two regions again reflects the fact that health services are based on different levels of technology. Further, the disease panoramas are not the same, partly because of different income levels and standards of living.

*Primary care and public health*

Although low efficiency and impaired quality are problems, a strength of the public funding of services under the communist system was the wide coverage of basic clinic services. For example, in the Russian Federation, although there are important geographical variations, by 1991 with over 21,000 polyclinics and other outpatient institutions there was generally a wide geographic distribution of clinics that provided a valuable potential infrastructure shell for the delivery of primary health programmes. In spite of the wide accessibility of clinics, preventive programmes and outreach activities are not well developed. International analysts have consistently identified substantial under-investment in public health and service weaknesses in the existing programmes.

Examination of expenditures by function reinforces the judgement that the capital invested in hospital services attracts most operating expenditures. In the Russian Federation in 1989, hospitals received 71 per cent of operating expenditures, ambulatory clinics and emergency care received 14 per cent, and public health

3 per cent, with the remaining 12 per cent going to a variety of other functions such as education and research. In Hungary and Poland the functional distribution of expenditures was similar. Within the hospital sub-sector, tertiary hospitals absorb the greatest part of expenditures, leaving modest budgets for first-level referral facilities.

## Western Europe

The mode of financing and organization of health care services is traditionally more pluralistic among countries in western Europe compared to eastern Europe. In the Nordic countries and in the UK most facilities, and almost all hospitals, have long since been owned and managed by public authorities. These public authorities have controlled the flow of investments and the accumulation of capital in the sector. In countries such as France, Germany and the Netherlands there is a split between the responsibilities of financing and providing health services. Many medical institutions, including hospitals, are private not-for-profit, but they have also been subject to a rigid regulatory framework in investment decisions. Although the modes of financing and organization in western Europe differ, the perceived problems with regard to present capital infrastructure, and more specifically efforts to scale down and restructure the hospital sector, are quite similar.

### Hospitals

As in eastern Europe, the number of hospital beds per capita in western Europe grew rapidly during the 1960s and 1970s. The turning point with respect to the total number of acute beds available came, however, in the mid- to late 1970s. Since then, the total number of beds and the number of acute beds has been reduced in most countries, although the number of beds in nursing homes has increased in many places. In parallel to this development, the volume of services provided increased steadily, and physicians per capita increased to around 25 to 35 per 10,000 population by the year 1990. Clear exceptions from this rough average are Ireland, Italy and the UK with about 15 physicians per 10,000 (OECD 1995).

Due to differences in definitions and the role of different medical institutions, it is difficult to compare measures such as occupancy rates and length of stay between countries. According to OECD statistics, occupancy rates average 60 to 85 per cent among countries in western Europe. The same variations can probably be found within each country, if rates at different types of institutions and in urban or rural settings are compared. Average length of stay is well below ten days in most western European countries for acute hospitals. This is substantially less than in central and eastern Europe. As has already been mentioned, the difference in part reflects the fact that health services in the two regions are based on different levels of technology. In western Europe, for example, the recent and widespread use of laporoscopic surgery has substantially decreased the average length of stay. Another explanation behind differences is that hospitals in central and eastern Europe also serve a social function, in part provided by other facilities such as nursing homes in western Europe. Yet another possible explanation is that hospitals in western Europe on average are more efficient in the provision of services.

Increasing health care costs are a problem shared by several countries in western Europe. The difficult financial situation together with technological developments has led to a common effort to try to reduce the total number of acute beds. In most western European countries, the number of beds have indeed been reduced during the 1980s, and several small acute hospitals have been forced to close or made to serve more limited health needs (Abel-Smith and Mossialos 1994). Other largely common problems in western Europe are connected with regional variations and geographical location of facilities. In many cases, the building of hospitals was the result of local initiatives and took place at a time when patterns of communication and the level of technology were quite different.

On closer inspection, there are differences in the current structures of the hospital sector as well as in the way those structures emerged. The Nordic countries, in comparison with Germany or the Netherlands for example, have a more planned structure, with area responsibility and sub-categorizations of hospitals. Another difference is in the number of acute hospitals in relation to the size of the population. In the early 1990s, Norway had 16 acute hospitals per million population. This was more than in the other Nordic countries (i.e. Denmark, Finland and Sweden), or in the UK, with 8–13 acute hospitals per million population, but less than in Germany with about 20 acute hospitals per million population (Anell and Claesson 1995). The average size of hospitals is inversely related to the total number. In Sweden and the UK hospitals are typically large, whereas German hospitals are much smaller in size. It should be noted, however, that direct comparisons are difficult to make. At best, statistical data from various countries may yield a rough idea of the differences.

Differences in the accumulation of capital in the hospital sector may be partly explained by different geographical conditions. Such a factor explains why Norway, with more difficult transportation routes, has more hospitals in relation to its population than does Sweden. Different institutional characteristics may play a part too. It is well recognized that the comparably long length of stay in German hospitals may be attributed in part to the fact that hospitals traditionally have been paid per diem, and that German hospitals prior to 1992 were not allowed to provide outpatient care. Comparing Nordic countries with the UK, public authorities in the Nordic countries go back a long time and by tradition hold powerful positions in the provision of health care services. This is in contrast to the British NHS, which was not formed until 1948. At that time the NHS took over some 3000 hospitals organized according to two entirely different systems: public and private not-for-profit institutions. Even today, differences with respect to hospital-care structure in the UK may partly be accounted for by referring to conditions that existed before the creation of the NHS.

Examination of expenditures by function reveals that the capital invested in the hospital sector attracts a large part of the total expenditures for health services. According to OECD statistics about 40–65 per cent of total expenditure on health relates to inpatient care.

## SOME CURRENT ISSUES

A common dilemma throughout Europe is that the dynamic link between investments and future expenditures for health services is usually not carefully addressed. The forces that have impelled the accumulation of capital differ in the private and public sectors. In many countries where the sector has been centrally directed and predominantly publicly managed, investment in new capital has been driven by central planning, and a budgeting process determined by population and service capacity norms. Public budgeting does not, however, always reflect the real cost of investments, which may be deflected to highly visible, politically attractive investments in large hospitals. Public investment may also flow into hospitals and equipment that duplicate facilities for different population or work groups in the same urban area. In the CEE/CIS countries, investment decisions under central planning have been too far removed from local environments to reflect local community needs accurately. With reforms, the separation of financing and provision of care will change the locus of investment control, and new problems in coordinating the structure of capital stock and investment policy are likely to arise.

In the private sector, financial incentives determine the size and type of investment. At least in principle, investment flows into technologies and infrastructure that provide the greatest profits. This response to market forces ideally results in an efficient use of resources. There are, however, important reasons that this principle is not always realized in capital investment in health. Market failures may restrict the efficient functioning of the market, and encourage a misallocation of capital that favours large hospitals over smaller-scale capital and public health capacity, as well as the indiscriminate accumulation of new technology. Information failures may make it difficult for payers of health services to make appropriate assessments and investment choices. Further, equity is also affected if one relies solely on the market to determine the allocation of capital. Public sector regulation, mandating and even provision of services may be required to generate adequate services in low-income or rural areas. Due to these market failures, governments typically regulate the private health sector, seeking to influence the size and type of investment.

The dynamics of technological change make it difficult to plan investment. Direct interventions, based on detailed sector planning and regulation of investment decisions, have generally not proven successful. The form of provider payment system provides incentives for both public and private investment decisions that can affect the flow of investments in a more indirect way (Weisbrod 1991). Fee-for-service, especially in combination with passive payers and freedom of choice for consumers, encourages supplier-induced demand, cost-escalating expansion of specialist services and investment in new technology. On the other hand, experience with line item budgeting in the public sector, especially when it is applied with service norms, demonstrates that it can also lead to over-investment in hospital beds and equipment. In many places ongoing health sector reforms are changing the payment system to alter these adverse incentives. Greater efficiency in the use of capital is being encouraged by various formulations of case-based fixed fees, capitation systems and global budgets.

In many countries, ongoing reforms will result in more self-administered providers. Changing the ownership and management of capital is an essential part of reforms in the CEE/CIS countries. The objective is to improve the incentives to provide efficient services. Depending on the structure of reform the change may involve transferring the ownership of capital to the private sector. Or, short of privatization, greater managerial autonomy may be achieved through contracts for the management of publicly owned facilities. In some systems, the ownership status may be distinguished by level and type of care. Hospitals may be publicly owned but autonomously managed and financed through global budgets or contracts. These future providers will be faced with less detailed regulations, but more demands with respect to efficient use of resources and the implementation of cost-effective strategies for treatment and diagnosis. This will also encourage more careful planning of the linkages between investment, capital, depreciation and operating expenditures, starting from the local level.

Throughout Europe there is a clear need to change the composition of capital. The number and type of hospital beds is usually a central and high political issue. In western Europe there has been a reduction in the number of beds from 1980 to the present. Some small hospitals and specialized facilities have been forced to close. However, the process is slow, especially when it comes to recent attempts to close or modify larger hospitals. The process is also characterized by uncertainty. Proposals to close down or scale down a hospital often mobilize local resistance. This seems to be the case irrespective of geographical prerequisites and available alternatives (i.e. resistance is as strong in the inner city of London as in rural Sweden). Second, decision makers are uncertain about the proper alternatives and how to structure the hospital sector. In part this uncertainty stems from limited knowledge about the extent to which hospital services based on modern techniques and methods are characterized by economies of scope and scale.

In the CIS the same changes as in western Europe (i.e. scaling down and integration of hospital capacity) to fewer units seem to have started in the 1990s. There has been a reduction in the number of beds from 1990 to the present. In many cases, the hospital closures and the reduction of the number of beds in existing hospitals have been modest because of political and practical difficulties in transferring resources from one use to another. Closing some specialized facilities and integrating their functions into general facilities is also an important current reform measure in other parts of central and eastern Europe. For example, in Estonia the functions of selected obstetric hospitals are being merged with nearby general hospitals. The result is to improve obstetric services by using the superior diagnostic, surgical and laboratory capacity of the general hospital. In Kyrgyzstan, adoption of short-term chemotherapy and outpatient treatment for tuberculosis (TB) will make it possible to reduce in-patient TB beds, and close or change the use of specialized facilities currently assigned for TB.

The effectiveness of hospital services in many CEE/CIS countries is adversely influenced by the poor quality of capital stock. Many of the small district hospitals in the CIS have no more than four or five square metres per bed. Some of the smallest hospitals also have low occupancy rates and a lack of radiology services, adequate heating or water. A 1989 survey of the state of health facilities found that 20 per cent of Russian hospitals did not have piped hot water, 3 per cent did not have piped cold water, and 17 per cent lacked adequate sanitation facilities. The survey also found that every seventh building, among hospitals and polyclinics, needed basic reconstruction. A similar inventory of facilities for 1988 found substantial under-investment in maintenance of polyclinics and hospitals with 19 per cent of polyclinics and 23 per cent of hospitals rated as either 'disastrous' or requiring full reconstruction (Table 7.2).

Due to problems of substandard care, reductions in the number and use of hospitals is an essential part of reforms in the CIS. Where facilities are not closed, or their use changed to nursing homes or

**Table 7.2**  Condition of hospitals and polyclinics in the Russian Federation, 1998 (per cent)

| Condition | Hospitals | Polyclinics |
| --- | --- | --- |
| Disastrous | 9 | 5 |
| Requires construction | 14 | 14 |
| Requires repair | 32 | 30 |
| Requires slight repair | 30 | 34 |
| Good condition | 15 | 17 |
| Buildings without: | | |
| • Sewer connection | 24 | 15 |
| • Central heating | 19 | 12 |
| • Bath/shower | 45 | 52 |
| • Electricity | 1 | 1 |

*Source*: USSR (1990)

other functions, they can be upgraded and used more effectively in the referral system.

It can be noted that governments and other purchasers of health services have experienced problems in their efforts to control investments in new technologies. New investments, at least for the most part, seem to be driven by the present system and incentives, with the result that additional resources are allocated to areas and forms of care which already have a large stock of capital. To break this pattern of past investments, cost-effectiveness of services has become an important principle of health sector reform. Many analyses have demonstrated the cost-effectiveness of primary health care, prevention and public health services in comparison with tertiary hospital services. The cost-effectiveness of additional prevention programmes is not always better than that of treatment, however, and this is especially true for a well-developed country which normally already devotes a lot of resources to preventive measures. Thus, the question of cost-effectiveness does not inevitably lead away from investment in hospitals but can support investment in hospital quality and availability as part of the need for a balanced distribution of resources across sector functions.

## CONCLUSIONS

Throughout the European region, the predominant investment emphasis in the health sector over the last several decades has been on halfway technologies in hospitals and curative care. Both in western Europe and in central and eastern Europe this has led to a rapid accumulation of beds. In western Europe, with higher income and more resources allocated to the health sector, the accumulation of beds has been accompanied and driven by rapid technological change, resulting in more intense care and increasing costs. In central and eastern Europe, the accumulation of beds has been accompanied by slower technological change and slower cost increases, but also less intense care, underfunding of health, inadequate maintenance of facilities and lower quality of services.

In contrast to the rapid development in new health technologies, adjustment of capital stock occurs only slowly over time. Once built, hospitals, or other health care facilities, are politically difficult to close. In a very real policy sense, the pattern of capital infrastructure in the health sector is subject to inertia. This inertia poses a core problem when it comes to securing efficient use of resources in the health sector. In a stable environment, the problem of inertia would be of minor importance. The health care sector is, however, associated with rapid developments as regards new possibilities for treatment and diagnosis, and this development in turn is linked to the optimal allocation of capital. Thus, health sector reform in relation to the allocation of capital should introduce incentives for payers and providers of services that result in optimal decisions as regards cost-effective investment in new technology and stimulate continuous change and critical revision when it comes to the existing allocation of capital. It remains to be seen if current health sector reforms, with deregulation of providers, new forms of payment for services and introduction of competition, will be successful in creating such decisions and stimulating innovative structural change among providers.

## REFERENCES

Abel-Smith, B. and Mossialos, E. (1994). Cost containment and health care reform: A study of the European Union. *Health Policy*, 28, 89–132.

Anell, A. and Claesson, R. (1995). *Svenska Sjukhus förr och Nu – Ekonomiska Aspekter på Struktur, Politik och Framtida förutsättningar.* Lund: Swedish Institute for Health Economics.

Fuchs, V. R. (1968). The growing demand for medical care. *New England Journal of Medicine*, 279, 190–5.

OECD (1995). *Health Data 95.* Paris: Organisation for Economic Co-operation and Development.

Thomas, L. (1975). *The Lives of a Cell.* New York: Bantam Books.

USSR (1990). *Health Protection in the USSR: 1989 Yearbook of Health Statistics.* Moscow: Goskomstat.

Weisbrod, B. A. (1991). The health care quadrilemma. An essay on technological change, insurance, quality of care, and cost containment. *Journal of Economic Perspectives*, 29, 523–52.

# 8

# PERFORMANCE-TIED PAYMENT SYSTEMS FOR PHYSICIANS[1]

## Lise Rochaix

The role and performance of the primary health care sector are currently being reviewed in a number of European countries. Among other reasons such as quality or access there is a belief that primary care physicians are better placed to curb unnecessary use of services. While some payment systems may meet this cost-containment objective, they may have also perverse effects on quality or access. It is therefore essential to analyse the impact of different payment systems on the performance of physicians. Increasingly, financial incentives have been introduced in payment systems. They may either be negative (in which case they are controls) or positive, in the form of performance rewards.

This general move towards performance-related payment systems constitutes the focus of this chapter. First, the chapter examines the features of this particular segment of the labour market (i.e. that of physicians). Next, the empirical evidence on the impact of different payment systems is reviewed. This is followed by a critical evaluation of current payment systems and a discussion on performance-related payment systems. Finally, the chapter outlines the main policy implications resulting from the analysis.

### WHY ARE PHYSICIANS' PAYMENT SYSTEMS DIFFERENT?

According to standard labour economics analysis (Elliott 1991) of payment systems, firms manipulate the level and structure of wages to induce workers to supply the desired quantity and quality of labour. Two main modes of payment can be defined. The simplest and most traditional form of payment system is time rates. Such systems are appropriate where each hour of labour supplied is equally productive and the firm is confident that the number of hours contracted for will be delivered. The alternative to time rates is payment by results (which directly relates pay to output). In the latter case, firms set a uniform price for each piece of output produced and pay the worker according to the number of pieces produced.

When applied to the health care field, the different types of payments to providers are one, or a mix, of the two basic systems: piece rates (fee-for-service) and time rates (salary-based payment). Yet, due to a number of special features of the market for physicians' services, neither of these systems is efficient. One of the most important features is the uncertainty and related *information asymmetry* which prevails between the physician and the patient. Arrow defined information asymmetry in terms of a differential in uncertainty between the physician and his patient with respect to the medical efficacy of the treatment (Arrow 1963).

Consequently, since patients' arbitrage cannot be relied upon for most health care services, in particular physicians' services, the definition of payment systems is likely to be the result of a three-way negotiation involving the physician, the patient and the state or the third-party payer for social insurance-based health care systems. The complex interaction between these three actors is best analysed through the 'Principal–Agent' paradigm.[2] Under this economic model, a principal delegates authority to an agent who then takes an action for which he or she receives compensation.

When applied to the health care field, at least two agency relationships can be defined: (1) the main (and historic) one, between the physician and the patient; and (2) between the physician and the regulator (be it the state or the insurance fund). In the first case *perfect agency* would imply that the physician recommends what the patient would have chosen, had he or she possessed the same medical information. Under the second and more recent agency relationship, the physician, as agent of the regulator, is entrusted with the optimal allocation of scarce resources to the community.

Imperfections in both agency relationships will mainly arise because physicians also pursue their own objectives.[3] A large number of economic studies of the market for physician services have centred around the Supply Induced Demand (SID) hypothesis, according to which physicians, as agents of their patients, can influence if not create demand for their own services. A corollary of SID is the 'target income hypothesis' according to which physicians use the discretionary power they derive from this information asymmetry to maintain a certain 'target' income level (Evans 1974). More importantly, even if physicians did not pursue their own interests in parallel to those of patients, conflicts would still arise between these two agencies inasmuch as the patient's individual interests often differ from community's interests.

The analysis in terms of a dual agency relationship underlines the interdependence between supply and demand in health care and its source – information asymmetry. Its main contribution, however, is to show that depending upon both the prevailing physician payment system and the patient's reimbursement system, collusive behaviour may arise, either between physician and patient or between physician and regulator. Thus, moral hazard on the physician's side (i.e. demand inducement) may be strengthened by the patient's moral hazard. This shows the importance of paying particular attention, in the analysis of payment systems, to the environment (*largo sensu*) in which physicians practice.

## EVIDENCE ON THE IMPACT OF PAYMENT SYSTEMS

The purpose of this section is to review selectively the literature on the advantages and disadvantages of different payment systems. For this purpose, a distinction is established between retrospective and prospective payment systems. In fact, the difference between capitation and fee-for-service is best understood with a reference to the notion of time – the payment of the resource (fee-for-service) is a retrospective type of payment, while the payment of the responsibility (capitation) is a prospective payment over the period covered by the agreement. Here, salary-based systems will be grouped with capitation inasmuch as total physician remuneration is known in advance and the incentives facing physicians are related.

For the purpose of evaluation, these two types of payment systems are compared with respect to:

- *micro-efficiency* which mainly refers to the individual agency relationship between the physician and his or her patient. It includes consumption or allocative efficiency (whether patients' preferences are duly considered in the allocation of care) and

productive efficiency (the allocation of given factors among the production of care);
- *macro-efficiency* which mainly refers to the physician–third-party payer agency relationship. Macro-efficiency is commonly identified with cost containment (OECD 1994) i.e. health spending should be restricted to predefined limits such as constant share of GDP; the rate of expenditure should therefore be adjusted to these limits.[4]

Due consideration will also be given to other desirable attributes of a payment system such as comprehensiveness of services, global health enhancing, professional freedom and case implementation.

### Retrospective payment systems

The advantages of fee-for-service are often phrased by providers themselves in terms of enhanced freedom and greater continuity of care. The latter issue has been documented, for instance, by Hicks who compared the impact of a random assignment of 18 paediatric residents to either fee-for-service payment or salary (Hicks *et al.* 1987). Results showed that fee-for-service physicians had more visits per patient enrolled with them (+22 per cent) than salaried doctors. In terms of continuity of care, results from another study (Kristiansen and Mooney 1993) indicate that patients were more likely to be seen by their regular doctor if he or she was under fee-for-service. For home visits, fee-for-service GPs were twice as likely to undertake a home visit and four times more likely to follow up patients at home than in the surgery.

The disadvantages are that fee-for-service payments are open-ended systems which give a blank cheque to providers, who can induce demand for their own services if they so wish. While it is beyond the scope of this chapter to review the evidence on SID (Rochaix 1991), it should be noted that most empirical tests, centred on medical density as the main explanatory variable, have suffered from methodological flaws which partly explain the ambiguous if not contradictory nature of their findings.

An alternative approach (Phelps 1986) uses natural experiments which are frequently being conducted in today's 'cost-conscious' health insurance market. Rice for instance looked into the impact of changing Medicare reimbursement rates on physician-induced demand (Rice 1983). The results showed that declining reimbursement rates were associated with an increase in the provision of more intensive services (both in terms of the quantity of services and their level of complexity): a 10 per cent decline in physician reimbursement for medical services, for example, would result in a 6 per cent increase in the intensity of medical services provided. Conversely, increasing reimbursement rates resulted in less intensive services. These findings applied for surgical services and laboratory tests, but not for medical follow-up visits or radiology services. The different elasticities derived for these classes of procedures suggest that the extent of physicians' discretionary power may vary from one activity to the other.

Another study (Labelle *et al.* 1990) provided evidence from Ontario on physicians' utilization responses to fee schedule revisions and found that although utilization can respond to fee changes, as evidenced in 13 of the 28 selected procedures, the response is neither inevitable nor widespread. These results are corroborated and extended in an econometric investigation of physician labour supply on Quebec GPs. The main results indicate that a tariff freeze leads to an increase in both the number and the complexity of procedures for all GPs, irrespective of their level of income (Rochaix 1991). The expenditure caps experiment (in the form of an individual quarterly GP's gross income ceiling implemented in 1976 and removed on two occasions over the study period) indicates that such a joint price and quantity regulation succeeds in reducing overall activity rates, although also affecting the actual mix of procedures used when the ceiling is reached. These results indicate that physicians have discretionary power and, in particular, they have the ability to hedge against fee cuts by increasing the quantity and altering the mix of services provided, thereby maintaining their target income. Concerning this latter point, a recent cross-sectional study of the determinants of physicians' target income (Rizzo and Blumenthal 1995) shows that targets are on average 17 per cent above actual income for the representative group of young physicians (below 40). Income targets were also found to respond directly to actual income, but this relationship is rather inelastic: a 10 per cent decline in actual income would only lead to a 3 per cent reduction of the target. This finding has important policy implications: any 'fee restraint will drive a wedge between actual and target income, giving physicians financial incentives to engage in volume offset[5] behaviour so as to get closer to their targets'.

The review of the evidence indicates that physicians' discretionary power is neither myth nor reality. It is a potential power that will be used if certain conditions prevail, relating to physicians' mode of remuneration, the level of physician supply, the patients' reimbursement system or other institutional variables. In particular, it is more likely when there is greater uncertainty about medical efficacy.

Furthermore, beyond sheer quantity inducement is also the issue of *fee creep*. Since it is very difficult to control the adequacy of the fee claimed in relation to the service performed by the physician, an inadequate use of the fee schedule may arise. Indeed, the negotiator is usually in a situation of imperfect information with respect to the true costs incurred by providers of care. Consequently, the negotiation process is likely to lead to a biased structure of fees, some procedures becoming more lucrative than others. Keeler and Brodie provide a good example of price distortions between procedures in obstetric decisions (Keeler and Brodie 1993). They compared the use of vaginal delivery versus caesarean section and indicated that the greater physician fee for caesarean section (an additional $500) is likely to be a significant factor in the choice between both types of treatment.

Another negative effect of fee-for-service is that physicians do not delegate to other health care providers (nurses in particular) as readily as if they were salaried or under capitation (Conseil médical du Quebec 1995).

**Prospective payment systems**

Prospective payment systems tend to give physicians incentives to control expenditures and develop more cost-effective styles of practice. 'Per capita payments also sever the link between amount of service provided and financial reward and hence involve minimal distortion of purely professional medical judgement' (Donaldson and Gerard 1989).

Early American research consistently pointed to lower per patient expenditures among recipients of prepaid care than among comparable patients under fee-for-service health care systems. Early findings (Luft 1978) are corroborated by more recent evidence from the Medical Outcomes Study[6] (Greenfield *et al.* 1992). However, there are a number of methodological flaws associated with comparing the impact of financial incentives on physician behaviour in different health plans (Hellinger 1996). In Europe, Kristiansen *et al.* studied the impact on the use of laboratory services of different payment systems and found that the total number of tests per encounter was slightly lower among salaried

GPs than among fee-for-service GPs (Kristiansen and Mooney 1993).

Yet, prospective payments may encourage providers to reduce the value of the treatment for which they receive a unit of payment by curtailing consultation time, leisure on the job, by excessive prescribing or by over-referral to hospitals. Also, prospective payments motivate providers to select out the sicker patients who will prove unprofitable (Ellis and McGuire 1990).

The earliest evidence, sometimes of a rather informal nature, came from the UK where it appeared that GPs lacked motivation under a capitation system, mainly defined on a geographical basis. Evidence also came from American experience with HMOs (Health Maintenance Organizations). Stearns analysed the change within an HMO from a fee-for-service-based system for primary care physicians to a capitation payment, with no parallel system change for specialists (albeit a significant reduction in the level of fees: 50 per cent) (Stearns *et al.* 1992). Beyond a reduction in hospitalization rates, the authors found that the number of referrals to specialists within the group increased significantly as a result of the change.

A more general question is to determine whether or not the successes obtained in cost containment under prospective payment systems can be replicated in the future. Indeed, it is sometimes argued that selection bias, under which prepaid care tends to attract patients in better health, still remains a possible explanation for the lower hospital utilization rates that were found in earlier studies. A recent analysis (Hutchinson *et al.* 1994) tried to control adequately for patient population comparability and analysed the impact of a change from fee-for-service to capitation payment on hospital utilization in Ontario over a long study period (three years before and as much after the change). The authors found that hospital utilization rates did not differ markedly between the two groups.

If such were the case, this would raise the issue of replication. Safran *et al.* (1994) argue that little evidence exists to show that the successes of prepaid care in relatively healthy populations can be replicated among sicker patients. They have developed a comprehensive analysis of the quality of primary care in fee-for-service (FFS) versus prepaid systems and the study design[7] is centred around chronic patients. The authors looked at five dimensions of care: (1) accessibility, either financial (1a) or organizational (1b); (2) continuity; (3) comprehensiveness; (4) coordination; and (5) accountability, either interpersonal (5a) or technical (5b).

To assess the effect of payment systems on each primary care dimension, the authors performed seven multivariate regression analyses, each with one of the primary care dimensions as the dependent variable. Independent variables included patient, physician and system characteristics. Results indicated that:

1a Patients with prepaid care reported better financial access than those with FFS coverage; indeed, payment system was the most important predictor of financial access and accounted for more than three-quarters of the variance explained by the model;
1b Organizational access (the logistics of obtaining care) was lower for prepaid care;
2 Payment system was the most important predictor of patient–clinician continuity, with FFS system scoring highest;
3 Prepaid care (particularly HMOs) scored lower than FFS on comprehensiveness of care but differences were not statistically significant;
4 Coordination of care was highest in prepaid care (particularly in HMOs);
5 No statistically significant differences were found on the two notions of accountability.

The results point to the difficulties of successfully incorporating each of seven elements of primary care into one payment system. 'In prepaid systems, we find increased financial access and improved coordination of care. However, these elements are countered by reduced patient–physician continuity and comprehensiveness of care and, in many cases, by diminished organisational access and interpersonal treatment that is less satisfactory to patients' (Safran *et al.* 1994).

In conclusion, on the relative merits of prepaid versus retrospective payment systems, neither system appears to be ideal. While fee-for-service payment systems lead to macro-inefficiency, prospective payment systems do not fare well on micro-efficiency (in particular, on allocative efficiency). A solution should logically be found in mixed prospective and retrospective systems of payments which will attempt to bring in incentives for performance and cost control. Indeed, as noted in the latest OECD report on health care reforms, 'It is hoped that mixed systems of payment will combine increased productivity with greater concern about consumer satisfaction and adequate control on costs' (OECD 1994). Against this theoretical background, it is now useful to turn to the evaluation of current payment systems.

## EVALUATING CURRENT PAYMENT SYSTEMS

When trying to set up a typology of payment systems which would encompass the environment in which physicians practice, it is useful to ask three questions: (1) what is paid for? (2) who determines the level of remuneration? and (3) who pays? (Contandriopoulos *et al.* 1990).

### What is paid for?

Three different payment systems can be defined:

- Remuneration of the actual resource i.e. the time spent by the physician. In salary-based systems the physician works within a predefined schedule and combines different activities (e.g. medical, administrative, teaching, research). Such systems often prevail in hospitals or in local health care centres. In some cases private practice under fee-for-service supplements physicians' salaries, but it is often restricted in time.
- Remuneration of the services that the resource (physician time) produces. Fee-for-service systems are organized around fee schedules which classify physicians' activity with varying degrees of precision.
- Remuneration of the responsibility for the health of the population covered for a certain period of time (capitation).

### Who determines the level of remuneration?

There are three different cases:

- Free-fee fixing by the physician him/herself. At present, this system is mainly applied in the US and to a limited number of physicians of *Secteur II*[8] in France.
- Negotiation between physicians' representatives and the third-party payer. Fee schedules are the result of a negotiation process between representatives of the medical profession and the third-party payer. The outcome of the negotiation will only determine total health care expenditure if systems are closed-ended (i.e. in the presence of global expenditure caps).
- Income-level definition by a central agency. Income definition and its evolution over time may simply depend on the number of years at work or may be related to actual performance.

**Who pays?**

Again, three cases apply here:

- the individual pays the service charge in full (e.g. France) and is later reimbursed for the total bill or part of it by his or her health insurance);
- the third-party payer;
- the institution employing the physician.

Combining these three dimensions yields up to 15 different settings (options) and allows a systems' approach: due consideration is taken here of the environment (the relationship with the third-party payer and the patient) in which the physician practises (see Table 8.1).

To characterize a national health care system fully requires combining options since each one often corresponds to a specific segment of the physician population. For instance, while Option 4 corresponds to US physicians with Medicare/Medicaid patients, Option 11 applies to public hospital physicians and Option 9 to HMO-salaried physicians. In some cases, payment systems are mixed at the level of the physician. Such is the case for UK GPs whose remuneration is a mix of Option 6 and Option 14, knowing

**Table 8.1** Typology of payment systems

| Setting/Option | What? | Who sets fees? | Who pays? |
| --- | --- | --- | --- |
| 1 | Services | Physician | Individual |
| 2 | Services | Physician | Third-party |
| 3 | Services | Negotiation | Individual |
| 4 | Services | Negotiation | Third-party |
| 5 | Services | Central agency | Individual |
| 6 | Services | Central agency | Third-party |
| 7 | Services | Central agency | Institution |
| 8 | Resource | Negotiation | Third-party |
| 9 | Resource | Negotiation | Institution |
| 10 | Resource | Central agency | Third-party |
| 11 | Resource | Central agency | Institution |
| 12 | Responsibility | Negotiation | Third-party |
| 13 | Responsibility | Negotiation | Institution |
| 14 | Responsibility | Central agency | Third-party |
| 15 | Responsibility | Central agency | Institution |

*Source*: Contandriopoulos *et al.* (1990)

that the fee-for-service component accounts for about 18 per cent of the total.

This typology enables more elaborate predictions about the impact of different types of payment systems. It suggests for instance that no less than seven different options ought to be considered when analysing fee-for-service. Indeed, the likelihood of SID will vary positively with physicians' degree of freedom: it should be maximum for Option 1 (fees determined freely and patients paying directly) and should reduce progressively to its lowest level in Option 7 (fees determined centrally and paid by the employer institution). Clearly, the aforementioned perverse effects of payment systems will be more or less pronounced according to the context in which physicians practice.

In an attempt to illustrate further the above typology, Table 8.2 shows the principal methods of paying primary health care physicians in selected European countries set in their respective institutional contexts. It shows the underlying relationships between providers' payment systems, the rate of visits per capita, the extent of cost sharing and the presence (or absence) of gatekeeping.

Prospective and retrospective payment systems seem to be spread evenly between western European countries. Many countries have a mix of payment systems. For instance, in France those physicians (a minority) working in health centres are salaried while the others are paid on a fee-for-service basis. In other countries the criteria for applying one payment system or another is the patient's economic status (as Ireland and the Netherlands) and the nature of the service covered (in Denmark and the UK, GPs are paid by fee-for-service for certain services that are to be encouraged).

Table 8.2 also shows that countries with gatekeeping and prospective payment systems (either capitation or salary) usually have low or zero out-of-pocket payments. By contrast, countries with fee-for-service only, never rely on gatekeeping and have to use out-of-pocket payments to reduce patients' moral hazard. This being said, some countries such as France allow partial or total refunding of out-of-pocket payments by private voluntary complementary insurance. In this case, no mechanisms are left to reduce moral hazard on the patient side and the system is clearly 'open-ended'.

This table also shows the great diversity which prevails in the European region. Payment systems are indeed the result of societal choices and power relations which lead to different starting points. Reforms will need to take this diversity into account.

**Table 8.2**  Characterizing the institutional set-ups in which primary health care physicians practise in selected European countries

| Countries | Type of payment | Annual visits per head | Gate-keeping | Cost sharing |
|---|---|---|---|---|
| Austria | Fee-for-service | 5.1[a] | No | 20% of population pays 10% or 20% |
| Belgium | Fee-for-service | 8.0[a] | No | Self-employed pay full cost |
| Denmark | 28% capitation (flat fee); 63% fee-for-service; 9% allowances | 4.4[b] | Yes | None |
| Finland | Salary | 3.3[b] | Yes | $0.17 |
| France | Fee-for-service; salary in health centres | 6.3[a] | No | 25%, including extra billing |
| Germany | Fee-for-service | 12.8[c] | No | None |
| Greece | Salary | 5.3[f] | No | None |
| Ireland | Fee-for-service if higher income; capitation (age-differentiated fee) if lower income | 6.6[d] | Yes | None if lower income |
| Italy | Capitation (age-differentiated fee) | 11.0[d] | Yes | None |
| Luxembourg | Fee-for-service | – | No | 5% |
| Netherlands | Fee-for-service if higher income; capitation (age-differentiated fee) if lower income | 5.8[e] | Yes | None if lower income |
| Portugal | Salary | 3.1[a] | Yes | None |
| Spain | Salary; capitation (age-differentiated fee) | 6.2[g] | Yes | None |
| Sweden | Salary | 3.0[a] | No | $6–9 |
| Switzerland | Fee-for-service | 11.0[e] | No | 10% of cost |
| United Kingdom | Capitation (age-differentiated fee); fee-for-service; allowances and target payments | 5.8[c] | Yes | None |

*Note*: [a] 1993; [b] 1991; [c] 1992; [d] 1988; [e] 1994; [f] 1982; [g] 1989

*Sources*: OECD (1994); Abel-Smith *et al.* (1995)

## MOVING TOWARDS PERFORMANCE-RELATED PAYMENT SYSTEMS

Most countries address the shortcomings of their payment systems by enacting reforms which usually imply a clear reference to, and assessment of, physicians' performance. Yet their starting point differs greatly. Countries with open-ended systems where fee-for-service prevails have had to address macro-efficiency objectives as a priority in their reforms. Rather than moving towards mixed payment systems at physicians' level (in order to combine both macro- and micro-efficiency objectives) they have had to implement expenditure caps or targets to pursue macro-efficiency at a collective level. The initial situation (fee-for-service) rarely confers the regulator sufficient room for manoeuvre to enforce such mixed payments. By contrast, countries which were already under closed-ended systems with either salary or capitation are attempting to solve micro-efficiency problems by a move towards mixed payment systems. So what may appear to be a move in opposite directions is actually motivated by the same desire to combine both micro and macro objectives, though starting from different initial situations. In both cases, they are addressing what has been called the 'transformation problem' – 'how should social conditions in health care be shaped in order to ensure that physicians' professional behaviour on the micro-level results in cost control on the macro-level ?' (Delnoij 1994).

### The pursuit of macro-efficiency

In their search for some form of cost containment, countries with open-ended systems have slowly moved towards expenditure caps or targets, linking payment to performance. Attempts at pursuing macro-efficiency by imposing some form of *ex ante* control over total physicians' expenditure vary in their application from one country to another. First, one may distinguish between expenditure caps and targets (Glaser 1993). While caps imply strong control, targets imply a flexible and voluntary collaboration between private payers and providers, with government limiting its role to that of provider of information and guidelines. Part of the 1989 Medicare reform includes expenditure caps: Medicare Volume Performance Standards (MVPS) which established target rates of growth for Medicare spending on physician services. If actual Medicare physician expenditures increase at a faster rate than the standard, the rate at which the Medicare programme raises physicians' fees will be reduced (and vice versa in the case of a slower rate of growth).

Second, controls vary according to the level at which they are defined: beyond the global or national level, regional or even individual caps may also be defined. Among the European systems which have developed expenditure caps in addition to price controls in the 1980s, Germany is possibly the first and most elaborate one. Physicians are paid a fee-for-service, subject to (1) a schedule of agreed fees, and (2) a global budget constraint for all physicians in a region. The fee schedule comprises a tariff of points, determined at federal level, for each of around 2500 items, and a price per point determined at regional level. There is a retrospective reduction if the regional budget is exceeded.

The Quebec experience is unusual in that it combines collective targets and individual caps. Since 1977, GPs have been subject to an individual quarterly gross income ceiling beyond which they receive a quarter of the going fee for each service produced. This helps meet the collective target negotiated annually between providers and payers, which is very similar to the MVPS.

Since 1991, the French government has attempted to alter the open-ended nature of the health care system by introducing expenditure caps for ambulatory care. Over time, the reforms have evolved from expenditure caps to targets, with both a regional and individual definition of sanctions. However, the 1995 Juppé plan turned out to be very controversial, and a large number of its proposals have not yet been implemented. At the centre of the debate is the issue of physicians' individual financial responsibility for excessive prescription of services and drugs (Rochaix 1997).

Finally, US managed care offers a number of ways in which macro-efficiency may be achieved in fee-for-service systems. Some health plans withhold a percentage of payments (10–20 per cent) until the end of the year and only distribute them to the physicians if overall costs fall at or below the budgeted level. Alternatively, some plans establish a capitation rate for a group of physicians rather than for each physician individually. Each physician within the pool is paid on a fee-for-service basis within the limits of available funds.

Clearly, there are many ways in which macro-efficiency considerations may be introduced into retrospective payment systems. Yet all forms of negative incentives (be it expenditure caps or targets) necessarily entail performance monitoring and often have to be negotiated with the profession. They are usually politically costly and therefore unstable.

**The search for micro-efficiency**

In their search for micro-efficiency, countries with prospective payment systems (capitation or salary) include positive incentives in the form of direct financial rewards to encourage particular procedures or lines of action. It is however difficult to predict from economic analysis what the impact of such mixed payment systems will be. Depending on the initial situation in terms of payment system, on physicians' preferences and on the size of the change, the introduction of financial incentives may or may not lead to the expected result. For instance, Hughes and Yule studied the effect of changes in British GPs' fees on the quantity of maternity and cervical cytology services over a 22-year period (Hughes and Yule 1992). Using secondary source data, they did not find that annual changes in real fees influenced the quantity of services provided.

Also, there is a whole array of determinants which will lead to the use of one type of treatment versus another, beyond their price. In the example quoted earlier in the chapter on obstetric decisions (Keeler and Brodie 1993), the authors also provide a wide-ranging analysis of all the elements which, beyond the fees differential, might determine obstetric decisions: physicians' costs, hospital versus HMOs' incentives, mothers' incentives and costs.

Beyond the early UK experience with mixed payment systems, some Scandinavian countries have also tried mixed payments: Sweden for instance recently introduced a payment per visit added on to salaries. A number of these experiments have been tried and some of them evaluated. For instance, Krasnik studied a change in GPs' payment systems in Copenhagen, Denmark (Krasnik *et al.* 1990). It entailed the change from a flat capitation fee over to a mix of capitation and fee-for-service. Using a quasi-experimental design, the authors compared the services provided by 72 Copenhagen GPs to those of a control group. While the number of visits remained stable, the number of diagnostic services per 1000 patients increased by 66 per cent in the experimental group (compared to 11 per cent in the control group) and the number of curative services increased by 80 per cent (8 per cent in the control group). The change encouraged doctors to reduce referrals to specialists and to reallocate their time to more profitable services. Interestingly, the authors found that the increase was not distributed evenly across the different diagnostic and curative services. In fact, they were able to establish a positive and significant relationship between professional uncertainty and the increase in the volume of services.

Again, US managed care offers ways of introducing micro-efficiency considerations into prospective payment systems (Robinson 1993). Some plans establish the capitation rate for a group of physicians rather than for each physician individually. Each physician within the pool is paid on a fee-for-service basis within the limits of available funds; many plans absolve capitated primary care physicians from direct financial responsibility for referral costs, but encourage them to reduce referrals by offering an end-of-year bonus from the budgeted funds for specialists' payments. In fact, some of the strategies entailing bonus/malus systems have also been evaluated. Hillman analysed the introduction of incentives in a subset of HMOs in the US which aimed at reducing the rate of hospitalization and visits per HMO enrolee. These incentives entailed a bonus/malus on physicians' incomes in case the budget was under/overspent. The results showed that being at risk for deficits in budgets was associated with lower utilization (Hillman *et al.* 1989). Hemenway also studied the impact of a change from salaried payment to a mix of salary and bonuses. These bonuses depended on the value of the gross charges GPs generated per month. Fifteen physicians were followed from a for-profit ambulatory care centre in the US. The results indicated a 23 per cent increase in the number of laboratory tests, a 16 per cent increase in the number of X-ray tests and a 12 per cent increase in the number of patients' visits per month. The income of physicians on bonuses rose by 19 per cent (Hemenway *et al.* 1990).

Undoubtedly, the way forward for prospective payment systems lies in mixed payments. However, their effects are not yet well documented. There is a need to continue carrying out experiments since most of the studies reviewed do not involve a control group, nor is the study population sufficiently large or representative. Neither is there any clear consensus on the 'ideal' mix. It may well be that only a small share of total activity should be under fee-for-service. Indeed, as suggested by Robinson, 'Every movement toward prospective reimbursement increases incentives for unbundling, undertreatment and risk selection. Every compensating movement back toward retrospective reimbursement revives the traditional incentives for cost-unconscious practice styles' (Robinson 1993).

## DISCUSSION AND CONCLUSIONS

The main objective of this chapter has been to shed new light on the issue of physicians' remuneration and to draw some policy implications for future reforms of payment systems. Before turning to the policy conclusions three issues central to any reform of physicians' payment systems need to be taken into account.

First, a successful reform of payment systems requires a clear understanding of the health systems context in which physicians practice. For instance, any attempt at reforming physicians' payment systems must also take into account demand-side features. In countries such as France, for example, where moral hazard is very important among some patient groups, there would be little point in introducing expenditure caps with no concomitant regulation of demand. Similarly, in health care systems with no gatekeeping, any attempt at introducing capitation for GPs will change the relationship with specialist services (in particular for maternity and paediatric services) from being substitutes to becoming complements.

Second, a single payment system cannot meet all the objectives of a health system. Mixed payments will allow more objectives to be taken into account but some trade-offs remain inevitable and have to be made explicit. The most difficult trade-off is given by the dual agency relationship, i.e. the conflict between individual and collective preferences. Depending on the relative emphasis placed on the micro- or macro-efficiency objectives, physicians will be inclined to give more weight to either patients' preferences or third-party payers' interests. The easiest trade-off to make explicit is that between equity and freedom of choice. Indeed, some countries are not prepared to forego the freedom to consult specialists directly by the adoption of gatekeeping (like France and the US). Yet the implicit cost of such an option value is the need to keep user charges – which are known to be regressive (van Doorslaer *et al.* 1993) – as a way to reduce moral hazard on both the physician and the patient side. To a certain extent, gatekeeping can be construed as an upstream moral hazard reduction mechanism while out-of-pocket payments are a more downstream one. It may be wise in these countries to make the trade-off more explicit and leave it to patients to decide whether they prefer one option or the other. Finally, there is a trade-off between simplicity and tailor-made mixed payments: gains in degrees of freedom through the use of mixed payment systems have to be balanced against losses in terms of simplicity of implementation.

Third, incentives display a number of characteristics which could render their use 'a mixed blessing' to decision makers (Stoddardt 1991). First, one of the main difficulties in using incentives is that they will be 'gamed' by the subjects whom they are intended to affect, so as to obtain the reward or avoid the punishment without adopting the desired behaviour. Second, incentives do not coordinate themselves, so it is difficult to synchronize behaviour across sectors. Third, incentives often have unanticipated consequences or, worse, may generate effects that are opposite to those intended. For instance, capitation payments, aimed mainly at discouraging overservicing, may in effect encourage underservicing. Fourth, incentives do not cost less to employ: some form of monitoring is required.

Overall, the analysis shows that no payment system (even a mixed prospective and retrospective payment system) will ever achieve all the objectives that one may wish to pursue and that some trade-offs are inevitable. To be credible, policy-orientated choices regarding physicians' payments ought to recognize that some objectives (and clearly some groups' preferences) will necessarily dominate others. It then becomes important to find a democratic way of making such choices explicit.

Changes in payment systems will inevitably have chain implications. When choosing fee-for-service payments, countries by the same token determine a number of features of their future system: some form of expenditure cap or target will be necessary to contain expenditure, and out-of-pocket payments may be unavoidable. Also, some choices are more irreversible than others: there is clear evidence from most fee-for-service systems that it is difficult to move on to individual mixed payment systems. Prospective systems, on the other hand, may easily move towards mixed payments which seem to be more successful in combining macro- and microefficiency objectives.

There is a need to continue carrying out experiments since the extent of research into this field is surprisingly small, and to urgently address the question of how changes in remuneration affect the health and welfare of patients. 'Policy makers have little evidence on which to base their recommendations' (Scott and Hall 1995). Indeed, most of the studies reviewed do not involve a control group, nor are the study populations representative. Valuable lessons can readily be drawn for the design of future experiments on the basis of existing studies. Consequently, in countries in which experiments take place, there should be a more systematic concern for some of the methodological points outlined above.

Finally, remuneration systems cannot do it alone. Other mechanisms such as selective contracting, peer review or physician information are important in determining physicians' practice and ought to be considered.

## NOTES

1 The author is indebted to Michael Marek for sharing his experience of reforms in CEE countries and to Josep Figueras for his comments on earlier versions of this chapter.
2 See Rees (1985a, 1985b) for a review of the theoretical models of agency derived from the economics of information.
3 The imperfect agency relationship may simply result from the fact that physicians are not fully aware of patients' preferences (Pauly 1980).
4 Achieving macro-efficiency would actually require an allocation of resources to health care based on the comparison of the marginal value of an ECU invested in the different collective functions of the state (education, housing, etc.).
5 Volume offset in response to mandated fee cuts is used here as a broader notion than demand inducement since it comprises both supply-side reaction (SID) and demand-side reaction (increased utilization in response to lowered cost).
6 The MOS was an observational study conducted in three American cities (Boston, MA, Chicago, IL and Los Angeles, CA) from 1986 to 1990. The study included adult patients of clinicians from prepaid and fee-for-service settings. The final sample of enrolled clinicians was 523 and included both a cross-sectional patient sample (n = 22,462) and a longitudinal panel (n = 2546) drawn from the cross-sectional sample and with five clinical tracers: hypertension, diabetes, congestive heart failure, recent myocardial infarction or major depressive disorders.
7 The data draws from the MOS (Greenfield *et al.* 1992) and is based on questionnaires filled in every six months by a cohort of 1208 adult patients with chronic disease whose health insurance was either through a fee-for-service plan or a prepaid health care system.
8 In France a new system (*Secteur II*) was created in 1980. Under this system physicians can freely set their fees, but face higher social insurance contributions than *Secteur I* physicians. About a quarter of physicians (mainly specialists) have elected to adopt this new system.

## REFERENCES

Abel-Smith, B., Figueras, J., Holland, W., McKee, M. and Mossialos, E. (1995). *Choices in Health Policy: An Agenda for the European Union.*

Luxembourg and Aldershot: Office for Official Publications of the European Communities and Dartmouth Publishing company.

Arrow, K. (1963). Uncertainty and the welfare economics of medical care. *American Economic Review*, 53, 941–73.

Conseil Médical du Quebec (1995). *Avis sur une Nouvelle Dynamique Organisationelle à Implanter: La Hiérarchisation des Services Médicaux*, Avis 95-03. Montréal: Conseil Médical du Quebec.

Contandriopoulos, A. P., Champagne, F. and Pineault, R. (1990). Systèmes de soins et modalités de rémunération. *Sociologie du Travail*, 1, 95–115.

Delnoij, D. M. J. (1994). *Physician Payment Systems and Cost Control*. Utrecht: NIVEL.

Donaldson, C. and Gerard, K. (1989). Paying general practitioners: Shedding light on the review of health services. *Journal of the Royal College of General Practitioners*, 39, 114–17.

Elliott, R. F. (1991). *Labor Economics: A Comparative Analysis*. London: McGraw-Hill.

Ellis, R. P. and McGuire, T. G. (1990). Optimal payment systems for health services. *Journal of Health Economics*, 9, 375–96.

Evans, R. G. (1974). Supplier induced demand: some empirical evidence and implications. In M. Perlman (ed.), *The Economics of Health and Medical Care*. London: Macmillan.

Glaser, W. (1993). How expenditure caps and expenditure targets really work. *Millbank Memorial Fund Quarterly*, 71, 97–128.

Greenfield, S., Nelson, E. C., Zubkoff, M. *et al.* (eds) (1992). Variations in resource utilisation among medical specialties and systems of care: Results from the Medical Outcomes Study. *Journal of the American Medical Association*, 267, 1624–30.

Hellinger, F. J. (1996). The impact of financial incentives on physician behaviour in managed care plans: A review of the evidence. *Medical Care Research and Review*, 53,3, 294–314.

Hemenway, D., Killen, A., Cashman, S.B., Parks, C.L. and Bicknell, W.J. (1990). Physicians' responses to financial incentives. Evidence from a for-profit ambulatory care center. *New England Journal of Medicine*, 322, 1059–63.

Hicks, G. B., Altimeter, W. A. and Peril, J. M. (1987). Physician reimbursement by salary or fee-for-service: Effect on physician practice behaviour in a randomised prospective study. *Paediatrics*, 80, 344–50.

Hillman, A. L., Pauly, M. V. and Kernstein, J. J. (1989). How do financial incentives affect physicians' clinical decisions and the financial performance of health maintenance organisations? *New England Journal of Medicine*, 321, 86–92.

Hughes, D. and Yule, B. (1992). The effect of per-item fees on the behaviour of primary health care. *Journal of Health Economics*, 11, 413–38.

Hutchinson, B., Birch, S., Hurley, J., Lomas, J. and Stratford-Devai, F. (1994). *Effect of a Financial Incentive to Reduce Hospital Utilisation in*

*Capitated Primary Care.* Paper 94–2. Ontario: Center for Health Economics and Policy Analysis.

Keeler, E. B. and Brodie, M. (1993). Economic incentives in the choice between vaginal delivery and caesarean section. *Millbank Memorial Fund Quarterly*, 71, 365–404.

Krasnik, A., Groenewegen, P. P., Pedersen, P., Van Scholten, P., Mooney, G., Gottschau, A. *et al.* (1990). Changing remuneration systems: Effects on activity in general practice. *British Medical Journal*, 300, 1698–701.

Kristiansen, I. S. and Mooney, G. (1993). The GP's use of time: Is it influenced by the remuneration system? *Social Science and Medicine*, 37, 393–9.

Labelle, R., Hurley, J. and Rice, T. (1990). *Financial Incentives and Medical Practice: Evidence from Ontario on the Effect of Changes in Physician Fees on Medical Care Utilization.* Ontario: Centre for Health Economics and Policy Analysis.

Luft, H. S. (1978). How do health maintenance organisations achieve their savings? *New England Journal of Medicine*, 298, 1336–43.

OECD (1994). *The Reform of Health Care Systems: A Review of Seventeen OECD Countries.* Paris: Organisation for Economic Co-operation and Development.

Pauly, M. (1980). *Doctors and their Workshops: Economic Models of Physician Behaviour.* Chicago: NBER University of Chicago Press.

Phelps, R. G. (1986). Induced demand – can we ever know its extent? *Journal of Health Economics*, 5, 356–65.

Rees, R. (1985a). The theory of principal and agent: Part 1. *Bulletin of Economic Research*, 37,1, 2–26.

Rees, R. (1985b). The theory of principal and agent: Part 2. *Bulletin of Economic Research*, 37,2, 75–95.

Rice, T. (1983). The impact of changing Medicare reimbursement rates on physician-induced demand. *Medical Care*, 21, 803–15.

Rizzo, J. A. and Blumenthal, D. (1995). Physician income targets: New evidence on an old controversy. *Inquiry*, 31, 394–404.

Robinson, J. C. (1993). Payment mechanisms, nonprice incentives, and organisational innovation in health care. *Inquiry*, 30, 328–33.

Rochaix, L. (1991). Adjustment mechanisms in physicians' services markets. Unpublished PhD thesis, University of York, York.

Rochaix, L. (1997). Recent reforms in the French health care systems, *Cahiers de l'ICI – Information, Coordination, Incitations – Université de Bretagne Occidentale*, no. 3, Août.

Safran, D. G., Tarlov, A. R. and Rogers, W. H. (1994). Primary care performance in fee-for-service and prepaid health care systems: Results from the medical outcome study. *Journal of the American Medical Association*, 271, 1579–86.

Scott, S. and Hall, J. (1995). Evaluating the effects of GP remuneration: Problems and prospects. *Health Policy*, 31, 183–95.

Stearns, S., Wolfe, B. L. and Kindig, D. A. (1992). Physician responses to fee-for-service and capitation payment. *Inquiry*, 29, 416–25.

Stoddart, G. L. (1991). Reflections on incentives and health system reform. In G. Lopez-Casanovas (ed.), *Incentives in Health Systems*. Berlin: Springer-Verlag.

van Doorslaer, E., Wagstaff, A. and Rutten, F. (1993). *Equity in the Finance and Delivery of Health Care: An International Perspective*. Oxford: Oxford University Press.

# 9

# FINANCING OPERATING COSTS FOR ACUTE HOSPITAL SERVICES

## Miriam M. Wiley

### INTRODUCTION

The acute hospital system constitutes the largest single component of health expenditure in the majority of developed countries. While economic pressures on health care resources are undoubtedly an important impetus for reform of this system in many countries, additional factors contributing to pressure within the system include technological and service advancements, together with increasing consumer expectations. Given the critical effect of hospital expenditure on the economic well-being of the health system in general, this review will concentrate on approaches to financing the acute hospital services in selected countries in the European region.

The predominant funding source and financing approach for acute in-patient hospital services are summarized in Table 9.1 for the 13 countries reviewed here. While the specifics of the approach to hospital financing vary between countries, an examination of Table 9.1 shows that financing approaches may be seen to fall into two broad categories, i.e. prospective global budgeting and service-based financing. Within each of these broad financing approaches there is further differentiation as countries may apply system-specific adjustments. Financing hospital services cannot be discussed in a vacuum as any approach will only be meaningful if viewed within the policy environment in which it has been developed and implemented. In the sections which follow, the range of applications for prospective budgeting and service-based financing will be explored by reviewing a number of country-specific systems within the European region. This review is followed by a concluding section briefly summarizing the relative advantages and disadvantages of the approaches discussed.

## PROSPECTIVE BUDGETING FOR ACUTE HOSPITAL SERVICES

Eight of the 13 countries listed in Table 9.1 can be seen to have directly adopted a prospective budgeting approach to financing hospital services. This grouping of countries includes Denmark, France, Germany, Ireland, Italy, the Netherlands, Norway and Poland. Though the approach to hospital financing in Sweden cannot be uniquely assigned to the prospective budgeting category, some of the characteristics of this model are in evidence within this system. While prospective budgeting is not necessarily pursued in the same way in each of these countries, there are a number of characteristics central to the adoption of this approach. These include: (1) determination of financing levels for service provision in advance; and (2) financing and time constraints are specified prospectively for the service providers.

As shown in Table 9.1, prospective global budgeting is not specific to any particular funding source. Health systems in Denmark and Norway are funded from decentralized, tax-based systems; Ireland, Italy and Poland are funded from centralized, tax-based systems; and social insurance prevails in France, Germany and the Netherlands. Adjustments for hospital activity within the prospective budgeting framework will be specifically examined when reviewing these country systems as the quantification of the relationship between resource inputs and hospital output is an essential precondition for an assessment of hospital efficiency. The range of approaches to the application of this adjustment will be addressed after the review of the more traditional approaches to prospective global budgeting which follows.

### 'Traditional' approaches to prospective budgeting

The two countries from among the group listed in Table 9.1 which apply the more traditional approach to prospective budgeting are Denmark and Poland. Prospective global budgets for Danish hospitals are mainly determined on an historical basis with

**Table 9.1** Predominant approach to funding and financing operating costs for acute in-patient hospital services in selected countries in the European region

| Country | Predominant funding source for acute in-patient hospital services | Predominant approach to financing operating costs for acute in-patient hospital services | |
|---|---|---|---|
| | | *Prospective global budgeting* | *Service-based financing* |
| Austria | Social insurance | | Based on length of stay (sickness fund) and lump-sum subsidies (Ministry of Health) |
| Denmark | Decentralized taxation | Based on historical expenditure | |
| Finland | Decentralized taxation | | Based on bed-days and services reimbursed by municipalities |
| France | Social insurance | Adjustment for activity/case mix | |
| Germany | Social insurance | Planned replacement of fixed budgets by adjustment for activity | |
| Hungary | Social insurance funding | | Performance-related financing system based on DRGs |
| Ireland | Taxation | Adjustment for case mix | |
| Italy | Taxation | Adjustment for case mix | |
| Netherlands | Social insurance | Adjustment for activity | |
| Norway | Decentralized taxation | Adjustment for case mix | |
| Poland | Taxation | Based on historical expenditure | |
| Sweden | Decentralized taxation | Prospective departmental budgets combined with activity-based financing | |
| United Kingdom | Taxation | | Based on activity determined by contracts |

adjustments for salary and price increases, service improvements and planned improvements in efficiency. The use of global budgets by county councils is identified by Petersen (forthcoming) as the reason why 'the Danish hospital sector has been able to control costs to a very great extent'. Greater flexibility in the more traditional approach to global budgeting was, however, considered necessary when attempting to address the problem of waiting times for elective services. The introduction of the 'free choice of hospital' scheme to reduce waiting lists and waiting time for elective surgery gave rise to greater responsiveness from the hospitals in addressing patient needs. In addition, the scheme engendered greater competitiveness among hospitals as additional funding could be acquired from the provision of the services required to reduce hospital waiting times. Where patients are treated outside the county of residence, the basis for payment is negotiated between the county councils and will generally be on a fee-for-service or a per diem basis.

While health care in Poland continues to be financed from tax revenue, the 1994 policy document *Strategy for Health* supports the commitment to the introduction of a mixed insurance/budget system (Ministry of Health and Social Welfare 1994). At the voivodship[1] level, the annual health budget is divided between pay and non-pay expenditure with resource allocation traditionally being undertaken on an historical basis. While the allocation to the voivodship is fixed, with restrictions on any change in staffing levels, this authority may determine the internal allocation of funds. There has been some experimentation with different methods of resource allocation with a view to improving the efficiency of the system and directing resources to where they are most needed. For instance, in 1994 and 1995 one voivodship allocated non-pay expenditure to hospitals on the basis of patient numbers and costs by specialty. As the health system reforms proposed for Poland support the introduction of incentives for health institutions to operate as autonomous bodies, there has been some consideration given in a number of voivodships to allowing the authority with responsibility for service provision (ZOS) to become the budget holder which buys hospital services where they are available at the best price (Ministry of Health and Social Welfare 1994).

The experience of Denmark and Poland with prospective budgets based on historical expenditure would suggest that while this method would seem to have performed adequately for cost-containment purposes, greater flexibility may be required for the pursuit of broader health system objectives such as efficiency. In addition, the potential within this approach to provide the necessary incentive basis to facilitate change such as a reduction in waiting lists has also been found to be limited. While continuing to support the traditional approach to prospective budgeting for hospital financing, the Danish and Polish health systems in particular would seem to recognize the need to integrate this approach within a more flexible financing model for the achievement of broader health policy objectives.

## Activity-adjusted prospective budgeting

The support for social insurance systems in Germany and the Netherlands means that the funding, payment and service provision functions tend to be separated at the institutional level. Any adjustments to the budget model should therefore facilitate application in a wide variety of institutional environments. The potential for greater autonomy at the institutional level within these systems may, in turn, facilitate greater innovation in approaches to resource deployment at this level. While generally applying an adjustment for activity within a budget framework, the approach pursued differs between these two countries.

A 'flexible' prospective budgeting system was introduced in Germany in 1985 on the basis that full cost coverage would be restricted to those hospitals assessed as working efficiently. Budget negotiations take place between the individual hospital, the regional association of the statutory sickness funds and the organizations of private health insurers (Leidl 1995). The negotiations refer to the services the hospital expects to render and to the associated cost. The prospective daily rate and the hospital budget are agreed at the same time. Under the 'flexible' budget system, where a hospital delivered less than the anticipated number of patient days, they still received 75 per cent of the daily rate for the missing days in the next round of budget negotiations. Hospitals delivering more than the planned level of patient days were expected to refund 75 per cent of the excess daily rates.

The accession of the German Democratic Republic to the Federal Republic of Germany in 1990 gave rise to a unique set of circumstances which had to be addressed in the reform of the health care system. The federal hospital financing law resulted from this process and came into force in the new German states in 1991. The Health Sector Act (HSA) took effect on 1 January 1993 and was associated with the enforcement of an income-oriented policy on growth in individual hospital budgets over the 1993–5 period. Taking the 1992 budget as the baseline, budget increases were to be limited to income growth of the sickness funds. This approach was actually extended to 1996 after which it has been planned to introduce again a 'flexible' budget mechanism which will be based on different types of payment units as the HSA has identified a greater role for payment options such as special daily rates for hospital departments, special fees for high-cost services and case-based lump sum payments. The coordination of the different components of payment within the hospital system remains to be finalized, though some advancement has been made towards the implementation of the new system as 73 case definitions and 149 special fees have been agreed within the framework of the hospital financing act (Leidl forthcoming).

In Germany, cost containment has featured as a major political problem since the mid-1970s with close to 60 cost-containment measures introduced in eight acts over the period up to 1989 (Schneider 1991). The HSA 1993 is the first major reform to go beyond the health expenditure issue and review the basic structure of the health care system. This act is also seen to represent a substantial advancement towards more fundamental reform given the requirements to strengthen the budgeting process, develop links to income development and expand performance-related financing mechanisms (Leidl 1995).

The blueprint for reform of the Dutch health care system prepared by the government-appointed committee chaired by Dr W. Dekker in 1987 essentially proposed that a two-part contribution system would replace the dual insurance system in operation at the time. The planned introduction of a compulsory basic health insurance scheme was to be partly financed by income-dependent contributions and partly by competitive flat-rate premiums. The income-dependent contributions would be paid into a central fund which would, in turn, contract with health insurers on the basis of risk-adjusted payments for service provision. The flat-rate contributions would be set and collected by the health insurers (Maarse 1995).

Budgeting on a fixed, historical basis which had been introduced in the Netherlands in 1983 was replaced by functional budgeting in 1988. While some form of functional budgeting has persisted within the hospital system since that time, there have been changes in the approach. The hospital operating budget is related directly to the volume of activity in the hospital, including admissions, outpatient visits, nursing days, day care and day treatment (Scheerder 1996). Annual agreements are reached between the hospital and the insurers and the sickness funds, regarding the amount of production units to be supported. The 'admissible' costs for the hospital are determined according to two types of tariffs: ancillary tariffs which are determined nationally and the daily charge for nursing which is determined by each hospital (Maarse 1995). If a hospital underspends relative to the budget, the surplus may be retained whereas if there is an overspend, the excess constitutes a negative reserve against the following year's budget.

As part of the overall proposals for health system reform in the Netherlands, there are attempts to integrate the fee-for-service payment system for specialists and the hospital budget into an integrated model. It is also proposed to test an alternative budget model based on the case-mix classification system, diagnosis related groups (DRGs). The approach to hospital budgeting is generally being reviewed with the objective of giving more flexibility to those involved in the negotiations at the institutional level, particularly with regard to the production levels, treatment volume, etc.

In reviewing the developments in hospital financing in the 1980s, it is interesting to note the replacement of service-based financing by global budgets in both Germany and the Netherlands. It is also noteworthy that this development represented the beginning rather than the conclusion of a process of reform which is ongoing. The reform process in these countries is based on the continued use of prospective budgets for financing acute hospital services. While there are differences in the financing model used, some adjustment for activity is applied within each system. There is also, however, a general recognition of the need to improve current financing approaches with a view to enhancing flexibility, efficiency and performance-related incentives within the respective hospital systems.

## Case mix-adjusted prospective budgeting

While the French health care system is grounded within a social insurance framework and the health systems of Ireland, Italy and Norway are all primarily funded from taxation, all systems apply some type of case mix adjustment within their respective prospective budgeting models. It is interesting to note that despite choosing a similar measure of case mix, these countries differ in the approach adopted for implementation.

Since 1984–5, public hospitals and private non-profit hospitals affiliated with the public sector (PSPH) have been financed on the basis of prospective global budgets in France. Under this system, hospitals receive an annual global allocation calculated according to historic expenditure levels and based on that proportion of expenditure which is to be supported by the sickness insurance funds. Because hospitals treat patients covered by a number of different insurers, the budget share required of each insurer is determined on the basis of the number of bed-days used within the insurer's catchment area (OECD 1992). The process for determining the global budget allocation involves extensive negotiation between the hospital, the supervisory authorities and the sickness insurance funds to agree on the payment rate and the level of activity to be supported. As these negotiations are part of an annual process, an average rate of increase (*taux moyen d'evolution*) fixed centrally by the Ministries of the Economy, the Budget, Health and Social Security may be applied. About 90 per cent of public hospital expenditure is met by the global budget allocation with the remainder coming from individual patient charges. Following the enactment of hospital sector reform legislation in France in 1991 (Republique Francaise 1991), the budgetary process has been subjected to detailed review in the interests of improving the speed, flexibility and efficiency of this procedure. In addition, provision has been made to enable a revision of the global budget during the financial year to reflect changes in volume which have been assessed on the basis of accepted measures of medical activity (Sourty-Le Guellec 1995).

The most important recent health care reform in France was introduced in the spring of 1996 and will be gradually implemented over the 1996 to 1998 period. This reform addressed a wide-ranging agenda and the specific objectives have been summarized by Rodrigues (1996) as including the progressive implementation of a universal health insurance system; the extension and development of medical information systems, accreditation and quality of care assessment; population needs assessment; and equity of resource allocation between regions and the implementation of cost-containment procedures together with experimentation of new hospital payment methods. As part of this reform, the French DRG system (*Groupes Homogènes de Malades* (GHM)) was used in the determination of 0.5 per cent of hospital budgets in 1996 and it is planned to gradually increase the impact of case mix on budget determination over time. While separate budgets for public and private hospitals will continue to be determined at the regional level in 1997, it is intended to include all hospitals within the regional budget framework by 1998.

Since 1993, a global budget framework incorporating a case mix adjustment has been used for the allocation of resources to the majority of acute general hospitals in Ireland. Within this model, hospitals are stratified according to teaching status and, using DRGs, the relative costliness of hospital case mix is estimated (Wiley 1995). In this context, the relative costliness of the hospital's case mix is assumed to indicate relative efficiency. An agreed proportion of the hospital's budget is determined on the basis of the case mix adjustment which may be negative or positive depending on the efficiency of the hospital relative to others in the reference group. The deployment of additional funds gained as a result of this process is at the discretion of the hospital.

The Irish approach contrasts with that proposed for Italy where the 1995 reforms aim to shift health service payment to a tariff basis (Mapelli forthcoming). For hospital services, tariffs based on DRGs are to be set on a prospective basis within predetermined budget constraints. There is, however, some discretion left to the region as to how this tariff system is to be implemented. This could mean that the choice for regions might range from a fee-for-service type system to one where tariffs would only be used to provide compensation for cross-border flows of patients. The objective for this initiative, however, is that hospitals are to be funded on the basis of the volume and quality of services actually delivered. As an additional incentive to promote increased efficiency, it has been proposed that local area units (USLs) retain any budget surplus which would be deployed according to objectives agreed with the region.

The financing of hospital services in Norway has historically been based on a system of fixed grants with the population-based global budgeting approach being introduced in 1980. An important impetus for the introduction of reforms in the 1990s originated with a political concern for waiting lists and efficiency at the hospital level. In determining the organizational response to these problems, it became clear that a system which was more flexible and incentive-based was required. As part of the process of addressing the efficiency issue, a pilot scheme begun in 1991 and expanded in 1993 tested an approach to hospital service financing involving the combination of fixed grants with a DRG-based, patient-related payment scheme.

Notwithstanding this development, the absence of controls on hospital expenditure in Norway continues to be a problem. The absence of any general monitoring or controlling programme to ensure that expenditure limits are not breached means that deficit budgeting for hospitals may still be found within some county councils. Increasingly however, within many areas hospital deficits result in deductions from the following year's budget. While such measures may be effective in the short run in facilitating some control over expenditure, a fundamental reform of the financing of hospital services will be required before the necessary incentives for improved efficiency become operational (Solstad and Nyland forthcoming).

In choosing to apply a case mix adjustment for hospital financing, some version of the DRG system has been the measure of choice in France, Ireland, Italy and Norway. Efficiency and productivity issues proved to have an important influence on the types of reforms introduced in these countries. The recognition that efficiency can be best assessed where resource deployment is directly related to service production was an important factor in the choice of a financing model. While the correct application of a case mix measure may both facilitate the measurement of efficiency and the operation of positive incentive effects for service production, the experience of these countries indicates that this procedure may actually be applied within a variety of financing models.

## SERVICE-BASED FINANCING

There is a considerable diversity in the approaches to hospital financing among the countries which fall within the general category of 'service-based financing'. For the basic approach observed here, payment is based on services delivered so the total level of investment in the service and the time period covered may be open-ended. While this may be problematic where the objective of cost containment is being pursued, the facility to relate resources to specific services may enhance the potential for measuring and improving efficiency. Where services are priced individually, this mechanism may be used to provide incentives for the delivery of particular types of services or the use of alternative sites of care. For example, increasing the delivery of screening services and/or day care might be facilitated where such services are priced with a view to raising productivity. The specific approach adopted by countries using service-based financing is summarized in Table 9.1 and briefly reviewed here.

In Austria, hospital payment is based on length of stay. In addition, the Ministry of Health provides a lump-sum subsidy to the hospitals which is determined according to the number of beds, special functions provided and any deficit carried forward. While in principle the hospital should support any shortfall in operating costs remaining after the income is received from the insurance fund and the Ministry of Health, in reality 'the hospital itself makes no losses and there are also no sanctions' (Pfeiffer 1995).

The fact that hospital costs have increased in Austria is perhaps not surprising given the perverse incentives associated with financing a service on the basis of length of stay and the absence of any incentives for cost control. Against this background the Ministry of Health has come to recognize the importance of developing new regulatory mechanisms for the financing of hospital services. In pursuing this objective, it is expected that a planned market for Austrian hospital services can be developed. One alternative hospital financing model which is currently being developed is based on a DRG-type classification system (Pfeiffer 1995). While the precise format of any alternative financing system has not yet been decided, it has been agreed that the aims of any new financing system should include: (1) ending hospital cost increases; (2) increasing hospital efficiency; (3) relating payment to diagnosis and therapy and not to length of stay; and (4) improving quality of care.

Pre-1993, financial responsibility for the funding of hospitals in Finland was shared between the state and the municipalities (WHO 1996a). As hospital revenues were mainly determined on an historical basis, there was no incentive to control costs and rising costs were increasingly borne by the state. The shift to reimbursement on an item-of-service basis in 1993 was influenced by cost-containment and efficiency objectives in the unfavourable economic climate. Under this system hospitals may determine prices for services which are paid directly by the municipality. While there is considerable variation in how hospitals specify services and estimate prices, the bed-day is commonly used as a unit of payment. Some hospital districts have introduced a form of prospective payment involving billing municipalities on the basis of specialty-specific prices for services provided.

Because they are unable to influence prices or the volume of services provided, municipalities are considered to be in a difficult position regarding the pursuit of cost-control objectives (WHO

1996a). In response to this problem, there are a number of pilot projects under way in which hospitals and municipalities enter into contracts specifying prospectively the price and quantity of services to be provided within an agreed time period. Most hospital districts have agreed on a fund equalization system whereby excessively high costs incurred in treating certain types of patients can be pooled between the municipalities in the district. Finally, a form of deficit financing has been agreed whereby the municipalities pay end-of-year deficits incurred by the hospital. This practice is, however, being reviewed as there is a view supporting the setting of any deficit against the following year's payment. Given continuing economic difficulties, it is likely that the financing of hospital services in Finland will continue to be reviewed with the objective of improving both cost containment and efficiency within the system.

The proposals for reform of the UK National Health Service (NHS) first presented in the White Paper *Working for Patients* were translated into legislation enacted in 1990 under the NHS Community Care Act. The most far-reaching effect of these reforms has been the shift from a budgeting system to one of contracting as a means of paying for hospital services. An important objective of this contracting system is the separation of the roles of the purchaser and provider of hospital services. There are a number of different ways in which this new type of relationship may be defined, though in each case the hospital fulfils the role of service provider within price- and quality-controlled service contracts agreed with the purchasing agent. District health authorities (DHAs) may act as the purchasing agent of hospital services and enter into block, cost/volume, or cost/case contracts with designated service providers for a defined and costed range of services. DHAs may also collaborate for the purpose of contracting.

While DHAs may continue to manage hospitals directly, the impact of the NHS reforms over time has involved the transformation of primary and secondary health care providers from directly managed organizations into independent trusts (Bartlett and Le Grand 1994). Trusts and other DHA-managed units have a statutory duty to operate within the income obtained from contracts. In drawing up contracts, trusts must set prices equal to average costs and ensure that there is no cross-subsidization between services (Bartlett and Le Grand 1994). Trusts compete with other providers for hospital service contracts irrespective of DHA boundaries.

An additional option within the purchaser/provider configuration is for general practitioners (GPs) in practices fulfilling particular conditions to become 'fundholders'. This means that GPs may adopt the role of purchaser on behalf of their patients and enter into contracts with hospitals for the provision of a specified range of services. Fundholding GPs have an incentive to secure contracts for hospital services at the lowest cost because any surplus earned on the budget assigned can be retained for improvements within the practice. Any budget overspend by GPs will result in the withdrawal of fundholding status from the practice.

In 1993, following the introduction of the reforms, the prospective budgeting system used in Hungary was replaced by a service-based payment method with the objective of improving the efficiency of the hospital system and enhancing quality of care (Nagy *et al.* 1994). Payment for hospital services is now based on a Hungarian adaptation of the DRG classification system. For acute in-patient care, reimbursement is based on the number treated in each patient group. The reimbursement level is determined by the cost weighting estimated for each patient group and agreed in a contract between the hospital and the Health Insurance Cashier's Office (Bordas 1994). Hospital departments treating long-term care patients may be reimbursed in proportion to the length of the in-patient stay having regard to daily quotas. Exceptional procedures like transplantation are funded on a case-by-case basis. The fact that this financing system is restricted to the allocation of operating costs is considered a drawback. Plans are therefore being developed to expand this system to take consideration of the balance between performance and investment in addition to addressing the relationship between amortization costs and reimbursement (Bordas 1994).

The categorization of national approaches to financing hospital services presented in Table 9.1 is intended to be indicative rather than conclusive. The points of differentiation between payment systems are becoming increasingly blurred as the range of approaches to financing this service expands and the pace of change accelerates. It is worth noting the increased use of contracting which may be seen as one way to address the problems caused by the open-endedness of service-based financing systems. As contracts may be based on the required service quantity/type and/or price and/or time period covered, there is some facility to place constraints on the investment. While the specification of investment constraints is to be welcomed, contract-based systems place heavy demands on activity and cost information systems and may also require considerable administrative resources to develop,

implement, manage and monitor. Contracting systems are therefore quite different from budgeting systems as contracts tend to be
institution-specific and represent the outcome of negotiations
between the purchasers and the providers.

The country classification in Table 9.1 is intended to indicate the
financing model which would appear to be the most dominant at the
time of this review. As there are exceptions to all rules, however,
the exception in this case would appear to be Sweden which seems
to straddle both the budgeting and the service-based financing
approach. The ongoing and recent reforms of the Swedish system
will therefore be briefly summarized.

## ACTIVITY-BASED FINANCING WITHIN
## DEPARTMENTAL BUDGETS

With the dawning of the era of cost containment for the Swedish
hospital system in the 1980s, a recognition of the need for tighter
control of hospital costs was associated with the introduction of a
clinical budgeting approach in some counties. In reforming the
approach to hospital financing, there has been a general tendency
towards the creation of internal markets for hospital services. This
has involved the development of a system whereby hospital departments are financed by activity-based revenues rather than fixed
budgets. In pursuing this objective, the separation of the purchasing and service provision functions may be logically undertaken at
the county council level with the objective of increasing productivity by competition.

By 1994, 14 county councils in Sweden had introduced some form
of purchaser–provider arrangement whereby purchasing organizations negotiated with hospitals to establish financial and activity-
based contracts (WHO 1996b). These contracts are often based on
fixed, prospective per case payments with controls for price, volume
and quality. The DRGs are the most common classification system
in use to set service prices within prospectively determined expenditure constraints, though other systems may also be used depending on the type of care. Specialties such as psychiatry and geriatrics
continue to be financed through global budgets and cross-boundary
care may be reimbursed on a fee-for-service basis. As all purchasers
and the majority of the providers of hospital services are still part of
the county council system, this means that most payments are
internal transactions at the local level (Paulson 1995). The reforms

introduced at the county council level in Sweden would seem to be attempting to combine the cost-control advantages of the budget mechanism with the flexibility of service-related funding.

## CONCLUSION

While the ordering of priorities may vary, the objectives most frequently cited for the reform of hospital financing methods in the countries reviewed here include the improvement of cost-containment mechanisms, the enhancement of quality service provision in an efficient manner and the achievement of community-wide access (Wiley 1992). The pursuit of these objectives is made all the more difficult by the dynamic nature of the hospital system, in particular, and the fiscal pressures exerted by ongoing technological advancements and expanding consumer expectations.

The way in which hospital services are financed in any health care system would seem to represent more of a pragmatic response to an ongoing policy challenge than a rational planning approach consistent with a clear theoretical framework. The hospital system is a visible and substantial component of all health care systems which means that it is significant politically as well as economically. The approach to financing hospital services must therefore attempt to meet the objectives which are considered a priority by any political administration within the prevailing economic environment. While the objectives of cost containment, efficiency and open access may now be considered almost universal, additional objectives such as the reduction in hospital waiting lists may also be prioritized and ultimately have an effect on the financing approach adopted.

The attempt in this paper to group country systems in a number of broad categories was intended to facilitate greater clarity in understanding the respective approaches. It is readily recognized, however, that the 'goodness of fit' with these categories varies considerably between systems which might be more appropriately considered as part of a continuum rather than a dichotomy. The summary information which is indicated by the broad categorization used is that eight of the 13 country systems reviewed use prospective budgeting, four use some sort of service-based financing and one country is developing what could be considered to be a combined budgeting and activity-based financing approach.

It is difficult to generalize about the service-based hospital financing systems because, by their very nature, they operate at a micro rather than a macro level. While this approach is generally characterized by the association of resource use with service use at the patient level, the approach to operationalization is subject to substantial variation. The most obvious disadvantage of the approaches within this category is their open-ended nature which makes cost control a difficult objective to achieve. Any constraint on utilization is also difficult to apply. The advantages are, however, clearly considered more important in those countries where they apply as they place a higher priority on the facility to relate resource and service use at the patient level and create an environment where increased competition may be expected to be associated with greater productivity. Where contracting is applied, conditions may be imposed for the achievement of specific objectives like cost control and utilization review at the service level. In addition, the service provider within these arrangements may have more autonomy and flexibility regarding the organizational, manpower, capital and financial aspects of service provision.

For the prospective budgeting systems, the most prevailing characteristic is that expenditure limits applicable over a predefined time period are determined in advance. The precise approach to managing and controlling services within these constraints may then vary between countries and increasingly include the incorporation of such factors as controls for case mix, output measures, administrative controls, etc. The prioritization of the cost-control objective has been associated with the application of the more traditional approach to prospective budgeting, with those countries concerned with improvements in efficiency applying some adjustment for activity/case mix within the budget framework. In addition, improvements in the budgeting mechanism may facilitate the enhancement of quality, autonomy and management flexibility. The implementation of any budgeting system must, however, have regard to potential problems with quality of care and complexity in implementation. Both the positive and negative characteristics apply to a greater or lesser extent depending on the country-model in question.

In conclusion, it should be noted that while the hospital financing models in the countries reviewed here have been placed at particular points on a continuum between 'pure types', what is becoming apparent with the advancement of the process of reform in this area is that the tools used for implementation may be increasingly interchangeable between models. Techniques like the separation of the purchaser and provider functions, the use of contracting and fixed price agreements have all been shown to be applicable within a variety of funding and financing settings. The dynamic nature of hospital systems specifically, and health systems generally, means that a 'snapshot' of a particular stage of development such as that presented here will rapidly become outdated. It would be hoped, however, that the specification of the prevailing models in this area will render the future planning process more effective by indicating the direction and the techniques which are most likely to be pursued by attempts to reform the financing of acute hospital services within the European region.

## ACKNOWLEDGEMENTS

Assistance provided by Ellie Tragakes in making available information on approaches to hospital financing in a number of eastern European countries and helpful comments on an earlier draft of this paper by Josep Figueras are gratefully acknowledged.

## NOTE

1 The geographical area with responsibility for health service provision in Poland is called the voivodship.

## REFERENCES

Bartlett, W. and Le Grand, J. (1994). The performance of trusts. In R. Robinson and J. Le Grand (eds), *Evaluating the NHS Reforms*. London: King's Fund Institute.

Bordas, I. (1994). Modification of the financing of hospitals in Hungary (from prospective setting to DRGs). Proceedings of the tenth PCS/E International Conference, Budapest, Hungary, October.

Leidl, R. (1995). Hospital financing in Germany. In M. M. Wiley, M. A. Laschober and H. Gelband (eds), *Hospital Financing in Seven Countries*. Washington, DC: US Congress, Office of Technology Assessment.

Leidl, R. (forthcoming). Hospital financing in Germany. In *Acute Hospital Care: Delivery and Financing*. Health Policy Studies Series No. 9. Paris: OECD.

Maarse, J. (1995). Hospital financing in the Netherlands. In M. M. Wiley, M. A. Laschober and H. Gelband (eds), *Hospital Financing in Seven Countries*. Washington, DC: US Congress, Office of Technology Assessment.

Mapelli, V. (forthcoming). Hospital financing in Italy. In *Acute Hospital Care: Delivery and Financing*. Health Policy Studies Series No. 9. Paris: OECD.

Ministry of Health and Social Welfare (1994). *Strategy for Health*. Warsaw: Ministry of Health and Social Welfare.

Nagy, J., Karolyi, Z. and Ladanyi, P. (1994). Experiences of the first year of the new hospital financing – the hoped for and the actual changes. Proceedings of the tenth PCS/E International Conference, Budapest, Hungary, October.

OECD (1992). *The Reform of Health Care: A Comparative Analysis of Seven OECD Countries*. Health Policy Studies, No. 2. Paris: OECD.

Paulson, E. (1995). Hospital financing in Sweden. In M. M. Wiley, M. A. Laschober and H. Gelband (eds), *Hospital Financing in Seven Countries*. Washington, DC: US Congress, Office of Technology Assessment.

Petersen, L. K. (forthcoming). Hospital financing in Denmark. In *Acute Hospital Care: Delivery and Financing*. Health Policy Studies Series No. 9. Paris: OECD.

Pfeiffer, K.P. (1995). The model of a new hospital financing system in Austria – its possible effects on hospitals. Paper prepared for the International Seminar on Health Care Management and Quality under Fixed Budgets, Hannover/Celle, Germany, March.

Republique Française (1991). *Loi No. 91-748 du 31 juillet 1991, portant sur la réforme hospitalière; Loi No. 91-738 du 31 juillet 1991, portant sur diverses mésures d'ordre social*.

Rodrigues, J.-M. (1996). The French connection. In Casemix and change – international perspectives. Proceedings of the eighth Casemix Conference in Australia, Sydney, 16–18 September.

Schneider, M. (1991). Health care cost containment in the Federal Republic of Germany. *Health Care Financing Review*, 12, 87–101.

Solstad, K. and Nyland, K. (forthcoming). Financing acute hospitals in Norway. In *Acute Hospital Care: Delivery and Financing*. Health Policy Studies Series No. 9. Paris: OECD.

Sourty-Le Guellec, M.-J. (1995). Hospital financing in France. In M. M. Wiley, M. A. Laschober and H. Gelband (eds), *Hospital Financing in Seven Countries*. Washington, DC: US Congress, Office of Technology Assessment.

Wiley, M. M. (1992). Hospital financing reform and case mix measurement: An international review. *Health Care Financing Review*, 13, 119–33.

Wiley, M. M. (1995). Budgeting for acute hospital services in Ireland: The case-mix adjustment. *Journal of the Irish Colleges of Physicians and Surgeons*, 24, 283–90.

WHO (1996a). *Health Care Systems in Transition: Finland*. Copenhagen: WHO Regional Office for Europe.

WHO (1996b). *Health Care Systems in Transition: Sweden*. Copenhagen: WHO Regional Office for Europe.

# 10

# CHANGING HOSPITAL SYSTEMS

## Nigel Edwards, Martin Hensher and Ursula Werneke

### INTRODUCTION

Growing public expectations, demographic change, the growth of technology and escalating costs have combined to make the control of health expenditure a key issue for many countries. In-patient care typically consumes 45–75 per cent of the resources dedicated to health provision. In several European countries it is perceived that there is scope for further reductions in the provision of hospital services and that there are more cost-effective alternatives. As a result hospitals have come under particular scrutiny as part of cost-containment policy.

Changes in the hospital network have also occurred for a number of other reasons such as the belief that people prefer to receive care in or near their homes. The trend towards sub-specialization, the need for expensive technologies, perceived economies of scope and scale and cost pressures have also tended to produce imperatives for fewer, larger hospitals providing acute or higher technology care with increased support in primary care or in sub-acute hospitals which may be more similar to nursing homes.

In spite of their importance in health systems, there is a paucity of research and evidence about hospitals as organizations, their future role and shape and how change in hospital systems can be implemented. There is an urgent need for more consideration to be given to the future of hospital systems in Europe and in particular into the policy instruments to bring about change.

There are various approaches to changing the hospital systems but in general policies appear to be aimed at achieving one or more of the following objectives: (1) increasing provider efficiency; (2) improving appropriateness of admission, utilization and discharge; (3) changing the shape of the network of hospital services to achieve a more efficient configuration. This chapter reviews the policies available to address these three areas and provides a review of trends in hospital care in Europe.

## TRENDS IN HOSPITAL CARE

Direct comparison of hospital data between countries is difficult since national statistics differ in terms of availability, completeness and denominators (e.g. per unit of time or population, unit of measurement, etc.). A further difficulty is that the role and the mode of provision of hospital care differs considerably between countries (Arnold and Pfaffrath 1993). Factors influencing these differences include reimbursement systems, the interface between primary and secondary care or the role and availability of social care.

The difficulties of comparing European countries are considerable, and comparisons between western Europe and the CEE/CIS countries are even more problematic because of institutional and other differences, such as the role of some hospitals and hospital beds, different public expectations about the role of hospitals or the approach to the management of patients.

In almost all western European countries the number of acute in-patient beds per head of population has fallen very significantly in recent years (see Figure 10.1). The reasons for these changes are not well documented but they have probably resulted from a combination of cost-containment policies, changes in technology or treatment modality and changes in the role of primary and social care. The impact of demographic and epidemiological factors do not appear to be particularly important although there is some evidence that an increase in the number of people with chronic illness may have contributed to a rise in admissions. An important policy lesson from these changes is that the large change in bed numbers has not led to a proportionate fall in expenditure on acute care. This may be due to the increased dependency of the patients in the

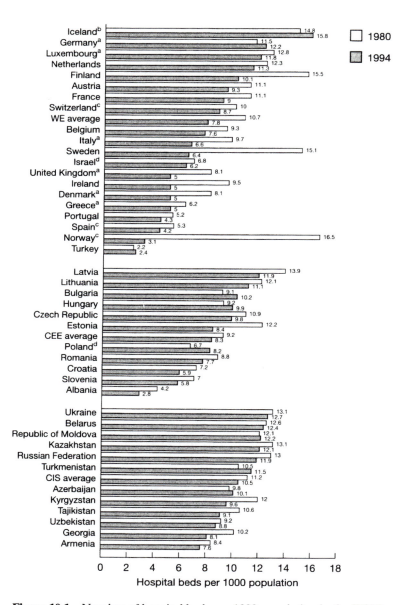

**Figure 10.1** Number of hospital beds per 1000 population in the WHO European Region, 1980 and 1994   *Note*: [a]1993; [b]1992; [c]1991; [d]1990

*Sources*: OECD (for western Europe); WHO Regional Office for Europe, *Health for All Database* (for CEE/CIS countries and for Israel, Norway and Sweden)

remaining beds, the high technology required to support them and the high costs of infrastructure which are only very indirectly influenced by changes in bed provision.

In most of western Europe there has been an increase in the admission rate from 1980 to 1994 and a reduction in length of stay with changes in the management of patients, improvements in clinical techniques such as minimally invasive surgery, and incentives to reduce lengths of stay and to discharge to other settings patients who no longer need acute care.

In the CEE/CIS countries there continues to be a large number of hospitals and hospital beds per head of population compared with western Europe. This has tended to be the result of norm-based planning which set hospital catchment populations at levels very much lower than elsewhere in Europe. This may have reflected a much heavier reliance on hospitals and a public preference for high levels of access combined with long distances and lower levels of private transport. The number of hospitals appears to be much more important than the size of the individual hospitals in explaining the high level of bed provision. This is a result of the large number of comparatively small hospitals.

There have been some falls in the number of hospitals and hospital beds although the fall has not been universal and has been less pronounced than that in western Europe. In general, small hospitals and maternity homes have been the main casualties where reductions have taken place. In many cases the bulk of the changes have taken place since 1990, reflecting a change in policy towards bed provision and in some cases changes in the total funding of the health sector. Overall, these data imply that there is still considerable scope for the closure of hospital beds and whole hospitals in the CEE/CIS countries.

The large number of hospitals and hospital beds is associated with very high levels of admission, very much greater than those in western Europe. It seems unlikely that this is purely the result of higher levels of morbidity or of underdeveloped primary and social care systems. It is probable that a substantial part of the difference can be accounted for by supplier-induced demand as a result of the large number of beds, and in some cases the short distances from hospitals that result from the high volume and density of provision in cities. A more concerning feature is the apparent collapse of admissions in some countries such as Armenia, Azerbaijan, Georgia, Turkmenistan and Uzbekistan. Some of this may be associated with the removal of incentives to record admissions to obtain payment but in a number of cases it is likely to be more associated with economic problems than policy changes.

## INCREASING EFFICIENCY OF PROVISION

There is general interest in measures to improve the efficiency with which hospitals are operated. A particular problem is the absence of a definition of what constitutes an efficient hospital (Braithwaite 1993) or how hospitals change (Shortell *et al.* 1995). Most of the literature in this field is from the US and suggests the use of indicators such as asset turnover ratios or the 'bottom line' (Fein 1990), which say little about the effectiveness with which care is delivered. Several approaches to improve the efficiency of hospitals have been adopted including (1) signalling financial constraints through techniques such as global budgets and performance targets, and (2) management improvements and adoption of measures to increase efficiency in service delivery such as the use of day-case and minimal access procedures.

### Signalling financial constraints[1]

The use of global hospital budgets is central to the changes in hospital systems in many western European countries. As budgets on their own do not necessarily provide incentives to improve performance they are sometimes combined with other mechanisms such as targets for key variables such as waiting times (Denmark, Spain, the UK), lengths of stay (Belgium, Italy, Slovakia, Spain, the UK), DRG or case mix systems (Germany from 1996, Hungary), bed quotas/occupancy (Belgium), staffing levels (Greece) and targets for levels of work (many systems).

Budgetary control is an indirect technique which relies on hospital managers and physicians responding appropriately to curtailed budgets. However, a number of conditions are required for such a response: (1) providing incentives to managers and clinicians to respond by improving performance other than simply constraining levels of work; (2) allowing hospitals to retain some of the savings achieved to fund developments; (3) allowing for the heavy costs of making adjustments such as staff terminations, rebuilding, centralization etc.; (4) monitoring financial performance and activity including levels of indebtedness; (5) involving clinical staff in introducing and managing change; and (6) giving unambiguous messages about the appropriate response to a budget (e.g. reduced income), including a belief that there are real penalties for failing to achieve it and a management capacity to respond. A feature of hospital management in a number of European countries is a belief (often demonstrated by experience) that hospitals will be rescued from bankruptcy. Furthermore, underdeveloped management capability combined with the absence of financial control systems has led to substantial and unsustainable indebtedness, often at the expense of staff and suppliers.

## Improving management

Hospitals have sought to increase technical efficiency through a series of management reforms to improve hospital performance. One trend has been the introduction of 'contracting out' for some support services. For instance, in the UK in the 1980s most hospitals competitively tendered their hotel services and while this has not been formally evaluated, there seem to be substantial cost reductions. This principle is now being extended and contracts for the full range of non-clinical support services (facilities management contracts) are being offered, and in some cases clinical services including pathology are being market tested.

A second trend is the adaptation of management techniques from other sectors to assist in improving the performance of hospitals. These include *benchmarking, business process re-engineering*, patient-focused care, quality-improvement techniques and internal-contracting models. Finally, there is a trend to develop general management expertise, supported by better information systems for decision making in clinical, financial and other managerial areas. There are several problems with approaches which concentrate exclusively on managerial changes and blanket efficiency targets. These can lead to concentration on marginal changes, diverting attention from more substantial efficiency improvements in the delivery of health care. Also, they may penalize organizations where attention had already been given to these issues and where the scope for further improvements in efficiency is lower.

## Day-case and minimal access procedures

In many European countries day-case procedures have been adopted as a major source of improved efficiency (Abel-Smith and

Mossialos 1994). Similar improvements are expected from minimally invasive surgery and the growth in diagnostic and interventional imaging techniques (Lee 1995). There is often an assumption that this work represents a pure substitute for in-patient care. However, at least some of this constitutes additional work made possible by the availability of new techniques, in particular endoscopy and MRI. Furthermore, if the capacity released by these new approaches is not closed, there may be an increase in admissions of other patients as a result of supplier-induced demand. Procedures which formerly required hospitalization and are now increasingly conducted as day cases include: inguinal hernia repair, varicose vein stripping, cystoscopy, arthroscopy, cholecystectomy and laparoscopy. Early experience suggests that growth of minimal access techniques requires a shift in the production function of hospitals from beds to operating theatres and from in-patient to community aftercare.

## IMPROVING THE APPROPRIATENESS OF ADMISSION, UTILIZATION AND DISCHARGE

A key part of a strategy for changing the role of hospitals is approaches designed to improve appropriateness of admission, use of services and discharge.

### Appropriateness of admissions

There are a number of approaches aimed at reducing the overall number of admissions. Clearly, primary prevention resulting in a reduced incidence of specific diseases offers the prospect of reducing disease-specific admission rates. Strategies involving primary prevention are explored in Chapter 5. This chapter focuses on three types of strategy for reducing the likelihood of inappropriate admission of those already ill: (1) primary care substitution; (2) raising admission thresholds; and (3) preventing admission through the provision of appropriate alternatives. Before focusing on these strategies a simplified model of the relationship between care modalities and disease severity is suggested below.

Figure 10.2 shows the hypothetical course of disease severity in a patient with a long-term condition. Region 1 (whose upper boundary is threshold A) represents, at any given time or level of technology, the degree of severity of disease which is managed routinely

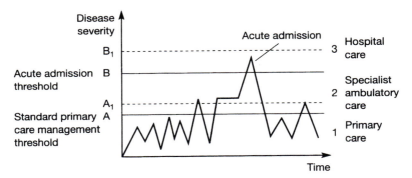

**Figure 10.2**   Schematic model – disease severity and management thresholds

within primary care as part of standard practice. Threshold B represents the degree of severity of disease which would be considered to warrant an 'appropriate' admission to hospital, thus Region 3 constitutes appropriate acute hospitalization. Region 2 consists of those patients who require specialist care but who do not require hospitalization. Thresholds A and B move over time (both upwards and downwards) and may well be 'fuzzy' lines (i.e. precise thresholds varying between practitioners, institutions and individual patients).

Raising the admission threshold (a move from B to $B_1$, i.e. an increase in the degree of severity required for admission) will reduce the proportion of cases of a given condition which will be admitted. Analogously, interventions (e.g. new drug therapies) may allow sufficient control of symptom severity that admission is no longer needed, pushing the severity 'peak' below the admission threshold. In Region 2, efforts to prevent admission will tend to centre upon 'enforcing' the admission threshold by ensuring that the services necessary to manage patients outside hospital are available and used effectively. Increasing the scope of conditions managed routinely within primary care (a shift in threshold from A to $A_1$) reduces the size of Region 2 – hence decreasing the number of patients in this region who might be vulnerable to inappropriate admission.

*Expanding the scope of primary care*

The diffusion of technology into primary health care has made possible the effective management of a growing range of conditions such as asthma, angina or diabetes. Arguably, however, the expansion in the scope of primary care is highly dependent on technology and technological change – essentially in the form of the development of new drugs, their diffusion into primary care use and the decline in their relative prices.

The evidence on the role of primary care as a partial substitute for secondary care derives mainly from the US, where access to primary care is closely linked to differing forms of insurance coverage. Recent US studies (Blumberg 1994) indicate that insurance coverage and access to health care appears inversely related to hospitalization rates for 'Avoidable Hospital Conditions' (AHC). Access to family and general practitioners in Pennsylvania (Parchman and Culler 1994) appears to be negatively correlated with hospitalization for AHCs. A similar result was found in a survey in a Norwegian county (Fylkesnes 1993). However, while primary care may be a direct substitute for certain types of *ambulatory* hospital care (Groenewegen 1991), the US studies do not necessarily imply a substitution relationship for conditions requiring *hospitalization*. It is possible that access to primary care has a categorical relationship with hospitalization (i.e. gaining access to basic primary care where none existed previously allows a 'one-off' reduction in hospitalization risk which has a much greater impact than any subsequent improvements in the scope or quality of primary care). Investment in primary care beyond the point of securing full coverage of basic services may therefore yield diminishing returns in its ability to prevent admission to hospital.

*Raising admission thresholds*

Hospital admissions can be prevented by raising the threshold severity for admission. Technological advances play an important role in this area. The development and expansion of day/ambulatory surgery has caused a fall in surgical admission thresholds. Cruder supply-side changes may also result in shifts in the admission threshold – when faced with a reduced bed stock due to bed closures, clinicians have little choice but to revise upwards their admission thresholds. Clinical, management and policy interventions can be designed to target the admission threshold directly. Short-stay observation units may safely separate out 'borderline' patients who will not actually require admission e.g. by ruling out acute myocardial infarction (Gaspoz *et al.* 1994). However, the assessment unit approach does not always reduce admission rates e.g. in asthma (Brillman and Tandberg 1994) and may be prone to becoming little more than an overspill bed pool when demand is high. Professional education and training on specific issues can be shown to reduce admission rates in certain circumstances: for example, a training programme for senior house officers in an English hospital facilitated a significant decrease in asthma admissions amongst children (Connett *et al.* 1993). In Italy, a combination of introducing diagnostic and therapeutic protocols, clinician training, observation beds and financial incentives for medical staff succeeded in reducing admissions (Rossi *et al.* 1993) in a large general hospital.

*Alternative interventions to admission*

A third family of approaches involves ensuring that patients in Region 2 of Figure 10.2 (i.e. those requiring specialist care but not admission) are prevented from 'slipping' over the admission threshold. Non-hospital specialist service provision can be facilitated by technological innovation or by deliberate policy changes in operating methods. Some approaches shown to achieve a reduction in admission rates include the development of a domiciliary management scheme using telephonic foetal heart rate monitoring for high-risk pregnancies (Dawson *et al.* 1989) or the introduction of community clinics and domiciliary visits by a team of specialist physicians and nurses (Swift *et al.* 1993). In Israel, weekly home visits by a physician to elderly patients with severe congestive heart failure halved annual admission rates (Kornowski *et al.* 1995). In Canada, enrolment of the elderly in a 'Long Term Care Program' (provision of health and social care at home or in nursing homes) resulted in reduced admission rates to acute hospital (Ellencweig *et al.* 1990). It may even be possible to use planned admissions to hospital-based respite care to avert acute medical admissions (Chang *et al.* 1992) in certain elderly patients with chronic conditions. However, annual comprehensive home health checks by specialist geriatric nurses in both California (Stuck *et al.* 1995) and South Wales (Pathy *et al.* 1992) did not result in any reduction in admission rates in patients over 75 years of age.

While these approaches may prevent acute admissions, they may also involve relatively resource-intensive interventions. The evidence is still substantially missing. Intensive home care may or may not be more cost-effective than admission but, even if cheaper, it may offer less real scope for resource savings than has hitherto been assumed (Hensher *et al.* 1996). Also savings resulting from prevented admissions arguably can only be realized if beds and inpatient capacity can be closed.

Admission may be avoided through the use of specific demand-side financing mechanisms.[2] For instance, Siu *et al.* examined the relationship between variation in the appropriateness of admission and differing levels of cost sharing by patients and insurers (Siu *et al.* 1986). They discovered a high level of 'inappropriate' hospitalization, but found that increasing levels of cost sharing by patients had the effect of reducing both inappropriate and appropriate admission indiscriminately. They argue that cost sharing alone is too blunt an instrument to prevent unnecessary admissions successfully without adversely affecting patients who genuinely require hospitalization.

**Utilization review**

Utilization reviews (UR) are an increasingly popular set of techniques for examining the appropriateness of admission and the use of in-patient beds. These techniques were first applied to contain expenditures in the US Medicare/Medicaid programmes (Payne 1987). In 1972, the federal government imposed a requirement for concurrent admission and length of stay review by a Professional Standard Review Organisation (PSRO). In the 1980s these techniques were further developed by insurers aiming to improve efficiency (Wickizer *et al.* 1989). In the US, financial incentives, e.g. fee-for-service payment, clinical incentives and legal incentives (defensive medicine), have encouraged the physicians to make heavy use of hospital services (Payne 1987). These incentives led to the introduction of pre-admission authorization. Patients who fail to obtain such authorization are often subject to financial penalties, but hospitals and physicians are rarely sanctioned.

Evaluations of the PSRO programmes have not produced consistent findings: some studies reported a reduction of hospital inpatient admission rates by 10–15 per cent, others did not detect any significant effect. Likewise, projections of cost savings differed considerably. Although UR may initially lead to reduction in length of stay and admissions, this effect seems to be greatest during the period following the review and to wane over time (Wickizer *et al.* 1989).

The realization that evaluation of utilization based on implicit criteria was arbitrary (and had only low to moderate inter-rater reliability), led to the development of instruments based on explicit criteria such as the Appropriateness Evaluation Protocol (AEP) and the Intensity Severity Discharge Protocol. These tools have been validated in the US but their applicability to other health systems has not been fully established. Thus, they should be applied with caution (Werneke and MacFaul 1996). The uncritical use of UR may induce barriers of access to appropriate care.

Any comparison of bed use between different providers or countries should take into account the following factors: (1) review instruments applied; (2) modifications of the review instrument; (3) method of data collection (case note review or interviews); (4) providers (primary, secondary or tertiary care facilities) and specialties sampled; (6) exclusion and inclusion criteria for patients; (7) seasonal patterns; and (8) time reference (retrospective, concurrent, prospective).

Table 10.1 gives examples of published UR. These results demonstrate the need for a more standardized and validated approach. UR techniques are in use in Europe, but mainly in health services research to audit clinical practice and increase the efficiency of hospitals.

### Improving discharge

A very large number of in-patient beds are occupied by a small proportion of patients, many of whom have ceased to benefit from the services of a hospital. Major changes to the size and role of hospitals could be effected if these patients could be dealt with more effectively. Therefore effective discharge is very significant. Two main approaches to improving discharge are improving the organization and clinical management of patients and adopting measures to expedite discharge once the patient has recovered. These may be indirectly influenced by the application of target-based systems such as the DRGs or other case mix systems (Czech Republic from 1996, Germany, Hungary), statistically-based targets (Slovakia), or targets incorporated into provider plans (UK). However these systems often offer considerable scope for gaming and may confirm sub-optimal practice if inappropriate mean lengths of stay are set or penalties are exacted for low but achievable lengths of stay as is the case in some DRG-based systems.

There appears to be more success in providing less detailed direction while providing incentives for physicians to develop audit and managerially-based approaches to improving length of stay. One

**Table 10.1**    Magnitude of inappropriateness of bed use

| Study | Location | Results |
|-------|----------|---------|
| Baré *et al.* 1995 | Barcelona, Spain | 9.1% of admissions |
| | | 29.2% of bed-days |
| Victor and Khakoo 1994 | Central London, UK | 0.7% of admissions |
| Victor *et al.* 1993 | Central London, UK | 14.6% of admissions |
| Namdaran *et al.* 1992 | Edinburgh, UK | 19% of beds for all specialties |
| | | 33.1% of beds for geriatric orthopaedic rehabilitation |
| | | 29.6% of beds for geriatric rehabilitation and assessment |
| McClaran *et al.* 1991 | Montreal, Canada | 19% of beds |
| Apolone *et al.* 1991 | Greater Milan, Italy | 41% of bed-days for all specialties |
| | | 12% of bed-days for surgery |
| | | 20% of bed-days for cardiology |
| | | 60% of bed-days for psychiatry,* geriatrics and neurology |
| Hynes *et al.* 1991 | Dublin, Republic of Ireland | 46% of beds for all specialties |
| Anderson *et al.* 1988 | Oxford, UK | 62% of bed-days |
| Coid and Crome 1986 | Outer London, UK | 10% of bed-days for all specialties |
| | | 22% of bed-days in medicine |
| | | 2% of bed-days in surgery |
| | | 9% of bed-days in orthopaedics |
| Popplewell *et al.* 1984 | Australia | 3.7% of admissions |
| | | 9.2% of length of stay |
| Seymour and Pringle 1982 | Dundee, UK | 4.2% of bed-days of all patients |
| | | 10.2% of bed-days in patients aged 65+ years |
| Murphy 1977 | Central London, UK | 16% of bed-days |
| Rubin and Davies 1975 | Liverpool, UK | 4.5% of bed-days |

*Note:* * AEP not valid for psychiatry

example is the integrated care pathways or anticipated recovery pathways developed in the US and now being implemented in the UK. The expected pattern of care for a patient is documented, variations are monitored and improvements developed as a result. The advantage of these systems is that they provide more clinically and locally meaningful information. These techniques are particularly useful when investigations or therapy are poorly programmed and happen sequentially rather than in parallel, as is the case in a number of models of hospital care in the CEE and CIS countries.

Another set of more effective measures aims at improving the ability of the hospital system to discharge patients who have ceased to benefit from the service of a fully equipped general hospital. As shown in the previous section many studies have found that a large number of hospital bed-days are used by these patients. Approaches available to deal with these patients include the development of home nursing (e.g. the Basque country, Denmark, Ireland, the Netherlands, the UK) and social care sectors; and more recently the introduction of 'Hospital at Home' initiatives. For instance, the growth in the nursing home sector in Ireland and the Netherlands has probably played a very significant role in the reduction in hospitalization. Also, many countries are converting small hospitals into nursing homes (e.g. in Belgium hospitals have been able to redesignate beds from acute care to nursing home use). Regression analysis as part of the resource allocation process in the UK found that nursing home provision had a significant effect on admission rates and bed-days used. The development of nursing homes can be promoted by changing payment systems to providers.

Measures have been introduced to improve coordination between the health and social care sectors by joint planning (Ireland, the UK) or by imposing financial penalties for delays in placing patients that require social care (Denmark, Sweden). Often, responsibility for these sectors is separated but experience suggests that joint management (Ireland and Northern Ireland) or a single purchaser (Hungary) is not a guarantee of improved coordination. These policies generally require cost shifting to individual users or their families, either directly in the form of co-payment (often required for nursing home care), or indirectly by requiring family members to provide some of the care. The growth in the number of women in the workforce, an increase in the proportion of people living alone and changes in expectations will make these policies more difficult to introduce.

## CHANGING THE CONFIGURATION OF THE HOSPITAL SYSTEM

A third set of policy approaches to changing the hospital system is aimed at improving the configuration of the hospital system. A number of issues arise, first, in planning hospital needs and second, in managing change.

### Planning hospital needs

There are major gaps in the evidence to inform the planning of hospitals. This represents a serious obstacle to change and presents the hazard that decisions will be taken which have very important long-term adverse implications for health systems. This section addresses a series of key issues that need to be considered in planning hospital needs.

### *Beds or hospitals – what is the correct unit of analysis?*

Many hospital reform programmes have focused on bed numbers. However, beds, or even wards, may not be the correct unit of analysis for policy formation, while hospitals may be a more sensible unit. There are some key issues that need to be considered. First, at least 30 per cent of the costs of hospitals are associated with the buildings, utilities and other facilities; this figure may be very much greater in the CEE/CIS countries. A further significant percentage of overhead costs are tied up in 'indivisible' assets and staff whose numbers are, at best, only very indirectly related to bed numbers. Second, the accuracy of bed statistics is such that many beds may only exist on paper or may be largely unoccupied. In a number of CEE/CIS countries large numbers of beds have been closed with only a small impact on the capacity of the system, as they have been declared as available but are not in fact staffed or used. Third, as noted above, if performance improves faster than bed numbers fall or occupancy rises, the real capacity of the system can increase, allowing admissions to rise. Low occupancy produces financial problems by depressing asset utilization ratios and increasing the unit price to purchasers.

Finally, large numbers of small cuts are damaging to morale, particularly in already efficient hospitals which may have less scope to make savings. In order to make the greatest impact on the costs of the hospital system, it appears that whole hospitals will need to be closed rather than adjustments made to the total bed stock.

*What constitutes an appropriate distribution of specialist services?*

The distribution of specialist services such as cardiac surgery, neuro-surgery, plastic surgery or cancer services is an issue of concern and has received particular attention in many European countries such as the UK where financial constraints and the shortage of medical staff have given the issues particular urgency. The pattern of distribution of treatment and diagnostic services (often wastefully duplicated) owes much to history and may have significant disadvantages in terms of lost economies of scale and potentially poorer clinical outcomes. The single specialty hospital, whilst still surviving, appears to be a particularly endangered species.

For example, London, with a population of 7 million, has 14 cardiac centres, 13 cancer centres and 13 providers of neuro-sciences. Budapest, a city of 2 million, has 10 cardiac units, 5 cancer units and 21 neurology units. Bishkek, a city of 465,000, has 7 cardiac departments/hospitals, 1 cancer unit and 8 neuro-sciences units (with neurology and neuro-surgery on different sites). In many cities the distribution of less specialized services is also an issue particularly in vascular surgery, maternity, neonatal and paediatric services.

Many European countries have systems for controlling the purchase of specialist and expensive medical equipment and the development of specialist services. However, these systems are less well developed for dealing with existing sub-optimal distribution. Markets are not well able to address the over-provision or duplication of specialist services as non-price competition for hospital care tends to encourage the development of specialist units. There are also perverse incentives in more planned systems; for instance, the possession of a specialist unit can be used to justify the presence of other support services, thus protecting the hospital from closure. As a result attempts to restructure specialist services face major difficulties.

- In general hospitals specialist services make substantial contributions to covering overhead costs. A specialist unit closure means that either the entire hospital's viability is threatened and/or the unit price and total cost rises.
- Specialist services often have a high profile and enjoy a high level of public support which creates a political barrier to change.
- The rationalization of these services often requires substantial investment in the hospital chosen as the site for centralization and the writing-off of capital assets in other hospitals.

- The poor record of planning systems in many countries means that it may be difficult to recruit support for a planning-based solution.
- The concentration of duplicated facilities in major cities and capital cities presents particular political problems. In a number of eastern European countries, dealing with over-provision in the capital would make a very substantial impact at national level.

### How do hospitals operate now?

Three key areas of uncertainty are the effects of economies of scale and scope on hospital efficiency and the lack of evidence on alternative models of hospital management.

- *Economies of scale.* If there are major returns to scale then the centralization of hospital services would be a sensible policy direction subject to considerations of accessibility. There have been few conclusive studies into the effect of scale on efficiency. Studies in this area suffer from substantial methodological difficulties such as assessing the value of outputs or identifying the correct level of analysis. Moreover, the complexity and style of the analysis that is available is such that it is hard to translate into locally applicable policy (Department of Health 1995).

  A second uncertainty relates to the relationship between the quality of outcomes and the volume of work undertaken. While there is evidence in this area (Black and Johnston 1990) the relationship is less strong than might have been expected and in some cases even non-existent (Sheldon *et al.* 1997). However, the problem for policy makers is that, whilst there is clearly an intuitive link, this may be difficult to apply convincingly in the case of an individual hospital without risk-adjusted outcomes data. A further difficulty is determining whether the relationship is related to the individual physician or the organization's competence (Lawton *et al.* 1991). Finally, users may be willing to trade actual waiting or travel times against the risk of a lower quality outcome.
- *Economies of scope.* The origin of hospitals as institutions has arisen from the need to group activities together to make best use of resources. In modern medicine patients are often referred between different specialties, and this allows those opposed to change the opportunity to construct arguments that individual services should not be relocated or closed because of the impact

this will have on remaining services. It is difficult to determine which of these arguments are true and which are special pleading by those who feel threatened. The evidence for economies of scope is very limited and rarely sufficient to justify a change in the pattern of provision (Sheldon *et al.* 1997).

- *Effective management.* Although the literature about clinical effectiveness is increasingly well developed there is little research-based evidence about the components of effective hospital management. There is not even an agreed definition of what constitutes an effective hospital. There are reasons to doubt whether the examples of excellence drawn from general management theory are applicable on any but the most superficial level. There is also insufficient understanding about the mechanisms available for changing hospital services. In the past many policies have had unintended consequences and even within the same system managerial approaches do not appear to be readily transferable: hospitals are complex systems and the way that they respond to internally generated change or external stimuli is contingent on culture, relationships and the interaction with external systems.

*What is the impact of technology on the way care is provided?*

Improvements in technology may result in centralization because of the high costs involved, or may allow the dissemination of a whole range of techniques outside hospitals (Banta 1990). Although there is an extensive literature about the effectiveness of technology, little consideration has been given to how it will be used and, in particular, what the impact of some of the expected developments might be. This applies to new medical technologies such as molecular medicine or minimally invasive techniques but also to the development of informatics including remote diagnosis, improved information for self-care and even remote treatment.

The literature on the future of hospitals suggests fewer, larger high-technology hospitals serving very large populations, perhaps supported by community hospitals, ambulatory care centres, home care and primary care. However, there is a lack of debate about the costs and benefits of alternative methods of providing acute care. Sometimes, bold statements about hospital at home, day hospitals, sub-acute beds and other alternatives are made and acted upon without sufficient evidence. An unresolved question concerns the role, function and relative cost-effectiveness of the small hospital.

Small hospitals can offer services ranging from general medical services, minor injuries treatment, simple surgery, diagnosis and investigation through to rehabilitation, terminal care and respite care.

### Are there limits to improved performance and substitution?

Clearly, current trends in reduction of length of stay and hospitalization cannot continue indefinitely. If they did, then as Vetter (1995) suggests, the last hospital bed in the UK will close in 2030, after 14 million patients will have passed through it in the preceding year! This paradox suggests that either there will be a quantum shift in how we provide care for people who currently use hospitals or there will be some plateauing of the trends. However, based on the US experience, there is no sign at present that in Europe the limits to reduced lengths of stay and reductions in hospital use have been reached.

In the CEE/CIS countries, hospital admission rates and lengths of stay are particularly high. Although primary care and home care is less well developed there appear to be no clinical or social reasons (other than clinical behaviour and patient expectations) why major change could not be implemented. However, to reach western European rates major changes in primary care, social care, patient expectations, informal care and other support systems are required.

### What will be the future demand for hospitals?

Finally, planners, purchasers, policy makers, investors and hospital managers have to contend with fundamental uncertainties about the future demand for hospital services. These include: (1) the impact of ageing and changes in population structure; (2) demand from migrant and ethnic minority groups; (3) social changes affecting the population's willingness to be cared for at home; (4) the impact of changing expectations about the role of hospitals and health systems; (5) and (6) the ability of primary health care to facilitate discharge, maintain patients at home and prevent admission.

## Managing change

The history of managing change in hospital systems is not very encouraging. An important reason for this is the political and financial costs of hospital closure. In a number of systems this is exacerbated by the absence of a banking function or the ability to hold reserves which means that it is difficult to fund large one-off expenditures such as capital investment or staff redundancy compensation. A second problem arises from the perceived importance of hospitals in the mind of the public, which makes even small changes contentious.

In a number of countries it is not clear who is leading the process of change in hospitals. For instance, the creation of insurance funds in a number of CEE countries and a less than clear set of relationships with other bodies such as health ministries, finance ministries or parliaments allows several institutions to assume they are leading the process. Organizations that have the mechanisms to produce change may not have a clear policy framework to help them define what the change ought to be.

The history and reasons for change in hospital systems are poorly understood. Although there have been a number of interesting policy changes and natural experiments these have often not been evaluated or even documented. There are a number of areas where further research is required:

- What is the impact of competition and ownership concentration on price and the costs of the system?
- How can support for change be recruited from key internal stakeholders, in particular doctors?
- How can effective mechanisms be developed for communicating with the public?
- How can change be managed in such a way that the debate about the future of hospitals is not unduly distorted by political factors (so that whilst policy makers remain accountable for the general policy direction they are not required to be responsible for decisions about individual hospitals)?
- Which models of hospital management are most effective in delivering change?
- What is the role of hospitals in the local economy?

## CONCLUSIONS

The development of hospital policy and policy making needs strengthening. It also must be appreciated that, whilst a number of the changes in the use of hospitals have originated from deliberate policy initiatives, many others were not explicitly planned but have evolved where the culture and policy framework has allowed it. A combination of market and planning mechanisms may be required, operating on both the demand- and supply-side of the system, to achieve this sort of change. It is rarely sufficient to rely on only one policy instrument such as reimbursement systems. A framework of approaches to changing hospital systems is shown in Table 10.2.

It has generally been found that unexpected consequences and gaming opportunities result from attempts to apply a single set of incentives to hospital systems. For example, reimbursing hospitals for days of care in CEE countries prior to recent reforms provided incentives to over-admit and to extend length of stay. Many of the measures described in this chapter are complementary and the challenge for policy makers is to build these into a system which will achieve the objective of increasing the appropriateness of hospital use and the efficiency of the system but which is flexible enough to allow innovation. It is very important that policy makers approach this as a systems problem and do not address elements of hospital

**Table 10.2**   Policy approaches to reform hospitals

| *Supply-side* | *Demand-side* |
|---|---|
| *Indirect mechanisms* | *Indirect mechanisms* |
| • Changing behaviour using reimbursement systems | • Payment incentives to encourage treatment of patients in primary care |
| • Changing market structure and behaviour by changing ownership (e.g. privatization) | • User charges |
| • Global budgets (possibly with other targets e.g. staffing targets) | *Demand management* |
| | • Appropriateness and utilization review |
| *Changing care delivery* | • Evidence-based purchasing or explicit rationing of hospital care |
| • Treatment protocols | |
| • Performance management e.g. target setting for length of stay | • Developing primary health care substitutes |
| • Business process re-engineering | • Social and home care solutions |
| • Cost-reduction/efficiency programmes | • Managed care or disease management |
| | • Prevention strategies including self-care and primary care interventions |
| *Planning approaches* | |
| • Hospital closure and reconfiguration programmes | |

provision individually without reference to their impact on the whole system.

Although reduced length of stay and increased day-case work allows either additional work to be performed or beds to be closed, their impact on costs is complex. To achieve shorter stays additional resources such as therapists, nurses or staff with other specialist skills may need to be deployed. Furthermore, unless the fall in length of stay is as a result of technologies which reduce the dependency of the patients (e.g. minimally invasive surgery), the need for skilled nursing care of the patients who remain in hospital will increase.

Unless the closure of beds keeps pace with the fall in length of stay or there are measures to control admissions it is probable that the threshold for admissions will fall and admission rates will rise. This is demonstrated by a recent study in two counties in the UK which showed a significant fall in the crude and age-standardized death rate of admissions. A threshold change appears to explain part of the major increase in emergency admissions experienced in a number of UK hospitals. In this case the hospitals are discharging patients who have a low cost per diem and replacing them with higher-cost patients who require a range of treatment and investigation. As a result total cost of the hospital system could increase.

Measures to improve the efficiency of hospitals and improve length of stay also need to take into account the impact on other parts of the system. If patients have high levels of dependency on discharge they are likely to make demands on primary care services or even, on occasion, require readmission. This may reduce the willingness or the ability of the primary health care system to prevent other admissions. The problem is likely to be more acute where there are institutional barriers between different types of care delivery, for example in Germany (until recently) and a number of other CEE countries where outpatients are generally followed up after discharge by doctors who were not responsible for the period of hospital care.

An important reason why an integrated approach is required is that the savings that can result from lower lengths of stay and reduced admissions may be difficult to realize. A strategy for identifying cost savings or reallocation is required. Savings may be significantly reduced by the high technology and the larger numbers of highly skilled (and more expensive) staff – at the bedside, in clinical support and in management – often required to achieve improved performance. The fixed costs of health provision are high, and very significant costs are associated with infrastructure. Therefore, marginal reductions in bed numbers may be of little assistance in making savings.

## NOTES

1 Hospital reimbursement and financing policy is a key part of any attempt to reform the hospital sector and is considered in detail in Chapter 7.
2 The use of cost-sharing mechanisms is explored in Chapter 3.

## REFERENCES

Abel-Smith, B. and Mossialos, E. (1994). Cost containment and health care reform: A study of the European Union. *Health Policy*, 28, 89–132.

Anderson, P., Brodhurst, S., Attwood, S., Timbrell, M. and Gatherer, A. (1988). Use of hospital beds: A cohort study of admission to a provincial hospital. *British Medical Journal*, 297, 910–12.

Apolone, G., Alfieri, V., Caimi, V., Cestart, C., Crispi, V., Crosti, P.F. *et al.* (1991). A survey of the necessity of the hospitalisation day in an Italian teaching hospital. *Quality Assurance in Health Care*, 3, 1–9.

Arnold, M. and Pfaffrath, D. (1993). *Krankenhaus Report '94*. Stuttgart: Gustav Fischer Veerlag.

Banta, H. D. (1990). Future health care technology and the hospital. *Health Policy*, 14, 61–73.

Baré, M. L., Prat, A., Lledo, L., Asenjo, M. A. and Salleras, L. L. (1995). Appropriateness of admissions and hospitalisation days in an acute-care teaching hospital. *Revue d'Épidémiologie et de Santé Publique*, 43, 328–36.

Black, N. and Johnston, A. (1990). Volume and outcome in hospital care: Evidence, explanations and implications. *Health Services Management Research*, 3, 108–14.

Blumberg, M. S. (1994). Impact of extending health care coverage to the uninsured. *Health Affairs*, 1, 181–92.

Braithwaite, J. (1993). Defining excellence in health services management: Evidence from an international study. *Journal of Health Planning and Management*, 8, 5–23.

Brillman, J. C. and Tandberg, D. (1994). Observation unit impact on emergency department admission for asthma. *American Journal of Emergency Medicine*, 12, 11–14.

Chang, J. I., Karuza, J., Katz, P. R. and Klingensmith, K. (1992). Patient outcomes in hospital-based respite: A study of potential risks and benefits. *Journal of the American Board of Family Practitioners*, 5, 475–81.

Coid, J. and Crome, P. (1986). Bed-blocking in Bromley. *British Medical Journal*, 292, 1253–6.

Connett, G. J., Warde, C., Wooler, E. and Lenney, W. (1993). Audit strategies to reduce hospital admissions for acute asthma. *Archives of Diseases in Childhood,* 69, 202–5.

Dawson, A. J., Middlemiss, C., Coles, E. C., Gough, N. A. and Jones, M. E. (1989). A randomized study of a domiciliary antenatal care scheme: The effect on hospital admissions. *British Journal of Obstetrics and Gynaecology,* 96, 1319–22.

Department of Health (1995). *Economies of Scope and Scale in Health Services: Summary of Evidence.* Leeds: NHS Executive.

Ellencweig, A. Y., Stark, A. J., Pagliccia, N., McCashin, B. and Tourigny, A. (1990). The effect of admission to long-term care program on utilization of health services by the elderly in British Columbia. *European Journal of Epidemiology,* 6, 175–83.

Fein, R. (1990). For profits look at the bottom line. *Journal of Public Health and Policy,* 11, 49–61.

Fylkesnes, K. (1993). Determinants of health care utilization – visits and referrals. *Scandinavian Journal of Social Medicine,* 21, 40–50.

Gaspoz, J. M., Lee, T. H., Weinstein, M. C., Cook, E. F., Goldman, P., Komaroff, A. L. and Goldman, L. (1994). Cost-effectiveness of a new short-stay unit to 'rule out' acute myocardial infarction in low risk patients. *Journal of the American College of Cardiology,* 24, 1249–59.

Groenewegen, P. P. (1991). Substitution of primary care and specialist care: A regional analysis in Denmark. *Social Science and Medicine,* 33, 471–6.

Hensher, M., Fulop, N., Hood, S. and Ujah, S. (1996). Does hospital-at-home make economic sense? Early discharge versus standard care for orthopaedic patients. *Journal of the Royal Society of Medicine,* 89: 548–51.

Hynes, M., O'Herlihy, B. P., Laffoy, M. and Hayes, C. (1991). Patients' 21 days or more in an acute hospital bed: Appropriateness of care. *Irish Journal of Medical Sciences,* 160, 389–92.

Kornowski, R., Zeeli, D., Averbuch, M. *et al.* (eds) (1995). Intensive home-care surveillance prevents hospitalisation and improves morbidity rates among elderly patients with severe congestive heart failure. *American Heart Journal,* 129, 762–6.

Lawton, R., Burns, R. and Wholey, D. (1991). The effects of patient, hospital and physician characteristics on length of stay and mortality. *Medical Care,* 29, 251–3.

Lee, S. (1995). *Hospital Care in Europe: The Challenge of a Changing Role.* Financial Times Management Report. London: Financial Times Business Information.

McClaren, J., Tover-Berglas, R. and Glass, K. C. (1991). Chronic status patients in a university hospital: Bed-day utilization and length of stay. *Canadian Medical Association Journal,* 145, 1259–65.

Murphy, F. W. (1977). Blocked beds. *British Medical Journal,* 1, 1395–6.

Namdaran, F., Burnet, C. and Munroe, S. (1992). Bed blocking in Edinburgh hospitals. *Health Bulletin,* 50, 223–7.

OECD (1996). *OECD Health Data 96.* Paris: Organisation for Economic Co-operation and Development.

Parchman, M. L. and Culler, S. (1994). Primary care physicians and avoidable hospitalizations. *Journal of Family Practice*, 39, 123–8.

Pathy, M. S. J., Bayer, A., Harding, K. and Dibbl, A. (1992). Randomised trial of case finding and surveillance of elderly people at home. *Lancet*, 34, 890–3.

Payne, S. M. C. (1987). Identifying and managing inappropriate hospitalisation. *Health Services Research*, 22, 709–69.

Popplewell, P. Y., Chalmers, J. P., Burns, R. J., Miller, C. D. and Mullins, P.G. (1984). Peer review of utilisation of medical beds at Flinders Medical Centre. *Australia and New Zealand Journal of Medicine*, 14, 226–30.

Rossi, P., Tosato, F., Franceschinis, P., Barberi, M., Zuddas, M., Barboni, E. and Perraro, F. (1993). Improving quality in emergency services to reduce hospital admission. *Quality Assurance in Health Care*, 5, 127–9.

Rubin, S. G. and Davies, G. H. (1975). Bed blocking by elderly patients in general hospital wards. *Age and Ageing*, 4, 142–7.

Seymour, D. G. and Pringle, R. (1982). Elderly patients in a general surgical unit: Do they block beds? *British Medical Journal*, 284, 1921–3.

Sheldon, T., Furguson, B. and Posnett, J. (1997). *Concentration and Choice in the Provision of Hospital Services*. York: Centre for Reviews and Dissemination, University of York.

Shortell, S. *et al.* (1995). Reinventing the American hospital. *Millbank Quarterly*, 73, 131–60.

Siu, A. L., Sonnenberg, F. A., Manning, W. G. *et al.* (1986). Inappropriate use of hospitals in a randomized trial of health insurance plans. *New England Journal of Medicine*, 315, 1259–66.

Stuck, A. E., Aronow, H. U., Steiner, A. *et al.* (eds) (1995). A trial of annual in-home comprehensive geriatric assessments for elderly people living in the community. *New England Journal of Medicine*, 333, 1184–9.

Swift, P. G., Hearnshaw, J. R., Botha, J. L., Wright, G., Raymond, N. T. and Jamieson, K.F. (1993). A decade of diabetes: Keeping children out of hospital. *British Medical Journal*, 307, 96–8.

Vetter, N. (1995). *The Hospital: From Centre of Excellence to Community Support*. London: Chapman and Hall.

Victor, C., Nazareth, B., Hudson, M. and Fulop, N. (1993). The inappropriate use of acute hospital beds in an inner London District Health Authority. *Health Trends*, 25, 94–7.

Victor, C. R. and Khakoo, A. A. (1994). Is hospital the right place? A survey of inappropriate admissions to an inner London NHS trust. *Journal of Public Health Medicine*, 16, 286–90.

Werneke, U. and MacFaul, R. (1996). Evaluation of appropriateness of paediatric admission. *Archives of Disease in Childhood*, 74, 268–74.

WHO (1996). *Health for All Database*. Copenhagen: WHO Regional Office for Europe.

Wickizer, T. M., Wheeler, J. R. C. and Feldstein, P. J. (1989). Does utilisation review reduce unnecessary hospital care and contain cost? *Medical Care*, 27, 632–47.

## 11

# REGULATING EXPENDITURE ON MEDICINES IN EUROPEAN UNION COUNTRIES

Elias Mossialos

## INTRODUCTION

The continuous rise in the cost of pharmaceuticals has caused increasing concern to governments since the 1970s. Expenditure on pharmaceuticals has risen faster than GDP in all Member States of the EU in the past 15 years and currently accounts for between 10 and 20 per cent of the total cost of health care.

The rise in drug costs has been fuelled by several factors, foremost among which are changing demographic patterns with an increase in elderly populations and patients with chronic diseases, and the introduction of expensive new medicines. In response to this rising expenditure, all countries have introduced measures to contain costs. In most cases, these measures have been introduced on an *ad hoc* basis and their effects have been difficult to evaluate.

This chapter compares pharmaceutical consumption and expenditure levels in EU Member States, describes the various cost-containment measures that have been introduced and analyses their impact. Drawing on this information, future policy options are then discussed. Evidence provided in this chapter is based on published descriptive and analytical studies obtained through databases (i.e. Medline, International Bibliography of Social Sciences), official publications of international organizations (OECD) and studies published by research institutes and organizations (WldO, CREDES). Pharmaceutical cost-containment measures change often and it was necessary to contact experts and policy makers in a number of countries to produce up-to-date comparative tables. The data presented in these tables are the most recently available at the time of writing. The chapter refers to developments up to the end of 1996.

## PHARMACEUTICAL CONSUMPTION AND EXPENDITURE

International comparisons of pharmaceutical consumption are usually based on the available units of measurement. These mainly include pharmaceutical expenditure, and/or number of boxes or number of counting units (i.e. tablets). Current pharmaceutical expenditure depends partly on the quantity supplied and partly on the price of goods (Lecompte and Paris 1994). Comparisons of pharmaceutical expenditure across different countries do not always permit safe conclusions about the amount of consumption since prices differ extensively between countries. Similarly, the number of boxes delivered does not take into consideration significant differences in the sizes of boxes. Lecompte and Paris estimated that in the case of analgesics, the average number of tablets per box ranges from 16 in Italy to 84 in the UK due to differences in delivery mode. The number of counting units is also not an ideal unit of measurement, since it is not always properly recorded and typically fails to reflect differences in dosages in different countries. Given these limitations, data from the OECD data bank and from a study conducted by the Association of German Pharmacists (ABDA) were used to estimate indirectly the level of pharmaceutical consumption in a number of EU Member States. The OECD figures do not always provide uniform definitions and data. In most cases, the 'over-the-counter' market is included but in some figures the data refers only to the ethical market.

In 1993, consumption measured in terms of prescription items per capita (described as boxes in the OECD data bank) ranged from 5.2 items in Sweden to 52 items in France. The relevant figures for Denmark and the UK were 7.6 and 9.0 respectively. The figure for Germany was 13.9 items per capita in 1992.

Pharmaceutical prices differ extensively between EU Member States. One attempt at comparison is shown in Table 11.1. This

**Table 11.1** Pharmaceutical price levels in Europe – the ABDA study

| Country | 1988 | 1990 | 1991 | 1992 | 1993 |
|---|---|---|---|---|---|
| Belgium | 88.6 | 92.6 | 100.5 | 107.7 | 116.2 |
| Denmark | 128.1 | 136.7 | 143.4 | 134.6 | 132.9 |
| France | 71.5 | 66.9 | 63.8 | 60.2 | 63.4 |
| Germany | 128.4 | 116.6 | 110.5 | 105.0 | 105.4 |
| Greece | 73.8 | 80.0 | 85.5 | 80.8 | 84.7 |
| Ireland | 130.5 | 132.2 | 129.8 | 129.5 | 133.2 |
| Italy | 79.1 | 89.4 | 96.1 | 102.8 | 95.5 |
| Luxembourg | 97.1 | 93.5 | 94.5 | 93.6 | 97.1 |
| Netherlands | 131.9 | 129.9 | 134.1 | 139.0[a] | 148.4[a] |
| Portugal | 67.5 | 57.9 | 57.7 | 60.9 | 67.0 |
| Spain | 71.6 | 76.6 | 83.7 | 89.4[a] | 93.5[a] |
| UK | 115.9 | 125.6 | 124.6 | 126.4 | 122.7 |

*Note*: Price index: EU = 100     [a] provisional figures

*Source*: IOO (1995)

table, produced by the ABDA, is based only on 129 products chosen in 1988 and thus excludes a number of new products. The calculation has been criticized for this and other reasons. For example, it includes a number of 'over-the-counter' drugs which are not reimbursable and excludes generic drugs. The results should therefore be interpreted as only broadly indicative (IOO 1995).

Table 11.2 shows pharmaceutical expenditure as a percentage of GDP and of health expenditure in selected EU countries. It also shows pharmaceutical expenditure per head in US dollars. What is striking is the high proportion of health expenditure apparently devoted to drugs in Greece; however this figure is based on OECD data (OECD 1996) which is likely to greatly underestimate total health expenditure. Using a country estimate (Abel-Smith *et al.* 1994) brings the figure down from 23.5 per cent to 16.7 per cent. Also significant is the fact that, in terms of US dollars, Germany spends on drugs per head more than twice the level observed in the UK, and the difference between the UK and France is nearly as great. This may result from higher volume in France and from both higher prices and volume in Germany. The Netherlands has the lowest percentage of health expenditure on drugs despite its high prices and a free pricing system. Expenditure is equally low in Denmark where prices are again high and a free pricing system operates, modified after 1993 by a reference price system affecting a

**Table 11.2**   Pharmaceutical expenditure in the EU Member States in 1994

| Member State | Pharmaceutical expenditure as a percentage of GDP | Pharmaceutical expenditure as a percentage of health expenditure | Pharmaceutical expenditure per head in US $ |
|---|---|---|---|
| Austria | 1.0 | 10.2 | 244 |
| Belgium | 1.4 | 17.5 | 323 |
| Denmark | 0.7 | 10.8 | 207 |
| Finland | 1.1 | 11.9 | 205 |
| France | 1.6 | 16.8 | 369 |
| Germany | 1.8[a] | 18.9[a] | 416[a] |
| Greece | 1.1[c] | 23.5[b] (16.7*) | 98[b] |
| Ireland | 0.9 | 11.5 | 132 |
| Italy | 1.5 | 17.4 | 258 |
| Luxembourg | 1.0 | 15.6[c] | 274[c] |
| Netherlands | 0.9 | 10.7 | 205 |
| Portugal | 1.9 | 25.2 | 168 |
| Spain | 1.3[c] | 18.2[b] | 194[b] |
| Sweden | 1.0 | 13.2 | 229 |
| UK | 1.1 | 15.4 | 186 |

*Note*: [a] 1993      [b] 1992      [c] 1991
        * based on the country estimate (Abel-Smith *et al.* 1994)

*Source*: OECD Health Data (1996)

small part of the market. The low level of expenditure reflects the low level of consumption of pharmaceuticals (Bartels-Petersen 1994).

The fact that France, Germany and Italy are high-consuming countries was confirmed by a comparative study of these countries and the UK undertaken in 1992 (Lecompte and Paris 1994). Using data provided by International Medical Statistics – an international market research company – the study measured pharmaceutical consumption levels for a number of therapeutic categories in four European countries. To overcome measurement problems, the authors estimated Defined Daily Doses (DDD) for all products examined. The DDD for a drug is established on the basis of the assumed average dose per day for the drug used for its main indication in adults. The results of the study are presented in Table 11.3.

**Table 11.3** Pharmaceutical consumption in DDDs per 1000 inhabitants and per day in Germany, France, Italy and the UK (1992)

| *Therapeutic class* | *Germany* | *France* | *Italy* | *UK* |
|---|---|---|---|---|
| Drugs for the treatment of peptic ulcer | 9.0 | 13.7 | 15.8 | 17.1 |
| Antihypertensives | 139.0 | 166.1 | 103.8 | 118.9 |
| • Hypotensives | 10.6 | 20.3 | 4.9 | 2.6 |
| • Diuretics | 47.6 | 46.9 | 24.1 | 62.0 |
| • B-blockers | 22.2 | 29.8 | 11.3 | 24.3 |
| • Calcium channel blockers | 40.3 | 33.9 | 32.4 | 20.9 |
| • ACE inhibitors | 18.2 | 35.3 | 31.1 | 9.1 |
| Peripheral vasodilators | 30.3 | 56.4 | 22.8 | 2.9 |
| Lipid-lowering drugs | 13.0 | 31.8 | 8.1 | 2.1 |
| Antibiotics | 10.6 | 26.2 | 14.0 | 13.3 |
| Non-steroidal anti-inflammatory drugs | 23.3 | 30.4 | 31.0 | 32.6 |
| Analgesics | 24.1 | 55.1 | 15.0 | 50.5* |
| Anti-epileptics | 4.6 | 5.8 | 2.7 | 5.6 |
| Psycholeptics | 36.3 | 128.5 | 51.2 | 33.2 |
| Psychoanaleptics | 11.8 | 27.3 | 11.2 | 13.8 |

*Note*: * This estimate takes into account only pharmacies' distribution of analgesics. It greatly underestimates the utilization of analgesics in the UK

*Source*: Lecompte and Paris (1994)

Consumption patterns differ significantly among the four countries, with higher consumption in France in most therapeutic categories. In the case of antihypertensive drugs, it seems that UK doctors are more 'conservative' and prescribe more diuretic drugs, whereas the French, German and Italian doctors prescribe more ACE inhibitors and calcium antagonists. It is shown that a number of products with ambiguous therapeutic effectiveness (such as peripheral vasodilators or hypolipidaemics) are heavily prescribed in France, Germany and Italy. This is not the case in the UK. It is also doubtful that the high consumption of psycholeptics and antibiotics in France reflects real therapeutic needs. A study in 1992 (Garattini and Garattini 1993) also showed that in France and Italy only about 50 per cent of the pharmaceutical expenditure for the first 50 products most sold by value goes on the purchase of agents showing efficacy. This figure rises to about 70 per cent in Germany and 95 per cent for the UK.

## COST-CONTAINMENT MEASURES

EU Member States' response to rising expenditure has been a series of *ad hoc* measures to contain costs. Cost-containment strategies in the pharmaceutical sector include measures aimed at influencing the supply- and demand-side of the market as well as addressing the problems created by the monopoly character of the industry. The industry has some features of monopoly power in a number of sub-markets where there are no therapeutic alternatives. Pharmaceutical producers also enjoy substantial monopoly power because of patent and regulatory barriers to competitive entry (e.g. significant costs for obtaining market authorization). The role of promotion of new products, which in many countries is entirely exercised by the industry, may also enhance its monopoly power. Demand-side strategies operate on patients (i.e. cost sharing, development of a market for over-the-counter (OTC) products) with the aim of making them price sensitive. Demand-side strategies also operate on health care providers (doctors and pharmacists who act as patients' agents) with the aim of minimizing the problem of induced demand and making the provision of pharmaceutical care more cost-effective. The objective is to change the behaviour of providers through financial incentives, penalties or other regulatory measures.

One way of attempting to influence providers' behaviour is by changing the method by which doctors are paid. Doctors paid on a salary or capitation basis have fewer incentives to over-prescribe because in general they have fewer incentives to over-treat. Another way is to introduce practice budgets for GPs or office-based doctors.

Supply-side strategies to deal with the pharmaceutical industry mainly include price controls seeking to keep prices down and/or to regulate the industry's profits. The UK Pharmaceutical Price Regulation Scheme (PPRS) is a profit control system that also indirectly regulates pharmaceutical prices. Other measures that may influence price level and stimulate price competition include the development of markets for generics and parallel imports as well as the imposition of revenue or fixed budgets for the industry. Controls on the number of products and promotion expenditure also aim at mitigating the industry's influence on providers. The aim of negative lists is to shift to the consumer the full cost of pharmaceutical care for certain treatments. Another aim is to reduce consumption of drugs whose effectiveness is questionable. However, an undesired effect may be to switch prescribing to more expensive products included in the positive list. Table 11.4 gives an account of

**Table 11.4** Alternative cost-containment strategies in the pharmaceutical sector in 1996

---

**Demand-side strategies**

- Demand-side strategies operating on patients

  Cost sharing (all countries but the Netherlands)
  Developing a market for over-the-counter products (France, Germany, the Netherlands and the UK)
  Health education programmes (the Netherlands, UK)

- Demand–proxy-side strategies operating on doctors and pharmacists

  *Payment systems*
  Capitation or salary payment for first contact doctor (several countries including Finland, Ireland, Italy, the Netherlands, Spain, Sweden and the UK)
  Paying pharmacist on a flat-rate not percentage basis (the Netherlands and the UK)

  *Budgets for pharmaceutical expenditure*
  Fixed budgets for doctors (fundholding GPs in the UK)
  Indicative budgets for doctors (Germany, Ireland and non-fundholding GPs in the UK)
  Fixed budgets for pharmaceutical expenditure (Italy)

  *Policies encouraging cost-effective prescribing and delivery of pharmaceuticals*
  Practice guidelines (France)
  Use of cost-effectiveness studies (mainly in France, Sweden and the UK, but not in a systematic way)
  Information and feedback to physicians (Denmark, Germany, the Netherlands, Sweden and the UK)
  Prescription auditing (several countries but not in a systematic way except in the Netherlands and the UK)
  Disease management (experiments in France and the UK)
  Encouraging generic substitution (several countries but mainly with doctor's agreement)

**Supply-side strategies operating on the industry**

- Price controls (all countries except Denmark and Germany for most patented products)
- Reference prices (Denmark, Germany, Italy, the Netherlands, Sweden)
- Profit control (UK)
- Industry contributions when budgets are exceeded (Germany in 1993)
- Revenue or fixed budgets for the industry (France, Spain)
- Positive and/or negative lists (all countries)
- Controlling the number of products (mainly Denmark and the Netherlands)
- Ceilings on promotion expenditure (Spain, UK)
- Taxes on promotion expenditure (France, Sweden)
- Promoting the use of generics and stimulating price competition (mainly Germany, the Netherlands, the UK)
- Development of a market for parallel imports (Denmark, Germany, the Netherlands, the UK)

---

the different approaches to cost containment introduced in the last ten years. A fundamental question is the long-term effectiveness of different measures.

The way health care is organized and delivered in different countries may also affect pharmaceutical regulation and provision. In this context, one would expect that where a monopsony buyer exists, regulation should be more effective at least in setting reasonable prices for new products and auditing the volume of products prescribed. However, with some exemptions, this is far from being the case.

In the UK, cost-containment measures focused on both the supply-side (e.g. PPRS) and the demand-side (e.g. GP fundholding and practice budgets). A number of countries where an NHS, with supposedly monopsony powers, exists, have failed to contain expenditure despite introducing measures aiming at controlling the supply-side of the system through price control systems. This is the case in Greece, Italy, Portugal and Spain.

When examining policy options in the pharmaceutical sector, the following policy dilemma confronts a number of governments, especially those with a significant pharmaceutical industry of their own: how does a state reconcile its attempts to contain costs, which in most cases constitutes a considerable proportion of health expenditure, with its efforts to increase jobs and exports? This dilemma is reflected in the price-setting schemes in several countries. Other governments, however, have no incentives to expand their industrial base since their home environment is not attractive for investments. The dilemma is becoming more important in the EU where policies for harmonization of pricing and reimbursement of pharmaceuticals have defied resolution due to the principle of subsidiarity (enshrined in the Treaty of the EU) which holds that governmental functions should be undertaken at the lowest practicable level. Pharmaceutical expenditure has been the 'usual suspect' in almost all cost-containment plans. However the effective life of different measures to contain expenditure is frequently shorter than the time required to develop and introduce them. Given accelerating changes in the way health care systems are organized, the lifetime of different measures may be even shorter in the future.

## ANALYSIS OF COST-CONTAINMENT MEASURES

### Demand-side measures operating on consumers

*Cost sharing*

Table 11.5 summarizes the payments which patients normally have to make out-of-pocket for pharmaceuticals. All countries rely on such payments, with the exception of Ireland (for General Medical Service patients) and the Netherlands. There are exemptions for those with low incomes and other categories which vary among EU countries. The proportion of the cost paid by the patient varies by type of drug in Denmark, France, Greece, Italy and Portugal and for certain classes of drug in Belgium. In Germany, the payment now varies according to pack size. It is a flat-rate sum in the UK

**Table 11.5**   Cost sharing in the EU Member States in 1996

| Country | Percentage of items exempted | Charges |
| --- | --- | --- |
| Austria | 18 | ATS 42 per prescription |
| Belgium | None | Flat rate plus 0/25/50/60/80/100% of price |
| Denmark | N/A | 0/25/50/100% of price |
| France | 9 | 0/35/65/100% of price |
| Germany | N/A | 3, 5 or 7 marks depending on pack size based on days of treatment |
| Greece | Negligible* | 0/10/25% of price |
| Ireland | GMS -100 | None for GMS patients; Category II eligibility patients: up to £(IR) 90 per quarter |
| Italy | 32 | Flat rate of 3000 lire (£1.20) for first two items or 3000 lire for first two plus 50% of price |
| Luxembourg | None | 0/20% of price |
| Netherlands | 100 | None |
| Portugal | 45 | 0/30/60% of price (15 and 45% for low-income persons) |
| Spain | 62 | 0/10/40% of price |
| Sweden | Negligible | SEK 160 for the first item and SEK 60 for further items |
| UK | 85 | Flat rate of £5.40 |

*Note*:   N/A = not available        * very low – just chronic sick and for some drugs in Belgium, while a standard proportion of the cost in Spain. There are extensive exemptions in Belgium, Denmark, Germany, Italy, Spain and the UK.

### Developing a market for OTC products

OTC drugs vary in kind among different countries, according to the criteria set by governmental agencies. In 1993 in the EU, the OTC market accounted for 22 per cent of the total market, with the largest markets being France and Germany (LSE Health 1995). However, the size of the market for OTC products is not easy to measure, since the rules governing OTC products, the funding systems and the outlets where OTC products are sold vary considerably between countries. There are no data available to estimate to what extent self-medication has resulted in less frequent visits to office-based doctors or GPs.

## Demand-side measures operating on providers

### Paying the doctor

Attempts can be made to influence the authorizing behaviour of doctors. One technique is to change the method by which doctors are paid. Payment schemes based on capitation give the providers incentives to reduce the cost of treatment and may minimize supplier-induced demand. This was also the conclusion of a recent cross-sectional study which estimated that capitation systems in primary health care tend to have lower pharmaceutical expenditure (OECD 1995). A fee-for-service payment scheme provides incentives for over-utilization of services and over-prescribing. Denmark, the Netherlands and the UK have always had a capitation element under the compulsory health insurance schemes. More recently, Finland, Ireland and Sweden also introduced a capitation scheme.

### Practice guidelines and the use of cost-effectiveness studies

In 1994, France started a system of 'medical references' (Références Médicales Opposables). These evidence-based medicine practice guidelines are used to assess medical practice outside hospitals. They specify when and how to use different procedures, including drug prescriptions related to a disease or health condition. Doctors who do not follow these references could be penalized financially or excluded from the social security system. To date, an initial list of some 200 references has been developed and accepted by the government.

The impact of cost-effectiveness studies and other types of evaluations comparing costs and outcomes on decision making concerning pricing and reimbursement decisions and on prescribing is still to be felt (Sloan and Grabowski 1997). In France, cost-effectiveness studies are considered by the committees dealing with pricing and reimbursement of pharmaceuticals but the real impact on decision making is still insignificant (Le Pen 1997). In Germany, there is no use of cost-effectiveness studies in reimbursement decisions (Schulenburg 1997). In the Netherlands, economic evaluation studies have played a limited role in reimbursement decisions. Elsigna and Rutten have reported and analysed a case study of one drug (simvastatine) for which cost-effectiveness had an impact (Elsigna and Rutten 1997). Drummond, Cooke and Walley reviewed the use of economic evaluation studies in the UK and concluded that the NHS reforms increase the potential for the use of economic evaluation (Drummond *et al.* 1997). However, cost-effectiveness studies have not as yet had a significant impact on pricing and reimbursement decisions.

### Promotion of generics

Within the EU as a whole, generic medicines in 1992 accounted for about 6.5 per cent of the total ethical pharmaceutical market and generated revenues estimated at $2.5 billion (Ball 1994). Over 80 per cent of these revenues came from sales in four markets (Denmark, Germany, the Netherlands and the UK). Generic prescribing is likely to grow further in countries which are encouraging it. It has been calculated that the potential market is 77 per cent of all drugs in France, 64 per cent in Germany and 63 per cent in the UK (Dukes 1997). A limited form of generic substitution is permitted in Germany, Italy, the Netherlands and Spain. Substitution with the physician's agreement is permitted in Belgium, Denmark, Ireland, Portugal and the UK. On the contrary, substitution is prohibited in France and Greece and permitted only for emergencies in Luxembourg. Generic prescriptions are strongly encouraged and promoted in Germany, the Netherlands and the UK. The use of generics is also encouraged in Denmark and Portugal. There is no governmental promotion of generics in Belgium, Greece, Ireland,

Italy, Luxembourg and Spain. The market for generics is more significant in countries where prices of the original products were high and in countries where firm or indicative budgets for doctors were introduced.

Methods of remunerating pharmacists generally do not provide any incentives for generic substitution even where substitution is encouraged. Only the Netherlands provides incentives for pharmacists to substitute since they can retain a third of the savings. The differences are important in the context of the spread of the generic market. Clearly pharmacists have no incentive to substitute when they are paid on the basis of a percentage of the price. One reason why generic penetration has been high in both the Netherlands and the UK is because pharmacists receive a fixed fee per drug item.

**Supply-side measures**

*Regulation of pharmaceutical prices*

Methods of regulating or influencing pricing are shown in Table 11.6. The underlying mechanisms are shown in the right hand column, even where they have recently, as in France, been superseded by budgets. Several countries have been introducing multiple systems for controlling pharmaceutical prices in the past few years. Most countries in western Europe control either the price or the profit margin of the pharmaceutical industry, with the exception of Denmark and Germany, and partial indirect control in Luxembourg. A type of convergence in pharmaceutical regulation can be seen in the use of a reference price system. This operates by grouping together similar products and specifying a price which will be fully covered by the insurance (reference price), subject to co-payment. The use of a reference price as a reimbursement benchmark indicates that the public payment system will only pay that particular price. Any additional amount above the reference price must be paid by the insured person. The issue remains as to the criteria used for the selection of the 'reference' price. This system was first used in Europe by Germany, where it now applies to about 70 per cent of all pharmaceutical expenditure and will be extended still further. It was introduced in the Netherlands in 1991, in Sweden in 1992, in Denmark in 1993 and in Italy in 1996.

A profit control system exists only in the UK. Prices are set by the pharmaceutical industry and are indirectly controlled through

**Table 11.6**  Main means of regulating or influencing medicine prices in 1997

| Country | Underlying mechanism to regulate or influence prices |
|---|---|
| Austria | Prices based on cost (based on production costs in locally based pharmaceutical companies) |
| Belgium | Prices based on improvement over existing therapy (a) |
| Denmark | Free pricing plus a reference price system excluding most patented drugs |
| Finland | Prices are regulated |
| France | Prices fixed on medical effectiveness and negotiation with each company |
| Germany | Free pricing plus a reference price system excluding most patented drugs |
| Greece | Prices fixed based on cost, transfer price and the lowest price in the EU |
| Ireland | Prices in Denmark, France, Germany, the Netherlands and the UK |
| Italy | Average prices of Germany, France, Spain and UK plus a reference price system |
| Luxembourg | Prices of Belgium, free pricing if no price in Belgium |
| Netherlands | Maximum prices are the average of those in Belgium, France, Germany and the UK, plus a reference price system including most patented drugs |
| Portugal | Lowest price among France, Italy and Spain |
| Spain | Prices based on 'cost' |
| Sweden | Negotiated price and a reference price system excluding patented drugs |
| UK | Profit regulation |

*Note*: (a) A product is reimbursed if its price does not exceed the price of any patent medicine containing the same active substance or 110–150 per cent of the price of a patent medicine with an equal therapeutic effect

the PPRS. The PPRS regulates the profits which companies make from their sales to the NHS. The scheme covers all branded pharmaceutical products sold to the NHS (including those whose patents have expired but are still sold by a brand name). The scheme measures profitability in terms of the return on capital employed. For companies which do not have any significant capital in the UK, it is assessed on the basis of return on sales. The use of return on capital employed reflects the regulator's objective to prevent pharmaceutical companies from making excessive profits from the NHS.

## Ceilings and taxes on pharmaceutical promotion expenses

A tax on total promotion expenditure (9 per cent) by pharmaceutical companies is used in France. The most complicated system is in the UK, where expenses above a certain level, defined by formula for each company, are disallowed for the purposes of calculating company returns for the PPRS. In Sweden, a tax of 11 per cent exists only on printed material with the company and/or product name. In Spain, promotion expenditure is limited to between 12–16 per cent of the retail price.

## Positive and negative lists

Positive and negative lists for drugs have been introduced in a number of EU countries. Some countries with positive lists may also have negative lists; however a positive list subsumes the negative one. Ireland in 1982 developed a negative list of drugs which cannot be provided for General Medical Services patients. Germany also removed certain minor drugs from coverage by health insurance in 1983 and more in 1991. In 1985, the UK removed from the NHS a range of drugs – mainly those obtainable without prescription – and extended that negative list in 1992. In 1993, Spain removed 800 drugs from the reimbursement list. From 1993, non-allopathic drugs were no longer reimbursed in the Netherlands. Positive lists of what may be paid exist in Belgium, Denmark, France, Greece, the Netherlands and Portugal but in the last it is not effectively enforced. In 1993, Italy removed from the positive list 55 per cent of the 9500 drugs then available on the market. The positive list has been modified several times since then.

## Number of products

Some countries control the market for products in order to reduce pressures from manufacturers on physicians to prescribe new products as well as to minimize pressure on regulatory authorities when the industry asks for price increases. It is notable that Denmark manages with only about 4900 brand-named products compared to 10,000 in the UK and 23,000 in Germany (Abel-Smith and Mossialos 1994).

## Expenditure ceilings

These can operate on top of other measures, such as the reference price system in Germany or the PPRS system in the UK (Table 11.7). Seven countries have established budgets that are either agreed with industry (France, Spain), or have incentives (Ireland and the UK) or penalties for doctors (France, Germany), or which are simply laid down by the government (Italy). Some countries also seek to change authorizing behaviour by giving doctors responsibility for budgets, as in the UK where general practitioners have been authorized to become fundholders, or by offering doctors part of any savings achieved on target as in Ireland (O'Donoghue 1994). Fundholding practices in the UK have an allowance for prescribing within the firm budgets allocated to them by regions, plus the added advantage of being able to allocate funds among drugs, staff and alternative treatments.

## Parallel imports

Parallel trade occurs due to the large differences in pharmaceutical prices between countries. The role of parallel imports is still relatively small – up to 6 per cent of the drug market in the UK and 12 per cent in the Netherlands, 3 per cent in Denmark and 2 per cent in Germany (Pickering 1996). The growth of the generic market makes parallel importing less attractive. One factor which may lead to an expansion of this market is the emergence of pan-European

**Table 11.7** The role of budgets for pharmaceutical expenditure in 1996

| Country | Budget |
| --- | --- |
| France | Revenue maximum per company. From 1996, target budgets for each doctor. If exceeded, the level of fees may be reduced |
| Germany | Indicative budgets for each doctor and for each region (doctors at risk for up to DM 280 million if budgets are exceeded) |
| Ireland | Target prescribing budgets for all doctors participating in the General Medical Service |
| Italy | Laid down by government |
| Spain | 7 per cent growth of expenditure for three years to be enforced by the industry from 1995 |
| UK | Indicative for non-fundholding GPs but firm for fundholders |

wholesalers, offering to supply a broad range of products at the lowest prices.

## Impact of cost-containment measures

Pharmaceutical expenditures have increased more rapidly through increases in volume and the introduction of expensive new medicines rather than due to a general increase in prices (Abel-Smith *et al.* 1997). Countries where the percentage of health expenditure is higher tend to be more rigorous in their attempts to control spending. It is typically less politically sensitive to control the price of drugs than to expand positive and negative lists or introduce fixed budgets, since these often generate opposition from patient organizations and political parties. It is also less politically sensitive than to attempt to interfere with the autonomy of doctors in what they authorize for their patients. Evidence can be found from particular EU countries about the effectiveness of specific measures. Some of the cost-containment measures have been short-term such as controlling pharmaceutical prices. Some have been likely only to achieve results on a one-time basis, such as increasing cost sharing or the introduction of negative and positive lists. Others have been more fundamental such as changing the incentives facing providers by altering the methods of remunerating doctors or imposing cash limited budgets for pharmaceutical expenditure.

Cost-containment measures are seldom introduced singly. Where more than one measure is introduced, it becomes difficult to evaluate the effect of each one separately. It is also difficult to quantify whether increasing pharmaceutical expenditure and care has an impact on other parts of the health system and to what extent it achieves significant efficiency gains. The growth of studies on comparative cost-effectiveness will help policy makers allocate resources on the basis of expected outcomes. At this stage, however, an overall quantification of the effects of different treatment alternatives is extremely difficult.

### Cost sharing

Increased cost sharing is likely to achieve results on a 'once and for all' basis. Several studies have shown that the demand for prescription drugs is reduced by a direct contribution from the patient. However, the price elasticities which measure the scope

of the decrease of drug consumption range at low levels from
–0.1/or –0.2 to –0.6 (Huttin 1994). It should be also emphasized
that most of these studies offer only preliminary answers and
focus only on a limited share of the population. A review of a
number of studies conducted in the UK shows that higher charges
are associated with a decrease in pharmaceutical consumption
(Fattore in press). These studies also suggest that the demand for
drugs is relatively inelastic. Evidence from the only randomized
control trial available – the RAND Health Insurance Experiment
(HIE) in the US – shows that lower levels of cost sharing were
associated with higher pharmaceutical expenditure overall (Leibovitz *et al.* 1985). This was not, however, combined with higher
levels of generic products utilization (Anderson *et al.* 1990).
Brook *et al.* (1983), based on the RAND HIE data, found that
low-income patients exempted from cost sharing had significant
improvements in visual acuity and significant reductions in blood
pressure compared with non-exempt patients.

### Practice guidelines

The examination of profiles of doctors' work and prescriptions only
seems to have limited effect. However this may depend on what
sanctions are applied and how often they are imposed. In France,
while the guidelines relating to drug prescribing had only a limited
effect on spending in 1994, some of them had a significant impact on
prescribing behaviour. It has been estimated that the 14 pharmaceutical guidelines could have a potential effect on 14 million prescriptions, equivalent to 1.9 per cent of all prescriptions issued by
office-based doctors in 1994 (Le Fur and Sermet 1996).

### The effect of price controls

In several countries, strict price control systems have been the
major cost-containment measure in the last 20 years. But price controls, if not combined with other measures (i.e. volume controls or
budgets), may also create perverse incentives which encourage
companies to introduce new products. In some countries, pharmaceutical companies have been trying to bypass strict price controls
on old products or competition from off-patented products by
launching new products that are not necessarily innovative. Strict
price controls in France have not prevented a significant increase in
the volume of pharmaceutical consumption. Two recent studies

confirmed that price controls failed to contain pharmaceutical expenditure in Spain and Sweden (Jönsson 1994; Lopez-Bastida and Mossialos 1997). Jönsson estimated that real drug expenditure in Sweden increased by 95 per cent between 1974 and 1993. During the same period, the relative price of drugs fell sharply, by 35 per cent. The number of prescribed drugs increased by 22 per cent but most of the increase in real drug expenditure can be attributed to a residual which increased by 146 per cent during the period 1974–93. Five factors were defined to affect the residual: (1) the introduction of new drugs into therapeutic areas where there were no other drugs available; (2) the switch from inexpensive to expensive drugs; (3) the introduction of new and cheaper generic drugs; (4) the sale of old drugs in larger packages; and (5) the sale of old drugs in smaller packages. Jönsson argued that the switch to more expensive drugs is the most important factor. Lopez-Bastida and Mossialos estimated that while real drug expenditure increased by 264 per cent between 1980 and 1996, the relative price of drugs fell by 39 per cent and the number of prescribed items increased by 10 per cent. Most of the increase can be attributed to a residual – mainly new products – which increased by 442 per cent between 1980 and 1996 (Table 11.8). Lopez-Bastida and Mossialos also found that most of these new drugs did not really offer new therapeutic potential.

*Fixed reimbursement systems*

The weakness of fixed reimbursement systems is that their introduction does not necessarily decrease the drug budget, as experience in Germany and the Netherlands has shown. Germany introduced in 1993 a range of further measures – including a cut of 5 per cent in prices not covered by the scheme and a firm drug budget with penalties for exceeding it – despite the continuation of the reference price system. In 1989, spending by sickness funds on pharmaceuticals rose by only 0.4 per cent. This was very low compared with an increase of 8.5 per cent in 1988. However, as Table 11.9 shows, the impact of the reference price system was short-term. The table presents the annual increases in pharmaceutical expenditure, volume of prescriptions and cost per prescription between 1988 and 1993 as a percentage over the previous year. According to Klauber (1994) a third component, the structural component (particularly the changes in the package size of prescription drugs), also contributed to increases in pharmaceutical expenditure. This led to the link of co-payments with package sizes.

**Table 11.8** Price and quantity in pharmaceutical expenditure in Spain, 1980–96

| Year | Real expenditure (1) | Relative price (2) | Quantity (3) | Residual (4) |
|------|------|------|------|------|
| 1980 | 100 | 100 | 100 | 100 |
| 1981 | 103 | 95 | 99 | 110 |
| 1982 | 113 | 85 | 99 | 134 |
| 1983 | 114 | 83 | 95 | 145 |
| 1984 | 114 | 81 | 93 | 151 |
| 1985 | 121 | 77 | 95 | 165 |
| 1986 | 124 | 73 | 95 | 179 |
| 1987 | 144 | 71 | 95 | 213 |
| 1988 | 165 | 71 | 99 | 235 |
| 1989 | 189 | 68 | 101 | 275 |
| 1990 | 212 | 66 | 106 | 303 |
| 1991 | 241 | 66 | 108 | 338 |
| 1992 | 270 | 64 | 107 | 394 |
| 1993 | 284 | 61 | 107 | 435 |
| 1994 | 294 | 60 | 105 | 467 |
| 1995 | 327 | 60 | 108 | 505 |
| 1996 | 364 | 61 | 110 | 542 |

*Note*: Index  1980 = 100
Column 1  Real pharmaceutical expenditure index, 1980–96
Column 2  Retail price index (VAT excluded) divided by consumer net price index (VAT excluded), 1980–96
Column 3  Prescribed medicines index, 1980–96
Column 4  Col.1/(Col.2*Col.3/100)*100

*Source*: Lopez-Bastida and Mossialos (1997)

One effect of the reference price system was that drug manufacturers made a major effort to promote drugs not covered by it and succeeded in increasing the market share of these more costly products. Companies could even raise the prices of these products to recover losses created by the reference price system. In Germany, pharmaceutical companies increased the prices of products not yet affected by the reference price system. Between 1991 and 1992 drug prices subject to reference prices decreased by 1.5 per cent while drug prices in the market segment free of reference prices increased by 4.1 per cent (Selke 1992). Reference prices were set on average at 30 per cent below the previous price of the brand name products. However the expected boom of the market for generics did not

**Table 11.9**   Germany: annual percentage increases of total pharmaceutical expenditure, volume of prescriptions, cost per prescription and 'structural component' (1988–93)

| Year | Pharmaceutical expenditure | Volume | Cost per prescription | Structural component |
|------|---------------------------|--------|----------------------|---------------------|
| 1988 | 8.5 | 4.1 | 4.2 | 2.7 |
| 1989 | 0.4 | –3.5 | 4.1 | 2.9 |
| 1990 | 6.5 | 5.3 | 1.1 | 1.3 |
| 1991 | 10.8 | 3.8 | 6.7 | 5.1 |
| 1992 | 9.8 | 3.2 | 6.3 | 4.0 |
| 1993 | –14.5 | –10.4 | –4.6 | –0.8 |
| 1988–1993 | 36.0 | 12.9 | 22.4 | 16.3 |

*Source*: Klauber (1994)

occur. In terms of sales revenue, the annual growth of 2 per cent of the generic market prior to the 1988 Health Care Reform Act has slowed down to about 1 per cent annually since. Reference prices did not prevent increases in volume in all market segments, and in some cases physicians prescribed expensive patented products and ignored cheaper alternatives. The Netherlands also successfully reduced prices by 5 per cent; however, pharmaceutical expenditures continued to rise after the introduction of reference prices for a part of the market (De Vos 1994).

In Sweden, in the year following the introduction of the fixed reimbursement system, the growth of pharmaceutical sales was 1.6 per cent less than the previous year. However, the next year, 1994, growth was at its highest during the last six years. A recent study (Zammit-Lucia and Dasgupta 1995) found that a fall in sales in the reference price segment of the market was more than outweighed by greater-than-average sales growth in the rest of the market, so that overall sales were largely unaffected. The study also found that changes in prescribing structure were the main driver of growth of pharmaceutical expenditure in Sweden. Following the introduction of the reference pricing, this contributor to growth became even more important. Trends in Sweden were, therefore, quite similar with those observed in Germany.

### Positive and negative lists

There is insufficient evidence concerning the impact of positive and negative lists on costs. The Department of Health in the UK estimated in 1984 that limiting prescriptions in the seven selected groups could save the NHS up to £100 million a year, but afterwards downgraded this to £75 million a year. These expectations were criticized since the Department never indicated how these figures were calculated. It was pointed out that assessing the impact of how many patients were shifted to products that remained available for prescription within the NHS is almost impossible (Bateman 1993). Reilly *et al.* observed an increase in orders for H2 antagonists following restrictions on prescriptions of antacids, suggesting that 'switching up' may occur, which could significantly limit potential savings from a limited list (Reilly *et al.* 1986). This example, however, is not the best one, because at the period of the observation the growth rate of prescriptions for H2 antagonists was high and has continued to be high for many years since then.

Two studies have shown that the introduction of the UK limited list resulted in a reduction in the rate of prescribing. One used a time series regression model to estimate that the introduction of the UK negative list resulted in a reduction in the rate of prescribing by 300,000 items per month (Ryan and Birch 1991). O'Brien estimated that the impact of the policy was to reduce the rate of prescribing by some 260,000 scripts per month (O'Brien 1989). The first study used data for January 1969 to December 1985. The limited list was introduced in April 1985. We do not know, therefore, to what extent the limited list had a lasting effect or resulted in a once and for all reduction of the rate of prescribing. Evidence from Ireland indicates that the introduction of the negative list in 1982 had a significant effect on pharmaceutical consumption, and that it took seven years before the actual prescribing rate returned to its previous high level although the rate of annual rise was regained by 1984 (Feely 1992). There were, however, confounding factors which diminished the extent to which financial savings were achieved. The removal of a number of products from reimbursement resulted in a significant increase in the prescription of other products which were retained on the list (Ferrado *et al.* 1987).

### Budgets for doctors or the industry

In the UK, several studies comparing fundholding practices and non-fundholding suggested that fundholding GPs have not reduced the cost of their prescribing in absolute terms, but also that the increase in the costs of their prescribing was slower than that of non-fundholders (Glennerster *et al.* 1995). There is also evidence that indicative budgets have not reduced the cost of prescribing in the UK (Brandlow and Coulter 1993; Glennerster *et al*. 1995). Maynard and Bloor argue that it is difficult to assess how financial incentives influence prescribing as most studies of fundholding have been descriptive and none is adequately controlled (Maynard and Bloor 1996).

In Germany, budgets may have created incentives for office-based doctors to refer patients for in-patient hospital care. The overall drug budget in 1993 seems to have been effective in its first year of operation, reducing overall expenditures by 2.2 bn DM. These savings are due both to a reduced number of prescriptions compared to 1992 (−10.4 per cent) and a reduced value of each prescription (−4.6 per cent). Nevertheless, referrals to other specialists increased by 9 per cent and referrals to hospitals where drug budgets do not apply increased by 10 per cent. It has been calculated that these alternative strategies incur additional direct costs of 1.3 bn DM to the sickness funds plus additional indirect costs (loss of productivity) of 1.5 bn DM (Schulenburg and Schoffski 1993).

In Spain, the agreement between the government and the Association of the Pharmaceutical Industries to limit the growth in social security expenditure on medicines to 7 per cent per annum for the period 1995–7 was not respected (Farmindustria 1996). In 1995, the market grew by 13.4 per cent and the industry had to pay back to the government the gross profit at 56.73 per cent on any sales exceeding the ceiling (Lopez-Bastida and Mossialos 1997). The industry has recently threatened to cancel this agreement.

In Italy, the fixed budget introduced in 1995 seems to have resulted in a reduction of public expenditure. However, it is not possible to disentangle its effect because an extensive negative list was introduced at the same time as well as a system of average prices for pharmaceuticals taking into account the prices in France, Germany, Spain and the UK. The expenditure ceiling for 1995 set at 9000 bn lire was exceeded by 520 m lire which was, however, less than the actual expenditure in 1994 (9772 bn lire) (Farmindustria 1996).

In France, it seems that the revenue maximum per company established in 1994 had a one-off effect. The target for the growth of the market for 1994 was set at 3.2 per cent. The actual growth rate was 2.1 per cent (0.7 per cent growth for the expenditure reimbursed by the *Sécurité Sociale*). However, in 1995 the expenditure reimbursed by the *Sécurité Sociale* rose by 6.9 per cent (Lancry and Sandier in press).

## CONCLUSION

Governments are faced with conflicting policies in the field of pharmaceuticals. They find costs difficult to curb, other than by acting directly or indirectly on prices or by user charges. While some governments (mainly the Netherlands and the UK) have established mechanisms to monitor prescribing, persuade doctors to adopt more rational prescribing and induce them to be more cost conscious, southern European countries have so far failed to introduce any of these measures. Hence these countries place greater reliance on price control and/or user charges, which in turn makes them more resistant to other measures. On the other hand, a number of governments are keen to increase investment and exports. In this context, the manufacture and development of innovative ethical drugs is a likely area for expansion in advanced societies with high educational and scientific standards. This may explain the reluctance of a number of countries to enact price-control schemes. The incomplete character of the Single European Market in the pharmaceutical sector plays a significant role in some countries' decision making concerning price setting for new drugs since these prices can be used by other countries as benchmark prices.

Countries which have not yet done so need to consider introducing measures which have proved effective in other countries. In the UK, firm budgets give a clear incentive for economical prescribing, since the fundholding doctors can retain half of any savings for approved expenses for their practice and any overspend has to be taken from other parts of their budgets. Some non-fundholding general practitioners are allowed to retain for practice improvements up to 35 per cent of savings below a figure slightly lower than their 'target budgets'. It is not surprising that fundholding general practitioners prescribe generics more than non-fundholders. Nevertheless, there is still room for a large growth in the generics market as there are wide variations in the extent to which doctors prescribe them (Audit Commission 1994). Also, budget controls can become more effective if they are rigorously enforced and, in some cases, backed up by practice guidelines. The impact of negative and/or positive lists for medicines may be negligible due to 'switching up' policies. These policies can be more effective if they are combined with prescription audit policies. Cost sharing can transfer costs from the public sector to the private sector and restrain total costs, providing this is not counteracted by extensive private or complementary insurance for co-payments. However, de-insuring patients in this way can have damaging effects on equity and increase inequalities in access to health care. More countries could encourage generic prescribing in a variety of ways and introduce positive lists based on cost-effectiveness studies.

If a balance is achieved through both supply and demand measures, then a volume–price trade-off may be considered. The issue, however, is to what extent this trade-off represents value for money and leads to a cost-effective provision of pharmaceutical care.

What is therefore important is a fundamental reassessment of the decision-making process. This could, in the long run, lead to significant efficiency gains and indicate clear priorities for the future. With more knowledge about the cost-effectiveness of different treatment alternatives, more reliable systems of policy and health outcomes measurement can be developed. One of the priorities, therefore, is to identify and fill gaps in present knowledge concerning cost-effectiveness.

## REFERENCES

Abel-Smith, B. and Mossialos, E. (1994). Cost containment and health care reform: A study of the European Union. *Health Policy*, 28, 89–132.

Abel-Smith, B., Calltorp, J., Dixon, M., Dunning, A., Evans, R., Holland, W. *et al.* (1994). *Report on the Greek Health Services.* Athens: Ministry of Health and Social Welfare of Greece: Pharmetrica SA.

Abel-Smith, B., Mossialos, E. and Hancher, L. (1997). *Regulation in Question: The Regulation of the European Pharmaceutical Industry.* London: LSE Health, University of London.

Anderson, G. M., Spitzer, W. O., Weinstein, M. C., Wang, E., Blackburn, J. L. and Bergman, U. (1990). Benefits, risks and costs of prescription drugs: A scientific basis for evaluating policy options. *Clinical Pharmacology and Therapeutics*, 48, 111–19.

Audit Commission (1994). *A Prescription for Improvement: Towards More Rational Prescribing in General Practice.* London: HMSO.

Ball, B. (1994). The current market for generics in Europe. Proceedings of a Meeting on Recent Changes Affecting the Development and Marketing of Generic Medicines, London, 27–28 September. Basle: International Pharmaceutical Congress.

Bartels-Petersen, J. (1994). Pharmaceutical consumption in a low consuming country: The case of Denmark. In E. Mossialos, C. Ranos and B. Abel-Smith (eds), *Cost Containment, Pricing and Financing of Pharmaceuticals in the European Community: The Policy-makers' View.* Athens: LSE Health and Pharmetrica SA.

Bateman, D. N. (1993). Selected list: Diversion rather than threat. *British Medical Journal*, 306, 1141–2.

Brandlow, J. and Coulter, A. (1993). Effect of fundholding and indicative prescribing schemes on general practitioners' prescribing costs. *British Medical Journal*, 307, 186–9.

Brook, H., Ware, J. E., Rogers, W. H. *et al.* (1983). Does free care improve adults' health? *New England Journal of Medicine*, 309, 1426–34.

De Vos, C. (1994). Financing of medicines in the Netherlands. In E. Mossialos, C. Ranos and B. Abel-Smith (eds), *Cost Containment, Pricing and Financing of Pharmaceuticals in the European Community: The Policy-makers' View*. Athens: LSE Health and Pharmetrica SA.

Drummond, M., Cooke, J. and Walley, T. (1997). Economic evaluation under managed competition: Evidence from the UK. *Social Science and Medicine*, 45, 585–98.

Dukes, M. N. G. (1997). Cresimiento y cambio en los medicamentos genéricos. In F. Lobo, G. Velásquez (eds), *Los Medicamentos Ante las Nuevas Realidades Economicas*. Madrid: Editorial Civitas SA.

Elsigna, E. and Rutten, F. F. M. (1997). Economic evaluation in support of national health policy: the case of the Netherlands. *Social Science and Medicine*, 45, 607–22.

Farmindustria (1996). *Indicatori Farmaceutici 1996*. Rome: Farmindustria.

Fattore, G. (in press). United Kingdom. In E. Mossialos and J. Le Grand (eds), *Health Expenditure in the European Union: Cost and Control*. Aldershot: Ashgate.

Feely, J. (1992). Influence of pharmacoeconomic factors on prescribing patterns in Ireland. *Pharmacoeconomics*, 2, 99–106.

Ferrado, C., Henman, M. C. and Corrigan, O. L. (1987). Impact of a nation-wide limited prescribing list: Preliminary findings. *Drug Intelligence and Clinical Pharmacy*, 21, 653–8.

Garattini, S. and Garattini, L. (1993). Pharmaceutical prescriptions in four European countries. *The Lancet*, 342, 1191–2.

Glennerster, H., Matsaganis, M., Owens, P. and Hancock, S. (1995). *Implementing GP Fundholding*. Buckingham: Open University Press.

Huttin, C. (1994). Use of prescription charges. *Health Policy*, 27, 53–73.

IOO (1995). *Beoordeling ABDA-Prijsvergelijking Geneesmiddelen [Evaluation of the ABDA Drug Prices Evaluation Study]*. The Hague: Institute of Public Sector Research (IOO).

Jönsson, B. (1994). Pricing and reimbursement of pharmaceuticals in Sweden. *Pharmacoeconomics*, 6 (Suppl. 1), 51–60.

Klauber, J. (1994). Entwicklung des Fertigarzneimittelmarktes 1983 bis 1993. In U. Schwabe and D. Paffrath (eds), *Arzeiverordnungs-Report*. Stuttgart: Gustav Fischer Verlag.

Lancry, J. P. and Sandier, S. (in press). France. In E. Mossialos and J. Le Grand (eds), *Health Expenditure in the European Union: Cost and Control*. Aldershot: Ashgate.

Le Fur, P. and Sermet, C. (1996). *Medical References: The Impact on Pharmaceutical Prescriptions*. Paris: CREDES-CES.

Le Pen, C. (1997). Pharmaceutical economy and the economic assessment of drugs in France. *Social Science and Medicine*, 45, 637–46.

Lecompte, T. and Paris, V. (1994). *Consommation de Pharmacie en Europe, 1992*. Paris: CREDES.

Leibovitz, A., Manning, W. G. and Newhouse, J. P. (1985). The demand for prescription medicines as a function of cost sharing. *Social Science and Medicine*, 21, 1063–9.

Lopez-Bastida, J. and Mossialos, E. (1997). *Pharmaceutical Expenditure in Spain: Cost and Control.* London: LSE Health, University of London.

LSE Health (1995). *Prescribing Patterns, Consumption and Use of Pharmaceuticals in Europe*. Report for European Commission. London: LSE, University of London.

Maynard, A. and Bloor, K. (1996). Introducing a market to the UK National Health Service. *New England Journal of Medicine*, 334, 604–8.

O'Brien, B. (1989). The effect of patient charges on the utilization of prescription medicines. *Journal of Health Economics*, 8, 109–32.

O'Donoghue, N. (1994). Pricing and reimbursement of medicines: The Irish experience. In E. Mossialos, C. Ranos and B. Abel-Smith (eds), *Cost Containment, Pricing and Financing of Pharmaceuticals in the European Community: The Policy-makers' View*. Athens: LSE Health and Pharmetrica SA.

OECD (1995). *New Directions in Health Care Policy*. Paris: OECD.

OECD (1996). *OECD Health Data 96*. Paris: Organisation for Economic Co-operation and Development.

Pickering, E. M. (1996). *Pharmaceutical Pricing and Reimbursement in Europe*. Halesmere: PRP Communications Ltd.

Reilly, A., Brown, D., Taylor, D. and Webster, J. (1986). Effect of the limited list on drugs use. *Pharmaceutical Journal*, 19 April, 480–2.

Ryan, M. and Birch, S. (1991). Charging for health care: evidence on the utilisation of the NHS prescribed drugs. *Social Science and Medicine*, 33, 681–7.

Schulenburg, J.-M. Graf von der (1997). Economic evaluation of medical technologies: From theory to practice – the German perspective. *Social Science and Medicine*, 45, 623–36.

Schulenburg, J.-M. Graf von der and Schoffski, O. (1993). *Implications of the Structural Reform of Healthcare Act on the Referral and Hospital Admission Practice of Primary Health Care Physicians*. Discussion Paper No. 34. Hanover: University of Hanover.

Selke, G. (1992). Auswirkungen der Arzeimittelfestbetrage. In U. Schwabe and D. Paffrath (eds), *Arzeiverordnungs – Report 1992*. Stuttgart: Gustav Fischer Verlag.

Sloan, F. A. and Grabowski, H. G. (1997). Introduction and overview. *Social Science and Medicine*, 45, 507–12.

Zammit-Lucia, J. and Dasgupta, R. (1995). *Reference Pricing: The European Experience*. Health Policy Review Paper. London: St Mary's Hospital Medical School, University of London.

# PART IV

## ON STATE, CITIZEN AND SOCIETY

# 12

# THE ROLE OF THE STATE IN HEALTH CARE REFORM

## Simo Kokko, Petr Hava, Vicente Ortun and Kimmo Leppo

### INTRODUCTION

Health care systems are often represented as the interplay of three actors: users of services, providers of services and financiers of services. In developed countries, collective financing is utilized since the need for health services is distributed across populations and individuals' life spans in patterns that require 'insurance' to secure adequate financing in all situations. Among the three actors, there are various modes of interaction. Users of services pay taxes or insurance premiums and receive services. Financiers pay or reimburse service providers, who in turn may be in a contractual relationship with the financiers.

This three-part picture best describes the setting in so-called Bismarck countries, where health care financing is organized through compulsory social insurance. In Beveridge countries, financing is predominantly collected through taxation and the provision of services has traditionally been organized through publicly owned and run institutions, although ambulatory services of these countries are often delivered by private practitioners under special contract. This latter situation is usually termed integration of financing and provision, in contrast to the separation of these functions.

In discussions of the Bismarck-style three-actor model, the state is not included in the picture. In the two-actor model, however, the user of services is dealing with a representative body of the state, although often the 'state' is represented by a regional or local public authority. The state (or its representative) is thus deeply involved in the two-actor model, holding all lines of authority basically in the same hands.

In practice, the role of the state cannot be reduced to this simple health system picture. The state sets and defines the macro framework through numerous elements of legislation. It helps regulate the actions of the ostensibly autonomous actors. Where financing is separate from the state, large proportions of insurance premiums or other types of contributions to the collective financing system typically are paid from state, regional or local taxes through various income redistribution, social welfare and other mechanisms.

The role of the state in Europe has been directly challenged in the 1990s. Current theories concerning effective management argue that removal of the state (or its representative) from direct service provision and/or operating management enhances efficiency. This is one fundamental argument in favour of separation of purchaser from provider in Beveridge-model countries. In the CEE/CIS countries, the political climate is opposed to the involvement of the state in any aspect of social life. Removal of the state as a principal actor in health care appears to be a goal *per se*.

A glancing acquaintance with recent health care reforms across Europe might suggest that transition towards less involvement of the state is one major common denominator in the reforms. Other analysts (Maarse *et al.* 1993; Saltman 1994) have, however, claimed that the issue is not whether the state is involved, but that state involvement is adopting new and more consistent forms that may lead to better outcomes from a health policy perspective.

This paper explores various ways that the state, usually through the ministries of health, or regional or local authorities as representatives of the same public interest as the state, is involved in health care. Second, it considers how these functions change before, during and after major health care reforms. Given that recent developments in established market economies and the CEE/CIS countries are very different, the paper is divided into two parts accordingly. In order not to get entangled with the particularities of which functions are literally functions of the ministry of health, as against which belong to subministerial organizations or other national organizations commissioned by the ministry, we refer simply to the 'state' in this article.

## Western Europe

The dividing line between Bismarckian and Beveridge health care systems has never been very clear, and recent reforms have further obscured the line. Beveridge-model countries usually finance their health services either through general taxation or tax-like earmarked financing mechanisms that are sometimes termed insurance. Beveridge countries have also traditionally kept provision of most services (certainly hospital services) as a public sector function. Involvement of the state had often been unquestioned until recent trends to decentralize planning, decision making and management to regional or local levels emerged. Separating purchaser and provider – an issue attracting much attention and rhetoric – is possible by definition only in Beveridge countries, since in Bismarckian countries this separation exists by definition. The UK and some regional authorities in Sweden have recently introduced such a separation.

Bismarckian systems finance their health services through compulsory social insurance and rely mainly upon private service providers, many of which are not-for-profit organizations. Integration of financing and service provision in private hands – whether on a for-profit (as in US HMOs) or not-for-profit basis – is not very common, although there are certain HMO-like developments currently under way in Switzerland. Several countries in southern Europe have crossed the line that has separated the Beveridge and Bismarck traditions. Both Portugal and Spain have recently moved over to the Beveridge side of the line.

## Common functions of the state

Given differences in the role of public financing and of the public sector in general, one might expect to find wide differences in the respective roles for the state. Thus roles of state and ministry for these two groups of countries will be considered separately. Table 12.1 presents a list of functions encountered both in Bismarck and Beveridge-model countries in European OECD countries (OECD 1992, 1994). While functions were surprisingly similar, differences in implementation were quite considerable. An additional common feature is state interest and involvement in containment of health care spending, regardless of the specific channels through which funds are dispersed. There are, however, major differences in cost-containment mechanisms employed in Bismarck and Beveridge-model countries.

**Table 12.1**   Functions of the state or other public authorities in health care systems in European countries

---

- Formulating health policy, with implications for legislation, planning and resource allocation; this policy-making process also may be regional, as in Germany, Spain and the Nordic countries
- Planning, enforcing and evaluating legislation
- Protecting public health, involving national, regional and local levels of public authority
- Establishing and operating special departments to carry out epidemiological research, keep relevant statistics and often participate in preventive and health promotive work at the population level. Sometimes these functions have been organized through governmental commissioning
- Coordination of capital investments
- Regulation of health services provision
- Medico-legal surveillance of the performance and conduct of health service providers

---

## STATE INVOLVEMENT IN BEVERIDGE-MODEL COUNTRIES

Although the formal health system structures differ between the Nordic countries and the UK, the overall role of the state and of public authority generally has been rather similar. In Finland, Norway and Sweden, due to historical and geographical factors, regional and local decision making has had a strong position. In spite of this tradition, however, the respective ministries of health as well as National Boards of Health have held substantial power in planning and resource allocation. In the UK, the National Health Service has been directly managed by the central government through the Department of Health. Due to the integration of financing and service provision within these countries, their ministries and/or decentralized public authorities have been directly involved until recently in planning and managing service delivery. In addition, through their role as managers of taxation, the public authorities have a central role in the financing of health services as well. In some countries, health care financing is through a special earmarked tax or a tax that is associated with health care in the minds of the taxpayers. In other countries, financing is from general taxes, either state or local.

Health planning became important in the Nordic countries and the UK with the expansion of epidemiology starting in the late 1960s. Epidemiological findings showed that the population was in rapid transition toward chronic non-communicable diseases, for which the proper policy responses lay in the areas of prevention and in health promotion. Evidence of health inequalities between socio-economic groups and geographical areas called for measures to counterbalance these problems. These countries also have long histories of trying to tip the overall health system balance more towards primary health care. Planning, together with legislative reforms, has been widely utilized to channel greater resources towards primary and ambulatory services.

Resource allocation has been a powerful policy tool in the Beveridge countries. In the NHS, allocating resources in the right proportion to the variable needs of populations has been a demanding task. International health service researchers have been interested in the national formulae (RAWP) that are used. In the Nordic countries, the regional and local authorities have their own right to taxation, financing most or at least part of health services directly. The state also steps in to level off differences between regions through state subsidies or through other similar mechanisms.

Direct involvement of ministries or other governmental authorities in the management of health services has been common in the Beveridge countries. This type of centralized management is hard to conduct, however, and is rapidly becoming obsolete. Among the Beveridge-model countries described in the OECD country studies, only Greece appears still to have direct central-level involvement. The UK and some counties in Sweden have introduced purchaser–provider splits within the public sector to enhance efficiency. However in Denmark, Finland and Norway, regional or municipal authorities participate in day-to-day management, although institutional managers may be given greater decision-making latitude than before.

## STATE INVOLVEMENT IN BISMARCK-MODEL COUNTRIES

The list of functions shared by public authorities in both Beveridge and Bismarck-model countries indicates that the state is far from a distant bystander in the interplay of the key actors (financiers, providers and users of services) in health care. Table

**Table 12.2**    Functions of the state in Bismarck-model countries

---

- Setting the general framework for health insurance and service delivery system
  - scope of benefits
  - determination of levels of insurance premiums, for example by ordering their growth to be kept in pace with the growth of GDP (France)
  - setting limits to patient fees and deductibles
  - requiring equalization transfers between insurance companies
  - ensuring that independent actors reach agreements or contracts
- Wide variety of cost-containment measures
  - control of capital investments
  - setting global budgets for hospitals, or otherwise ensuring that hospital expenses are capped
  - launching programmes to cut down the number of hospital beds including promotion of ambulatory care
  - negotiation of drug prices; use of size to achieve negotiation power for drug prices
  - setting ceilings to key supply-side determinants: numbers of medical students or graduates, numbers of general practitioners, numbers of pharmacies
  - direct involvement in hospital costs by regulating payments, wages, numbers of employees
- Accreditation and quality control
  - keeping accreditation within a governmental body or setting and monitoring standards of accreditation
  - accrediting insurance companies
  - establishing new quality control programmes
- Direct management of public hospitals
- Financing of care for those outside insurance systems

---

12.2 describes typical types of state involvement in insurance-based countries. Central governments have spread these functions between ministries of health and regional and local authorities in many countries. In Germany, the federal government has delegated key regulatory functions to sickness funds and professional bodies that have a legally acknowledged status through the process of 'Sicherstellungsauftrag'. These functions include pricing, planning of supply of ambulatory care, and definition of quality standards. The state acts as a referee if the independent actors neglect their duties, or if contracts for service provision and pricing cannot be reached.

## STATE, MINISTRIES AND HEALTH CARE REFORM

International rhetoric sometimes gives the impression that 'all countries' are proceeding on a rather similar path in reforming their health care systems. The same rhetoric describes these reforms as rapid innovations highlighting radically different things that can be done. This is an unwarranted picture, possibly presented by interested parties who would like to see such changes take place. Looking at western Europe, only reforms of the UK and some counties in Sweden could be characterized as being rapid and fundamental. The Dutch proposal for reform constitutes the most widespread and most radical in Europe, but it remains uncertain whether key elements of that proposal will ever be implemented.

### Types of reform

While the scope of reform can be questioned, there is broad interest in engaging in health system changes. It is hard to find a country that considers itself satisfied with the status quo. Many of these changes, however, are slower and more incremental. Some countries have started their reform programmes early in the 1980s, often as a part of a wider social reconstruction of society. Good examples of this approach are the health care systems in Portugal and Spain. Some countries have colourful histories of successive reforms initiated by different political cabinets with rather divergent health policy goals during the past 15–20 years.

Two features are very common. First, countries are struggling with rising health care expenses and are resorting to tightening measures of cost containment. Second, decentralization of planning, decision making and operating management is taking place widely, regardless of the basic model of health care (see Chapter 13). Reform-related policy issues reflect these two major undercurrents. The following issues have attracted wider international attention.

- Tipping the balance toward primary care. Portugal and Spain have established National Health Services; Sweden is trying to build a system of general practitioners 'underneath' a network of strong hospitals; the UK introduced general practitioner fundholding.
- Introduction of tailored purchasing has been a special feature of the British reforms. It is also an attempt to combine a health gain

orientation with the dynamics of separating purchaser and provider.

- Reduction of hospital overcapacity has become a frequent policy objective, especially around large cities.
- Enhancement of patient choice is often mentioned as one common feature in the reforms of many countries. Sweden has swung from one extreme to another in this respect.
- Giving patients guarantees of certain types of care – often targeted to get rid of politically embarrassing waiting lists.
- Introduction of internal markets as well as competition and privatization (where applicable) have been radical new elements, both to Beveridge and Bismarck-model countries. There seems to be much more rhetoric than real change, however.

Some countries with previously integrated financing and service provision functions have introduced separation of purchaser(s) and providers. This seems to serve many of the policy objectives above, but it may have become an ideological end in itself. Important policy objectives such as strengthening prevention and health promotion, as well as pursuit of equity, have not been very high on reform agendas.

### Role of the state and ministries

All the reform processes described here have been initiated and led by governments and ministries of health in those countries where the reforms originally began. Sometimes reform ideas have attracted supporters in new countries, where ministries may not be willing or ready to follow suit.

Some elements of reform are seen to be sufficiently imperative that changes of political parties in power do not change the fundamental course (although new parties may feel it necessary to place their own fingerprints on the reforms – for example in the terminology used). Some reform policies are politically more neutral than others, for example strengthening primary care and the reduction of excess hospital capacity. On the other hand, such objectives as introduction of internal markets, competition and patient choice can be highly political. The reforms in the UK and certain elements of the Swedish reforms were strongly driven by the parties in power at the time of initiation. The role of governments and ministries varies accordingly.

## Less state involvement?

Some states have actively adopted policies that move towards less involvement of the state. The notion that the Netherlands' health care system, despite its pluralism, had become too regulated and over-bureaucratized has spurred its reform plans. In Germany, physicians are by law organized into associations that have considerable power over individual physicians. These associations have received a legally defined role from the state and thus there is genuinely less direct state involvement.

States and ministries have delegated power and duties to regional public authorities. Some cynical critics have pointed out that decentralization is very popular now that reductions are required in public expenditure (e.g. governments and ministries do not mind transferring unpleasant decisions to regional or local bodies).

## More state involvement?

The state has pursued tighter regulation in several insurance-based countries including Austria, Belgium, France and Germany. It has interfered by demanding that independent actors use methods of payments and incentives that have been shown to be helpful in cost containment. As a consequence, the use of global budgets for hospitals is becoming more common, as is prospective payment instead of open-ended reimbursement. Quality development represents another new line of state requirements in many countries.

In England and the UK, the state has been active in setting goals and preparing the framework for internal markets. In Sweden, however, many county councils (responsible since 1982 for health services) have not been as keen to introduce markets as the state. Both countries have also experimented with various types of guarantees regarding patient access to service.

Efforts to develop new managerial tools are expanding in many countries as rapidly as central command-and-control planning and direct involvement in management retreat. There is great enthusiasm for 'management by benchmarking' in those countries with information systems that allow for the development of such detailed information.

**New kind of state involvement?**

Saltman postulated that there is a general pattern observable in western national health systems: governments and ministries retreat from direct planning and management, but they maintain a role that is at least as active and demanding as before in regulating, setting standards and ensuring that the now more autonomous actors act correctly in the new internal market (Saltman 1994). Maarse does not yet see such changes taking place, but he recommends that, instead of taking a *laissez-faire* attitude, states should be active players in the field – although in new ways (Maarse *et al.* 1993).

Does the European scene of health care reforms warrant Saltman's generalization? Due to the smaller number of countries that have undergone more radical reforms, the answer would have to be 'no' (although for Sweden and the UK, given developments in the first half of the 1990s, it would be 'yes'). Instead there is a broad adoption of decentralization, with the introduction of various – often unpleasant – cost-containment measures, and with countries moving in opposite directions. Portugal and Spain, for example, have become tax-financed countries, while CEE/CIS countries are in the process of establishing social insurance-funded systems. Switzerland is introducing new ways to integrate financing and service provision in privately owned HMO-like organizations, whereas other countries which currently have publicly administered integration are avidly pursuing the separation of purchaser from provider.

With all these changes, what is happening to those functions that should be maintained as state or public authority functions? A description of recent events in the health ministry in Scotland could provide a cautionary example. While the overall number of senior employees in the ministry has been reduced, many experts in public health and health promotion are now employed full-time on the particulars of reform organization such as invoicing purchasers, monitoring providers, etc. Of course reforms may create new rules of the game which will require more referees than before. However, if the new referees must be recruited from among the same experts that formerly worked with broader health issues – or with the same money spent for these wider purposes – health protection and promotion may suffer.

**Health care systems in transition in CEE/CIS countries**

The CEE/CIS countries had a uniform model of organizing health services until the end of the 1980s. This model was introduced successively in these countries after the Second World War, and is often referred to as the 'Semashko model'. These countries officially financed their health services entirely through the state budget. Health care facilities were both publicly owned and the services publicly provided. Different levels of state administration – central, regional and local – were responsible for planning, allocation of resources and managing capital expenditures. The health services had a number of parallel subsystems: the general hospital and outpatient services for the majority of population as well as services provided by large enterprises or some state sectors that employed large numbers of persons, for example the army, railway systems and police. Ministries of health were directly responsible for the administration of national public health and hygiene services, and for highly specialized institutions in the area of health, medical research and postgraduate education. This soviet model was vertically structured, with precisely defined responsibilities.

The following features have frequently been deemed to be problems of the Semashko model as it was applied in CEE/CIS countries:

- services were unresponsive to the needs of patients;
- services were relatively underfunded by international standards in spite of the rhetoric of health being a high priority. Following from this, the availability of modern technologies, both pharmaceuticals and equipment, was a major problem;
- services were inefficient in terms of their structure, management and in the allocation of resources;
- hospital care and medical specialization were emphasized instead of outpatient services and primary health care. By international standards, there was an excess number of hospital beds and consequently excess use of in-patient care;
- the number of physicians was very high in relation to the population, along with the number of hospital specialists. The potential of other health professionals was not optimally employed;
- certain small groups in the population – usually based on political criteria – had better access to higher-quality services. A grey economy also existed in health services;
- CEE/CIS countries had a poor record of success in preventing illness and promoting health. These countries participated in the WHO health for all process, but their participation was only formal. These countries had also developed large environmental pollution problems.

On the other hand, the following features have been often referred to as advantages or strengths of the Semashko model:

- equity of access was relatively high, with lack of money not an obstacle;
- a network of structurally integrated services covered the countries well and even now provide an existing infrastructure for the future (Preker and Feachem 1994);
- the range of services was comprehensive;
- certain public health programmes, such as immunization, were successfully carried out.

### State and ministry until the end of the 1980s

The main role of central planning was to set the financial framework and establish limits to spending. Ministries of health and finance were often responsible for resource allocation to the level of regions. This tight control of spending resulted in a rather stable level of expenditure development, usually below 5 per cent of the GDP. All money was carefully earmarked for the purposes of ambulatory care, hospitals, pharmaceuticals and other similar sectors. The system was held in control through careful monitoring of costs and the state was usually successful in containing costs.

Ministries and other governmental authorities were not directly responsible for management of health services, which was left to the regional and local institutions of health care administration. State administrators used simple, but efficient, incentives to control service operations – financial results, reinforced by adherence to the set annual plan. The appointment of managers loyal to the regime was under the control of the leading political party. The ministries kept a wide range of statistics on the operation of health services, but these were not used for health policy development.

### State and ministry in transition

At the beginning of the 1990s the economic systems of CEE/CIS countries began a transformation from centrally planned to more market-oriented systems. The legislation regulating the economy has been changed at various speeds in different countries. In a number of instances, liberalization has gone too far, markets have been left unregulated and there have been instances of supply-induced demand. The position of the government has become

**Table 12.3**   Functions of the state in CEE/CIS countries until the end of 1980s

- Ensuring equity in access to health services
- Cost-containment policy
- Resource allocation through budgeting and planning
- Strict control of capital investments
- Monitoring of health, health services supply and crude financial indicators
- Further education of health professionals
- Organization and financing of research
- Setting the income levels of physicians and other health professionals
- Price setting (drugs, material, equipment)

relatively weak, as new actors have entered the scene (for example, professional unions and insurance companies).

In the area of health services, the transition has offered exceptional opportunities for many entrepreneurial activities and for making profit. This has led to new forms of allocative inefficiency in health systems, particularly in the area of new technology and the use and selection of medicines. Newly privatized health care providers and physicians have gained greater autonomy, either through new types of contracts or new grounds for reimbursement. Physicians have also gained more power in the policy-making process. These transformations in the CEE/CIS countries differ from health sector reforms in western Europe in that they did not seek to restore or reform the previous system, but rather to build an altogether new one.

**Table 12.4**   New roles and responsibilities for ministries of health in CEE/CIS countries

- Negotiation with new actors (associations of physicians and chambers) involved in policy making
- Negotiation and regulation of price setting in the new mechanisms of reimbursement
- Strengthening equal access to health services through constitutional changes
- Adoption of a more realistic role in the restoration of the health of the nation
- Better collecting and processing of health-related data

The previous centrally planned system was simpler from the point of view of state bureaucrats, and the state was successful in cost containment. The new bureaucracies are under more complex political pressures to change legal, organizational and economic features of entire systems of health during very short periods of time. The following objectives seem to have first priority: provider autonomy, introduction of new reimbursement schemes, freedom of choice for patients and introduction of new technologies. There are numerous vested interests behind these objectives, including physicians as well as the producers and distributors of new technology and pharmaceuticals.

Vertical systems of central planning were changed into networks of health care providers with relatively high autonomy and with their own contracts with health insurers (e.g. a purchaser–provider split). In a number of CEE/CIS countries, obligatory public insurance schemes have been introduced. Ambulatory health services and pharmaceutical distribution are now usually privately owned and operated. The new financing and reimbursement schemes are administratively complicated, however, generating frequent technical errors in price setting which are quickly exploited by physicians. State bureaucracies have not been able to monitor adequately the necessary cost indicators or to correct errors.

The state has been faced with new types of decision-making processes. In many cases, the responsible persons have not been under effective democratic control. Individuals within the bureaucracy have had almost unilateral power over decisions like the contents of the lists of medicines covered by health insurance. This situation has created opportunities for corruption. All CEE/CIS countries now have high pharmaceutical expenditures, typically over 20 per cent of their expenditure on health (see Chapter 11). A related problem has been the high rate of turnover among key persons in some ministries. Their position has been correspondingly weak and they have not been able to negotiate efficiently with well-organized associations of health professionals.

The newly established organizations that run public health insurance have not been sufficiently prepared for their work. They often continue to act as passive reimbursement institutions rather than adopting rational control mechanisms or setting limits on the contracting processes. They also do not employ methods of assessment of needs for health services. A number of such 'financial institutes' have found themselves after a short period of operation with substantial deficits, as happened in the Czech Republic and Hungary.

As an illustration of the issues that governments and ministries have confronted in the CEE/CIS countries, the process of transformation in the Czech Republic is described in the following case study.

### Czech health care sector (a case study)

The transformation of the health care sector in the Czech Republic began in 1990. The core of the transformation was the shift from a public health care system financed by the state budget to a system of primarily independent health care providers (taken from the state and transferred to private ownership) financed by mandatory public health insurance. As a result of this decentralization, practically all health care providers became independent legal and physical entities that entered into contractual relationships with an equally new entity, the public health insurance company (later (1993) several independent health insurance providers rose within the system of public health insurance). Concurrently with this 'privatization process',[1] property belonging to spas, pharmacies, ambulance companies and hospitals[2] was also privatized. The property belonging to spas was privatized most quickly, followed by that of the pharmacies and ambulance companies. The slowest privatization was of hospitals, which was reduced further by the government in 1996.[3]

With the exception of large regional and teaching hospitals, the privatization process of all other hospitals was evaluated and carried out. This organizational transformation rested on two fundamental alternatives: the hospital ownership could have been transferred from the state to counties or cities, or transferred from the state to private companies (i.e. to the for-profit sector). At the time when privatization projects were being processed, no legislative framework governing the private non-profit sector existed. Therefore, this third option was not utilized and the majority of privatization projects were made to fit the existing legal framework for for-profit companies. For example, the spas have been privatized under this for-profit regime.

From the beginning of this transformation, not enough attention was paid to the accessibility of care and to the rules of management, control, and administration of these new companies. Institutionally-based health care services research was stopped. Health policy making was not data-based. Management training to deal with these new conditions was also neglected. Within only a few years, the insufficient legal framework combined with inadequate management and availability of services led to a number of problems, especially in the sphere of hospital services, but also in the new health insurance institutions. The result was the halting of the process of hospital property privatization in mid-1996, and to date no alternative solution has been put forward by the government. This case study is a vivid example of the consequences of overlooking the experiences of other states, as well as a country's own experience of the relationship between public and private sectors. In the Czech Republic, a liberal approach was chosen, which stemmed from the assumption that it is possible to transform the entire health care sector simply and rapidly into private, profit-making institutions financed by public funds (i.e. by the public health insurance system) with only formal state control mechanisms.

Over time, the system of public health insurance gradually became the object of narrower corporate interests. A greater number of health insurance companies emerged within the public health insurance system. These newly formed insurance companies have their own legal make-up which facilitates commercial or quasi-market ventures. They can be seen as models of doing business without risk (having a state or public cushion). The first phase of such business ventures is under the protection of the public system; only after withstanding the initial steps can an attempt be made at commercial status. However, such transformation has not yet occurred – the Ministry of Health is working on policy alternatives and a new health insurance act is being prepared during 1997.

With regard to the management of their finances, hospitals are not systematically audited, and therefore health care policy makers cannot pinpoint the causes of poor financial results. Apart from the provision of mechanisms of public control and supervision, the political will of the current national government is also evidently lacking. Hospitals preparing to be privatized are attempting to broaden their range of activities and equip themselves with expensive modern technology in anticipation of expected competition. A section of the parliamentary opposition has demanded that the government work out an overall scheme for the further development of a health system.

## Similarities with health care reforms in western European countries

The experiences of CEE/CIS countries can provide useful lessons for western European countries, since CEE/CIS countries introduced market-based reforms faster and in more radical forms. It is now possible to see the outcomes of these policies. The *laissez-faire* approach of the Czech Republic in particular is an important experiment not too different to the situation in the US at its most unregulated phase. In both cases, the operation of a competitive health insurance system became very expensive. For example, in 1996, health care expenditures in the Czech Republic probably rose to close to 10 per cent of GDP. The Czech case illustrates well the crucial importance of using needs assessment as the basis of prospective financing, employing precise cost estimation and price-setting methods as well as using global budgeting. Also tools for assessment of microeconomic (or technical) efficiency and effectiveness and for outcome measurement need to be developed.

After several years of health care reforms in CEE/CIS countries, the key question is not simply the choice between fee-for-service and capitation-based methods, but about health economics in a wider sense. Policy making and its subsequent implementation is a considerably more complex issue than the simplified paradigm of three actors suggests. In CEE/CIS countries, one can see the importance of vested interests and interest groups as well as the political culture and value orientation. At the same time, or perhaps as a consequence, there has been an inability to use the results of international research effectively.

## CONCLUSIONS

The above review suggests that certain principles or alternative methods in health care reforms tend to become ends in themselves, rather than tools with which to attain health policy objectives. Health policy issues should be on top of the national agenda, and health service reforms should be tailored to lead to the desired policy objectives. Health policy building is, and should be, a state and ministry responsibility, although it requires wide discussions and consultations within society.

There also is adequate evidence to warn against separating state involvement from the interplay between the key actors of health care. The state should have its role in setting the framework in financing of health care, in payments from third-party payers to service providers, in health care delivery and in regulating relationships between different actors.

European countries have for historical and political reasons chosen different models of health care, and these models differ considerably in the degree and manner in which public authorities are involved in financing, management and delivery. However, the state should – at a minimum – have a similar regulatory role in all models, and should also safeguard those policy objectives established to protect disadvantaged groups. If the state delegates key functions to non-governmental organizations, it might be wise not to give a message that the state will not come back and interfere, if needed.

Public health and general concern for the population's overall health are mainly functions of ministries or other public authorities. In some countries, the prospects for the promotion of public health have turned rather pessimistic. Involving the best expertise in the health sector in the particulars of health care reform may do a serious disservice to public health: not only does this consume resources, but it tends to reinforce the message that health depends primarily upon the activities of the curative health sector.

## NOTES

1 The first step in privatization was the privatization of activity – its result was independent health care providers. The second step was the privatization of property.
2 Hospital privatization was a rather complicated process and as a result only some hospitals were privatized during the process, which lasted several years.
3 The privatization of Czech medical property is a long-term process taking several years if all of the following steps are included: making political decisions, creating a legal framework, defining its scope, deciding which property is to be privatized, the preparation of projects and feasibility studies, different privatization committees decision making in several levels (district, ministries, cabinet, Czech National Property Fund (CNPF), contract between CNPF and new owner).

## REFERENCES

Maarse, J., van der Horst, A. and Molin, E. (1993). Hospital budgeting in the Netherlands. *European Journal of Public Health*, 3, 181–7.
OECD (1992). *The Reform of Health Care: A Comparative Analysis of Seven OECD Countries*. Health Policy Studies, No. 2. Paris: Organisation for Economic Co-operation and Development.

OECD (1994). *The Reform of Health Care Systems: A Review of Seventeen OECD Countries*. Paris: Organisation for Economic Co-operation and Development.

Preker, A. S. and Feachem, R. G. A. (1994). *Health and Health Care*. New York: World Bank.

Saltman, R. B. (1994). A conceptual overview of recent health care reforms. *European Journal of Public Health*, 4, 287–93.

# 13

# OPTIMAL BALANCE OF CENTRALIZED AND DECENTRALIZED MANAGEMENT

David J. Hunter,
Mikko Vienonen and
W. Cezary Wlodarczyk

## INTRODUCTION

Decentralization is typically a central plank of health sector reform. It is seen as an effective means to stimulate improvements in the delivery of services, to secure better allocation of resources according to needs, to involve the community in decisions about priorities and to facilitate the reduction of inequities in health. Whether the claims for decentralization outweigh the disadvantages, notably fragmented and duplicated services as well as high transaction costs, requires examination. Further, a tendency to discuss centralization and decentralization as if they were two distinct and therefore alternative categories also needs careful consideration.

Decentralization is attractive because a central administration is typically not close enough to the users of services to allow appropriate responses to expressed preferences. Disappointment with large, centralized and bureaucratic institutions is widespread throughout Europe. In many countries, the same drawbacks of centralized systems have been identified: low efficiency, slow pace of innovation and inadequate responsiveness to changes in the external environment affecting health and health care. The susceptibility of centralized systems to manipulation by politicians is also regarded as a cause for concern. It would, however, be naive to think that decentralization is automatically a solution to this problem. Decentralization can take many forms and is usually politically inspired.

The objectives of decentralization have been diverse. It has been seen as an important political ideal, providing the means for community participation and local self-reliance, and ensuring the accountability of government officials to the population. It has also been seen as a way of transferring some responsibility for development from the centre to the periphery and, in consequence, a way of spreading the blame for failure to meet local needs.

In many developed countries, local government has historically been strong with central government powers often being developed somewhat later than those of local government. However, central government has tended to place increasing restrictions on local government. A common theme in the expansion of the powers of central government has been the need to promote greater equality of public services throughout the country using central policies, regulations and grants. Decentralization nevertheless has remained a continuing cry, although often raised against a background of strong influences promoting centralization. Recently, faced with economic recession and a wish to control public expenditure, some central governments have tried to limit local discretion further.

Decentralization cannot be regarded simply as a technical matter. It arouses strong emotions, with the result that discussion of the concept is perhaps less balanced than it should be. Too often, only the advantages of decentralization are identified while those of more centralized systems are ignored.

## CONCEPTS OF DECENTRALIZATION

Decentralization is a term that is overused while at the same time not fully understood. Its lack of precision makes it fashionable but also unhelpful when attempting to consider its particular strengths and limitations. It can be defined in general terms as the transfer of authority or dispersal of power in public planning, management and decision making, from the national level to subnational levels, or more generally from higher to lower levels of government (Rondinelli 1981). A dictionary definition describes decentralization in these terms: 'to withdraw from the centre: to transform by transferring functions from a central government, organisation or

head to local centres'. It therefore involves a shift in power relationships and in the distribution of tasks between levels of government
and the various stakeholders to be found at each level.

Decentralization places responsibility for making decisions at the
lowest possible level of the organization. At one extreme, in completely decentralized institutions, all decisions would be taken at
the lowest operational level, where possible at the point of application. At the other extreme, in wholly centralized institutions, all
decisions would be made at the highest level of management. In
actual practice, organizations do not exist in a pure form at either
end of the continuum, but may be arranged at various points
between the two extremes. Decentralized models of health care
systems are therefore those displaying characteristics which place
them at the greatest distance from centralized models and vice
versa.

Each model has its own particular characteristics and expected
outcomes. A decentralized model is based on a more entrepreneurial philosophy whereas a centralized model relies heavily
on central government involvement. Patients' choice is likely to
be most restricted in a centralized model and, conversely, may be
less restricted in a decentralized one. Centralized models function
according to a constant stream of directives, mandates and orders
while decentralized models tend to give greater attention to
negotiated decisions between key interests which may include
patients. Generally, Beveridge-type health care systems tend to be
centralized while those of a Bismarckian persuasion are typically
decentralized.

Few health care systems are exclusive examples of one type or
the other in respect of all their components. In Sweden, the overall
health care system is centralized but only from the regional level
downwards. Yet dental care is highly fragmented and decentralized.
In Germany and the Netherlands the curative health services are
clearly decentralized, although many preventive and public health
services operate according to a centralized model. Even the regulation of hundreds of health insurance funds through a small
number of central agencies bears some of the characteristics of a
centralized system. Further, over time, health care systems may
veer towards centralization or decentralization.

## TYPES OF DECENTRALIZATION

Various forms of decentralization can be identified (Cheema and Rondinelli 1983). Four main ones – *deconcentration, devolution, delegation and privatization* – are briefly described here. The distinction between these types of decentralization is based on their legal status. Other factors such as financial authority, means of representation of the local community and geographical conditions are also important in classifying the type of decentralization.

Although studies of decentralization frequently include privatization as a form of decentralization, this classification has been questioned on the grounds that transferring of authority to the private sector constitutes a shift to a different system of organizing activities, rather than a shift between various forms of organization within a single system (Collins and Green 1994). Decentralization and privatization are conceptually two different processes which may or may not be interrelated. Here privatization is included as a form of decentralization, although acknowledged as substantially different from the other forms identified. This issue can become further complicated where there is a public–private mix and public bodies become purchasers of care provided privately (through either for-profit or not-for-profit organizations).

A summary of the different types of decentralization is presented in Table 13.1.

- *Deconcentration* (administrative decentralization) refers to the redistribution of administrative responsibilities only within the

**Table 13.1**   Types of decentralization

| *Type of decentralization* | *Definition* |
|---|---|
| Deconcentration (administrative decentralization) | Decision making is transferred to a lower administrative (civil servant) level |
| Devolution (political decentralization) | Decision making is transferred to a lower political level |
| Delegation | Tasks are allocated to actors at a lower organizational level |
| Privatization | Tasks are transferred from public ownership into private ownership |

*Source*: Modified from Borgenhammar (1993)

existing structure of central government. Only administrative, and not political, authority is transferred to one or more lower levels. This has been termed the 'ministerial' model (Regan and Stewart 1982), whereby administrative responsibilities are handed over to locally based offices of central government ministries. Since deconcentration involves the transfer of administrative rather than political authority, it is seen as the least extensive form of decentralization. Nevertheless, it is frequently used in many countries. The local administration set up under deconcentration can be of two different types. In the vertical pattern of local administration, local staff of each ministry are responsible to their own ministry. The second type of local administration may be referred to as the integrated or prefectoral form, in which a local representative of central government responsible to one ministry (e.g. the ministry of interior or local government) is made responsible for the performance of all government functions in that area. Sectoral government ministries exercise only technical supervision over their staff.

- *Devolution.* In implementing devolution (political decentralization), governments relinquish certain functions to new or different organizations outside their direct control. Devolution means the creation or strengthening of subnational levels of government that are substantially independent of the national level with respect to a defined set of functions. They may be called regional or local government.

  Devolution thus implies a greater restructuring than deconcentration. Two major issues arise. First, health makes a heavy demand on recurrent expenditure, yet local governments often have restricted possibilities to raise revenue. One trend has thus been to shift health services ownership and financing out of local government control, as health services have become too expensive for them to maintain. On the other hand, if the cost is covered by central government grants to local governments, then this implies heavy dependence and a likely reduction in autonomy. Such a situation, especially within budgets covering actual expenses, offers health services an incentive to overspend and become inefficient. Second, devolution may complicate efforts to construct a logical hierarchy of health services and to set up a regional structure.

- *Delegation.* In delegation the emphasis is on giving an authority the right to plan and implement decisions relating to particular activities without direct supervision by a higher authority. This form of decentralization relates only to defined tasks and not to all activities. The attraction of delegation is that it allows government regulations and bureaucracy to be bypassed in order to permit more efficient and flexible management.

If the management of an entire, nationalized health service is delegated to a parastatal organization, the role of the ministry of health is restricted to strategic and policy issues. This can happen under devolution as well as full-blown insurance-based health care provision. There is, however, a danger of duplication of services.

- *Privatization.* Privatization involves the transfer of government functions to a non-governmental organization which may be either a voluntary agency or a private company. It may refer to production (provision) of services, to financing of services, or to both (Barr 1987). In practice different combinations of these two elements can be found. Privatization may refer to support functions like maintenance, cleaning, transport, catering, and so on.

Privatization does not remove from the government all burdens of health care management. In practice, a strong regulatory authority will be needed to monitor the supply and quality of both health services and supply industries (e.g. pharmaceuticals) and to ensure the effective coordination of services on a geographical basis.

## PATTERNS OF DECENTRALIZATION

Countries employ different patterns of decentralization simultaneously for different functions. For instance, in the UK the model of organization is one of deconcentration. However, the chain of command from centre to periphery is interrupted by appointed district health authorities which are agents of the Secretary of State for Health.

With regard to devolution, the outcome depends on the strength of local governments. Countries which have successful regional and/or local government in health care typically have had it for a long time. Local democracy is not something which can be put in place overnight. Transferring decision-making power to weak local bodies is risky if a local 'dictator' can distort local democratic control for personal gain. In eastern Europe, for example, due to the weak democratic tradition, it has been difficult to understand the different roles of elected and nominated bodies.

The case of the UK nicely illustrates another version of this dilemma. The district health authority is accountable through the regional office to the Secretary of State for Health (the Minister). Although health authority members are appointed, some confusion exists as to whether they should be agents of the centre or represent local communities. In reality they fall into the former category, since they possess no local legitimacy in that they are centrally appointed rather than locally elected bodies.

In the Nordic countries, by contrast, health boards at either regional level (Denmark and Sweden) (Anell 1996; Anell *et al.* 1996) or municipal level (Finland and Norway) (Martikainen and Uusikylä 1997; Saether and Hertzberg 1997; Saether and Olsen 1997) are democratically elected and directly responsible to their local populations. Managers and other professionals are employees who have only as much decision-making power as is delegated to them by the health boards.

The point is that whatever the composition of the decision-making body, it should be clear from where the mandate to operate comes. The fundamental question remains whether the head of a hospital or a district is allowed to exercise decision-making power and managerial (implementation) power at the same time. In principle, this should not be possible.

## RATIONALE FOR DECENTRALIZATION

Decentralization has acquired considerable appeal because it is seen as a means of resolving problems in complex public bureaucracies. These were criticized for being monolithic, sclerotic, inefficient and insensitive to the preferences of users. Figure 13.1 summarizes some of the expected positive effects of decentralization.

Popular management thinking has been infused with notions of delegated or devolved responsibility in order to get 'close to the customer' (Peters and Waterman 1982). Decentralized institutions have a number of advantages (Osborne and Gaebler 1993): (1) they can respond quickly to changing circumstances and customers' needs; (2) they can be more effective since frontline workers are closest to most problems and opportunities; (3) they can be more innovative than centralized institutions; and (4) they can generate higher morale, more commitment and greater productivity.

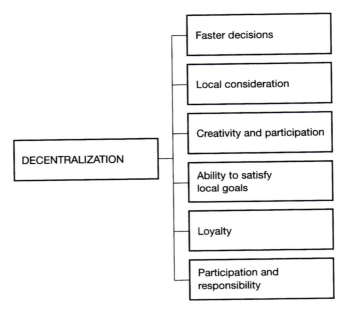

**Figure 13.1** Expected effects of decentralization

Governments sought to apply these management principles to public sector organizations through the 'New Public Management' (NPM), which emphasizes the centrality of competition, separating purchasing from provision and performance measurement (Hood 1991). Decentralization is an inevitable consequence of an NPM approach. In theory, the purchaser–provider separation also allows the provision of services to be transferred from the public to the private sector, although there may be good reasons for not doing so (Kettl 1993). Decentralization provides the opportunity for the principles of delegation, responsiveness and accountability – the so-called hallmarks of general management – to be taken down to the lowest possible level (Dalley 1987). The introduction of clinical directors exemplified the belief in, and commitment to, decentralization. Table 13.2 summarizes the main expected results from decentralization.

**Table 13.2**    Benefits of decentralization

| Type of decentralization | Benefits |
| --- | --- |
| Deconcentration | The need for central administrative bodies is reduced |
| | Local innovations are implemented |
| Devolution | More local decision-making power and more people can gain influence |
| | Less central power |
| Delegation | Faster implementation |
| Privatization | Activities become independent from 'incompetent politicians, who are incapable of making decisions and unclear of their role' |

*Source*: Modified from Borgenhammar (1993)

## DECENTRALIZATION: LIMITS AND BARRIERS

Decentralization is not a universal panacea to all flaws in contemporary health systems, even if seen in this way by some politicians. To take advantage of decentralization certain conditions in the social and cultural environment must be met. Borgenhammer has identified the following: sufficient local administrative and managerial capacity, ideological certainty in implementation of tasks and readiness to accept several interpretations of one problem. Institutions themselves also have to change. 'Organisations that decentralise authority also find that they have to articulate their missions, create internal cultures around their core values, and measure results' (Osborne and Gaebler 1993).

Decentralization can have negative effects including: fragmented services, weakening of central health departments, inequity, political manipulation to favour particular interests or stakeholders and a weakening of the position and status of the public sector. The experience of many countries in recent years demonstrates that there are certain areas where decision-making power should not be decentralized. Four such domains may be identified. First, general provisions concerning health policy. Second, strategic decisions on the development of health resources. Third, specific arrangements concerning regulation. And fourth, monitoring, assessing and analysing the health of the population and health care provision.

The first of the four domains is a fundamental part of the activities of the state. Essential decisions should be restricted to the national government. Since health policy involves basic values which can affect many spheres of social life, core strategic matters should conform to the same procedures that govern all other public policy. The second domain concerns resources devoted to health which will shape the system's future. Such infrastructural concerns include qualified personnel (training and accreditation, licensing), major capital developments, expensive equipment and research and development.

A considerable degree of centralization in these areas is justified by the lengthy time horizon to obtain information not readily accessible at lower levels, and to overcome local resistance and vested interests. For example, forecasting numbers of highly trained health care professionals can only be done sensibly at a national level. Economies of scale also justify centralized decision making. Procuring capital equipment centrally should result in lower prices, better servicing and more intensive usage. Research and development as well as training also should be organized on a regional or national scale.

The third domain concerns decisions that relate to the protection of the public interest. The regulation of new drugs and the maintenance of quality standards are regarded as matters for central control. The final domain focuses on monitoring, assessing and analysing health sector activities. Particularly if the government has decided to decentralize health care provision, the monitoring of equity between different geographical regions and social strata may become an effective tool to influence behaviour on the periphery. Since decentralization by definition means giving up power to new decision makers, it is paramount to monitor whether these new bodies meet the expectations placed on them. Such monitoring and publicizing of the results can be a powerful incentive to prevent undesired behaviour.

Various forms of decentralization can produce specific disadvantages. These are presented in Table 13.3.

Generally, decentralization generates additional costs due to the need for coordination. Typically, it is more difficult to guarantee a sufficient level of uniformity of decision in decentralized institutions than in centralized ones. Decentralization can also harm economies of scale, and both specialists and equipment may be underused.

**Table 13.3**   Risks of decentralization

| Type of decentralization | Risks |
|---|---|
| Deconcentration | • The right hand does not always know what the left hand is doing<br>• Risk for many kinds of practices being implemented |
| Devolution | • Lack of political oversight |
| Delegation | • Less professionalism<br>• It can be difficult to maintain quality and efficiency if the decentralized units are too spread out |
| Privatization | • Private monopolies can emerge which may exploit their power |

*Source*: Borgenhammar (1993)

## DECENTRALIZATION: KEY QUESTIONS

Important questions in implementing decentralization include: to what level, to whom and which tasks? The choice of *level* of decentralization defines the centre–periphery relationship and the mode of accountability adopted. The more local the level, the more likely that dilemmas will arise over scarcity of management skills, fragmented provision due to the large number of small operating units, and difficulty in providing services efficiently for large populations. One solution to these problems is to establish a hierarchy of levels between the centre and periphery (e.g. regions and districts). However, what may look like decentralization from a central perspective may not seem so if a patient has to confront seemingly equally remote district- or region-based agencies.

As regards *to whom* to decentralize, decision makers within a devolved system will be elected and accountable to the electorate. Local government, for example, functions in this way. However, a deconcentrated organization, where health policy and management remain the responsibility of central government, may have some type of appointed board. Health boards can be seen as a way of making local health services more responsive to their local community without actually devolving power to a local government structure or completely removing the line of accountability to the centre (Mills 1994). Appointed boards, such as those operating in the British NHS, have been criticized for having no democratic legitimacy and for being administrative arms of the centre (Stewart

1992). Despite the rhetoric of devolved responsibility, governments retain, and exercise, considerable power over local health authorities through the appointments system and by other means. Accountability is therefore firmly upwards even if delegation is downwards. Decentralizing responsibilities while maintaining a degree of central influence appears to be the optimal form of decentralization for many countries.

*Tasks* to be decentralized include revenue raising, policy making and planning, resource allocation, funding of service provision and interagency and intersectoral coordination. For the most part, central influence over funds and their distribution remains intact. Some minimal delegated responsibility over resources may be permitted e.g. in the UK, general practitioner fundholders are allowed to retain savings from the budgets delegated to them, although not for personal gain but rather to improve patient services.

Policy making and planning are usually split between central and subnational levels, although the precise mix will vary between countries and over time. In general, local freedom in policy making and planning is constrained by the requirement to operate within a centrally determined framework which seeks to establish priorities. For instance, in the UK the national health strategy has set down targets in five key areas and local health authorities' performance is monitored against progress towards these. There is limited scope for varying the national targets in the light of local circumstances. However, a new health strategy is being introduced with fewer national targets and with scope for local targets to be set.

Decentralization is often favoured as a means of improving the coordination of services and activities at the local level. It is also recognized that health is about more than health care and that agencies besides health care delivery ones must be involved in any rebalancing of the policy agenda. But joint working is not easy when the different agencies involved have their own agendas and cultures as well as different accountability structures.

## EVALUATION OF DECENTRALIZATION IN THE LIGHT OF EQUITY, EFFICIENCY AND CONSUMER CHOICE

It has not been customary to assess the outcome of decentralization in the light of health gain, equity, efficiency, quality of care and consumer choice. As a rule it has been taken for granted that the outcome of decentralization automatically brings about positive changes. Furthermore, the expected outcomes with regard to these parameters are usually not well defined in advance. It would be a major step forward if policy makers would explicitly define what improvements are expected.

### Equity

If decentralization fosters the development of local health centres and improves the geographical distribution of resources it can contribute directly to equity. However, if decentralization undermines the uniformity of decision making then it could jeopardize equity. This risk is real but so far no direct link between decentralization and rising inequalities has been established. If they occur, they seem to depend on other factors such as broader economic processes. It should also be emphasized that there is no direct link between centralization and equity. There are many examples in the CEE/CIS countries, among others, which show that centralized health care systems may be unfair with respect to accessibility and utilization, and extremely ineffective in terms of securing equal health status.

Privatization as a form of decentralization is more problematic. In the sense of increasing the role of private enterprise in health services, privatization has become an ideological issue, especially in the CEE/CIS. As a slogan it conveys the ideal of a free market, which is considered the ultimate form of decentralization by proponents of a market system of health care. Nevertheless, it can also be used as an effective managerial solution to achieve better utilization of resources. Usually, privatization of service provision does not hamper equity. Privatization of financing carries a higher risk. One of the core prerequisites for a market to function and the 'invisible hand' to operate is that people can afford to pay, thereby denying access to those who cannot afford to pay. Thus privatization of financing may contradict equity of access to health care. A decision to privatize thus requires close consideration of the government's ability to regulate the resulting market.

### Efficiency

There is growing evidence that an efficient provider of health services ought to possess the basic properties of a firm rather than a bureaucratic office. According to Saltman and von Otter, 'it would be relatively free to design its own structure and make its own judgements concerning scale advantages, forward integration of production or market links with other stages in the health care production chain' (Saltman and von Otter 1992). Since decentralization can provide health care establishments with such properties, it thus can improve efficiency. However, when provision of services is privatized but a substantial proportion of the cost is paid by public funds, a difficult dilemma concerning efficiency arises. Experience in Europe and the US indicates that under these circumstances it is notoriously difficult to encourage cost control and prevent cost escalation (Smith and Lipsky 1992).

**Consumer choice**

Various forms of decentralization increase possibilities for consumer choice in different ways. Devolving power to lower political levels, i.e. to local government, puts it closer to people. Local voters can more effectively influence local governments and shape decisions according to consumers' preferences. Also, health providers may be more responsive to expectations expressed by people.

It is broadly agreed that the prospect of receiving privately provided primary services enlarges consumer choice (OECD 1994). However, the choice is a real one only if no financial barriers inhibit access. Due to the role financial mechanisms play in making health care available, their privatization is more problematic. Private financing as a result of decentralization may increase choice for those who are well off (at least in the short term), but drastically reduce choice for those with insufficient financial means.

## CONCLUSIONS

Decentralization can bring benefits as well as difficulties. The principal potential benefits include:

- allowing local communities greater involvement in the management of their own health as well as improved opportunities to influence priorities and resource allocation policies;
- assisting in establishing a clearer relationship between primary, secondary and tertiary services (e.g. the 'hub and spoke' concept whereby it is clear which services should be provided centrally and which locally);
- reducing inequalities within countries, between regions, and between rural and urban areas if accompanied by the allocation of resources according to local needs;

- allowing national ministries of health to be released from administrative responsibilities and tasks of an operational nature in order that they can concentrate on policy and strategic planning functions;
- aiding the implementation of health policy by reducing central interference and encouraging local ownership;
- facilitating, or at least helping to create the conditions for, intersectoral coordination between health care agencies and others influencing health such as local government;
- helping overcome communication problems and delays due to features of distance, lengthy hierarchies, multiple organizational layers.

Ministries of health seriously considering, or committed to, decentralization in the health sector should address a number of issues. Unless these are acknowledged, and attention is paid to them, decentralization is unlikely to succeed. Experience of decentralization in a variety of different contexts suggests that the following issues are of particular importance:

- clarity about the nature of decentralization, the functions to be decentralized and those which are not;
- management capacity and capability, including regulatory and monitoring skills;
- the requisite number of management levels in a decentralized system;
- financial issues;
- workforce issues.

It is essential to be clear at the outset about the nature of decentralization in a given context, the functions to be decentralized and those which are to remain under central control. There is often a vagueness about such matters which can cause confusion at a later stage.

Capacity and capability issues are important because management expertise will be required to implement a policy of decentralization. However, once decentralization has occurred, different skills will be required which may include the need for strengthened regulatory instruments to monitor the activities of newly decentralized arrangements. A balance is needed between the regulation required to ensure compliance with national health policy priorities while avoiding over-regulation which might stultify the creativity which decentralization is at least in part intended to achieve.

A further issue of importance concerns the number of management levels below the national one. Having more than four (including the national level) commonly results in a cumbersome structure which may hamper the achievement of effective decentralization.

Clarity about the functions to be decentralized is not confined to the national level. Subnational levels – regions and districts – also need to be clear about their respective responsibilities. There is a tendency for subnational health authorities to centralize power at their level, going against the spirit of decentralization to the local level. This would be of particular concern if the aim of decentralization is to give primary care enhanced responsibility.

If health finance is devolved it may be more difficult for the national government to implement its policy priorities as well as to monitor expenditure and control costs. There will be a debate about how much freedom to allow decentralized agencies to spend funds according to their own priorities.

Finally, decentralization will raise human resources issues concerning the workforce. One relates to the capability concerns mentioned earlier. Decentralization can reveal a deficit of senior management and health planning skills. Training and development opportunities will thus need to be an important part of decentralization.

In the last analysis, decentralization is a means to an end and not an end in itself. The key question to ask is not *whether* to use this policy and management instrument but *how* and *to what* effect so that the central objectives of national health policy may be most effectively achieved.

## REFERENCES

Anell, A. (1996). *Decentralization and Health Systems Change: The Swedish Experience*, IHE Working Paper 1996: 7. Lund: The Swedish Institute for Health Economics.

Anell, A., Rosén, P. and Svarvar, P. (1996). *Health-Care Reforms in Sweden: Striving Towards Equity, Efficiency and Cost Containment*, IHE Working Paper 1996: 8. Lund: The Swedish Institute for Health Economics.

Barr, N. (1987). *The Economics of the Welfare State*. London: Weidenfeld and Nicolson.

Borgenhammar, E. (1993). *At vårda Liv: Organisation, Etik, Kvalitet [Looking after Life: Organization, Ethics, Quality]*. Stockholm: SNS Förlag.

Cheema, G. and Rondinelli, D. (1983). *Decentralisation and Development.* Newbury Park: Sage.

Collins, C. D. and Green, A. T. (1994). Decentralisation and primary health care: Some negative implications in developing countries. *International Journal of Health Services,* 24, 459–75.

Dalley, G. (1987). Decentralisation: A new way of organising community health services. *Hospital and Health Services Review,* 83, 72–84.

Hood, C. (1991). A public management for all seasons? *Public Administration,* 69, 3–19.

Kettl, D. F. (1993). *Sharing Power: Public Governance and Private Markets.* Washington, DC: Brookings Institution.

Martikainen, T. and Uusikylä, P. (1997). *Reforming Health Policy in Finland: A Critical Assessment.* Helsinki: Ministry of Health and Social Welfare.

Mills, A. (1994). Decentralisation and accountability in the health sector from an international perspective: What are the choices? *Public Administration and Development,* 47, 281–92.

OECD (1994). *The Reform of Health Care Systems: A Review of Seventeen OECD Countries.* Paris: Organisation for Economic Co-operation and Development.

Osborne, D. and Gaebler, T. (1993). *Reinventing Government.* Reading, MA: Addison Wesley.

Peters, T. J. and Waterman, R. H. (1982). *In Search of Excellence – Lessons from America's Best Run Companies.* New York: Harper and Row.

Regan, D. E. and Stewart, J. (1982). An essay in the government of health: The case for local authority control. *Social Policy and Administration,* 16, 19–43.

Rondinelli, D. (1981). Government decentralisation in comparative theory and practice in developing countries. *International Review of Administrative Sciences,* 47, 133–45.

Saether, E. M. and Hertzberg, A. (1997). *Decentralisation and Health Systems Change: The Norwegian Case,* 1997: 2. Oslo: Diakonhjemmets Internasjonale Senter (DIS).

Saether, E. M. and Olsen, I. T. (1997). *96% Public? The Private/Public Mix in the Norwegian Health Sector,* 1997: 1. Oslo: Diakonhjemmets Internasjonale Senter (DIS).

Saltman, R. B. and von Otter, C. (1992). *Planned Markets and Public Competition. Strategic Reform in Northern European Health Systems.* Buckingham: Open University Press.

Smith, S. R. and Lipsky, M. (1992). Privatisation in health and human services: a critique. *Journal of Health Politics, Policy and Law,* 17(2), 233–53.

Stewart, J. (1992). *Accountability to the Public.* London: European Policy Forum.

White, J. (1993). Markets, budgets, and health care cost control. *Health Affairs,* 12(3), 44–57.

# 14

# CITIZEN PARTICIPATION AND PATIENT CHOICE IN HEALTH REFORM

Michael Calnan,
Janoz Halik and
Jolanta Sabbat

## INTRODUCTION

A continuing theme associated with health reform is the need to take into account the views of the citizen and the user in the provision of health care. It is difficult to judge to what extent these policies have been prescriptive, resulting from political values and philosophies about either the importance of democratizing the health service through public participation or, quite differently, the importance of consumer sovereignty and choice in the market economy for health care. Alternatively, these policies may have emerged in response to demands from the public, or segments of it (the so-called 'consumer' movement). This might reflect the public's increasing interest in the type of health care which is provided and which they pay for through tax, insurance contributions or a mixture of both.

Ideas about citizen participation and patient choice in health care traditionally tend to be linked to different political philosophies about the organization of health care. Some have argued that taking the views and opinions of citizens 'collectively' into account, such as through increased 'participation' in the policy-making process or decision-making process, may serve as a means of democratizing health services, thus making the medical profession and the state more accountable (Calnan 1987). This approach is usually associated with the view of health care as a 'public utility' found in national health service systems.

In contrast, the concern with patient choice is traditionally associated with health care systems where emphasis is placed on market economy principles such as competition. Patient choice is usually associated with the idea of 'consumer sovereignty' and the importance of tailoring health care systems to meet the 'individual' demands of its users. One can summarize these two different logics by suggesting that the notion of participation has traditionally been limited to patient *needs* while the concept of choice of provider has been connected to patient *wants*.

This analysis is, however, incomplete because in some systems where market economy principles have been introduced and 'rationing' of health care has become more 'explicit', increasingly the 'public' and 'community' are being asked about their views on priorities for health care. In this case, however, emphasis is being placed on the public being responsive rather than on active community participation and representation in the policy-making process.

An alternative approach to the market economy model can be called democratic–political (Saltman 1994). This approach portrays patient choice as an exercise in democratic rather than commercial rights. Patient choice becomes a mechanism whereby individuals can exercise more influence over what happens to them inside a publicly operated system. The choice of hospital and physician gives individuals the ability to influence the provision of service. Patient choice becomes a political characteristic in which patients, through their participation, help legitimate the underlying authority/appropriateness of the service delivery system. In this view, patient choice is an important concept for examining users' approaches to health care systems irrespective of whether they are privately or publicly funded (Saltman 1994).

One useful analytical framework for examining approaches to participation (Arnstein 1966) constructs a ladder of participation to describe the different degrees of power potentially available to the 'user'. This ranges from manipulation and therapy, through informing, consultation and placation, to partnership, delegated power and citizen control, where power is held by citizens rather than governments or service providers.

A similar typology classifies the different degrees of authority that can be considered to create 'empowered patients' (Saltman 1994). Starting with patient advice and appeals, it moves from the least to the most empowered position for the individual patient. It begins with moral persuasion (the ability only to ask to be heard) through formal political control to the ability to control one's own organizational destiny. Thus at the least empowered end of the continuum is patient advice and appeals. Moving along the scale are legal remedies, then on to annual patient selection of insurance carrier, to patient choice of physician and hospital (without budgeting link), to elected democratic control over finance and provision, to patient influence over treatment modality and finally patient choice of physician and hospital with budget links. In this typology, the key to understanding empowerment is the degree of individual leverage over specific service delivery decisions. To become empowered, therefore, patients have to wrest substantial control over resource allocation from managers and doctors. This typology focuses mainly on the individual and emphasizes the importance of patient control over decisions.

There are, however, a number of unresolved issues associated with choice in health care. The first concerns whether choice is as important for the user as some policy analysts impute it should be. To what extent is choice important for all health care provision or is it only important in certain areas such as maternity care? A related issue is whether, given the special characteristics of health care (Calnan *et al.* 1993), users will have access to enough information (McKee *et al.* 1995) to make informed choices. Finally, there is the question of inequality of access to choice: those people with the most resources (finance, time and energy) will have the greatest choice. Hence choice is a complicated concept at least in the context of health care and it should not be taken for granted that 'choice' is something that patients value highly.

## EUROPEAN EXPERIENCE

### Citizen participation/representation

Two key questions are first, how the citizen's voice is heard in relation to health care in different countries and second, how much power citizens have in influencing decisions. Approaches taken in countries have been at both the collective level and the individual level. In Finland, citizens have a formal influence through its elected health boards. The municipal council responsible for health care delivery is elected and that council then elects the 'boards' responsible for decision making about health care. The health board consists of a mix of local lay people representing citizens' views as well as the Chief Physician from the municipal health centre. The UK has adopted a different approach. While health authority members are not elected but nominated and do not automatically include citizen representatives, local community health councils (CHCs) have been in existence for 20 years. These are agencies set up specifically to represent citizens' interest in health care. Unlike in Finland, representatives of CHCs are appointed, not elected, and the councils tend to act in an advisory and informative role. A more recent initiative put forward by the UK was to attempt to portray local people as 'advisers' to the new purchasing authorities and consortia. Each 'purchaser' would act as a 'champion of the people'. A number of means by which purchasers might consult local people were cited in *Local Voices*, an advisory document produced by the National Health Service Management Executive (1992). Suggestions include the use of 'focus groups' drawn from the local population, surveys, and health forms. These suggestions were not incorporated into statutory mechanisms.

In the countries of central and eastern Europe, there has been a rapid development of the voluntary sector including a variety of patient support groups. Concurrently, the advent of independent media has given publicity to issues of patient participation and choice. In Poland, an important role played by the press can be seen in the formation of a patients' rights movement.

One of the more successful reforms in Poland has been the re-establishment of local democracy in the form of local self-government councils with health committees. Despite centralized financing and provision of health care, many local self-governments have now taken over some responsibilities for health care, typically at the level of primary care. In the majority of cases, these responsibilities are delegated from a higher governmental level and this limits empowerment. These local self-governments must, however, be consulted concerning the closure or establishment of health care facilities in their area.

Poland's Act on Health Care Institutions (1991) provided for the transformation of the state health system into a public one and introduced supervisory boards for health care institutions. Membership of the boards should represent the local community and self-governments. The boards have a responsibility to represent the views of the population and should act on behalf of patients, ensuring that patient rights are observed. Many health facilities still do not have these boards and it has taken time for them to become active. Nonetheless there is potential for the development of greater patient representation through this mechanism.

In Hungary, representatives are elected to the Boards of the Health Insurance Fund through periodic general elections. In Poland, draft legislation provides for representation at every organizational level of the Health Insurance Funds.

## Patients' rights and quality of care

One common policy in a number of European countries has been the introduction of mechanisms for protecting patients' rights. While this type of approach does not necessarily involve public participation, it is an attempt to make health service provision more responsive to patient demands. In Poland, for instance, an Act was passed in 1991 which ensures that patients are entitled to a level of care appropriate to current medical knowledge; to be informed of their state of health; to express their informed consent or refusal of specific components of health care; to privacy and dignity; and to a peaceful and dignified death. In addition, when undergoing inpatient treatment, the patient has a right to personal telephone and correspondence communication with the outside world; to be nursed by near ones; and to receive spiritual care. There was no provision for implementation of these rights, however. A Charter of Patients' Rights is currently being developed in Poland, although as yet it has not become law.

In the UK in 1992, a Patients' Charter was introduced which sets out ten rights (three new ones) and calls for the setting of national and local standards to improve the quality of care provided for patients. The emphasis is on standards, not on legal rights. Thus the success of the UK Patients' Charter will depend on the quality of the procedures developed to give substance to the Charter principles and the significance attached to those procedures by those responsible for their implementation. Without effective mechanisms, the Charter will do little to empower citizens who will continue to have limited influence on policy making in the UK.

In contrast to the approach taken in Poland and the UK, Finland has defined the rights of patients by law (1993) which constitutes a landmark in the development of legislation in this area in Europe (Fluss 1994). The law gives patients the right to good health and medical care and related treatment; access to care; information; and self-determination. The status of patients who are minors, emergency treatment and appropriate clinical competence are also covered. One important aspect of the Finnish legislation is the role of the patient ombudsman, which stands in marked contrast to the role of the ombudsman in the UK and Poland. Under the Finnish scheme, every health care institution must nominate a patient ombudsman who can be responsible for a number of local health care units. The patient ombudsman's role is to advise the patients on all practical matters concerning the implementation of the Law in Patients' Rights; to assist the patient in writing a complaint, or application for compensation; to provide information about patients' rights; and to facilitate implementation.

A different approach to patients' rights has been adopted in Italy through the Tribunal for Patients' Rights. The Tribunal is comprised of ordinary citizens who voluntarily use their interest to monitor the quality of health services, resolving patients' complaints as well as lobbying for more humane methods of administration and respect for existing laws, regulations and the Patients' Charter. Representatives of the Tribunal are involved in every health authority throughout Italy. This is an example of public participation and involvement having emerged from a social movement.

### Complaints mechanisms

One mechanism through which users' dissatisfaction can actively be voiced is a formal complaints procedure. In some European countries such as the UK, there is evidence of a rapid increase in rates of complaints. It is difficult to identify the root cause of this, however, and in particular whether it is due to a real increase in grievances, a rise in users' expectations or easier procedures for voicing a complaint. How far complaints are strong indicators of quality is still uncertain.

Most countries do have systems for channelling complaints, although the array of channels can be bewildering for the potential complainant. In the UK, the complicated system has recently been reviewed (Department of Health 1994). Recommendations have been accepted that a common system of complaint be introduced comprising an internal, and then if required an external, inquiry which would involve a panel consisting of a majority of lay people (Department of Health 1995; Wratten 1996).

One issue associated with systems of complaint was that the agencies dealing with complaints are only able to make decisions about disciplinary measures, since financial compensation tends to be dealt with by the courts. An attempt to resolve this problem has been made in Finland through the No-Fault Liability and Patient Insurance Law in 1987. The Patient Injuries Board was set up within the Ministry of Social Welfare and Health. The task of the Board is to recommend whether compensation should be paid and to give an opinion about the compensation payable. Sweden has had a no-fault structure for several decades, administered by its National Board of Health and Welfare and funded by a small per capita contribution made by the country council to a central fund.

Several complaints mechanisms exist in Poland. The old system of complaints concerning the state bureaucracy, rooted in administrative law, is largely discredited. Complaints procedures for patients also exist within the system of professional self-regulating associations and patients may complain through the 'Ombudsman for Patients Rights'.

## Choice of health care

The question of choice in health care is complicated. In the UK, there have been attempts to increase patient 'choice' both directly and indirectly. Tax concessions for subscription to private health insurance were introduced as part of the reforms for those at retirement age but have recently been abandoned. The emphasis on partnership between the public and the private sectors has indirectly encouraged patient choice and exit from the National Health Service, although the range of services available in the private sector is still limited. In 1993, the percentage of the population covered by private health insurance stood at 15 per cent (Bosanquet 1994). Private health insurance is the major method of paying for private health care in the UK. More directly, through the introduction of the new GP contracts, attempts were made to give patients better choice by providing them with more information about the services GPs offer, together with more competition among GPs and easier arrangements for changing doctors. The new purchasing role of general practice fundholders created through the reforms also aimed to extend choice, with general practitioners acting on behalf of their patients by shopping around between providers in the internal market for the most appropriate care. The GP is also able to make extra contractual referrals should the need arise.

In Poland, where direct access to specialists is possible, there is evidence of multiple consultation and also of 'informal' channels of referral for those with higher educational status. Strict adherence to catchment area contributes to the weak position of the patient in Poland, particularly for those who do not have access to the informal sector. Increased choice is provided for in draft legislation on health insurance, with free choice of medical practitioner and hospital within the territory covered by the insurance fund.

## EVALUATION: IMPACT OF THESE POLICY CHANGES

What impact have these changes had on the level of public participation and choice? The available evidence largely comes from studies done in the UK. Survey evidence (Bruster *et al.* 1994; Bosanquet 1994) suggests that the influence has been mixed. For example, Bruster *et al.* in their national study of patient views about hospital care show that Patients' Charter rights were not being met in a number of areas: (1) explanation of treatment proposed; (2) access to health records; (3) choosing whether they wish to take part in student training; and (4) being guaranteed admission within two years of being placed on a waiting list. There was also evidence that five of the national charter standards were not met.

Evidence from the Social Attitude Survey (Bosanquet 1994) shows that the reforms seem to have reduced the demand for health spending and have helped restore confidence in the performance of the service. However, they also seem to have failed to convince the public that their views now count more in how the service is run. In 1987, nearly two-thirds thought if a hospital had to choose between making life a bit easier for patients or a bit easier for doctors, the hospital would opt to make life easier for patients. In 1993, only just over half thought they would make that choice, and only just over one in four believed that they would definitely or probably have a say in which hospital they went to if they needed an operation. Also, it has been suggested (Cartwright and Windsor 1992) that the limit on waiting list times may be focusing on the less important aspect of waiting for an operation: they found that patients were more dissatisfied with the delay between referral by the general practitioners and being seen at an outpatient department and, to a lesser extent, the decision to put them on a waiting list. More recent evidence from the British Social Archives Survey in 1994 (Central Statistical Office 1996) shows that while two in three people thought that the quality of medical treatment in hospitals was satisfactory or very good, the proportion who were dissatisfied with in-patient treatment and care rose from 7 per cent to 16 per cent between 1983 and 1994.

What impact has the introduction of fundholding had on patients' choice? The evidence available is limited and thus it is difficult to judge (Coulter 1995). The idea that the introduction of fundholding would lead to money following patients, that fund-holders would enhance patient choice by 'shopping around' for health care, has not yet materialized as fundholders tend to support their local hospitals. However, some claims have been made that patients from fundholding practices have better access to hospital care through a reduction in waiting lists. One study showed GPs were no more likely to take account of patients' preferences after the implementation of the reforms in either fundholding or non-fundholding practices (Mahon *et al.* 1994).

There are a number of other areas where UK government poli-cies have attempted to extend choice. One was in choosing a GP, and the new reforms have sought to encourage patients to shop around for their health care. However, several authors (e.g. Leavy *et al.* 1989) are sceptical of this happening. They question patients' motivation to act as consumers and their enthusiasm for shopping around. They argue that most people only change their doctor when circumstances force them to do so, either because they have moved or because their general practitioner has moved, retired or died. For those with chronic conditions, a relationship of trust and confidence may have been built up during the course of an illness which provides a powerful incentive to stay put. A recent study (Jones *et al.* 1994) found the new system had led to no increase in the rate of movement between GPs.

Similarly, while the upward increase in the proportions covered by private health insurance in the UK has slowed down, it still remains the preserve of the well off. Does the use of private health insurance increase 'consumer choice'? The evidence (Calnan *et al.* 1993) suggests that choice is extended only slightly. Certainly, those who had experienced private health care stressed the quality of the facilities, the individualized nature of care and the timing of visits, but there was little evidence of shopping around between the pri-vate and public sectors. Also, subscribers had limited knowledge of the costs of treatment and felt they lacked the competence to evaluate the skills of different consultants in order to make an informed choice. Rather than shopping around for the best deal, they depended on their NHS GP to decide whether they should go privately and if so which consultant they should see. Thus, the notion of consumer sovereignty in this context was problematic and individuals did not feel more empowered. This suggests that patients will almost always be dependent on medical professionals, making the issue how to regulate this dependence (Flynn 1992).

What of the effects of the new attempts by purchasing authorities to consult local people? Certainly, there is a voluminous literature on methods of consultation adopted by health authorities (Sykes *et al.* 1992) ranging from surveys and rapid appraisal techniques to 'neighbourhood forums' and user groups. Evidence available to assess the impact of these methods in consultation is in short supply (Milewa *et al.* in press). It is difficult to know whether they are genuine attempts to take on board the public views or 'token' strategies reflecting managerial manipulation (Winkler 1987). There is also the question of the internal organizational structure of the health authority and to what extent 'public views' once elicited actually shape health authority decision making.

One area where the role of the public is clearer is in the rationing of services. With the growing emphasis on 'explicit' rationing, purchasers have increasingly invited the public to prioritize their preferences (Bowling 1993). This is a role that the public seems reluctant to perform (Heginbotham 1992), given that they feel it is mainly the responsibility of the medical profession. The methodology adopted in many of these studies has been criticized for ethical reasons and also as to whether it accurately represents all segments of the community.

## CONCLUSIONS

Returning to the analytical framework described above, it appears that the UK is still on the lower rungs of the ladder of participation and at the moral persuasion end of the continuum of empowerment. How effective such an approach is, with its emphasis on advice and unelected representation, is a question which remains to be answered. However, while discussion has focused on 'top-down' prescriptive policies, there is evidence of the development of organized groups who have protested against or pressed for change in the provision of health care or against professional medical decisions (Williams and Popay 1994). In these circumstances the pressure for change has emerged from public initiative.

The Finnish system of democratically elected municipal health boards is in principle a good example of how to ensure citizens' participation and empowerment. However, those who get their mandate from political parties are not always representative of the population as a whole (Vienonen 1994). Young families, the elderly, unemployed and some 'minority' groups are less likely to be representatives because they are not politically active. Also, the health service in bigger cities is a complex system which is difficult for lay people to grasp, thus shifting power to administrators. Bigger cities have started to establish smaller administrative units with similar types of citizens' representation from the local area.

Decision making in the hospital is also, in principle, democratic although once again the technical nature of the issues limits the influence of 'lay' representatives and increases the power of managers and doctors. However, a similar system to the GP fundholding initiative in the UK has been taken up in Finland in that the municipalities are, at least in theory, able to purchase secondary care services wherever they wish, or they can provide them themselves. Vienonen reports that this has made the secondary services more sensitive to the needs of the municipalities, although not necessarily to the needs of citizens (Vienonen 1994). It is too soon to assess the impact of the new Law on Patients' Rights, with its objective of securing the status of the patient as consumer of health services. Time will show if it is a better approach than less interventionist policies aimed at supporting professional codes of conduct.

In summary, Finland has adopted more 'interventionist' government legislation aimed at enhancing patient rights and public participation. The latter approach is believed more likely to empower users (Saltman 1994) and enable effective public participation (Arnstein 1966). However, there is still limited evidence on which to base judgements about the most effective mechanisms for reflecting citizens' views about health care.

In Italy, an evaluation of the impact of the Tribunal for Patients' Rights points to the success of the Tribunal in altering relations between the public services and their users (Cimatti 1994). The Tribunal has enhanced user participation by providing users with a range of instruments which enable them to shape the provision of services. It also appears to have an impact on access to services by improving first aid services or reducing the amount of time people wait to receive treatment at hospitals. Its impact on quality of health care is difficult to judge, although it may lead to a broader concept of quality that includes comfort and interpersonal relations. It has specifically improved the provision of services for women.

In Poland, despite the major objective of reform in 1990 of maintaining health security, the average citizen feels lost and confused by the system's transformation. Present reforms have not been negotiated with citizens. The initial political consensus of 1989 gradually gave way to partisan fragmentation and the policy process became slow. Many proposals remain on the drawing board. Health services research is poorly developed in Poland and there is no funding to support such research or training in this field, so adequate evaluation of the impact of policy changes is not possible. An important role in this regard can be played by the international health services research community. Collaborative research could provide a useful framework for the transfer of know-how and for the development of research skills in Poland and other countries of the sub-region.

This brief review, based on selected countries' experiences, shows the similarities and differences in policies adopted and some evidence of effectiveness. Some, like the UK, have taken the 'moral persuasion approach' whereas others, like Finland, have adopted more 'interventionist' government legislation aimed at enhancing patients' rights and public participation. In Italy, the policy was generated from a social movement rather than a top-down prescriptive policy. Despite these different approaches, there is still limited evidence on which to base judgements about which are the most effective mechanisms for representing citizen views about health care. Similarly, the evidence available to show the most effective method of enhancing patient choice is in short supply and there are still doubts about how much priority should be placed on the notion of 'choice' in health care.

## REFERENCES

Arnstein, S. R. (1966). A ladder of citizen participation. *American Institute of Planners Journal*, 35, 216–24.

Bosanquet, N. (1994). Improving health. In R. Jowell *et al.* (eds), *British Social Attitudes: The 11th Report*. Aldershot: Dartmouth.

Bowling, A. (1993). *What People Say about Prioritising Health Services*. London: King's Fund Institute.

Bruster, S. *et al.* (1994). Survey of hospital patients. *British Medical Journal*, 309, 1542–6.

Calnan, M. (1987). *Health and Illness: The Lay Perspective.* London: Tavistock.

Calnan, M., Cant, S. and Gabe, J. (1993). *Going Private: Why People Pay for their Health Care.* Buckingham: Open University Press.

Cartwright, A. and Windsor, J. (1992). *Outpatients and their Doctors.* London: HMSO.

Central Statistical Office (1996). *Social Trends.* London: HMSO.

Cimatti, G. (1994). *Citizens' Voice and Choice in the Italian Health Service.* Copenhagen: WHO Regional Office for Europe.

Coulter, A. (1995). General practice fundholding. *European Journal of Public Health*, 5, 233–9.

Department of Health (1994). *Being Heard: The Report of a Review Committee on NHS Complaints Procedures.* London: HMSO.

Department of Health (1995). *Acting on Complaints.* London: HMSO.

Fluss, S. J. (1994). *Patients' Rights, Informed Consent, Access and Equality.* Sweden: Nerenias and Santeris Publishers.

Flynn, R. (1992). Managed markets: Consumers and producers in the national health service. In R. Burrows and A. Marsch (eds), *Consumption and Class, Divisions and Change.* Basingstoke: Macmillan.

Heginbotham, C. (1992). Rationing. *British Medical Journal*, 304, 496–9.

Jones, D., Lester, C. and West, R. (1994). Monitoring changes in health services for older people. In R. Robinson and J. Le Grand (eds), *Evaluating the NHS Reforms.* London: King's Fund Institute.

Leavy, R., Wilkin, D. and Metcalfe, D. H. M. (1989). Consumerism and general practice. *British Medical Journal*, 298, 737–9.

Mahon, A., Wilkin, D. and Whitehouse, C. (1994). Choice of hospital for elective surgery referral: GPs and patients' views. In R. Robinson and J. Le Grand (eds), *Evaluating the NHS Reforms.* London: King's Fund Institute.

McKee, M., Strong, P. and Gardner, P. (1995). Leap of faith over the data tap. *Lancet*, 345, 1449–50.

Milewa, T., Valentine, J. and Calnan, M. (in press). Incorporating public views into the health service purchasing process. *Social Science and Medicine.*

National Health Service Management Executive (1992). *Local Voices: The Views of Local People in Commissioning for Health.* London: NHSME.

Saltman, R. B. (1994). Patient choice and patient empowerment in northern European health systems: A conceptual framework. *International Journal of Health Services*, 24, 201–29.

Sykes, W., Collins, M., Hunter, D. J., Popay, J. and Williams, G. (1992). *Listening to Local Voices: A Guide to Research Methods.* Leeds: Nuffield Institute for Health Services Studies.

Vienonen, M. (1994). *Reorienting Health Care for Health Gain through Citizens' Voice and Choice: The Experience of Finland.* Copenhagen: WHO Regional Office for Europe.

Williams, G. and Popay, J. (1994). *Lay Knowledge and the Privilege of Experience.* London: Routledge.

Winkler, F. (1987). Consumerism in health care: Beyond the supermarket model. *Policy and Politics*, 15, 1–8.

Wratten, L. (1996). When things go wrong. *Health Matters*, 25, 10–11.

# 15

# VALUES, NORMS AND THE REFORM OF HEALTH CARE SYSTEMS

André-Pierre Contandriopoulos, Marju Lauristin and Ellen Leibovich

## INTRODUCTION

The reform of health care systems[1] is a central preoccupation for all developed countries. If consensus exists on the necessity of reform and even in a general sense of what must be done (Saltman 1991; Saltman and von Otter 1992; World Bank 1993; Barr 1994; Angus *et al.* 1995), implementation remains a problem. Specifically, how do we transform large social systems, and in particular health care systems, around which modern democracies are based, without jeopardizing the foundations of these societies? How can we make possible the creative opportunities needed by those who must overcome the paradoxical situation[2] within which they currently function (Contandriopoulos 1994)?

The Canadian situation is, in this respect, very revealing. In 1995, 60 per cent of the Canadian population was very satisfied with the existing health care system and, amongst all social programmes, they considered it to be the greatest contributor to quality of life and to national identity (National Forum on Health 1997). However, due to the increasing debt, the proportion of public spending allocated to paying interest costs continues to grow (in 1995 it will have reached 18 per cent of total public expenditures in the Province of Quebec). Since health care costs constitute nearly a third of government expenditures, the government, reluctant to increase taxes, finds itself forced to cut its public health care spending.

Canada and its provinces thus face a paradox. Economic imperatives (Saltman 1997) oblige their governments to reduce spending and to balance their budgets. If unable to do so, their dependence upon internal and external financial markets (the debt in foreign currency constitutes 40 per cent of the total) limits the autonomy needed to govern democratically and to maintain a competitive position in international markets. However, budget cuts to social programmes jeopardize the legitimacy of the state, leading one to question its ability to put in place a new order in line with economic priorities.

This situation is not unique to Canada and is evident in developed countries including the US,[3] as well as existing in an inverse manner in the eastern European countries where the question is: how can the state, whose legitimacy is questioned in the aftermath of communist regimes, be able to reorganize equitable and efficient health insurance programmes?[4]

It is not possible to choose between one side of this paradox (maintaining the status quo in the health system) to the detriment of the other (balancing the budget) because either choice would call into question the fundamental existence of society. We must consider Cameron's statement that 'no choice need be made between two or more contradictions. Both contradictions in a paradox are accepted and present. Both operate simultaneously' (Cameron 1986). Because we cannot resolve a paradox nor eliminate it we must master its richness. 'A paradox is an idea involving two opposing thoughts or propositions which, however contradictory, are equally necessary to convey a more imposing, illuminating, life-related or provocative insight into truth than either factor can muster in its own right. What the mind seemingly cannot think it must think; what reason is reluctant to express it must express' (Slaatte 1968: 4 cited by Cameron 1986). For Barel, this means that it may be appropriate 'to apply a paradoxical or *double* strategy to a paradoxical situation. This double strategy, while producing and reproducing the actual, also produces and reproduces the potential. It demands that we seriously consider the idea that there exist two forms of social "reality": an actual and a potential form' (Barel 1989: 301–3). When a decision is taken, immediate effects are seen in the 'actual' world while future possibilities are opened in the 'potential' world. In other words, the only way to deal with a paradoxical situation is to innovate (Langley 1995; Denis *et al.* 1996).

The difficulties democratic societies have in reforming their health care systems are tied to complex and paradoxical relations which exist between the values of society, the norms that societies have adopted in order to operationalize these values and the existence of individuals simultaneously autonomous and dependent on these values and norms. In this context, the reform of the health care system cannot be reduced to a mechanical exercise which consists of implementing a rational plan aimed at improving the effectiveness with which resources are used. This is not to say that the objective of rationalization is futile, rather that it does not address the real problem.[5]

What is at stake here is much more fundamental. It is a question of maintaining the health care system which is perceived by individuals as a central element to society and simultaneously creating profound changes to it so as not to mortgage the survival of society. This can only result in a difficult process of negotiation between actors in each society (defined by its history, traditions and culture). This balance of forces in tension can lead to new solutions, each focused on its context. These solutions will permit a redefinition of roles in the health care system and a redeployment of resources. These solutions will define and be defined by changes carried out in all of society, in its values and institutions.

In order to discuss more formally the questions associated with the implementation of change, we begin by showing that the stable evolution of social systems is assured by the institutionalization[6] of values and the creation of norms. In the second section, we present the actors, their strategies and the framework within which they interact as well as the role played by the internalization[7] of society's values and norms in their decisions and interrelations.[8]

## THE INSTITUTIONALIZATION OF VALUES AND THE STABILITY OF LARGE SOCIAL SYSTEMS

The stability of large social systems and in particular that of the health care system is a result of the coherence that exists between society's values (referred to as the dominant belief system) and the social and material structures of the health care system (Figure 15.1). This structure is composed of the organizational forms of health care systems which include all of the processes, laws and regulations that structure the manner in which resources and authority are distributed (Benson 1975) as well as the volume and type

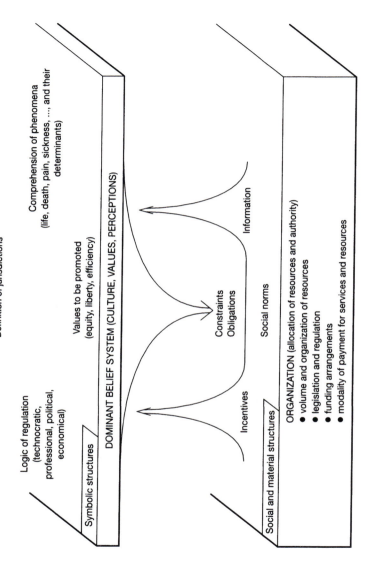

**Figure 15.1** Dominant belief system and organizational modalities

*Sources:* Benson (1975), Sabatier (1987), Lomas (1994), Bourdieu (1992, 1994)

of resources available. These resources and the manner in which they are organized are in some measure a reflection of society's values.

## Dominant belief system

The concept of the dominant belief system does not signify that there exists a unique system of beliefs and values shared by all. Rather, this concept implies that the tension and negotiation existing between differing values and beliefs has a certain stability. This tension between divergent values can be best understood by grouping them around four poles. The relationships between these poles constitute the symbolic structure that allows actors to interpret the world and to give it meaning (Habermas 1987: 243).

### Pole 1: Values

In democratic societies, three central values exist in tension with each other:

- *Equity*. This value refers to a collective concern for justice between individuals. Equity can be defined, in very general terms, as an appreciation of what collectively is just to distribute equally between individuals or groups (Sen 1992). This value shows that for each judgement that is made to divide something equally (resources, services, health) there corresponds another decision which will distribute something unequally. To distribute health care resources equally between regions does not mean that health, for example, has been equitably distributed. The concept of equity is thus paradoxical.
- *Individual autonomy*. Autonomy is one of the unavoidable values of the health care system and the social sphere in general. It is currently taken as a synonym of independence and freedom, in contrast to the collectivist viewpoint of society defined by the concept of equity. But the notion of autonomy is so complex that it is attributed a number of meanings in literature. These include: self-determination, individual freedom, independence, self-rule, acting according to one's own principles or following one's own plan of life (Clark 1988). This concept covers two basic notions: the first is autonomy of action, the possibility to act in a voluntary and intentional manner; the second is the capacity to act independently relying on one's own judgement and to have the necessary resources to reach a desired result. Individual autonomy is

driven by the idea of self-respect and human dignity and, in western societies, is a value vigorously defended by professionals and the population.
- *Efficiency*. Efficiency is the will to maximize a social outcome (health, quality of care) in the most economical way possible. Every definition of efficiency corresponds to a principle for the allocation of resources. It is useful to distinguish three levels of efficiency (technical, allocative and social). However, effici-ency is not solely the definition of a means of allocation. The concept of efficiency is not operational unless it is situated in a context of equity. For example, classical utilitarianism considers that the optimal social goal is reached if collective well-being is maximized, whereas Pareto's optimum defines an optimal allocation when one cannot improve the condition of certain members of society (at least one) without aggravating other members.

## *Pole 2: Understanding of phenomena*

An understanding of phenomena such as life, health, sickness, death, pain and their determinants constitutes a way of interpreting the object of the health care system. This perspective evolves over time (Canguilhem 1966; Foucault 1976; Evans *et al.* 1994) and is not uniform. The concept of health covers realities that are very different and cannot be superimposed.

Thus, if we choose to describe the health of a population by indicators that have been constructed around the concept of mortality (life expectancy, standardized mortality rates), it is difficult to appreciate health as it is perceived by individuals in pain or who are worried about being sick. However, if it is the latter perspective which is held, it is almost impossible to assess biological functions (on the level of organs, tissues, cells, molecules) that modern methods of diagnosis enable science to identify and biological technology to treat.

All of this raises two basic considerations. The first concerns the definition of what is normal and pathological (Canguilhem 1966; De Vries 1981) and, therefore, what constitutes health and disease for individuals, professionals and society. The second concerns the relationships between these two concepts. These considerations very quickly refer us to basic conceptions about the world and about knowledge.

Classically, medical science is based on the idea that disease is the result of a quantitative disturbance in one of the functions of a living organism. Through the use of scientific methods, this disturbance can be analysed and its causes discovered. By acting on these, normal functioning can be restored. In this perspective, disease is an observable and quantifiable phenomenon. Each disease may be studied separately and when the disturbance is corrected the disease disappears. This vision of disease is based on a positivist conception of the world. The question of what is normal may be reduced to the empirical finding of an average value; there is no difference in nature between the pathological and the physiological (Canguilhem 1966). Progress resides in the constant refinement of techniques that enable us to observe biological phenomena and to act upon them. This concept has been the source of extraordinary development in biomedical science and the capacity to diagnose, treat and sometimes prevent specific diseases at the individual level. The legitimacy of current health care systems rests on it.

But despite its success, this approach is more and more frequently challenged. The disparities in health between population groups, far from diminishing, seem to be greater. Diseases do not seem to be independent from one another. 'No cure can bring back biological innocence' (Canguilhem 1966: 156). Every disease leaves its mark. For example, children cured of diarrhoea are more susceptible to other diseases than those who have never been sick (Mosley and Becker 1991). It is becoming clear that disease is a state that is different in nature from health. There is a qualitative difference between pathology and health. Disease cannot be reduced to the malfunctioning of an organ.

'One new and important area of investigation is the study of the exceptionally healthy individual who seems to escape every epidemic of influenza, has an exceptionally high performance capacity, is mentally highly gifted, or remains healthy up to an old age. One advantage of such investigation is that health and the condition promoting health become a primary focus rather than disease and conditions conducive to disease. Such investigations would represent the beginnings of a general health science which would serve as a complement to traditional general pathology' (De Vries 1981: 61–2). Health and its determinants must, therefore, be understood directly, as it is perceived and felt by the person. Health is not the inverse of illness as defined by biological norms that are inevitably relative and circumstantial.

The operationalization of health at the individual level is very difficult. In fact, health seems to be a concept which is best suited to characterize populations. The more that is known (Evans *et al.*

1994) on the determinants of a population's health, the clearer it appears that the concepts of illness and health, while not independent, are not synonymous. The increased health of a population does not mean that the need to diagnose and treat disease is reduced. The challenge for any developed society is to be able to give to each individual access to high-quality treatments when needed and at the same time to develop public policies which promote the health of the population.

## *Pole 3: Definition of jurisdictions and allocation of resources*

This pole concerns the perception of the role and the functions of different individuals that work in the health care sector and of the allocation of resources between sectors. On the one hand, this reflects the opinions prevalent in society regarding the responsibilities and positions that each professional must hold, on the resources that he or she must acquire and on the education that he or she must attain. On the other hand, it reflects the best allocation of public resources between health and health care and within health care between prevention and care, between hospital and ambulatory care, between public and private.

## *Pole 4: Logics of regulation*

The roles and interaction of the participants in the delivery of health care are set by four typical regulatory models.[9] Each model emphasizes a different set of values. The dominant model of a given system reflects the priorities chosen by society.

In the *technocratic model*, trained experts guide the system by relying on their specialized knowledge and their dominant position within political and economic institutions (Fischer 1990). This regulatory approach, also called the 'command-and-control planning model' (Saltman 1991), is based on normative analysis produced by experts who are responsible for structuring, monitoring and assessing the activities of the health care system in order to decide the extent to which these activities are likely to achieve the system's objectives. The normative analysis consists of making judgements on the gap between the system's resources, activities, results and what had been forecast or planned. This model implies the direct intervention of the state in the operation of the health care system in order to achieve rationalization and to limit shifts in the system's goals caused by the irrational behaviour of its actors (Fischer 1990). Thus, the justification for technocratic intervention is based on its capacity to present itself as an apolitical and rational action in the public interest. This model is, therefore, fundamentally opposed to reform proposals aimed at producing new types of relationships between policy makers, service providers and consumers.

In the *professional self-regulatory model*, the physician is at the centre of the health care system and the utilization of health resources rests upon his or her decisions. Acting as the patient's agent, he or she is able to define the patient's needs and is expected to provide care based on these. The quantity and variety of care being provided is under control. Any limit to the accessibility of the health care system represents a potential danger to the patient. The role of public officials is to eliminate economic barriers to health care by establishing a system of insurance. Their second role is to guarantee sufficient health care personnel and equipment and to create health promotion programmes for the population.

This model assumes that control over the health care system must be delegated to the medical profession. Given the imbalance of information and knowledge in favour of the physician, the physician's central role in determining how resources are used and the absence of any real legal framework controlling medical practice, limits to physician abuse can only be set by the medical profession itself. This control is exerted through education and training that ensures standardized skill acquisition. It is, as well, exerted through a strong professional code of ethics that emphasizes medical practice based on patient needs that avoids both over- and under-utilization of services. Control of medical practice is further influenced by the socialization of professionals to certain ethical norms. In this process, experience results in generally accepted norms within the profession. These norms give rise to a professional code of ethics through which norms of practice are defined. In this model, regulatory mechanisms are thus implemented by the very profession which controls conformity of physician practice to the established norms.

In the *market-based model*, regulations are established in accordance with supply and demand in competing markets and on condition that certain constraining postulates are accepted. This type of regulation leads to what may be considered a Pareto-optimal allocation of resources in the sense that it is impossible to change that allocation without penalizing at least one economic agent. This is a powerful model mainly because of its normative and ideological aspects. The approach is based on a doctrine that affirms the autonomy of the economic realm and thus considers that government intervention in economic affairs must be minimal.

In the *democratic model*, each citizen possesses the right and has the responsibility to influence socio-political decisions and actions within society. This democratic right can be exercised directly or indirectly. Most often it is exercised indirectly through representatives who are either elected or co-opted. The democratic model links the population with the process of formulating needs, problems, priorities and solutions to the management and administration of the health care system.

### Institutionalization of values

This brief listing of what constitutes a dominant system of beliefs shows that there cannot be one consensual model around which everyone rallies. In reality, it is an immense intertwining process of negotiations and discussions that from time to time can crystallize into an ensemble of organizational modalities. These organizational modalities constitute the legal, administrative and material structure of the system. They define how material resources are allocated and how authority and power (what Bourdieu calls the symbolic capital) are distributed (Benson 1975).

The organizational structures produce a vast system of incentives, constraints, obligations and norms that at any moment reinforce a specific set of values, perceptions and beliefs. The social and material structure produces a 'field of incentives' like that created by the forces in a magnetic field in which actors struggle to transform the existing order to better serve their own interests (Bourdieu 1994: 55). According to Wacquant, the recursive interplay of the material and social structure with the dominant belief system is a guarantee of a dominant order. Various classes and groups of individuals will continuously struggle to impose their own vision of society to promote their particular interests (Wacquant 1992: 22). The dominant belief system which exists in a given society and the organizational forms which are coherent with it are producing incentives, constraints and obligations, information and social norms that reinforce the existing orders and the interests of the groups of actors that the system favours.

### Crisis

It is possible to imagine that the organizational structure is a reflection, at a given moment, of the equilibrium and tension that exists between the beliefs and perceptions of the various actors in the system. Therefore, it is also plausible that the organizational and symbolic structures have different evolutionary rhythms. As time passes, a break can occur between the two. It is clear that the greater the break the more these organizational forms can be considered inadequate. A situation of crisis is thus created. This can be resolved by the transformation of an organizational form without questioning the equilibrium of forces in tension that characterizes the system as a whole. However, it is also possible that this crisis is more profound if it affects the four poles that structure these symbolic representations. In this situation, marginal transformations of organizational structures are insufficient to resolve this crisis. Profound changes are needed. This is probably the situation that presently prevails in developed countries (Contandriopoulos 1994). In essence, the crisis which affects all health care systems is major; it is not only a financial crisis, it is a crisis of knowledge, of values and of regulations as well.

In order to understand how these systems are reproduced and transformed, consider Figure 15.2. The 'field of incentives' created by the interdependence of the dominant belief system and other organizational forms is permanently traversed by an uninterrupted flow of new information, new knowledge, new techniques (new technology, new way of managing etc.) as well as the problems that the system must manage. It is this interaction of knowledge, of technological development and of the problems that go with it that gives birth to new policies, interventions and decisions. These policies in turn modify the dominant belief system and organizational forms. However, contrary to what Figure 15.2 suggests, it is not a simple circular system where from time to time the organizational structure and the cognitive structure adapt in response to a problem. In order to have a truer picture of what is happening, imagine that as time passes, the dominant belief system and the organizational infrastructure move not at the same speed and not always in the same direction but that the speed and the direction of one is always dependent on the speed and direction of the other; they remain simultaneously dependent upon each other. Each new decision leads to a situation that is not the one that we knew from the point of departure.

Given that 'this field of incentives' results from the interplay between beliefs and organizational forms, how does it influence the decisions which will in return transform these organizational forms? It is important to realize that any policies that will transform the health care system will at the same time question the dominant

system of values and the interests of groups of actors that profit from the status quo.

To understand these phenomena, we need to introduce the notion of actors and the role played by the internalization of values which are the roots of the stability of social systems.

## THE INTERNALIZATION OF VALUES BY ACTORS AND THE TRANSFORMATION OF SOCIAL SYSTEMS

Actors can be individuals or organized groups of individuals e.g. the medical corporation, personnel, administrators, the local population. In their relationship with one another, each actor has an objective to maintain and increase his or her power with respect to the critical resources of his or her field. The ability of these actors collectively to put into place efficient strategies in a given field depends on their capacity to mobilize different groups around common projects to create a culture of reciprocity and trust.

Actors can be considered agents (or organized groups of agents) that interact with others (Crozier 1963; Young and Saltman 1985; Friedberg 1993) and are simultaneously characterized by four poles:[10] their culture, intentions and strategies, dispositions or ability to act and the resources that they use or control (Figure 15.3). Change in one of the poles creates change in the other three and in the relations that actors undergo with their environment. Actors can transform themselves and participate in the transformation of the field in which they interact if new information modifies their perception of things, if the techniques that they use change, if laws and regulations change, if their projects evolve, if their beliefs and values are modified or if the economic forms of regulation evolve i.e. modification in the method of payment to doctors, in the method of financing hospitals.

Actors, such as general practitioners, are simultaneously defined by the relations that they maintain with the other actors and by the symbolic and material resources that they control. These resources and their practices constitute their material and social structure: their values, their beliefs, projects and strategies, their mental and cognitive structure. This cognitive and mental structure is (Bourdieu 1992, 1994) comprised of the categories of perception that an actor unconsciously uses in a given society, at a given moment, in order to interact with others. The more his or her mental and cognitive

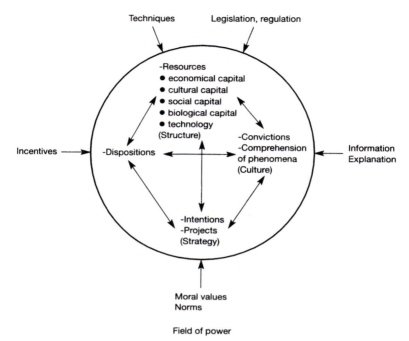

**Figure 15.3** An actor and forces that affect his or her interactions with others

*Source*: Contandriopoulos (1996)

structure conforms to the dominating system of beliefs, the more this actor will be inclined to find 'normal' and 'natural' the established order and the relations of power that prevail. 'The interaction between a doctor, an intern, a nurse is underscored by the relationships of power that are not always apparent immediately in the interaction or in the way that it is observed' (Bourdieu 1992: 53). The more actors internalize the values and the norms of the system within which they interact, the more they will contribute unconsciously to maintaining the status quo. What we call status quo is not the absence of change. It is a situation in which changes are highly predictable and in which the relative positions of actors are at stake.

As indicated earlier, actors do not interact in a vacuum. They are deeply rooted to a society that is characterized not only by its laws, its regulations and its institutions but by its own history and culture. According to Wacquant, repeated exposure to social conditions and values will profoundly influence the actions of individuals. These individuals will internalize society's values and behave in accordance with them (Wacquant 1992: 21).

The restructuring and the transformation of a domain such as the health care system results in strategies of concurrence and cooperation between the various actors to acquire and control critical resources. These strategies are dependent on the characteristics of each of these actors and in particular on the degree of internalization of these collective norms and their initial situation. They are influenced by three groups of factors.

The first group is comprised of the forces which characterize the field of incentives in which the actors are placed. This system of incentives reinforces the position of actors who are in a situation of authority and can enact general rules governing the distribution of resources critical to this domain (e.g. financial regulations, conditions necessary for the exercise of the practice of medicine, planning). It also reflects a dominant system of beliefs. These rules give form to the strategies (e.g. authoritative, incentive) of the dominant actors such as the ministry and the regional health board. The second group is comprised of the continuous flux of information and knowledge as well as new technologies and problems that traverse the field of power. These first two groups of factors guide the evolutionary trajectory of the health care system.

The third group of factors is tied to the local dynamic of relations among actors. It depends on their specific strategies and on the initial distribution of resources among them. They modify from within the interaction among actors and the distribution of critical resources in the domain considered. The strategies can be grouped into four types:

- *Cooperative strategy.* Adhesion of different actors to common projects.
- *Opportunistic strategy.* There is an absence of consensual projects but development is assured by exterior factors. The actors use, more or less voluntarily, the opportunities that are presented to them.
- *Authoritative strategy.* One actor dominates in the definition and in the implementation of a project (the emergence of leadership).
- *Competitive and confrontational strategy.* There is competition between actors in order to obtain a dominating role in the definition and in the implementation of opposing projects.

The periodic restructuring of a domain is thus simultaneously and recursively the result of this interplay between actors. This is influenced by the transformation of and the evolution of knowledge, the development of new techniques and the strategies of the actors.

In order to understand how the health care system can transform itself, the various players must be placed in this field of incentives (Figure 15.4). For reform to take place, actors must align their strategies, their intentions, convictions and perceptions around a project. These actors must accept the fact that the reform, represented here in the form of a project, will modify the system of allocation of resources and the power relationships in place. If the transformation is of any importance, certain actors will lose while others will profit. These transformations are aimed at modifying the power relationships in place and it is evident that their implementation will pose problems for those holding a position of dominance.

**An example: the situation in eastern Europe**

The situation in eastern European countries is an elegant example of this crisis. Although the fall of the communist regimes was accompanied by a radical transformation of the dominant belief system, adjustment to organizational modalities cannot be made as rapidly. Today, many researchers have characterized the situation as one of overwhelming social stress. This stress has caused a worsening of the health situation in CEE countries and in the NIS. For example, shortened life expectancy, increased death rate and declining birth rate, re-emergence of diseases like tuberculosis and the growing number of suicides are among the trends which indicate a close link between social stress and the health situation. At the same time, the system of health care, which was based on state financing and which guaranteed full and free access to all health services in spite of the incomes of individuals, is now being reformed due to strong pressure from both market forces and international finance agencies. Health care reforms are discussed in these countries mainly as an economic rather than a social or medical issue.

The principles of the communist health care system denied individual rights and stressed, in spite of this, the worthiness of people for the state workforce, as defence force and as demographic resource. The health care system in communist countries was part of the state's power. Its tasks were defined by the state: to guarantee the health of the workers, the conscripts to the army and the health of the children as future citizens. The state-centred ideology of

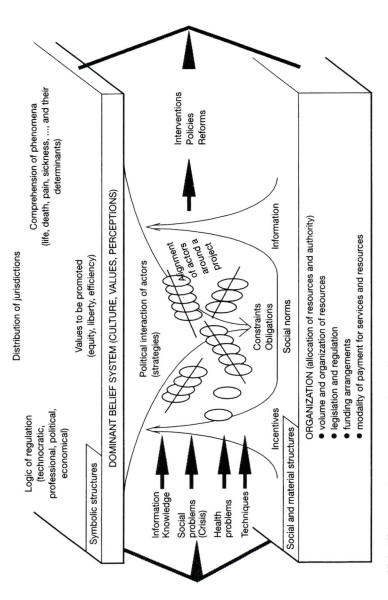

**Figure 15.4** Alignment of elements around a project

*Sources:* Benson (1975), Sabatier (1987), Lomas (1994), Bourdieu (1992, 1994)

health care meant that health services were free of charge. The doctors, not the patients, were considered part of the state authority and were in charge of it. However, lack of citizen responsibility meant lack of patient rights. Patients were considered passive objects of the health care system whose treatment was differentiated according to their status in the ideologically determined state hierarchy. The system of health care institutions was built up according to the hierarchy of the state (i.e. the special polyclinics, hospitals and sanatoriums for the party nomenclature, for the military, for the state railways, for the industrial and agricultural workers, for the artistic unions). On the lowest level of treatment were those who did not have any value for the state (e.g. old people with chronic diseases, patients with mental illnesses, handicapped children and prisoners).

In post-socialist society, one of the major changes is connected with the status of the individual as it is defined by the concept of universal human rights. Unlike the state-centred ideology, individual risks and responsibilities connected with people's health are now the focus of attention. The importance of the individual as the subject of the health care system is raised.

The economic differentiation of the population is rapidly growing along with rising costs of medical services and drugs. The social differentiation of patients according to their incomes is replacing the differentiation of patients according to their political merits which was typical in the communist world. Although implementation of compulsory health insurance should guarantee access to health services, the number of people for whom health care is no longer a universally accessible good is becoming larger in all central and eastern European countries. Health care reforms are directed at economic efficiency. They are creating the dilemma where individuals have to make choices between paying for health care and other needed expenditures such as clothing, education, food and housing. This could mean that needed care is postponed as long as possible. Health which is highly valued could be, in practice, a much lower priority than consumer goods.

Understanding health as a universal human value and health care as a human right, health care development in post-socialist countries should be matched with the new social situation. Hence, the needs of the most vulnerable groups (i.e. the elderly, families with small children, people with chronic diseases and the handicapped) could be taken into account. The social guarantees for universal access to health care services is not the only solution. The rising price of curative health care stimulates a change of mentality connected with health. People accustomed to receiving free health care during the communist era came to understand the value of health in economic terms. The new paradigm of health policy, prioritizing healthy lifestyles and public health as an alternative to the development of expensive secondary and tertiary levels of curative services, will have popular support only after the price of disease has become considerably higher than the price of health, not only for society but also for patients.

## CONCLUSION

In conclusion, what we seek are changes to the status quo that will favour a fundamental transformation in thinking with respect to health and its determinants. According to Guattari, these changes are needed in order to realign actors so that innovative ideas can germinate and grow. Without this transformation, our material and social environment will remain unchanged. Without a change in the environment there will be no change in attitudes (Guattari 1992). We are thus caught in a vicious circle.

It would be futile to search for a simple solution to the problems of the health care system. Rather, a more profound transformation is needed. To do this, we must envision a long iterative process during which changes in attitudes open the door to innovation which will in themselves contribute to new transformations of structures.

A utopian vision of the future that gives meaning and direction must be proposed alongside this change. As François Furet suggests, it is difficult to live without a utopia. Health is an example of a new problem which we may face. Man's desire to live longer and the increasing average life expectancy will lead to an intense battle for care. A new battle between generations will emerge replacing the one between classes (Furet 1995).

Thus, the challenge consists of putting in place a complex strategy that will profoundly change health care systems and their evolution. This trajectory is specific to each country and is largely influenced by its values, history, culture and traditions. The process of reform, therefore, must be specific to each country. In certain countries, this reform will be the result of regular and repetitive adjustments to the structure and to the dominating system of values. In these countries, new innovative practices will emerge which will permit actors to accept more easily the risks of change. In other countries, there exists a rigidity in which the room to innovate is blocked. The reform in this instance can only result in a rupture and a reconstruction. The form that the reform will take in a specific country is, in itself, a reflection of the dominant values of its society.

## NOTES

1 Health systems are constituted, on the one hand, by a system of care whose goal is to correct health problems, to prevent their appearance and to conceal their consequences. On the other hand, they are formed by a system whose goal is to promote the health of the population. The health system is conceived as the interaction between these two systems – the system of care and the system of health promotion (Contandri-opoulos and Pouvourville 1991; Evans *et al.* 1994; Pineault and Daveluy 1996).

2 A social system is by nature complex and paradoxical. It is a social order that attempts to simplify, orient and determine the diversity of society but never manages to do so. Society comprises the elements of order and disorder which it cannot separate and this is the heart of its paradox (Barel 1989: 19). This is the same idea that Cameron proposes: 'To be effective, an organization must possess attributes that are simultaneously contradictory, even mutually exclusive' (Cameron 1986: 544–55). An organization is thus fundamentally paradoxical.

3 The example of the US where public health care expenditure represents only 40 per cent of the total shows that what is at stake is not only public expenditure but the total cost of the health care system. The growth in costs may prevent society from involving itself in programmes which have a considerable influence on the health of the population. These programmes pertain to employment, education of disadvantaged youth, working conditions, etc. (Evans *et al.* 1994). These escalating costs will, as well, prevent them from balancing the budget's deficit.

4 'Repairing the damage caused by the last three decades of communist rule and closing the gap in health status must, therefore, be the central objective for human resource policy throughout the region. This will be neither easy nor quick' (Preker and Feachem 1994: 295).

5 The rational argument does not stipulate who will be in charge of implementing the plan nor does it indicate who decides on the rules which define its rationale. More fundamentally, it does not take into account the complexity of the social organization.

6 The institutionalization of values and the creation of norms is only an approximate representation of the complex and paradoxical character of the symbolic structure of society. The organizational modalities cannot fully portray the complexity of this structure.

7 The internalization of society's values and norms is always subject to the critical reflection of its actors. The acceptance of these norms is never absolute. In their interaction with each other, actors conform to these norms while simultaneously questioning them. This behaviour contributes to the renewal of the existing order and to its transformation. The individual is not a passive instrument in the transmission of society's norms nor is he or she completely impermeable to these forces. The internalization of values and of norms refers to Bourdieu's concept of 'habitus' (Bourdieu 1994).

8 The argumentation presented in Sections 2 and 3 was, in part, elaborated in Contandriopoulos 1996; Contandriopoulos and Souteyrand 1996.

9 The ideas presented in this section have been developed by Contandriopoulos (1996).

10 These four poles can be used to define a paradigm. They describe the same dimensions as the one presented previously. Culture refers to the area of epistemology; intentions and strategies to teleology; ability to act to methodology and resource and jurisdictions to ontology (Levy 1994, 1996).

## REFERENCES

Angus, D. E. *et al.* (1995). *Sustainable Health Care for Canada.* Ottawa: Queen's and University of Ottawa Economic Projects, University of Ottawa.

Barel, Y. (1989). *Le Paradoxe et le Système.* Grenoble: Presses Universitaires de Grenoble.

Barr, N. (ed.) (1994). *Labor Markets and Social Policy in Central and Eastern Europe. The Transition and Beyond.* New York: A World Bank book, published in association with the London School of Economics and Political Science, Oxford University Press.

Benson, J. K. (1975). The interorganizational network as a political economy. *Administrative Science Quarterly,* 20, 229–49.

Bourdieu, P. (1992). *Reponses.* Paris: Seuil.

Bourdieu, P. (1994). *Raisons Pratiques.* Paris: Editions de Minuit.

Cameron, K. S. (1986). Effectiveness as paradox: Consensus and conflict in conceptions of organizational effectiveness. *Management Science,* 32, 539–53.

Canguilhem (1966). *Le Normal et le Pathologique.* Paris: Presses Universitaires de France.

Clark, D. G. (1988). Autonomy, personal empowerment and quality of life in long-term care. *Journal of Applied Gerontology,* 7, 279–97.

Contandriopoulos, A. P. (1994). Réformer le système de santé: Une utopie pour sortir d'un status quo impossible. *Ruptures,* 1, 8–26.

Contandriopoulos, A. P. (1996). Transformer le système de santé. *Ruptures*, 3, 10–17.

Contandriopoulos, A. P. and Pouvourville, G. (1991). *Entre Constructivisme et Libéralisme: La Recherche d'une Troisième Voie.* Montreal: University of Montreal, GRIS, cahier N91–03.

Contandriopoulos, A. P. and Souteyrand, Y. (1996). La construction de l'offre local de soins dans l'hôpital stratégie. In A.P. Contandriopoulos and Y. Souteyrand, *L'hopital Stratége?* Paris: John Libbey.

Crozier, M. (1963). *Le Phénomène Bureaucratique.* Paris: Le Seuil.

Denis, J. L, Brémond, M., Contrandiopoulos, A. P., Cazale, L., Leibovich, E. (eds) (1997). Organiser l'innovation, imaginer le contrôle dans le système de santé. *Ruptures*, 4(1), 96–114.

De Vries, M. J. (1981). *The Redemption of the Intangible in Medicine.* London: Institute of Psychosynthesis.

Evans, R. G., Barer, M. L. and Marmor, T. R. (1994). *Why are Some People Healthy and Others Not?* Berlin: de Gruyter.

Fischer, F. (1990). *Technocracy and the Politics of Expertise.* Newbury Park: Sage.

Foucault, M. (1976). *Histoire de la Sexualité: La Volonté de Savoir.* Paris: Gallimard.

Friedberg, E. (1993). *Le Pouvoir et la Règle.* Paris: Le Seuil.

Furet, F. (1995). Interview in *Le Devoir*, pp. B1.

Guattari, F. (1992). Pour une refondation des pratiques sociales. *Le Monde Diplomatique*, 463, p. 26.

Habermas, J. (1987). *Théorie de l'Agir Communicationnel.* Paris: Fayard.

Langley, A. (1995). *Innovativeness in Large Public Systems.* Département des sciences administratives, Montreal, Université du Québec à Montréal.

Levy, R. (1994). Croyance et doute: Une vision paradigmatique des méthodes qualitatives. *Ruptures*, 1, 92–100.

Levy, R. (1996). Editorial – La mission de la santé publique ... sur les traces de Shakespeare. *Rupture*, 3, 3–8.

Mosley and Becker (1991). Demographic models for child survival and implications for health intervention programs. *Health Policy and Planning*, 6, 218–33.

National Forum on Health (1997). *Canada Health Action: Building on the Legacy.* Ottawa: National Forum on Health.

Pineault and Daveluy (1996). *La Planification de la Santé: Concepts, Méthodes, Stratégies.* Montreal: Edition Nouvelles.

Preker, A. S. and Feachem, R. G. A. (1994). *Health and Health Care.* New York: World Bank.

Sabatier, P. (1987). Knowledge, policy-oriented learning, and policy change. *Knowledge: creation, diffusion, utilization*, 8, 649–92.

Saltman, R. (1997). La mondialisation de l'économie et l'avenir de l'hôpital. *Ruptures*, 4, 1186–90.

Saltman, R. B. (1991). Emerging trends in the Swedish health system. *International Journal of Health Services*, 21, 615–23.

Saltman, R. B. and von Otter, C. (1992). *Planned Markets and Public Competition. Strategic Reform in Northern European Health Systems.* Buckingham: Open University Press.

Sen, A. (1992). *Inequality Reexamined.* Cambridge, MA: Harvard University Press.

Slaatte, H. A. (1968). *The Pertinence of the Paradox.* New York: Humanities Press.

Wacquant, L. J. D. (1992). Introduction. In P. Bourdieu, *Réponses.* Paris: Seuil.

World Bank (1993). *World development report 1993. Investing in health.* New York: Oxford University Press.

Young, D. W. and Saltman, R. B. (1985). *The Hospital Power Equilibrium – Physician Behaviour and Cost Control.* Baltimore and London: Johns Hopkins University Press.

# PART V

# IMPLEMENTING HEALTH REFORM

# 16

# IMPLEMENTING HEALTH CARE REFORM: A FRAMEWORK FOR DISCUSSION
Gill Walt

## INTRODUCTION

Much attention on health care reforms has focused on the components of reform: financing strategies and changes in public sector organization and procedures. Although many have noted the fact that reforms have been harder and slower to implement than expected (Cooper 1994; Saltman 1994; Chernichovsky and Chinitz 1995; De Leeuw and Polman 1995), and can have unintended consequences (Golinowska and Tymowska 1995; James 1995), there has been little systematic analysis of the problem of implementation.

This chapter suggests that if policy analysis precedes or accompanies policy choice, the chances of effective implementation are greater. It uses a simple framework of policy analysis (see Figure 16.1) which sees execution of policy as an integral part of the policy process. In this approach, while notice is taken of the *content* of policy (the appropriate design of a social insurance system for example), more attention is put on the *context* in which policy is introduced, the *process* by which policy is formulated, implemented and evaluated, and the *actors* who are affected by and influence policy content, context and process. Figure 16.1 is a highly simplified framework of an extremely complex set of interrelationships, and gives the impression that each can be considered separately. However, while it is analytically convenient to distinguish the four

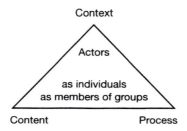

**Figure 16.1**    A framework for health policy analysis
*Source:* Walt and Gilson (1994)

concepts from each other, no analysis will be complete without considering their inter-relationship. Other caveats are in order as well. Policy analysis is clearly dependent on particular circumstances and time periods, and policies are not static. No attempt has been made to define health care reforms – they vary according to the setting, period of time considered, and are at different stages of monitoring and execution. Finally, this framework does not provide a way of assessing whether some policies are 'as good as' or 'better than' others. Ethical considerations and policy analysts' own values and perceptions clearly affect which policy options are preferred.

Using this framework, this chapter focuses on the *implementation* of health care reforms, explores specific contextual factors, processes and actors, and briefly considers their relationship with content. It ends by demonstrating how the framework can be used to plan strategically so that policies may be more effectively executed. While the framework is described largely at the national, central level, it can as easily be applied to the subnational or institutional level.

## HOW DO CONTEXTUAL FACTORS AFFECT IMPLEMENTATION?

Context in the framework refers to the historical and existing environment within which policy making takes place, taking account of a number of factors which influence the policy process and its outputs – in this case, health care reforms. The range and number of factors that influence or determine what governments do, or what they choose not to do, are virtually infinite. Health care reforms may be influenced, among other things, by prior policy commitments, international tensions, economic wealth, the nature of political institutions, degree of ethnic conflict, strength of religious culture and personality of its leadership. Some of these influences will be central, others peripheral, and they will differ from country to country and over time.

Policy analysts have been concerned with making explicit the political factors that influence policy. Their central debate (Mackintosh 1992) is between 'public interest' views of the state (the state, although not neutral, has a central role in promoting the public interest) and public choice or 'private interest' views (the state exercises power in favour of dominant classes, and is made up of self-seeking bureaucrats and politicians). These are fundamental debates about social and political values concerning the role of the state, for which there are no easy answers. They currently permeate all societies and affect thinking on collective versus individual, and state versus market relationships, and expectations of what support the state should provide its citizens (Marmor 1993; Pierson 1994). Such debates have been presaged and stimulated by the economic instability and uncertainties of the 1980s and 1990s, in which recession or slow growth in many industrialized countries has constrained economies. They have had particular relevance for the health sector, leading to uncertain health policy environments and considerable conflict in values about health care.

## Uncertain policy environments

The policy environment differs from country to country depending on its form of government, the strength of government and the extent to which participation is facilitated or discouraged by the political system.

Policy environments have been starkly affected by a fundamental questioning of the scope and functions of government (Leach 1995: 247). Where there was once considerable consensus about the legitimate sphere of state activity, the last 15 years have seen major debate about what the state should be doing in health care among other sectors. A somewhat technical orientation of health policy (despite the move towards a primary health care approach in the late 1970s) raised few objections while the policy environment was characterized by consensus about the role of the state, as it was until the 1980s. The state played a strong central role, medical elites dominated health policy making, and health policies were largely uncontroversial, receiving broad (if passive) support from the population, and appearing as 'low politics'[1] issues on the political agenda, although much depends on which country is in the spotlight. Health policies were almost entirely concerned with content (improving access and coverage, increasing efficiency in the use of hospital beds or in vaccine regimes) and any changes were largely rearrangements of organizational furniture (Collins *et al.* 1994).

However, with economic recession from the 1980s the health policy environment became more uncertain and less harmonious, as governments sought ways to rationalize retrenchment. Fundamental questions were raised about the values underlying chosen policies (choice, equity and privatization), changes were introduced in power relations between health sector workers (for example, between managers and health professionals), resulting in conflicts of interests between groups. Debates about health care were increasingly characterized by public dissension, making them, relative to past decades, 'high politics' agenda items. This conflict inevitably generated considerable uncertainty around appropriate policy choices, both for consumers and health workers. Table 16.1 encapsulates the change in the health policy arena from low politics to high politics, although shifts between 'high' and 'low' politics policies have differed between countries at different times.

Health care reforms have been introduced in a period of global and domestic retrenchment, which contrasts strongly with the preceding four or five decades of expansion. This has led to greater exigency on public expenditure (the search for cost containment

**Table 16.1**   The shifting policy arena

| *Consensus* | *Uncertainty* |
| --- | --- |
| Period of incremental policy making, of small changes, characterized by consensus and expansion of the health sector | Period of major reforms, change, characterized by crisis and contraction of the health sector |
| Focus was on technology: vaccines, restricted drugs lists, day surgery, and clinical procedures | Concern is with performance, accountability, consumer choice, plurality of service delivery |
| Central issue was service delivery, organizational restructuring, equity | Central issue is cost containment: liberalization and cost sharing |
| Doctors dominated | Managers dominate |

and efficiency) and attempts to shift financial burdens – in some countries from central state bodies – to individuals, semi- or autonomous institutions, regional or local authorities. Retrenchment has been accompanied in some countries, especially in central and eastern Europe, by considerable political upheaval and instability. Long-established institutions are themselves the subjects of reform, creating uncertainties of employment and procedures. Where reforms have been introduced in relatively stable political systems, they have generally been implemented incrementally, although the *pace* has differed, as for instance between Sweden, the Netherlands and the UK (Ham and Brommels 1994). However, even incremental implementation may have far-reaching effects in the long term.

In political systems which have undergone regime change, such as those in the countries of central and eastern Europe, reforms may be welcomed by the new middle class and some health professionals – perceived as an opportunity to challenge over-centralized, bureaucratized, initiative-stifling health systems. However, while reforms may be seized on as an opportunity, they may be extremely difficult to implement because they are opposed by significant groups who see themselves losing (the elderly), and also because they depend on a range of different management skills, commitment and information systems that do not exist. Further, any reforms may be undermined by tensions between the old and new guard, both within professional groups and among citizens.

### Conflicting values

Value systems are seldom explicitly taken into account when policy implementation is considered. Yet in relation to health care reforms, there is evidence of considerable conflict in values between policy makers, professionals and the public, and within each of those groups – for example overusing market versus welfare mechanisms in health care. Where values clash with reform objectives, there may be considerable resistance to executing policies. For example, hospital doctors may refuse to cut hospital stays in order to achieve greater efficiency.

Value systems are embedded in political systems. In the liberal democracies of western Europe which established 'welfare states', the introduction of reforms to the health sector (often in concert with reforms to other social policies) has been relatively unpopular with the public and influential professional groups (Pierson 1994; Mohan 1995). In these countries the health system achieves high coverage of the population and is perceived by the public to be working relatively satisfactorily. There may be some dissatisfaction with the quality of care, but there is little support for reductions in care and still less if these are gained through induced market mechanisms. Where the objectives of reform are tax containment and sharing costs, couched in ideological, pro-market terms, governments have had to face direct opposition from groups strongly attached to public health policies or collectivist, non-market values at least for health care.

On the other hand, where government *raison d'être* for reform is based on improving access to, or quality of, health care, basic social values may be shared and widespread. But even where the motivation for reform is perceived as improving the system, there are still pitfalls between policy formulation and implementation because of the need for trade-offs between public and private control, freedom of choice restricted by budgetary constraints and availability versus affordability (Peabody *et al.* 1995). Implementation may be highly affected by the extent to which governments can persuade the public that their reform programmes are driven by positive intentions rather than purely by economic constraints.

Reluctant implementation may occur where government implementers do not accord reform policy high legitimacy. In some Latin American countries, reforms have been seen as imposed from the outside (Martinez and Sandiford 1995); in the Russian Federation ideas for reforms have been imported without any test of their applicability (Curtis *et al.* 1995); a World Bank report on implementation suggested that negotiations on policy were often seen as a 'coercive exercise designed to *impose* the Bank's philosophy' (Wapenhans 1992: 16).

## THE PROCESS OF POLICY MAKING

'Policies are a process as well as a product' (Wildavsky 1979), and public policy making the process by which government decides what to do and how to do it. Processes of policy making can be divided into four overlapping (but not linear) phases: (1) *problem identification* (or agenda setting i.e. how the need for health care reforms was recognized and placed on the policy agenda); (2) *policy formulation* which centres around which individuals and groups take part in the formulation of policy, the process by which they participate and their role in influencing policy outcomes; (3) *policy implementation*; and (4) *policy evaluation*.

To understand the policy process it is useful to consider two basic theoretical models. The *rational* (or top-down) model sees policy making following a linear progression of these four phases with a feedback loop at the point of evaluation. Implementation is often perceived as an administrative or managerial part of the process. The model implies a centralized view of the health system, whereby policy is made at the national level, but implemented at lower levels, by authorities which have a duty to implement directives and little discretion in execution.

The *interactive* (or 'bottom-up') model rejects this linear view of the policy process which separates policy formulation from implementation. The policy process is seen as political (not rational) and iterative: with problems being defined at different points of the process (during implementation for example); with policy formulation not restricted to national level policy makers; and with considerable authority and discretion (to distort, divert, adjust, amend) during implementation.

The extent to which there is discretion in implementation depends on the system of government and central–local relations. Almost all governments transfer authority or disperse some power in public planning, management and decision making from national to subnational levels, or from higher to lower levels of government (Mills *et al.* 1990). In practice the system of decentralization varies enormously between countries. Many governments have moved to decentralize responsibility to lower-level authorities. However, in societies where tight control has been historically held by a central bureaucracy it may take a generation to change attitudes at the local level. Officials unused to taking decisions, or inexperienced in negotiating or consulting with interest groups, may be quite reluctant to exercise any devolved discretion they have gained. For instance, Golinowska and Tymowska describe how the 1990 law on local self-government in Poland transferred primary social institutions to local authorities, which were 'politically immature bodies, lacking the required social and organisational experience and, even more significantly, constrained by regulations relating to the collection of local taxes' (Golinowska and Tymowska 1995: 141).

Implementation of policy is clearly dependent on the extent to which the centre can expect lower-level authorities to follow its guidelines. This will depend on how much political authority is vested in the system of government, and what mechanisms the centre can use to influence subnational authorities: mechanisms may be through regulations or legislation (whether discretionary or mandatory) or financing inducements or sanctions. For instance, in Russia weak authority and guidance from the centre has left much health care reform to regional authorities, which has affected implementation (Curtis *et al.* 1995). In many Latin American countries ministries of health are weak in comparison with social security or health insurance agencies. Fiedler (1991) notes that in Ecuador funds for health programmes are channelled by the Ministry of Finance directly to the local level, bypassing the Ministry of Health. This pattern is also found in Kyrgyzstan. Clearly local-level authorities may exercise significant power over policy and its implementation in such situations.

In those countries where the centre can use financing mechanisms – as one-off incentives or for ongoing control – the chances of implementation are improved. The UK government, for example, made available resources for institutions introducing reforms such as resource management systems in hospitals (Keen *et al.* 1993) and to encourage general practitioners to move towards fundholding practices.

While the structure of authority and the exercise of control and discretion between central and local-level institutions influences implementation, there are other factors which clearly affect implementation of policies. If it is unclear how to make policy objectives operational, implementation may falter. For example, in devising health reforms, many governments have developed lofty policy objectives, but have found it much more difficult to say how these objectives are to be achieved. Marmor suggests this is because most political systems give much greater rewards to 'shrewd deployment of symbols and generalised arguments' than to detailed analysis and forecasting (Marmor 1994: 217). Certainly most analyses of health care reforms point to the gap between policy intent and strategies for making policy work. Borissov and Rathwell suggest that while a new national health insurance system has been introduced in Bulgaria, with overall Ministry of Health monitoring, there has been little discussion on *how* to ensure that the state will consult and collaborate with the institutions in the new system (Borissov and Rathwell 1995). Yet health reforms are *process-oriented*. They are aimed at restructuring relationships between public and private sectors, managers and policy makers, providers and consumers. Any refiguring depends on understanding *how* change should be implemented, and *who* is likely to favour or resist reform.

**Table 16.2** Factors affecting the process of implementation

| *Facilitating factors* | *Current health care reforms* |
|---|---|
| *Simple technical features*<br>Knowledge, technology exist<br>No new resources needed | *Highly complex*<br>Experience lacking<br>Training needed<br>Information/cost systems need to<br>  be developed<br>Costly |
| *Marginal change from status quo*<br><br>Incremental change easier to get<br>  agreed | *Reforms require major change<br>  from status quo*<br>Major change may be strongly<br>  opposed |
| *Implementation by one actor*<br>Collaborating across sectors<br>  complicates process | *Reforms often pluralist*<br>Public and private sector<br>  collaboration difficult |
| *Goals of policy clearly stated*<br>One main objective mitigates<br>  against confusion or conflict | *Reform goals often in conflict*<br>Multiple objectives, some of which<br>  conflict with political and<br>  societal values |
| *Rapid implementation*<br>Short duration limits build-up<br>  of resistance, distortions of<br>  policy | *Reforms complex, and execution slow*<br>New systems (procedures,<br>  institutions) have to be devised<br>  and established |

*Source*: Adapted from Cleaves (1980)

In Table 16.2, Cleaves's model of the factors that facilitate implementation has been adapted to sum up some of the difficulties that face the introduction of reforms in the health sector (Cleaves 1980).

## THE ROLE OF ACTORS IN IMPLEMENTATION: POWER AND INFLUENCE

Actors form a key part of policy analysis, and can be broadly categorized as: governmental actors (e.g. politicians, civil servants, bureaucrats); non-governmental actors (e.g. professional bodies, trade unions); pressure or interest groups (e.g. pharmaceutical

industry); international actors (e.g. multi- and bilateral international agencies, multinational corporations); and others such as
the media, academic institutions etc.

Actors also include a more amorphous group of citizens or individuals – members of civil society – whose views are represented
through 'public opinion' in the media, through representatives, or
through their own actions (for example, street demonstrations or
switching between public and private health services). They may
not join particular interest groups, but may form social movements
with common identities and concerns, which can be mobilized to
support a particular cause.

If individuals want to influence policy, they usually do so *through*
one (or more) of the above groups, but the extent to which citizens
*can* influence policy depends to some extent on the level of sophisti-
cation of civil society: the independence of the media, their culture
of investigation, what access members of the public have to political actors or the media. It will depend on the perceived legitimacy
(by government and civil society), of both sectional and cause interest groups,[2] and their experience in lobbying. It will depend on how
much legitimacy the citizenry accord channels of influence and particular government policies: they may take to the streets to demonstrate. Many citizens (whether in formal government positions or
outside government) of formerly centrist and authoritarian regimes
lack experience in the mechanisms of dialogue, negotiation and
pressure that characterize democracies.

Most policy analysis, however, focuses on policy elites – the
senior politicians and bureaucrats who formulate and implement
policy: key questions revolve around the relative power and interests of each group. Attention on bureaucrats is justified because of
the strategic roles they play in the implementation of reforms. Their
response to reforms may be positive or negative. Grindle and
Thomas suggest that policies with benefits that are apparent only in
the long term (as in the case of many health care reforms) may be
perceived negatively by those implementing the reforms – the
officials and managers who have to introduce new systems, break
old habits, relinquish accustomed forms of security, control,
responsibility or even graft (Grindle and Thomas 1991). Bureaucrats who understand the costs long before the public sees any benefits may find ways of delaying or amending policy. To avoid such
action, politicians have to mobilize support from outside the
bureaucracy.

In considering the role of policy elites, it is important to consider at what level they are working. Central-level bureaucrats may be relatively distanced from the day-to-day concerns of managers, or 'street-level bureaucrats' at local authority level: in formulating policy they do not necessarily consider the feasibility of policy implementation, and even if they do, they may not be aware of common hazards. Developing country participants at a World Bank discussion on the problems of implementation suggested that their governments often sent the wrong people to negotiate with the Bank – 'policy makers rather than the *soldiers* who could make the project work' (Wapenhans 1992).

While concentrating on policy elites (including business elites) in those political systems where power has been concentrated in few hands is understandable, the increased role of interest groups must not be ignored. In Europe, the growth in the number of interest groups has led some to talk of an 'overcrowded policy environment' (Richardson 1982), and where interest groups are particularly powerful – such as the health insurance industry in the US – decision making may become very difficult. Health reforms have been easier to introduce in those countries in which there are few stakeholders. In Taiwan (with a centralized political system and still developing civil society) for example, the absence of a strong private health insurance industry made it politically feasible for the government to legislate in order to amalgamate three insurance programmes into one (Peabody *et al.* 1995).

The media and academic groups may be important players in supporting or opposing health reforms in general, and certain reforms in particular. At one point in the attempts to reform health care in Kenya, the media launched an attack on the level of fees being introduced in hospitals, to which the President responded by withdrawing the change in fees – at least initially. In contrast, in Mexico, a survey which established considerable public support for health reform was used deliberately to give the people a voice and make them protagonists for health reform (Mwabu 1993; Fundación Mexicana para la Salud 1995). Persuading the public of the need for reform can have an important effect on the implementation of reform. For example, Tendler and Freedheim suggest that the state's publicity drive to promote health reform was one of the factors that helped transform part of the health sector in northeast Brazil (Tendler and Freedheim 1994).

In all countries there are what Peterson calls representational communities – organized interests such as consumer groups, trade unions, professional groups (medical or nursing), researchers, the media (Peterson 1993). Peterson sees these representational communities varying over time and across different policy issues. Stakeholders generally benefit by the status quo, or are threatened by revisions to it; stake challengers, on the other hand, want to change the status quo because they do not benefit from it, or are even harmed by it.

Table 16.3 summarizes four distinct representational communities. When stakeholders are allied, and stake challengers are not present, the community is homogeneous, and implementation should proceed. Where stakeholders are allied, and stake challengers confront them, the community is polarized (a dyad of opposed coalitions). However, when stakeholders are competitive with each other and stake challengers are absent, there may be amalgams of differentiated interests which will slow implementation or allow incremental change only. If stakeholders are competitive and stake challengers are strong, however, then there is what Peterson called a heterogeneous network, which draws a great deal of attention to the particular issues under consideration, and may aid implementation.

These analyses of health care reforms stress the importance of political leadership. Not only is having an overall image of reform necessary – a policy package rather than isolated reform options (Chernichovsky and Chinitz 1995; Gilson and Mills 1995) – but identifying a leader committed to reform may also make a difference to the way (or even whether) reforms are implemented. Authoritative leadership may be more important in established systems reluctant to change.

**Table 16.3**   Types of representational communities

|  | *Stake challengers* | *Present* |
| --- | --- | --- |
| Characteristics of stakeholders | No | Yes |
| Allied | Block (homogeneous) | Dyad (polarized) |
| Competitive | Amalgam (differentiated) | Network (heterogeneous) |

*Source*: Peterson (1993)

## THE LINK TO CONTENT: DOES PAST POLICY AFFECT POLICY CHOICE?

Up to now we have argued that policies are the outcome of politics affected by the complex inter-relationship between actors, processes and contextual factors. But how far are politics the result of policies? How far do previous policy choices affect current policy choices?

Pierson argues that not only do interest groups shape policies, but policies shape interest groups (Pierson 1994). The emergence in the US of what is now a formidable pressure group, the American Association of Retired People, was facilitated by policies which had neglected health care benefits for the elderly. Also cumulative commitments affect what policy options are perceived to be feasible. Marmor and Oberlander suggest that the enactment of Medicare created a political constituency that now makes the creation of a universal health insurance programme more difficult (Marmor and Oberlander 1995).

Policy makers may thus be 'locked-in' by prior policies. For example, if policies create incentives and commitment to particular services, it may be very costly to alter such services or even consider alternatives which were once possible. Policies which have required massive investments of infrastructure or training over a long period may constrain reforms in the shorter run. Pierson argues that:

> Lock-in effects are likely to be important when public policies encourage individuals to make significant investments that are not easily reversed, or when individuals face strong incentives to co-ordinate their activities with other social actors and adopt prevailing or anticipated standards.
>
> (Pierson 1994)

Pre-existing policy frameworks affect the extent to which policies are adopted. In countries where the private sector is small, and where a traditional public sector ethos denigrated the private sector (as Ngalande-Banda and Walt (1995) describe for Malawi), groups may be slow to respond to entrepreneurial opportunities in an expanded private sector. In Nicaragua Fiedler suggests privatization has been slow because health care organizations have been unwilling to take risks in an unfamiliar arena (Fiedler 1996).

Societal or historical values may have a strong influence on what sorts of policies are considered feasible to execute. For example, Potucek suggests that after 1989 prevailing political values in the

Czech Republic were suspicious of state control, and favoured a pluralist approach and clear reform strategy (Potucek 1994). This led to the establishment of health and social insurance funds separate from the state. However, in Slovakia, a greater 'dependency' culture, more reliance on the state and no clear reform strategy led to the development of a single, state national health insurance system. Altenstetter and Bjorkman (1997) suggest that the social insurance model favoured by the Czech Republic is a revival of the 1980s health insurance – a historical inheritance about which the Czechs feel comfortable.

However, while past policies may affect current policy negatively, they can also have positive effects on the implementation of reforms. In some Latin American countries, where the private sector was long established, excess capacity has influenced the extent to which physicians have been willing to cooperate with the public sector, so that privatization of parts of existing social security systems has led to greater choice for members and to shorter waiting times (Fiedler 1996).

## STRATEGIES FOR IMPLEMENTATION

Much analysis of health care reforms has focused on technical features of policy and has neglected contextual factors, the roles of actors and the process of policy making. This could explain why a number of policy changes have been implemented ineffectively and expected policy outcomes have not been achieved.

In today's uncertain policy environment policy analysis can be a tool to help influence policy outcomes (and not merely to understand them). Implementing policy reform in an environment characterized by retrenchment may be a matter of identifying strategies to weaken or outflank political opponents (Pierson 1994). In other words, implementation should be anticipated and planned for. As Grindle and Thomas put it '. . . decision makers and policy managers can analyse their environment, in the context of a political economy framework, to see if the conditions and capacity exist for successfully implementing a reform' (Grindle and Thomas 1991: 141).

Policy analysis thus becomes part of a strategic participatory planning process. White refers to interactive policy inquiry in which a process approach is used to plan and carry out policy changes (White 1991). Brinkerhoff talks of strategic management of change

(Brinkerhoff 1995). Drawing on interested groups at all levels of the health service, it ensures policy makers take responsibility for designing appropriate policy responses and implementation strategies. Klitgaard (1991) has used such an approach to help public sector officials tackle the problems of corruption, and Reich has developed a political analysis approach to use in analysing health policies (Reich 1996). These different approaches all apply similar methods, which have to be adapted to particular circumstances and settings. Some of them are covered in Table 16.4.

**Table 16.4** Instruments in policy analysis which can be used for planning and managing the implementation of change

| Area of analysis | Planning action |
|---|---|
| Macro-analysis of the ease with which policy change can be implemented | Analyse conditions for facilitating change and, where possible, make adjustments: (one implementing agency; clear goals, one objective; simple technical features; marginal change; short duration; benefits are visible; clear costs) |
| Making values underlying policy explicit | Identify macro- and micro-level values underlying policy decisions. If values conflict with policy, support will have to be mobilized; costs minimized |
| Undertake stakeholder analysis | Review interest groups (and individuals) likely to resist or promote change in policy at national and institutional levels; plan how to mobilize support by consensus building or rallying coalitions of support |
| Analysis of financial, technical and managerial resources available | Consider costs and benefits of external funds; assess 'rent-seeking' behaviour, review salary levels, incentives to change behaviour; review need for training, need for new information systems or other resources; inducements and sanctions |
| Build strategic implementation process | Involve planners and managers in research and analysis of how to execute policy; identify networks of supporters of policy change, clinical champions; manage uncertainty; promote public awareness campaigns; institute mechanisms for consultation, monitoring, 'fine-tuning' |

In all these attempts at policy analysis and the implementation of change, it must be acknowledged that policy analysts are not themselves necessarily disinterested or neutral: they often represent the interests of particular groups. It is probably a necessary, but not sufficient, condition in any policy analysis exercise to identify how far the policy analysts are (intendedly) objective, or are seeking to promote a particular policy.

Using the instruments outlined in Table 16.4 can help to avoid pitfalls in implementation. By undertaking the macro-analysis of any particular reform, some actions may be taken before implementation is expected: for example, it may be preferable to introduce a change which is marginal (uses existing administrative procedures) and can be put into effect quickly, rather than a more radical change which provides the opportunity for resistance because new methods have to be devised for execution. On the other hand, radical change introduced quickly may be successful.

Similarly, by making values explicit, policy makers (and researchers) are assisted to recognize their own and others' perspectives, and how they may be influencing policy, or conflicting with each other. Making values explicit helps in the design of policy. For instance, at the micro level, if policy makers assume that responsibility for contraception lies with women, they will design policies that are aimed at female contraceptives offered in maternal and child health centres. If they assume, on the other hand, that contraception is the responsibility of both men and women, resulting policies will make contraceptives freely available and not gender-focused. Policy makers often do not consider what assumptions (or values) lie behind suggested policy options.

By undertaking stakeholder analysis, it is possible to map the contours of likely support and opposition, and act to change the map. In political mapping, Reich suggests that completing a stakeholder analysis is just one of five steps that need to be taken to influence implementation (Reich 1993). It involves several qualitative assessments about the representational community. The first is to assess for each organization identified its objectives – what does the organization gain from a particular decision? And what is the organizational priority (high, medium or low) for each objective identified? Based on the information collected on organizational structures, the next step is to sketch a policy network map which identifies connections and alliances among the organizations involved in the specific health decision. This mapping does not explicitly divide the interested organizations into stakeholders and stake challengers, which might be useful in a given situation (see Table 16.3).

Having identified and analysed the positions of stakeholders (and stake challengers), policy makers can employ several tactics (Freeman 1990: 165): they may ignore the stakeholder (taking the risk – and precautions should it occur – that implementation may be derailed); they may take the 'public relations' approach (build images, 'sell' the need for policy change, woo opinion leaders); they may use 'implicit negotiation' (anticipate objections, and design policies which meet those objections); and finally they may use 'explicit negotiation' by working with stakeholders on the design of policy.

Analysis of financial, technical and managerial resources should be part of planning the execution of any policy. Grindle and Thomas suggest that proponents of reform have to take into account two scenarios of reaction or response to policy change (Grindle and Thomas 1991). The first is when the policy is 'high politics' and visible, the stakes are critical for government and political elites and resources to sustain the reform are considerable. Skills in political management are essential. The second is where stakes are lower and, while the sorts of resources necessary are also considerable, the brunt is borne at a relatively local level. Here guaranteeing successful implementation depends on incentives, management skills, training, information.

Building a strategic implementing process means involving planners and managers in monitoring and controlling the progress of reforms: for example, establishing milestones by which the programme will be executed, looking at variances from budgets and other resources allocated, monitoring results (Freeman 1990). It may also mean identifying and supporting clinical (or other) champions to lead with reforms. Lomas has shown that when acknowledged leaders accept innovation, others follow. Indeed, the success of much implementation will depend on identifying strategies that help to change behaviour: having codes of practice that establish expected standards of service provision; or inventing incentives to change (Lomas 1993). Public campaigns to explain the reason for reforms, and to publicize their benefits, as occurred in Mexico and Brazil (Tendler and Freedheim 1994; Fundación Mexicana para la Salud 1995) may also be important tools.

Planning implementation may also mean managing uncertainty: uncertainties about the working environment mean more information is needed; uncertainties about guiding values mean objectives need to be re-thought, clarified; uncertainties about related decisions mean that more coordination is necessary (Friend and Hickling 1993).

Policy analysis thus provides a number of different instruments which can be useful at different stages of the policy process: from getting an issue onto the agenda, to planning how a particular policy will be implemented. Health care reforms are on the policy agenda in most countries: the next stage is to ensure they are implemented as desired.

## NOTES

1 The terms 'high' and 'low' politics are borrowed and adapted from the international relations literature, and compare issues of crucial importance (often crisis engendered) with low-key, routine, politics-as-usual policies (Walt 1994).
2 *Sectional* groups are those which represent the interests of their members, such as trade unions, professional or industrial associations. *Cause* groups are those which try to influence policy in relation to a specific cause, such as nuclear disarmament or abortion law reform.

## REFERENCES

Altenstetter, C. and Bjorkman, J. W. (eds) (1997). *Health Policy Reform, National Variations and Globalization*. Hampshire, UK: Macmillan Press.
Borissov, V. and Rathwell, T. (1995). Health care reforms in Bulgaria: An initial appraisal. *Social Science and Medicine*, 42, 1501–10.
Brinkerhoff, D.W. (1993). *Linking Applied Research and Technical Cooperation in Strategic Management of Policy Changes*, IPC Research Note no. 2. Washington, DC: USAID.
Chernichovsky, D. and Chinitz, D. (1995). The political economy of health system reform in Israel. *Health Economics*, 4, 127–41.
Cleaves, P. (1980). Implementation amidst scarcity and apathy: Political power and policy design. In M. Grindle (ed.), *Politics and Policy Implementation in the Third World*. Princeton, NJ: Princeton University Press.
Collins, C., Green, A. and Hunter, D. (1994). International transfers of National Health Service reforms: Problems and issues. *Lancet*, 344, 248–50.
Cooper, M. H. (1994). Jumping on the spot – health reform New Zealand style. *Health Economics*, 3, 69–72.

Curtis, S., Petukhova, N. and Taket, A. (1995). Health care reforms in Russia: The example of St Petersburg. *Social Science and Medicine*, 40, 755–65.

De Leeuw, E. and Polman, L. (1995). Health policy making: The Dutch experience. *Social Science and Medicine*, 40, 331–8.

Fiedler, J. (1991). Child survival and the role of the ministry of health in Ecuador: progress, constraints and reorganization. *Health Policy and Planning*, 1, 32–45.

Fiedler, J. (1996). The privatization of health care in three Latin American social security systems. *Health Policy and Planning*, 4, 406–17.

Freeman, R. E. (1990). *Strategic Management*. Boston and London: Pitman.

Friend, J. and Hickling, A. (1993). *Planning under Pressure*. Oxford: Pergamon Press.

Fundación Mexicana para la Salud (1995). *Health and the Economy – Overview*. Mexico City: Fundación Mexicana para la Salud.

Gilson, L. and Mills, A. (1995). Health sector reforms in sub-Saharan Africa: Lessons of the last 10 years. *Health Policy*, 32, 215–43.

Golinowska, S. and Tymowska, K. (1995). Poland. In N. Johnson (ed.), *Private Markets in Health and Welfare*. Oxford and Providence: Berg.

Grindle, M. and Thomas, J. (1991). *Public Choices and Policy Change*. Baltimore and London: Johns Hopkins University Press.

Ham, C. and Brommels, M. (1994). Health care reform in the Netherlands, Sweden, and the United Kingdom. *Health Affairs*, 13, 105–19.

James, J. H. (1995). Reforming the British National Health Service: Implementation problems in London. *Journal of Health Politics, Policy and Law*, 20, 191–210.

Keen, J., Buxton, M. and Packwood, T. (1993). Doctors and resource management: Incentives and goodwill. *Health Policy*, 24, 71–82.

Klitgaard, R. (1991). *Adjusting to Reality*. San Francisco: ICS Press.

Leach, R. (1995). *Policy-making in Britain*. London and New York: Routledge.

Lomas, J. (1993). Retailing research: Increasing the role of evidence in clinical services for childbirth. *Milbank Quarterly*, 71, 439–75.

Mackintosh, M. (1992). *Questioning the State*. Milton Keynes: Open University Press.

Marmor, T. (1993). Understanding the welfare state: Crisis, critics and countercritics. *Critical Review*, 7, 461–77.

Marmor, T. (1994). *Understanding Health Care Reform*. New Haven and London: Yale University Press.

Marmor, T. and Oberlander, J. (1995). Review Essay. Political analysis and the welfare state: Can we learn from history? *Journal of Health Politics, Policy and Law*, 20, 211–25.

Martinez, J. and Sandiford, P. (1995). *Health Sector Reforms in Central America*. Liverpool: Liverpool School of Tropical Medicine.

Mills, A., Vaughan, J. P., Smith, D. L. and Tabizzadeh, I. (1990). *Health System Decentralization: Concepts, Issues and Country Experience*. Geneva: World Health Organization.

Mohan, J. (1995). *A National Health Service?* New York: St Martin's Press.

Mwabu, G. (1993). Health care reform in Kenya 1963–1993: Lessons for policy research. Paper presented at the conference on Health Sector Reform in Developing Countries, September 10–13, 1993, Durham, New Hampshire, USA.

Ngalande-Banda, E. and Walt, G. (1995). The private sector in Malawi: Opening Pandora's box? *Journal of International Development*, 3, 403–21.

Peabody, J. W., Yu, J. C., Wang, Y. R. and Bickel, S. R. (1995). Health system reform in the Republic of China. Formulating policy in a market-based health system. *Journal of the American Medical Association*, 273, 777–81.

Peterson, M. A. (1993). Political influence in the 1990s: From iron triangles to policy networks. *Journal of Health Politics, Policy and Law*, 18, 395–438.

Pierson, P. (1994). *Dismantling the Welfare State?* Cambridge: Cambridge University Press.

Potucek, M. (1994). *Markets, States and Social Citizenship in Central and Eastern Europe.* Unpublished paper, Prague, Institute of Sociological Studies, Charles University.

Reich, M. R. (1993). *Political Mapping of Health Policy.* Boston: Harvard University.

Reich, M. R. (1996). Applied political analysis for health policy reform. *Current Issues in Public Health*, 2, 186–91.

Richardson, J. (1982). *Policy Styles in Western Europe.* London: George Allen and Unwin.

Saltman, R. B. (1994). A conceptual overview of recent health care reforms. *European Journal of Public Health*, 4, 287–93.

Tendler, J. and Freedheim, S. (1994). Trust in a rent-seeking world: Health and government transformed in Northeast Brazil. *World Development*, 22, 1771–91.

Walt, G. (1994). *Health Policy: An Introduction to Process and Power.* London: Zed Books.

Walt, G. and Gilson, L. (1994). Reforming the health sector in developing countries: The central role of policy analysis. *Health Policy*, 9, 353–70.

Wapenhans, W. (1992). *Effective Implementation: Key to Development Impact.* IBRD, Washington.

White, L. (1991). *Implementing Policy Reforms in Less Developed Countries.* Boulder, CO: Lynne Rienner Publishers.

Wildavsky, A. (1979). *Speaking Truth to Power: The Art and Craft of Policy Analysis.* Boston: Little, Brown.

# 17

# IMPLEMENTING HEALTH CARE REFORM: A REVIEW OF CURRENT EXPERIENCE

Tom Rathwell

## INTRODUCTION

The reform of health care systems is a key issue on the policy agenda in many countries. This chapter reviews relevant efforts of various governments in the European region in reforming their health care systems. It does not seek to describe the reform mechanisms themselves, since this is well documented elsewhere (Artundo *et al.* 1992; Saltman and von Otter 1992; Zarkovic *et al.* 1994; Gilson and Mills 1995; Rosleff and Lister 1995; Seedhouse 1995). Rather, the thrust of the discussion here concentrates on the neglected aspects of policy analysis: context, process and actors (Walt 1996). This paper utilizes the framework of context, process and actors to examine the experience to date of health systems reforms in the European region and selected other countries, in terms of the lessons for implementation. The chapter begins with the context, goes on to explore the process and continues with an examination of the impact that various actors have had on the emerging health care reform policies.

## UNDERSTANDING THE CONTEXT

The position and role of the state in health care is fundamental. A significant feature of the health systems reforms in European

countries is the lessening of direct state involvement in the organization and delivery of health care through the introduction of self-
regulated, managed markets (Ensor 1993; Hurst and Poullier 1993).
Reducing state involvement in health care systems in return for
granting greater autonomy to those responsible for organizing and
delivering health care is an untested and untried strategy which
may or may not deliver the promised benefits (Hurst and Poullier
1993; Saltman 1994). Many governments have difficulty adopting
an indirect role in policy; namely, a regulatory and supervisory role
which will increase with the decentralization of health care delivery
systems (see Chapter 13). There is growing consensus that the
movement towards market-oriented health system reform requires
a change in style of government, not an abdication of government.
Maarse argues that better government, not less government is
needed (Maarse 1994), while Saltman and von Otter assert that
solidarity, 'so long a feature of European public funded health care
systems, has acted as a brake' on moves towards more market-
oriented policies as governments are constrained by what is politically acceptable (Saltman and von Otter 1992). The purpose here is
not to question the political decisions of the state to introduce self-
regulating, managed markets in health care, but rather to note that
the state will continue to have a responsibility to ensure that such
reforms are properly planned and evaluated – an important issue
which affects implementation.

The nature and scope of health system reform and its degree of
success is strongly influenced by key characteristics of the government in power. Setting aside the ideology of particular reforms, the
ability of governments to push through health systems reforms
reflects a variety of factors. Strong stable majority governments as
in New Zealand and the UK are far more able to ensure adoption
of health reform policies than are minority and relatively unstable
governments. Even stable coalition governments have to tread
more carefully in undertaking health system reform. In countries
such as Finland, Germany, the Netherlands and Sweden where
coalition governments are often the norm, health system reform
has been more incremental than that introduced in Canada, New
Zealand and the UK. The Dekker Report in the Netherlands illustrates this nicely in that while it proposed a radical reform of the
health care system, what actually occurred was considerably more
modest (Groenewegen 1994). Similar pictures can be painted for
Finland, Germany and Sweden, where the respective governments
have been reluctant to take major political risks.

In CEE countries, the result of unstable governments or governments hamstrung due to the composition of parliament has sometimes been little or no action on health system reform. There has also been a purging of administrative staff at all levels of the policy process, and those who replace them often are unprepared and/or unqualified for the task of implementing change. Even where administrative staff have not been purged, administrative efficiency has declined as the previous rigid hierarchy and party discipline is replaced with a different and to some extent alien decision-making culture (Wlodarczyk 1993). Moreover, the lack of an independent administrative (civil) service often means that as the parties in power change so too does the administrative machinery, which serves to replicate the inbred inefficiency of the former system (Heginbotham and Maxwell 1991). The close association between political parties and the administrative structure somehow must be broken if health system reform is to be effective. Bulgaria, Poland and Romania, for example, have all had considerable expert assistance and technical advice regarding health system reform, yet due to a varying combination of political instability, economic crisis, and short terms of office for ministers of health, progress in reforming the health care system has been slow (Balicki and Sabbat 1994).

## MAKING SENSE OF PROCESS

As the paper by Walt in this volume notes (Chapter 16), the process for determining the policy agenda is essentially political and value-laden. Often, however, values conflict between different key actors, and governments sometimes ignore the potential difficulties this can create for implementation. The health system reforms in the UK, for example, were enacted in spite of strong opposition by the British Medical Association. Indeed, such was the belief of the government in the appropriateness of the reforms that it 'proceeded without ... demonstrations and projects and with a minimum of consultation' (Gladstone and Goldsmith 1995). In acknowledging the potentially damaging effect that opposition to the reforms could create, the British government used financial incentives to help lubricate the process. For example, they made resources available to hospitals to set up resource management systems (Keen *et al.* 1993) and provided early general practitioner recruits to fundholding with monies to computerize their patients' records and office accounting systems (Glennerster *et al.* 1995).

The restructuring of the New Zealand health system followed a similar pattern to that of the UK, in that the reforms when introduced were highly contentious and faced considerable opposition (Ashton 1995). The New Zealand reforms parallel those of the British National Health Service, but are acknowledged as going further and with a pace of change much faster than that in the UK (Ashton 1995). The conclusion of commentators on the health system reforms in both New Zealand and the UK is that their introduction owes more to ideology than to policies based on sound empirical evidence (Borren and Maynard 1994; Robinson and Le Grand 1994).

In contrast to the unilateral approach taken by politicians in New Zealand and the UK, reforms in Finland, the Netherlands and Sweden were more consultative. In the case of the Netherlands, the 1987 Dekker Report set out a detailed agenda for restructuring the health care system which, in effect, advised the government to drop its comprehensive health care planning approach and to rely on market forces for effective cost containment of health care expenditure (de Roo 1995: 55). Political, institutional and public opposition has meant that by 1997 only partial implementation has occurred of the Dekker proposals. As de Roo wryly observes, 'we are witnessing an ongoing process of pragmatic socio-political adaptation of a political value to new social conditions' (de Roo 1995: 63). Thus, in the implementation of the Dutch health care reforms, political pragmatism has been very much the order of the day.

Both Finland and Sweden are pursuing an incremental approach to health system reform. The overarching objective of the reforms in both countries is the decentralization of the public sector (Brommels 1995: 105). The Swedish reforms are essentially county-specific with each county developing a different approach or model. Stockholm County Council, for instance, decided to establish an internal market for hospital services in which hospitals are paid for the services they actually provide (Glennerster and Matsaganis 1994). This has been characterized by Ham as 'bottom-up reform'. Due to the decentralized nature of the health system, reforms have been driven from the bottom (county level) up resulting in a wide variation between the reforms pursued in different counties (Ham 1997).

Finnish health system reforms transferred to the municipalities responsibility for policy in addition to their long-established role in service delivery (Sinkkonen and Kinnunen undated). This has resulted in a variety of municipality-initiated developments with no overall structure or model being imposed nationally as in the UK. Thus innovations in Finland and Sweden, though reflecting aspects of the British reforms (Glennerster and Matsaganis 1994; Brommels 1995) are locally derived and focused. In a further distinction from British reforms, it appears that the locally based Swedish and Finnish reforms are undergoing some form of formal evaluation (Anell 1995; Rosleff and Lister 1995).

An additional factor here is that unintended policy changes may occur as a consequence of the publication of a strategy or plan for reform. Groenewegen, for instance, in commenting on the health reform process in the Netherlands, notes that policy publication can lead to change even before policy implementation (Groenewegen 1994). Proposals contained in the Dekker Report in the Netherlands led to a wave of mergers between health insurance companies and among some of the larger hospitals. This was done in order to protect their market share when the proposals became policy. Groenewegen comments that this behavioural response to reform means that new policies will probably be implemented in an environment different from the one in which they were proposed (Groenewegen 1994: 145). Thus to talk of reform can lead to anticipatory change even if no policies emerge.

## THE CENTRALITY OF ACTORS

Although context and process are important, a majority of commentators concerned with policy analysis highlight the centrality of actors as a determinant of policy change. Actors, or stakeholders, are those with a vested interest, however large or small, in the policy process, and who have the ability to affect either positively or negatively the implementation of policy (Chapter 16). In the public sector, the role of actors or stakeholders is often more important than would appear to be the case elsewhere. This is particularly true of the medical professions, which can have a major bearing on the implementation of policy.

As countries work their way through a health care reform, the influence of the health professions can be undermined, however, and in places usurped by a growing ascendancy of bureaucrats and managers. The effect and impact of the changes in the British

National Health Service on the health professions is documented by Harrison and Pollitt (Harrison and Pollitt 1994) who conclude that, although managerial control over health care professionals has increased, health professionals still exercise substantial control over their clinical departments and the supply of their labour.

The ability of particular actors to affect the manner in which policies are implemented can be further illustrated by the examples of the general practice fundholding initiative in the United Kingdom and of contracting in countries such as New Zealand, Sweden and the UK. Despite efforts by the UK government to promote fundholding, including adjusting the criteria and addressing stakeholders' concerns, achieving an overall majority of both general practices and population covered by the scheme continues to be elusive. This difficulty highlights the ability of major stakeholders to use their influence to modify policy. Scepticism among general practitioners about the benefits to them and their patients was one factor in the slow pace of change. Another was the pressure exerted by some practices who did not meet the initial qualifying criteria for a relaxation of the rules. A third factor was concern in government circles that a major plank of its health reform policy could be in danger of becoming derailed. This history suggests that governments need to be flexible about the criteria for policies if they wish to bring key stakeholders along with them.

The procedure of contracting and the concomitant purchaser–provider split are key features of health reforms being introduced in countries with centralized or planned health care systems. In New Zealand, Sweden and the UK, stakeholder interests were critically important in the process of implementation. In the case of the UK, managerial authority has been enhanced because the change in organizational environment created new leverage for both purchaser and provider managers over medical professionals, by putting additional levers of power and persuasion into managers' hands (Harrison and Pollitt 1994: 122–3). It could be argued that the UK government successfully implemented radical reform by creating a situation whereby one set of actors (managers) perceived for themselves particular advantages in supporting change in terms of enhanced prestige and influence, such that they chose to discount the concerns of other actors (Peck 1991).

The New Zealand reform was implemented by the government in the face of widespread opposition from the health professions, but in the knowledge that the business community generally favoured it (Ashton 1995). This suggests that a divide-and-rule policy was also employed in this instance to ensure that controversial change was put into practice.

In contrast to New Zealand and the UK, Sweden adopted a different and more incremental approach. Thus, instead of a national reform package being imposed, a variety of separate initiatives were taken by the county councils who have responsibility for the provision and financing of health care. Diversity in the Swedish context may be advantageous in that different models can be tested but, as Diderichsen notes, there is a balance to be managed: between equity and efficiency, between equity and broad political loyalty, and between broad political support and cost control (Diderichsen 1995: 152). The decentralized structure of the Swedish health care system, and the strong public support for it, significantly constrains both the ability of national or county government to introduce sweeping radical reform and the range of reactions to those reforms by key actors within the system including health professionals. The public is a significant stakeholder in the Swedish health care system, and is recognized as such politically (it is they who elect the county council and approve their tax-raising policies). Given this distribution of stakeholder roles, it is most likely that the system will only undergo incremental change along lines already initiated (Carlsson 1994).

Historically, CEE health care systems were characterized by strong central control (Preker and Feachem 1995). With the demise of the old centralized system of political control, new CEE governments have been searching for a different structural paradigm for their health care systems. One consequence has been the replacement of the prior administrative elite with untrained and/or inexperienced personnel as well as opening up the health care system to influence by a range of new stakeholders. New in this sense means that health professionals, managers/administrators, local politicians and the public (users/consumers) all believe that they should have a greater role to play in the restructuring of the health care system. Indeed, Zarkovic and colleagues argue that adopting a pluralistic health care system is essential in order to meet new needs and improve overall efficiency (Zarkovic *et al.* 1994). While structural change is well under way in most of the CEE (Ensor 1993), what is not clear is the extent to which these changes have opened up the policy process to the influence of other relevant stakeholders.

An important actor often missing from health reform analyses is the user of health care services. Alford's seminal work (1975) documented how professionals and administrators/managers combined to exclude the patient from the policy process, on the grounds that the decisions they took, either collectively or individual, were always done in the best interests of the user. It is an interesting perspective on the health systems reforms being implemented in the European region that the user view is missing. Despite the emphasis within many European reform proposals to enhance patient choice and competition between health service deliverers and, sometimes, insurance providers (Groenewegen 1994), the patients' perspective is itself often missing.

## SUCCESS OR FAILURE IN HEALTH SECTOR REFORMS IMPLEMENTATION

As the previous section suggests there seem to be a number of attributes that make some governments more successful than others in implementing reforms. It is these attributes and the circumstances behind them which are the focus of this section.

### Big-bang vs. incrementalism

On the evidence available about the British and New Zealand approach to health system reform, the top-down imposition of a grand plan (big-bang approach) may not be the most appropriate way to introduce change.

A notable feature of the Swedish reforms is its incremental nature, with changes occurring at the county council level. As Brommels (Brommels 1995) notes, the role of the politicians was an important factor in the Swedish reforms. Given that county councillors are directly elected by the populace, it is not surprising that some counties in Sweden have implemented changes to the health care system, whereas others have not. This places the various counties in Sweden in an interesting position of being able to compare the different approaches being pursued by other counties, such that those reforms which seem best able to meet desired objectives are the ones most likely to be adopted more broadly. This approach in Sweden, where change is tested locally before being extended to the rest of the country, may be a more effective mechanism than a big-bang unitary model (Borren and Maynard 1994). One observation arising from the Swedish experience is that experimentation with change may in the long run lead to more acceptable policies than the radical changes introduced rationally in New Zealand and the UK, where political counter-pressures resulted in a subsequent slowing down of the reform process (Ashton 1995; Gladstone and Goldsmith 1995). The incrementalist model based on local pilot projects also may provide a better paradigm for CEE/CIS countries that are restructuring their health care systems, and where the political infrastructure required to impose major national change appears weak and relatively unstable (Wlodarczyk 1993).

## The relevance of political will

Perhaps the most significant factor affecting policy implementation is political will. Strong political will can lead to situations as in New Zealand and the UK where major health sector reforms were introduced despite substantial opposition. Neither government felt it necessary to consider evaluating the results of such radical change, being convinced that the outcome would be beneficial. This was a high-risk political strategy and one which could have foundered had it not been, at least in the UK case, for the support of health services managers (Gladstone and Goldsmith 1995).

The difficulty in introducing health system reforms in many CEE countries is often a function of a lack of political will. Governments have been short-lived and rapid changes in administration have led to differing reform proposals being considered. Poland is a good case in point as there have been several changes in government since the overthrow of the previous authoritarian rule. One of the tendencies of the new government has been to try to replace most of the systems established under the communist regime with a different approach. A further complicating factor is that many politicians have only a general idea of what they want and consequently may be persuaded by others to introduce poorly thought-out policies. Jonczyk describes the difficulties that arise when different groups, with different objectives and agendas, are involved in producing proposals for health systems reforms (Jonczyk 1993). He suggests that in an unstable political environment, such as existed in Poland, multiple approaches to policy formulation and implementation may lead only to inaction.

Brommels's assessment of the Finnish and Swedish health systems reforms is that, despite the common goal of decentralization of the public (health) sector, there has been a marked reluctance by politicians to let go of their direct involvement in the provision of health services (Brommels 1995). Here progress towards the goals of health care reform is being hampered by the same actors who argue for reform. Political stakeholders thus seem to be caught on the horns of a dilemma: how to retain public accountability for health care services while loosening their hold on direct involvement in both strategic and operational matters. The consequences for health care reform in Finland and Sweden, according to Brommels, are that the overall goals are unlikely to be achieved until the actors involved realize that their interests, and those of the population, can best be served by separating political from professional responsibility (Brommels 1995: 108). Politicians as stakeholders can be thus both a force for as well as an obstacle to change. As Brommels implies, politicians must have the courage of their convictions (Brommels 1995).

The tendency of politicians to advocate change for all but themselves is, in Potucek's contention, hindering the development of health sector reform in much of central Europe (Potucek 1994a). In his view, CEE countries are neither prepared nor willing to move directly from state paternalism to social citizenship (1994a: 24). This political intransigence poses particular problems for the implementation of health care reforms. For instance, in such a political vacuum, others become more influential – as happened in the Czech Republic where the medical profession became both the driving force for and agent of reform (Potucek 1994b). Here was a set of actors who took advantage of the changing political context in the Czech Republic and used uncertainty to change policy so that providers would be reimbursed on a fee-for-service basis from health insurance funds (Potucek 1994b). This particular policy change had a significant impact on the health insurance fund, which became bankrupt in less than six months of operation (Preker and Feachem 1995). Clearly, the process of health system reform should not be left to those with a particular vested interest in their own welfare.

**Understanding the environment**

The management of policy implementation requires a range of skills. One of these is doing one's homework by assessing the environment to identify possible obstacles which may impede the implementation of the policy as well as facilitating factors which can smooth the process. Another is to marshal locally available technical skills and expertise in support of the health reform process. Lithuania has used such an approach quite effectively. It established the Health Care Reform Management Bureau, a quasi-independent organizational unit, whose remit was to provide technical support for the reform of the health care system.

For many countries, the main environmental constraint on implementing health system reform is the economy. This is as true of countries in western Europe as of those in central and eastern Europe. Indeed, it has been argued above that in many cases it was financial conditions and circumstances which triggered the process of reform. Yet if health system reform appears to be directed only at saving money, then there is a danger that it could unravel, as events in several countries demonstrate.

It is typically easier to introduce change in new areas where established services or entrenched vested interests do not yet exist (Rathwell 1988). However, if the external environment is supportive, it is possible to make changes in the established configuration of services as well. One example was the Finnish national health for all policy which prioritized development of its primary health care sector (Ministry of Health and Social Welfare 1986). The shift in emphasis towards primary health care came at a time of a growing economy, such that the resources required to support it were additional to, and not taken from, existing funding for the secondary care sector. As a result, the secondary sector did not feel threatened by the growth of primary health care. However if the resource situation had not been favourable and the secondary sector's economic base had been reduced to fund the primary care initiative, the developments which occurred in Finland would have been much harder to achieve. The message from the Finnish example is that governments may have to be prepared to invest additional resources in specific areas in order to affect particular reforms to their health care systems. The old adage that to save money one must first spend money may well apply to the process of implementation of health systems reforms.

### Strategic alliances and public support

Establishing alliances of people/organizations/agencies who support the change is a key task. Gladstone and Goldsmith describe how the UK government undermined the opposition of the medical profession to the 1991 reforms through the use of health sector managers who stood to gain financially and professionally from them (Gladstone and Goldsmith 1995). The Lithuanian Health Care Reform Management Bureau also was designed to be a participatory mechanism which would connect to both patients and providers in the development of health care reform initiatives.

The lack of broad public support for reform can be a major barrier to change, yet governments can and have pushed through health system reform without widespread public support for such measures. As examples, both New Zealand and the UK pursued this course of action. They informed their respective publics about the changes being introduced to the health care system and sold these reforms largely on the grounds that they would result in a better, more effective health care system and give people greater choice over how and where they would access services. This strategy meant that the government was able to instigate change quickly, however it did not mean that public concerns were muted and that when they did arise they went unheeded. In New Zealand, there was so much public disquiet about a proposal to allow for alternative (private sector) health purchasers that it was not implemented, though it remains on the statutes (Lovelace 1995).

The public backlash in many provinces in Canada against the widespread nature of health system reform highlights the inherent dangers for governments and politicians in taking for granted that their reform package has broad political support. This seems especially true when the reforms being implemented lead to a conflict between social and market values. This has been a factor in the limited success of health care reform in the Netherlands (Groenewegen 1994). It has also tempered the way in which health system reform has been implemented in the UK; in particular, the shift in policy from covert privatization to one which stressed the importance of a managed (regulated) market (Ham and Brommels 1994).

In most countries of central and eastern Europe, it is unclear as to whether or not there is public support for health system reform. This lack of consensus for reform coupled with the dire (for many) economic situation makes for a very unstable policy environment, and considerable difficulty in implementing reform. As a result, a variety of agencies, organizations and groups seek to push the health system reform agenda toward changes that are more acceptable to themselves. The irony is that there is a need for strong leadership just at the time when it is often found most wanting.

## CONCLUSION

This chapter has outlined the evidence regarding the current state of reform implementation in the European region. The picture it paints is a varied one. This reflects many factors: different ways in which systems are organized and structured; different starting times for reform; and different approaches to reform. CEE countries face an additional constraint: the adjustment to pluralistic government while seeking to restructure the economy and the public sector. Overall, this diversity of approaches to health system reform makes it difficult to point to any one factor as crucial and of fundamental significance to implementation. However, the combination of strategic alliances coupled with political will do seem to be the major driving force behind the implementation of many reforms.

## ACKNOWLEDGEMENTS

I am grateful to the following for their helpful comments on earlier drafts of this paper: Josep Figueras, Richard Saltman and Gill Walt. I alone am responsible for any errors and/or omissions that remain.

## REFERENCES

Alford, R. (1975). *Health Care Politics*. Chicago: University of Chicago Press.
Anell, A. (1995). Implementing planned markets in health care: The case of Sweden. In R. B. Saltman and C. von Otter (eds), *Implementing Planned Markets in Health Care*. Buckingham: Open University Press.
Artundo, C., Sakellarides, C. and Vuori, H. (1992). Health Care Reforms in Europe. Paper presented at the first meeting of the Working Party on Health Care Reforms in Europe, Madrid, 23–24 June.
Ashton, T. (1995). From evolution to revolution: Restructuring the New Zealand health system. In D. Seedhouse (ed.), *Reforming Health Care: The Philosophy and Practice of International Health Reform*. Chichester: John Wiley.
Balicki, M. and Sabbat, J. (1994). The state's responsibility for health care in Poland. *Antidotum*, Supplement No. l, 81–8.
Borren, P. and Maynard, A. (1994). The market reform of the New Zealand health care system: Searching for the Holy Grail in the Antipodes. *Health Policy*, 27, 233–52.
Brommels, M. (1995). Contracting and political boards in planned markets. In R. B. Saltman and C. von Otter (eds), *Implementing Planned Markets in Health Care*. Buckingham: Open University Press.
Carlsson, P. (1994). *Swedish Health Care is Still at the Crossroad*. Paper presented at Ditchley Foundations Conference, Oxford, 20–22 May.

de Roo, A. A. (1995). Contracting and solidarity: Market-oriented changes in Dutch health insurance schemes. In R. B. Saltman and C. von Otter (eds), *Implementing Planned Markets in Health Care*. Buckingham: Open University Press.

Diderichsen, F. (1995). Market reforms in health care and sustainability of the welfare state: Lessons from Sweden. *Health Policy*, 32, 141–53.

Ensor, T. (1993). Health system reform in former socialist countries of Europe. *International Journal of Health Planning and Management*, 8, 169–87.

Gilson, L. and Mills, A. (1995). Health sector reforms in sub-Saharan Africa: Lessons of the last 10 years. *Health Policy*, 32, 215–43.

Gladstone, D. and Goldsmith, M. (1995). Health care reform in the UK: Working for patients? In D. Seedhouse (ed.), *Reforming Health Care: The Philosophy and Practice of International Health Reform*. Chichester: John Wiley.

Glennerster, H. and Matsaganis, M. (1994). The English and Swedish health care reforms. *International Journal of Health Services*, 24, 231–51.

Glennerster, H., Matsaganis, M., Owens, P. and Hancock, S. (1995). *Implementing GP Fundholding*. Buckingham: Open University Press.

Groenewegen, P. P. (1994). The shadow of the future: Institutional change in health care. *Health Affairs*, 13, 137–48.

Ham, C. and Brommels, M. (1994). Health care reform in the Netherlands, Sweden, and the United Kingdom. *Health Affairs*, 13, 105–19.

Ham, C. J. (ed.) (1997). *Health Care Reform: Learning from International Experience*. Buckingham: Open University Press.

Harrison, S. and Pollitt, C. (1994). *Controlling health professionals. The future of work and organization in the National Health Service*. Buckingham: Open University Press.

Heginbotham, C. and Maxwell, R. (1991). Managing the transitions: A Western European view of health care development in Eastern Europe. *European Journal of Public Health*, 1, 36–44.

Hurst, J. and Poullier, J. P. (1993). Paths to health reform. *OECD Observer*, December 1992/January 1993, 4–7.

Jonczyk, J. (1993). The Polish dilemma and proposals for change. *Antidotum*, 1, 81–4.

Keen, J., Buxton, M. and Packwood, T. (1993). Doctors and resource management: Incentives and goodwill. *Health Policy*, 24, 71–82.

Lovelace, C. (1995). The Implementation of Health Reforms: A Framework. Canada (British Columbia) and New Zealand. Paper presented at the Workshop on Implementation of Health Systems Reforms, Copenhagen: WHO Regional Office for Europe, 10–11 November.

Maarse, H. (1994). State intervention in health care: Aspects, effects and prospects. Paper presented at the Third Meeting of the Expert Network on Health Care Financing Strategies, Bratislava, 24–26 May.

Ministry of Health and Social Welfare (1986). *Health for All by the Year 2000: The Finnish National Strategy*. Helsinki: Valtion Painatuskeskus.

Peck, E. (1991). Power in the National Health Service: A case study of a unit considering NHS trust status. *Health Services Management Research*, 4, 120–30.

Potucek, M. (1994a). Markets, states and social citizenship in central and eastern Europe. Unpublished paper, Prague.

Potucek, M. (1994b). The transformation of the Czech health care in 1990–1992. An abbreviated English version of the study written for the project 'The transformation of the Czech Health Care of the Social Transformation Advanced Research Trust'. Unpublished paper, New York.

Preker, A. S. and Feachem, R. G. A. (1995). *Searching for the Silver Bullet: Market Mechanisms and the Health Sector in Central and Eastern Europe*. Washington, DC: World Bank.

Rathwell, T. (1988). A management partnership for the mentally handicapped. *Health Policy*, 9, 80–91.

Robinson, R. and Le Grand, J. (1994). *Evaluating the NHS Reforms*. London: King's Fund Institute.

Rosleff, F. and Lister, G. (1995). *European Healthcare Trends: Towards Managed Care in Europe*. London: Coopers and Lybrand.

Saltman, R. B. (1994). A conceptual overview of recent health care reforms. *European Journal of Public Health*, 4, 287–93.

Saltman, R. B. and von Otter, C. (1992). *Planned Markets and Public Competition. Strategic Reform in Northern European Health Systems* Buckingham: Open University Press.

Seedhouse, D. (ed.) (1995). *Reforming Health Care. The Philosophy and Practice of International Health Reform*. Chichester: John Wiley.

Sinkkonen, S. and Kinnunen, J. (undated). Finnish health care system. Unpublished paper, Kuppio.

Walt, G. (1996). Implementing health care reforms: a framework for discussion. Paper presented at the Workshop on Implementation of Health Systems Reforms, Copenhagen: WHO Regional Office for Europe, 10–11 November.

Wlodarczyk, C. (1993). Expert network on health and health care financing strategies in countries of central and eastern Europe, or on the advantages of neighbourly cooperation in health care reforms. *Antidotum*, 1, 8–21.

Zarkovic, G., Mielch, A., John, J. and Beckmann, M. (1994). *Reform of the Health Care Systems in Former Socialist Countries: Problems, Options, Scenarios*. Neuherberg: Institut für Medizinische Informatik und Systemforschung (Medis).

# ASSESSING THE EVIDENCE

Richard B. Saltman,
Josep Figueras and
Constantino Sakallerides

The cross-national transfer of ideas has been at the very heart of the European experience since the end of the Middle Ages. In art, architecture, literature and music, in military technique and diplomacy, even in cuisine, one can discern the impact of outside influences within nearly every national context. Among the more prominent examples are Italian renaissance painting and music, seventeenth-century Flemish and German architecture, and nineteenth-century French cuisine, all of which have substantially influenced the perceptions and expectations in these fields elsewhere in Europe. Further, the impact of outside ideas was not limited to intra-European exchange. One can readily trace the legacy of Byzantine, Moorish, Chinese, and, most recently, North American influences across large swaths of European cultural and social activity.

This process of cross-fertilization can similarly be observed in the much shorter history of health policy in Europe. One of the best-known examples was the adoption by Lloyd George in 1911 in Great Britain of a similar model of social insurance to that introduced by Otto von Bismarck in Germany in 1883 – this despite England and Germany being only three years from going to war with each other. A more recent, more explicit, example was Finland's strategy in the early 1960s for developing a national health insurance programme. Recognizing that they were among the last in western Europe to introduce health insurance, the Finns formed a high-level group to study the experience of other countries, with the mandate to make policy recommendations based on what had been learned elsewhere (Haeroe and Purola 1972).

This Finnish exercise was important in that, unlike earlier essentially impressionistic efforts, it took an evidence-based approach to cross-national experience in the health sector. The Finnish team set out to evaluate systematically what had been learned elsewhere and sought to apply those lessons to the construction of an insurance system that would be culturally, politically, and financially appropriate in their own national context. While European policy makers have embarked upon many international study tours since then, the Finnish example was one of the earliest precursors in the health sector of a systematic cross-national approach to the generation of evidence-based public policy.

The essays in this volume represent just such a systematic cross-national effort to summarize the available evidence about making health policy as of the mid-1990s. The separate chapters deal with a variety of conceptual and practical issues involved in raising funds, allocating revenues, and delivering services in contemporary European health care systems. Beyond the specific conclusions at the end of each essay, the evidence points toward two broader patterns of experience in the construction of health care reforms generally (WHO 1997). One pattern concerns where reforms have been more successful in achieving their objectives as against where they have been less so, while the second concerns the underlying role of the state in the development of sustainable health sector reform. While these two patterns have at various points a close connection with each other, national policy makers as well as students of health systems may find it helpful to consider each pattern in its own right.

The first pattern concerns approaches to health system reform that have had relatively more success, as against those that have had less. Success can be defined here in two senses. Normatively, success requires the proposed reform to help generate health gain for the broad population as well as to sustain overall equity and solidarity within the health system. Operationally, success refers to a particular reform having achieved the technical objectives set out for it by its designers. The range of objectives typically involves a mix of fiscal, social, and political as well as health system organizational goals.

The cross-national evidence presented in this volume indicates that reforms have been less successful when they have focused on the application of market-style incentives to individual patient-based demand (Part II). This observation reflects an analytic split in the concept of demand between aggregate population-based and individual patient-based forms of demand for health services.

Organized efforts to reduce aggregate population-based demand typically focus on public health measures, and have been ongoing since the advent of improved sanitation and immunization (Chapter 5). Since the 1970s, additional interventions on lifestyle issues such as smoking reduction, reduced consumption of fat, and increased exercise, as well as on environmental issues such as airborne and ground water pollution, have been pursued with varying degrees of success by policy makers in many countries. These various population-based interventions contrast sharply with reform strategies in the 1980s and 1990s that focus directly on individual patient-based demand. Indeed, advocates in Europe of a broadly based inter-sectoral public strategy frequently contend that health reform proposals in the 1990s have largely ignored aggregate population-based demand to concentrate predominantly on the individual-based portion of the demand for health-related resources.

In assessing the impact of reforms on individual-based demand, we need to consider the institutional framework through which it is expressed (Saltman and Figueras 1998). Despite complicated arrangements in different national systems for funding health services, it is nonetheless possible to classify the predominant source of revenue in terms of the system's broad financial and social structure. Only slightly oversimplified, one can distinguish between funding systems based predominantly on publicly accountable payers (whether constructed on taxation or statutory social insurance), characterized by bedrock principles of universal access for all citizens (or all below a high income threshold) and sustainable system-wide financing, as against funding systems based predominantly on privately accountable payers that are not responsible for ensuring either universal access or sustainable system-wide financing. Nearly all western European countries have had some form of publicly accountable payer for all or most of their citizens prior to the current reform period, and all western European countries remain committed to the bedrock principles of universal access and sustainable financing. Despite occasionally heated debates, no western European country has shifted from a publicly accountable to a privately accountable funding system.

In CEE/CIS countries severe financial pressures as well as newly adopted market-oriented theories have contributed in many countries to a shift away from their prior taxation-based funding arrangements for health services. While some countries have retained publicly accountable payers through a statutory social insurance framework, others have established privately accountable funding arrangements based on competing private insurers. Those countries which maintain a publicly accountable funding structure, however, do not in most cases have adequate public revenues to provide stable or sustainable health sector funding, and the continued role of 'informal payment' mechanisms indicates that universal access has in practice broken down.

The few western European countries in which recent funding-side reforms have attempted to incorporate privately accountable payers within what was to remain a publicly accountable funding structure have encountered serious difficulties (Chapter 2). In the Netherlands, successive Dutch governments have struggled largely in vain for ten years to devise a scenario that could introduce competitive private funders while still maintaining a high level of solidarity (de Roo 1995; van der Ven *et al.* 1994). In Israel, the effort to consolidate an existing structure of privately accountable payers into a new system of universal national health insurance (Chinitz 1995) has generated growing deficits and a rapid increase in restrictive governmental regulation. In some CEE/CIS countries, competing payers have contributed to rapid and unsustainable escalation of expenditures as well as serious breaches of solidarity.

Another set of funding-side reforms have sought to reduce demand for publicly financed services by shifting a proportion of health care costs on to the individual by introducing cost-sharing schemes and/or removing services from the public package of care. To the extent that reforms would require the introduction of incentives for cost-reducing behaviour through shifting a share of provider-generated costs directly onto the patient, these proposed reforms either have not been introduced or have been sufficiently buffered that, in most cases, their demand-reducing effect has been effectively neutralized (Chapter 3). Many European countries reject cost sharing as a significant tool for either improving efficiency or containing cost for hospital and physician services due to problems related to supply-induced demand together with concerns about equity. Cost sharing may reduce the utilization of services initiated by the patient, but such reductions may not be very effective in achieving cost containment. This reflects the reality that one of the main drivers of health care costs is service intensity, which is generated predominantly by providers rather than by funders. Compensating administrative procedures such as exemptions for low-income or chronically ill citizens can partly address resulting inequities, yet at the same time they also reduce the impact of cost-sharing measures, thus defeating their ability to reduce utilization and contain costs. With regard to rationing (Chapter 4), in western European countries few explicit measures have actually been adopted. As with cost sharing, policy makers instinctively recognize the two-tier consequences of de-listing a service from the publicly reimbursed package and are unwilling to accept such a breach of solidarity in the health sector. Again, in CEE/CIS countries, the situation differs due to inadequate public funding for health in a time of economic transition. However, the result has often been severe rationing of access to necessary services, rather than the type of reasoned reduction in provision that western health ethicists seek to promote. One useful outcome from both western and eastern European countries engaged in the rationing debate has been a heightened interest in assessing the effectiveness of existing levels of care, including technology assessment and quality initiatives such as medical practice guidelines and continuous quality development. Overall, the evidence from the European health reform experience indicates that attempts to affect provider behaviour indirectly by generating financial pressure through individual patient-based demand or on competing privately accountable payers has not worked well either financially or socially.

Conversely, the cross-national evidence suggests that reforms pursued on the supply-side (e.g. allocation and production components (Part III)) fared relatively well in both normative and operational terms.[1] In the area of allocation, efforts to recalibrate incentives for providers included the introduction of contracting and/or commissioning within public-operated health systems (Chapter 6), new methods to allocate capital investments (Chapter 7), performance-tied payment systems for professional and institutional providers (Chapters 8 and 9), and the use of regulatory measures to control pharmaceutical expenditures such as reference pricing, positive lists and indicative budgets (Chapter 11). In the area of production, relatively successful policy interventions included initiatives like continuous quality development, technology assessment, medical practice guidelines, and the substitution of less intensive for more intensive services (day surgery, home care, etc.). Also deserving mention is the restructuring of hospital configuration (Chapter 10) and the reorganization of budget-driven public hospitals into various types of public firms (e.g. publicly owned but managerially independent institutions funded on production-linked criteria).

The supply-side reforms currently under way in the European region have been designed and introduced predominantly by public sector officials, at either national or regional levels of government. While there continues to be substantial interest in the use of competitive mechanisms between different public providers, these public officials have rarely sought to privatize the core health functions or ownership of public institutions. This reflects a realization among many national policy makers that the issue of provider competition is conceptually distinct from the issue of private ownership (Saltman and von Otter 1992). In terms of the results achieved, one concludes that it is somewhat less important whether the reforms pursued are regulatory or competitive in their basic structure. The crucial element for success appears to have been that the reform focuses directly on providers (e.g. allocation and provision) in the health system.

This leads to a second major pattern that emerges from the essays in this volume: the balance between the roles of state and market in health care (Part IV). This issue of 'state or market' is in many respects a 1990s reprise of the intense debate in Europe about public versus private during the 1980s (McLachlan and Maynard 1982). The recent period of health system reform has served to concentrate policy makers' attention, however, on the degree to which the proper relationship between state and market is not a strictly reciprocal one. Contrary to the writings of neo-classical economists (which in this matter strongly resemble those of Marxist theorists before them), the advent of the market in health services does not appear to lead to the withering away of the state any more than did soviet-style communism. Reform experience in the European health sector has demonstrated that the greater the reliance placed upon market mechanisms, the greater will be the need for a continued strong role for the state. Several CEE/CIS countries found it necessary to develop a state regulatory apparatus to reduce the negative consequences of giving market forces free rein, and even Sweden found that it lacked an adequate regulatory structure to rein in the self-interested behaviour of fully private providers (Orn 1996).

This renewed role for the state, however, requires a fundamental shift in emphasis. Instead of controlling inputs, the state should be monitoring outputs and – in the health sector – outcomes. Instead of directly managing hospitals, governments in CEE/CIS countries and in Israel, as well as in Spain and the UK, are realizing they should focus on setting the broad strategic framework for the entire health system. To meet this objective, the state must not only continue to function, but it must work more effectively (Kettl 1993): the state needs to 'row less and steer more' (Osborne and Gaebler 1991).

These two broad patterns in health sector reform – where reforms have been successful and the continuing role for the state – establish a useful framework with which to measure the likely future impact of a variety of different health reform measures. They suggest, for instance, that proponents of patient choice and patient rights may have more fruitful long-term results if they concentrate their efforts on better delineating the relationship between patients and the providers of services, rather than focusing on the role of patient choice in selecting among different funders of care. Similarly, it implies that the introduction of contracting with providers for services – creating what has been termed the 'purchaser-provider split' – may be more successful if the purchaser is some type of unitary publicly operated agency – or, perhaps, local primary care provider – rather than large competing risk-bearing insurers as in the managed competition model of health care funding that has emerged in the US.

This assessment of existing evidence also carries implications for the important process of implementing reforms. Successful introduction of reforms will likely be more rapidly achieved if reforms focus on changes that, substantively speaking, conform with what other countries have found are easier and/or more readily accepted reform measures. One clear advantage of systematic cross-national analysis is that health sector decision makers might become more hesitant about adopting policy proposals that could lead to a repetition of, say, the Dutch experience with the introduction of a competition-based funding structure (Chapter 2) or the CEE/CIS experience with inadequately regulated private providers (Chapter 12). Of course, adopting a relatively successful reform developed in a different country context is itself a challenge, and the process of implementation can have a major impact on the outcome (Part V). The evidence discussed in Chapters 16 and 17 nonetheless also suggests that policy makers can minimize their exposure to failure by learning from other country experiences with implementation. Several factors have played a key role in bringing about or creating obstacles to health sector change. These include the choice of an appropriate time for reform, the availability of financial resources and technical capability, the existing political will and leadership in introducing change, the establishment of strategic alliances with key actors and the active management of the process of change.

If evidence-based policy making is to emerge as an important dimension of the overall health reform process in Europe, a variety of political and social as well as informational barriers will need to be overcome. It will, however, be particularly important to expand the evidentiary foundation upon which such policy making needs to be based. The essays in this volume should thus be viewed as a contribution to an analytic process that requires a variety of further cross-national studies, and a field of scholarly endeavour which is still nascent.

## NOTE

1 In this analysis, allocation is combined with production, forming the supply-side of the system, leaving funding as the source of demand. This placement of allocation reflects the reality that in most European health systems, in practice, allocation and production are administered jointly or closely regulated in a coordinated manner by one or another public sector agency.

## REFERENCES

Chinitz, D. (1995). Israel's health policy breakthrough: The politics of reform and the reform of politics. *Journal of Health Politics, Policy and Law*, 20, 909–32.

de Roo, A. A. (1995). Contracting and solidarity: Marketing-oriented changes in Dutch health insurance schemes. In R.B. Saltman and C. von Otter (eds), *Implementing Planned Markets in Health Care*. Buckingham: Open University Press.

Haeroe, A. S. and Purola, T. (1972). Planning and health policy in Finland. *International Journal of Health Services*, 2, 23–34.

Kettl, D. F. (1993). *Sharing Power: Public Governance and Private Markets*. Washington, DC: Brookings Institution.

McLachlan, G. and Maynard, A. (1982). *The Public/Private Mix for Health*. London: Nuffield Provincial Hospitals Trust.

Orn, P. (1996). Flera hundra förfalskade provsar laamnade laboratorie företaget. *Läkaretidningen*, 93, 532.

Osborne, D. and Gaebler, T. (1993). *Reinventing Government*. Reading, MA: Addison Wesley.

Saltman, R. B. and von Otter, C. (1992). *Planned Markets and Public Competition. Strategic Reform in Northern European Health Systems.* Buckingham: Open University Press.

Saltman, R. B. and Figueras, J. (1998). Analyzing the evidence on European health care reforms. *Health Affairs*, 17, 85–108.

van de Ven, W. P. M. M., Schut, F. T. and Rutten, F. F. H. (1994). Forming and reforming the market for third-party purchasing of health care. *Social Science and Medicine*, 39, 1405–12.

WHO (1997). *European Health Care Reform: Analysis of Current Strategies.* Edited and written by R. B. Saltman and J. Figueras. Copenhagen: WHO Regional Office for Europe.

# INDEX

NOTE: Page numbers followed by *f* or *t* refer to figures or tables